THE SLIP/PPP CONNECTION

THE SLIP/PPP CONNECTION

The Essential Guide to Graphical Internet Access

Paul Gilster

John Wiley & Sons, Inc.

NEW YORK • CHICHESTER • BRISBANE • TORONTO • SINGAPORE

Publisher: Katherine Schowalter
Editor: Phil Sutherland
Assistant Editor: Allison Roarty
Managing Editor: Frank Grazioli
Copyeditor: Janice Borzendowski
Book Design & Composition: North Market Street Graphics, Lancaster, PA

Library of Congress Cataloging-in-Publication Data
Gilster, Paul
     The SLIP/PPP connection : the essential guide to graphical
Internet access / Paul Gilster.
          p.   cm.
     Includes index.
     ISBN 0-471-11712-9 (acid-free paper)
     1. Internet (Computer network)   I. Title.
TK5105.875.I57G57   1995
005.7'13—dc20   95-7398
                                                                   CIP

Printed in the United States of America
10 9 8 7 6 5 4 3 2 1

This book is dedicated to my mother,
Inez G. Gilster, whose support has always
encouraged my explorations.

Contents

Preface

How we access the Internet has always been a conundrum. In the early days, using the net meant tying in to a local network, usually at a research organization or government agency; later, universities signed on through their own campus networks. Modem users were more or less left to their own devices until the advent of SLIP—Serial Line Internet Protocol—which allowed anyone with a modem to exchange data packets directly with the network. Later, PPP—Point-to-Point Protocol—refined the model and provided an alternative mechanism for remote access through modems.

But with the cost of such connections high, most modem users opted for a so-called shell account, one which allowed you to sign on to a computer run by your service provider and tap the resources it provided. It couldn't be said you were actually on the Internet this way; after all, the network traffic passed only as far as your provider's machine, and you accessed it by logging on and downloading what you needed, or by running programs your provider made available at his or her site. It was a workable solution, and it offered a considerable degree of power for modem users, but it lacked a critical element: with a shell account, you couldn't run graphical software, and were limited to a command-driven interface.

Not too long ago, that wasn't a problem. True, the Internet was conceptually challenging, given its origins in operating environments like Unix, which require users to master command sequences to perform their work. But MS-DOS expected the same of its users, and people managed to work with WordPerfect, Lotus 1-2-3, and the other DOS tools. And the benefits of Internet access so outweighed the difficulties that mastering a shell account was just part of the initiation process. You might not enjoy it, but it was worth the effort.

Mosaic changed all that. By offering a graphical front end to many Internet functions, it gave users the opportunity to move about the Internet and be productive without learning all those complicated commands. And when you tied Mosaic in to the World Wide Web, you had at your disposal a communications medium that allowed you to read fully formatted text on-screen, with typeset quality presentation. You could include graphics in such a document—photographs, maps, paintings—and because the Web used hypermedia, you could even tap sound files, playing them back on your machine. Click on a resource and you went there; that was the model.

It was a model that changed the way we look at the Internet. Suddenly, that shell account looked too confining. You can't run Mosaic, or Netscape, the second-generation Web browsing tool, over a shell account, because both programs need a direct Internet connection. Only SLIP/PPP can provide that to modem users, and that put the pressure on the service providers. SLIP/PPP prices plummeted as demand soared. Soon, we moved beyond the command line issue of shell accounts and hit another wall—how do you configure the necessary software to make a SLIP/PPP connection work? And how do you find the software tools which run under its environment?

This book was written to address those issues. We begin with a look at what SLIP/PPP is all about, and then plunge into a discussion of implementing it on both Microsoft Windows machines and Macintoshes. The rest of the book then works through client programs that run under SLIP/PPP. These are tools that can provide access to any Internet resource, from FTP sessions for file transfer, to Telnet logins at remote computer sites, to WAIS searches of full-text databases. Whatever your need, there's a software program that can handle it in the SLIP/PPP world. And, of course, we don't neglect Mosaic, Netscape, and the other World Wide Web browsers.

Here's the layout of the book:

- Chapter 1 shows you examples of SLIP/PPP at work, explaining the difference between this form of access and the more conventional shell account.

- Chapter 2 deals with the issues that SLIP/PPP provokes; in particular, the ways in which the Internet needs to function to make the client programs we'll consider work properly on your remote PC over a modem. Equipment issues form a major section of this chapter, because a poorly equipped machine is going to have insufficient power to run these programs.

- Chapter 3 addresses Microsoft Windows users, and explains how to install the major shareware program for SLIP/PPP access, Trumpet Winsock.

- Chapter 4 deals with MacTCP, the Macintosh software you need to implement your connection. We also look at InterSLIP and MacPPP, two programs that work with MacTCP to handle the actual login at your service provider's site.

- Chapter 5 begins our look at client software with an examination of FTP programs for both Microsoft Windows and the Macintosh. I present full directions for finding and running these programs.

- Chapter 6 shows how you can use superb software like Eudora and Pegasus to organize and manage your electronic mail.

- Chapter 7 deals with Telnet, an Internet protocol that lets you log in at a remote computer and use whatever resources the system administrators there have made accessible, from library catalog searches to weather reports.

- Chapter 8 examines Wide Area Information Servers (WAIS). Using a WAIS database, you can search for information in a full-text environment, using a variety of search techniques.

- Chapter 9 focuses on Gopher, a system of menued information that lets you pick items from a list to explore the resources available at sites all over the world.

- Chapter 10 presents the USENET newsreaders most likely to win your support in both the Microsoft Windows and Macintosh environments. A good newsreader spells the difference between keeping up with the news and letting priceless information slide past.

- Chapter 11 is all about the World Wide Web, and the full panoply of tools, including Netscape, Mosaic, and Cello, that make accessing it both enjoyable and productive.

Overall, this book attempts to build an Internet toolbox that you can use under your SLIP/PPP connection. By the time you are through, you will have access to all the major tools that the Internet has to offer. You can then use these tools to develop a network presence that will keep you abreast of what is happening on the Internet, and will inform you of the arrival of new software programs that may provide still further features. Once you have experienced using these programs under SLIP/PPP, you're unlikely to want to return to the standard shell environment.

Acknowledgments

I owe much to my good friend Joseph Ragland, the man who built the Internet in North Carolina through his unceasing labors at the Microelectronics Center of North Carolina. Also playing a major role as a technical reviewer was Marty Schulman of the Internet Society, whose comments were always on the money; this book has benefited greatly from the expertise of both these men, while any errors in it must be attributed to its author rather than the reviewers who tried to straighten him out.

My friends at John Wiley & Sons did their usual competent job in getting me through the production process, particularly Allison Roarty, who I never caught in a bad mood despite my frequent calls and questions. Phil Sutherland provided valuable insights into shaping the book for its target audience. Frank Grazioli and Liane Carita made the galley process painless (well, almost), while Janice Borzendowski once again proved that good copyediting requires a sharp eye, a keen intelligence, and a sense of humor, all of which she possesses in abundance. Thanks, guys, as always.

1

The Nature of the Connection

The Internet has been around since 1969, but only recently has its use exploded. Why? The answer is partly evident when you examine the offerings of any number of Internet service providers. The Net is getting easier to use. It doesn't really matter whether we're talking about a commercial on-line service with Internet connections (DELPHI was the first of these, but CompuServe and America Online are jumping in with significant offerings) or an Internet-only access provider like Interpath, the one I use here in North Carolina. The trend is toward some kind of user-friendly interface—by interface, I refer to what you see on the screen when you log in. Interfaces can make your life easier or more difficult; lately, they've made trekking through the Internet a simpler task than it's ever been before.

You can trace the same development in technology in general. Computers running MS-DOS, which required you to enter commands at a system prompt to make things happen, have steadily moved in the direction of greater user-friendliness. DOS itself changed, offering features like an optional interface with pull-down menus (in version 4.0) and a variety of other tools that made using the operating system less intimidating. The Macintosh, from the other side of the great operating system divide, went immediately to a graphical interface upon its release in 1984 and has remained graphical ever since. People who've used both often insist that the Mac has always been easier to use than DOS machines, at least until the advent of Windows.

Ah yes, Microsoft Windows. Put aside the legal controversy between Apple Computer and Microsoft over who owns this kind of interface (it really seems to have come out of the research Xerox did at its Palo Alto Research Center, the famous PARC, way back in the 1970s), the success of Windows has brought computers into the home in record numbers, and the arrival of

Windows 95 brings computer networking home in the same way. Windows 95 contains network hooks that allow you to jump onto the Internet once you've established an account with a service provider. More significantly, Windows 95 allows you to view the Internet through an interface that makes sense. That interface is made possible by something called SLIP/PPP.

As you'll soon see, SLIP/PPP connections make all the difference. The Internet is fully accessible for people without such connections—but at a price. As with MS-DOS, the Internet tends to offer a cryptic command line to those without SLIP/PPP, in place of a graphical environment that the latter makes possible. Once again, you're forced to type a command to make things happen. Being a command-line kind of person, I rather enjoy this, but I sympathize with my friends, most of whom don't share my passion for digital tinkering and simply want to get on with things. They have jobs to perform, or hobbies to cultivate; they don't want to spend half their networking time figuring out what to type next. This book is for them.

Why You Want SLIP/PPP

Let's dispose of the acronyms first: SLIP stands for Serial Line Internet Protocol; PPP stands for Point-to-Point Protocol. The two are different animals, but because they make many of the same things possible, I tend to use them interchangeably, and you'll see the designation SLIP/PPP throughout this book. It really means "either SLIP or PPP," and you can plug in whichever of these you happen to use. Both are ways to achieve a new degree of graphical freedom in your experience of the Internet. Both allow you to choose your own tools for on-line work and to change them when you please. Both enable a user environment that is accessible and intuitive.

Take a look at the difference. In Figure 1.1, I have logged on to a standard Unix-driven Internet account without SLIP/PPP. I am looking for information on the worldwide collection of discussion areas called USENET. The program I am using to do this is called trn, and to invoke it, I typed the command **trn** at the user prompt for my system. That prompt itself is nothing more than the name of the local computer. It looks like this:

mercury:

After the colon, I am on my own; I need to know what to type or I could sit there staring at the prompt all day long.

What a difference SLIP/PPP makes. In Figure 1.2, you can see the same USENET newsgroup available for display. But now the articles are shown to me in a field in the bottom two-thirds of the page, while the various newsgroups I've subscribed to are listed at the top. I can pull down menus from the top of the screen to perform actions, or I can click with a mouse along the button bar at the bottom of the screen. I can double-click on an article to call it up

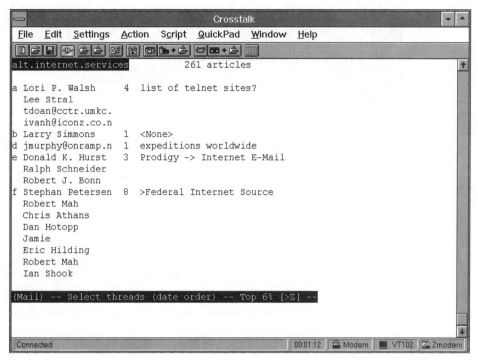

Figure 1.1   USENET through a Unix shell account presents a lean, character-based interface.

for viewing, whereas with the regular, non-SLIP/PPP account, I had no such option because I couldn't use a mouse with it. In short, SLIP/PPP lets me be exploratory as I learn how to perform actions, while regular dial-up connections make this process more difficult.

Of course, SLIP/PPP doesn't limit us to USENET newsgroups to do our work. The benefits of the graphical environment extend to almost all of our network tasks. One of the pleasures of preparing this book was the discovery of just how much software development is going on in the area of new client programs. I discovered one of the best newsreader programs I've ever seen, Newswatcher for the Macintosh, and a sharp program that manages Gopher connections under Microsoft Windows (Gopher is a menu-based information-browsing system). Take a look at HGopher, as seen in Figure 1.3.

Notice the variety of icons, pull-down menus and other touches, including, as seen along the top of the screen, the bookmarks menu, which is a customized list of your most frequently visited sites. HGopher lets you set up any number of such collections around the theme of your choice. As you'll see in Chapter 9, a commercial program called WinGopher brings even more customization features to your bookmark list.

In Figure 1.4, you see an example of File Transfer Protocol, or FTP, as run through a SLIP/PPP connection (FTP allows you to download files from sites

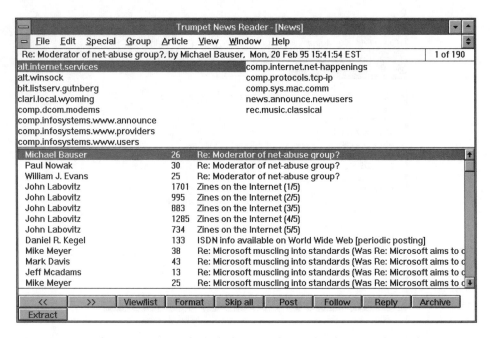

Figure 1.2 Looking at USENET through the eyes of a graphical newsreader in the SLIP/PPP environment.

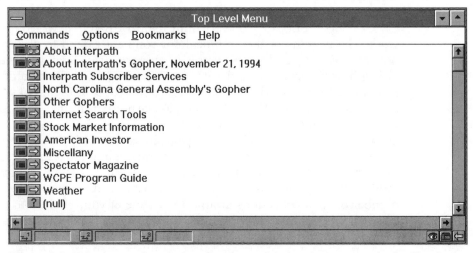

Figure 1.3 HGopher overlays the benefits of a graphical environment on the familiar Gopher menu.

worldwide). The program is Fetch, a superb FTP engine for the Macintosh that was developed at Dartmouth College. On the left of the screen I have a list of files and subdirectories in a particular directory at the site **ftp.ncsa.uiuc.edu**. I can pull down menus to move back and forth in the directory structure here, examining the file archives and finding just what I need. When I track down the program I'm after, retrieving it is a matter of clicking on the Get File button. No more typing in Unix commands. In fact, if you'll examine the bottom center of the screen, you'll see that I don't even need to tell the remote computer whether my transfer will be in binary or ASCII mode. Fetch can make that decision for me when I click on the button marked Automatic. Equally impressive FTP tools exist for Microsoft Windows. Figure 1.5 shows a program called WS_FTP; here, I am at the same site, National Center for Supercomputing Applications, and am about to download the latest version of the World Wide Web browser called Mosaic.

Each Internet protocol has one or more corresponding applications that can be run over a SLIP/PPP connection. Maybe you want to search an on-line database. A search engine called WAIS—Wide Area Information Servers— makes this possible. But in the Unix environment, WAIS is hard to search because the swais program you need to use is counter-intuitive and requires a

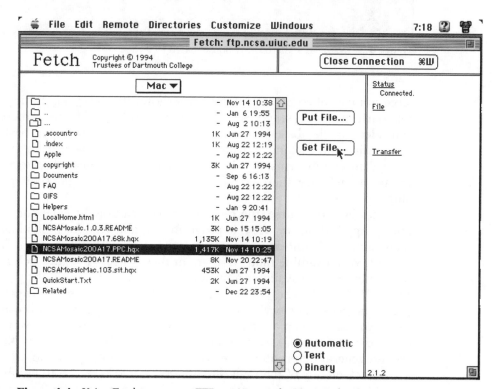

Figure 1.4 Using Fetch to manage FTP sessions on the Macintosh.

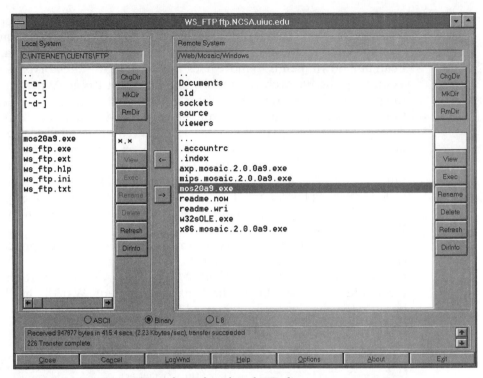

Figure 1.5 WS_FTP, a Microsoft Windows-based FTP client.

large number of commands. Figure 1.6 shows WinWais, a graphical program that performs WAIS searches. Notice how many helpful features there are. You can select the database you want to query and run your search past it simply by pointing and clicking on what you need, filling in keywords in the field that holds your search terms. In this case, I am about to query a directory of servers to find out whether there are any databases on the Internet that specialize in anthropology.

And then, of course, there's Mosaic. The National Center for Supercomputing Applications makes this program available free for individual use, and there are any number of new commercial browsing programs coming to market. We'll examine many of them in these pages. The idea behind them is the same: to make available a browsing tool that can exploit the power of the World Wide Web. The Web is a hypermedia environment in which you can point-and-click your way from one resource to another by following hyperlinks. You can call up an image, listen to a sound file, play a short movie clip, or read text files on-screen. Figure 1.7 is an example of what Netscape, a second-generation product based on Mosaic technology, can do.

A click on any of the underlined items would take you to it, whether it is located on the same host computer or on a computer halfway around the

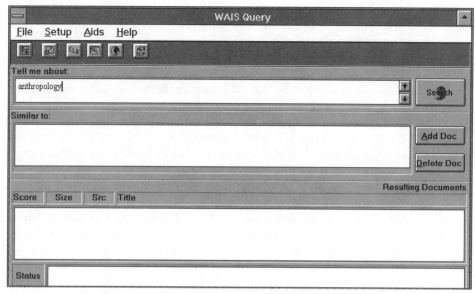

Figure 1.6 WinWais lets you search a wide range of databases by entering keywords and moving between sources with ease.

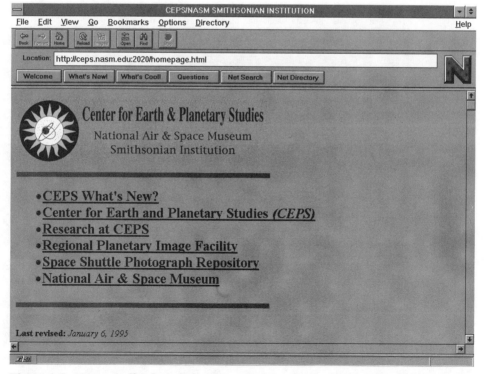

Figure 1.7 Netscape offers hyperlinks to Internet data; point-and-click and you're there.

world. In Figure 1.8, you see another example of a World Wide Web browser, this time the original Mosaic program. Here, I am about to take an electronic tour of Paris.

Hypermedia is a wonderful electronic publishing tool, but the power of Mosaic and its various counterparts, like Netscape and Cello, is that they all allow us to display formatted hypermedia on our screens along with graphical tools that make using these resources easier. You can use Mosaic to read USENET newsgroups, or to examine the holdings at a Gopher site. We still don't have a completely all-in-one Internet interface, but the Mosaic format comes close, which doubtless accounts for its phenomenal popularity in recent times.

And let's not leave electronic mail out of the picture. Most of us who cut our teeth on Unix systems mastered one or more mail programs. The basic program, called, simply, mail, allows you to send and reply to messages, and provides a surprising amount of power, but in a command-driven interface with little by way of a help system. A more sophisticated program called pine brings greater ease of use and an elementary menu structure to the process. Numerous programs exist to manage your mail under the SLIP/PPP environment. Figure 1.9 shows one of them, Eudora, as seen running on my 486. Notice that I have a wide range of menu options running across the top of the

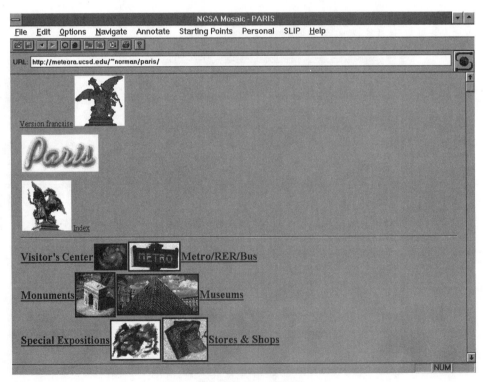

Figure 1.8   Mosaic can take you on a "virtual" tour of Paris.

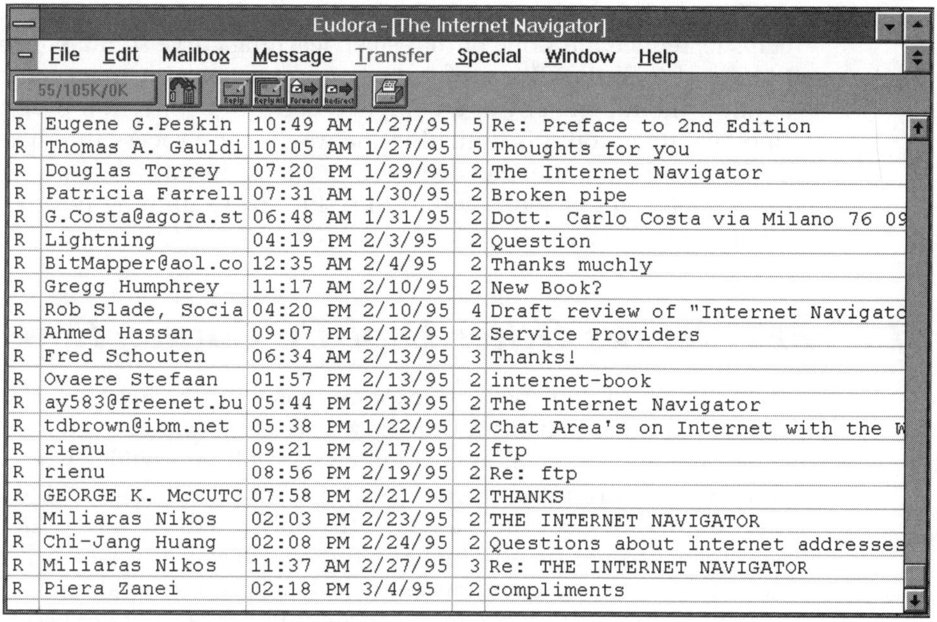

Figure 1.9 Eudora makes using e-mail manageable by providing pull-down menus and easy-to-do customization options.

screen. Viewing any of these messages is simply a matter of clicking on its subject field, and I can manage mail by moving to any number of customized mailboxes. Comparable programs, which I'll discuss soon, provide the same functionality for the Macintosh.

Whatever your operating system, SLIP/PPP can make your on-line life both more productive and more interesting. And there is another benefit: With your SLIP/PPP connection, you have the ability to open several different connections at the same time. I might know, for example, that I have quite a few messages waiting for my review in the various USENET newsgroups to which I subscribe. I'd also like to run a Telnet session (a way to log on to a remote computer) with a library in Singapore so that I can search its catalog. And it would help to be able to check the local Gopher for an address.

You might not think such wizardry would be possible with a single telephone line, but it is. I fire up Trumpet for Windows and let it begin pulling in headers for my newsgroups, even as I launch a Telnet session with a client program called Ewan. Up pops the Telnet screen, allowing me to log on at the remote site in Singapore. I do so, launch my search there, and then click on the HGopher icon to launch my Gopher application. By now I can see headers available in Trumpet, so it's back to that program to begin skimming for news. Then back to Singapore for the results of my search. And so it goes, a bit of globe-hopping courtesy of SLIP/PPP. Each *virtual connection* shares the same bandwidth.

Clearly, this kind of connectivity offers a boost to our Internet work and helps us reduce the slope of that steep learning curve so many new users fear. In fact, what SLIP/PPP does for the home and small business computer user is to allow the full benefit of a complete network connection over a modem. A Unix dial-up account is limited in the way it can process Internet data and in the way your computer can deal with that data, in ways that now need explaining. Let's begin our journey into SLIP/PPP by examining how it differs from other forms of access.

SLIP/PPP versus Other Dial-Up Connections

Most of us begin our network explorations with the lowest-cost option, a so-called *shell* account using a Unix-based access provider. Even if you choose an alternative source, such as a commercial on-line provider like CompuServe, you are still using a basic menu system without graphical capabilities to access the Net. And indeed, this has been the only practical way, until recently, for newcomers to get on the Internet. When I began my network explorations some years ago, you could purchase a shell account for about $35 per month, usually set up as a flat rate for a certain number of hours of use (this cost varied, as you might imagine, depending upon the service provider in question; some charged more; a few charged less). SLIP/PPP cost significantly more than a shell account, and was rarely used.

Today, the price of SLIP/PPP is plummeting; one access provider in my town is now down to $25 per month, and I know of providers elsewhere who make SLIP/PPP available for as low as $18 per month. Many people are beginning to take the upgrade path, wondering how their previous connection differs from the new SLIP/PPP access they're about to receive. The differences are critical for understanding what is happening when you invoke a program under SLIP/PPP.

There are three ways to use the Internet over a modem:

- By using a shell account.
- By logging on to a commercial on-line service like CompuServe or America Online.
- By using a SLIP/PPP account.

Let's talk about each. What is a shell account, and how does it differ from other forms of modem access, such as using CompuServe or America Online to reach the net through a gateway? And how does SLIP/PPP differ from both?

The Shell Account Defined

A *shell account* is your authorization to connect to the Internet through somebody else's computer. This means that you are given an account on a computer, usually a Unix machine, that you access to perform Internet work. On that machine, you use a Unix shell, which means that you can tap the Unix operating system to run programs and perform tasks, everything from file management to downloading software from the Internet or using Internet tools like Gopher and WAIS.

Note: What's a shell? It's the basic interface provided for you when you sign on to your Unix account. In the world of Unix, the operating system needs an interpreter that can translate the commands you type into something the computer understands. There are a variety of such shells available, with names like the C shell, the Bourne shell, and the Korn shell. Fortunately, you don't have to make distinctions between them, because every time you sign on to your service provider's computer, a shell program is launched automatically. The system then provides you with a prompt that means it is ready to accept your commands. The most familiar prompts are % and $, although the user can change the prompt to whatever he or she wants. You can see the similarity between this concept and the familiar C:> prompt of MS-DOS; both indicate it's your turn to tell the computer what to do.

A shell account is the lowest-cost option for getting onto the Internet, but it does place you in an environment where entering commands (and, therefore, knowing which ones to enter) is necessary. There is no "point-and-click" in a shell environment, using a mouse to click on what you need. Nor do you have a real connection to the Internet. When you dial up a shell account, you are using your service provider's computer. It is that computer that has a presence on the Internet.

When you log on to pick up your Internet mail, for example, that mail is stored for you on the Unix machine, and you must run a program on that machine to read it. Thus you move to the command prompt and type a command. Typing **mail** runs a Unix program called mail that displays your messages and allows you to reply; typing **pine** runs another Unix program, more complex but considerably easier to use, that does the same thing.

The key point is, you're using a computer that is on the net, but your computer is not. Download a file by using File Transfer Protocol (FTP) and it winds up not on *your* machine, but on that of your service provider. Thus, file downloads become a two-step process: First, you give the **ftp** command on your service provider's system. The file is transferred. Then you activate a download from your service provider's computer to your own. Now the file is actually transferred to your machine. The system works fine, but you've added an intermediate step. It is this step that SLIP/PPP eliminates, by giving you an actual network presence. Your machine goes directly onto the net, and maintains its own Internet address.

Note: When I spoke of command prompts just now, you may have noticed that various service providers use different ones. A shell account can be set up to show virtually any command prompt. If my service provider displays the name of the machine I'm on, another might simply show you a symbol. You log on and see this:

%

What does it mean? The same thing that C:> does. It's a prompt waiting for you to do something. Whatever the prompt, the principle is the same. A shell account provides access to a computing resource over telephone lines. You can use that resource by typing in commands, and that means mastering a set of Unix statements that will work in your dealings with the Internet. SLIP/PPP accounts can do away with all of that.

Because a shell account involves using resources on a different computer to do your Internet work, it also includes the necessary tools and disk space to help you do that work. You are given a home directory, which is where you wind up when you first log in. You also receive default files for your e-mail, and the ability to use system tools for file management. After all, if you retrieve a file by FTP and it winds up on your service provider's machine, you need some way to transfer it to your own computer. Tools like sz and sx, which are implementations of zmodem and xmodem respectively, allow you to do this. Other tools, like mv and rm, are used to change the names of files, or to remove them from the disk altogether. Using a shell account effectively means mastering these and other commands.

Logging On to a Commercial On-Line Service

The second way to access the Internet through a modem is by connecting to one of the big commercial on-line services. If you're a user of one of these, chances are you've never run across the term "shell account" before—and for good reason. The operating system on the computers you connect to when using Prodigy or CompuServe is hidden from you; you log on only to access a menu or a graphical interface (if you use a product like CompuServe's CIM software for either Windows or the Macintosh, or if you use America Online, which has a well-established graphical interface). You must master whichever commands the system makes available to you, but this is done in an environment that is usually more user-friendly than Unix.

Until recently, many commercial services provided only e-mail access to the Internet. This limited you to sending messages and using some of the ingenious "e-mail only" tools for various tasks, such as retrieving computer files in

ASCII format as messages and then decoding them on your own computer. But in recent times, all of the commercial services have begun to offer expanded Internet access. DELPHI and BIX have provided full access to the major Internet tools for some time, while CompuServe has just opened USENET and FTP gateways, and America Online makes both USENET and Gopher available, with the clear intention of moving into the realm of the World Wide Web.

Can you use a commercial on-line service as an Internet provider? The answer is yes, but only if you accept the fact that the graphical touch provided by SLIP/PPP will be unavailable to you. Both shell accounts and commercial service accounts are hampered by the way in which they move Internet data. You can move back and forth in menus and receive graphics through in-house products like WinCIM, but the wide variety of shareware, commercial, and public domain Internet programs discussed in this book will be unusable (you are limited to what your service provider can send). To understand why, we need to look at something called *terminal emulation.*

Terminal Emulation: The Limiting Factor

When you emulate something, you do the best job you can of acting like that thing. *Terminal emulation* means getting your computer to act like a terminal that is hooked up to another computer. Your communications software, like Crosstalk or Procomm Plus or Microphone, is used to perform this emulation. When you sign on to a computer over a modem, the remote machine "thinks" it has received a login from a terminal. Terminals are a different breed than PCs; they contain no central processing unit, no RAM, and no hard disk. In the absence of these tools, they cannot run programs, but can only display what is sent to them by the host computer, and send back whatever you type on their keyboards.

Your communications software can provide further functionality, allowing you, for example, to download files and capture on-line sessions to disk. But by and large, terminal emulation is a limiting factor. You are restricted to running whatever software is provided by your service provider on his or her computer, since the assumption of the server is that your machine has no processing smarts of its own. The programs you are able to run this way are limited as well, since they can't rely on your machine's native power. More sophisticated software, such as that provided by America Online, sends data that can be used by a "smarter" terminal, one that understands graphics.

VT-100 is the name of a particular type of terminal emulation that grew out of work done by Digital Equipment Corporation (DEC) computers. It has become more or less a standard for terminal emulation on the Internet. Programs to manage most Internet tasks, from Gopher to Internet Relay Chat (IRC) to WAIS, are available through VT-100 emulation, but it is clear that the trend of software development is toward full-featured software tools with graphical interfaces that can exploit the local computer to the maximum.

When you use a modem, SLIP/PPP can provide this kind of functionality, as can ingenious workarounds like The Internet Adapter or SlipKnot (both provide the ability to run programs like Mosaic without a SLIP/PPP connection, but at a cost in speed). We'll discuss these options in Chapter 11.

What SLIP/PPP Does

If SLIP/PPP is preferable, what does it do that is more advantageous? The answer is, SLIP/PPP allows network traffic to be routed directly to your machine. When you turn on your modem and activate your SLIP/PPP connection to the Internet, you establish a two-way link. Run your mail program now and the messages you retrieve will be routed directly onto your computer. If you want to save one, you simply activate the Save command in your mail software. To do that with a shell account, you would have to save the message to your service provider's hard disk and then download it to your own.

The same thing happens with file transfers. When you use a program to go out over the net and open an FTP session, the file you download is sent directly to your machine, rather than through the intermediary of your service provider's computer. As we'll see, your computer has gone from being a terminal on somebody else's computer to being a full-fledged host on the network, with its own Internet Protocol address. That address is active whenever you are logged on; when you log off, the IP address no longer handles your traffic, but data like electronic mail is still queued for you at your service provider's site and can be accessed the next time you log on. SLIP/PPP may not be as fast as a direct, dedicated line to the network, but for anyone using a modem, it's the next best thing; it provides the same power, though without some of the speed.

How is your data routed? Your call is answered at your service provider's site by a *terminal server*, which is a computer that accepts your incoming IP traffic. The terminal server prompts your computer for a user ID and password (all of this happens transparently through a script; you don't necessarily see the process on the screen). Having accepted this information, the terminal server begins transmitting the raw TCP/IP data from your computer to your service provider's Local Area Network. That network, in turn, is connected to the Internet by a *router*, which manages the task of moving Internet data to and from the provider's site and ensuring that it goes where it's supposed to on the net.

From your point of view, nothing much has happened; the login proceeds behind the scenes, leaving you connected but looking at no prompt or other identifiable marker. But the all-important link has been established. With TCP/IP now implemented on your computer, you can run any of the graphical software programs for Internet access, from Mosaic or Netscape to Gopher, from WAIS to FTP, and let these programs provide you with a user interface and the capability of running the various Internet tasks. Your Internet address is now active.

Direct Network Connections

To illustrate how SLIP/PPP works, let's also consider it in relation to a dedicated network connection, one that does not use a dial-up modem for your computer to be on the Internet. With a direct network connection, your computer contains a network interface card, an expansion board that fits into the machine, and allows it to be connected to your office's Local Area Network (LAN). The LAN, in turn, is connected through a router to the Internet; via leased circuits the router directs messages between the two networks.

In the DOS environment, this kind of connection normally involves a type of software called a *packet driver*, which is included with the software that runs the interface card. The packet driver runs as a terminate-and-stay resident (TSR) program that is loaded under MS-DOS; its function is to allow that card to work with the kind of data packets used by the Internet. When using Microsoft Windows, another TSR, called a virtual packet driver, is frequently used to serve as the interface between TCP/IP and the DOS-based driver. TCP/IP, in turn, uses its own driver to interface with the packet driver.

By contrast, SLIP/PPP does not require the drivers associated with a LAN interface card. But the connection functions just as if the computer were logged on to an Ethernet network through a network interface card. To demonstrate how a computer moves data out onto the network, Chapter 2 examines the way traffic flows on the Internet itself. But first, there are several issues that newcomers need to address. If you're just starting out, how do you get all this great software in the first place? And is there something to be said for a shell account as an entry-level gateway to the greater wonders of SLIP/PPP?

A Newcomer's Strategy for Internet Access

Assume for the moment that we live in a perfect world (I know, but never mind). And in this world, a person who has absolutely no experience with the Internet comes to me and asks how to get connected. (This happens, in fact, quite frequently.) This person has heard about various access options and wants to know which is best for the beginner—SLIP/PPP or a shell account? The answer is by no means obvious, nor is the progression of access types clear. In other words, it just isn't true that everyone needs a SLIP/PPP account right off the bat. A month or two of shell access may prove valuable.

While I advocate SLIP/PPP as the closest thing to a hard-wired network connection, my advice to the newcomer is this: if you have patience, start with a shell account and get to know the ropes—use it to download the graphical software and the TCP/IP stack you will later use with your SLIP/PPP account. A shell account has this virtue: it looks and feels closer to the conventional on-line service you may have used in the past. Many such accounts are set up with menu systems for easier access; those that are not will require that you master the basic set of commands before you proceed, but what of that? The point is, the shell account will teach you something about the Internet, and that is all to the good. People I have worked with who go straight to SLIP/PPP often become frustrated with the Internet, because they don't understand its nature. A shell account is a quick—and cheap—way to explore.

Most service providers will then let you take the upgrade path, usually simply by making a phone call. Some people maintain both shell and SLIP/PPP accounts because there are some things that shell accounts do better. When I want to read my mail, for example, I often use pine, a mail reader that runs under Unix on my service provider's machine. The pine mail reader is fast and easy to use; it is a perfect case of a program that possesses many of the advantages of SLIP/PPP, even though it runs over a conventional dial-up connection. FTP is also easily managed under a shell account, so that I often download files in the Unix environment rather than using a graphical client program.

But assuming you don't want the expense of running two different kinds of account at the same time, why not use a shell account for a month or two to learn about the Internet before moving on into SLIP/PPP? The shell account will make it easy for you to access the SLIP/PPP tools that I discuss in this book; you can download them now for use when you activate your new connection. I use Trumpet Winsock to manage TCP/IP on my 486 machine, and the combination of MacTCP and InterSLIP to run the SLIP/PPP connection on my Power Mac. I retrieved the Trumpet and InterSLIP software by anonymous FTP in my shell account, and you can do the same. You can also retrieve most, though not all (some are commercial), of the programs I discuss in the chapters on Gopher, WAIS, FTP, mail, and the rest.

Not convinced? Okay, if you're sure that a shell account would be too difficult to work with, there is another route. Everyone I've ever talked to who wants to get on the Internet has some experience with commercial on-line services. The usual progression is to start with a CompuServe or America Online account (or DELPHI or Prodigy). In any case, these are services that have been around for a while and have built up a substantial following among home and business users. For many, they serve as the introduction to using a modem.

The good news is that the software you will need to get up and running in the SLIP/PPP environment is also available on such services. I can download the Trumpet TCP/IP stack from America Online or CompuServe, and the Inter-SLIP program is likewise available there for the Mac (MacTCP, being part of the operating system, is available only through Apple Computer). Once you have activated your SLIP/PPP account with a full-service Internet provider, you will be in position to then go out over the net using a graphical FTP client to retrieve any of the client programs I discuss in these pages.

And if you do want to go straight to SLIP/PPP, your service provider should be able to offer a basic startup software package that will get you on-line; you can then use its tools to access the software programs discussed in this book. The gratifying and exciting thing about SLIP/PPP access is that it makes you the master of your own network fate. Programs exist for everything you want to do on the Internet; in the Microsoft Windows environment particularly, several implementations are available for each task, an embarrassment of riches that give you the chance to explore and customize your own environment to your heart's content. I have Microsoft Windows running as I write, using the Norton Desktop for Windows to create a desktop in which I have set icons for all my Internet tasks. Netscape and Mosaic are there, as is Trumpet Winsock; I have icons for newsreaders, Gophers, WAIS clients, and FTP programs. Not a month goes by—frequently, not a week—when I don't try something new.

That's the fun of SLIP/PPP, and it's sure to continue as more developers, both from the shareware/freeware camp and the commercial side, continue to work on software. In the Internet world, shareware has never lost its allure; in many cases, it remains the cutting edge of software development. Stay away from all-in-one packages of software, then, and opt for the freedom that roaming the Net can give you. Learn to use one on-line tool (like FTP) to access another tool, and so on, building up a desktop customized for your particular needs. It is a journey that never ceases to fascinate, and if you will abandon the notion, so often hammered home by the media, that the Internet is all but impossible to understand, you may come to find the same enjoyment in it. The Internet is complex, but that is because it contains great riches, and the time spent in mastering it will pay for itself over and over again.

How to Use the Addresses in This Book

In each of the following chapters of this book, I will be examining not only the issues involved with SLIP/PPP, but also the software necessary to make the connection and to use it to perform Internet tasks. The information I specify here can be used to retrieve these programs right off the net, but there are certain caveats you need to bear in mind. These vary depending upon your method of retrieving the software.

If You Already Have Internet Access

FTP sites are set up by local system administrators, who have decided to make a portion of their computing resources available to the public. As a noncommercial service, an FTP site is under no constraints to be consistent with other sites. The directory structure you find there will depend upon what seems logical to the powers that be at the site. Some directories are well-nigh universal; you will almost always, for example, find a */pub* directory, which is often a good place to begin looking for interesting materials.

But system administrators always have an eye for what will streamline operations on their computers. It is more than likely that a printed specification about which directory you turn to as you look for a file will be out of date by the time you read it. The program is probably still on the computer at the specified address, but you will need to look around for it.

What to do? As an author, I think the best thing to do is to lead you to the right site, and to show you where a given program is located at that site *today*. This will give you a sense of the directory structure you will find at that site, and some clues as to where to begin looking if your program isn't exactly where you thought it would be. If you log on and simply can't find the program in question, look in the directory to which FTP logs on for help information. Most sites maintain a file that explains where things are. It might be called README, READ.ME, INDEX, or some variant of any of these; in any case, its name should be self-explanatory.

Another possibility is a file with the bizarre name ls-lR, which is a listing of all the files available at that site (ls-lR is a Unix command with parameters that pull all file information out of all available directories). The thing to do is to download this file and read it. There are ways to read files on-line at FTP sites, but I don't advocate using them for this reason: FTP is not a *connectionless* protocol. By this I mean that, when you log on to a site, a connection between your computer and the site remains active until you explicitly close the connection. Why tie up the site when you can read what you need off-line? This contrasts with, say, Gopher, which is connectionless. When you examine a Gopher menu, the program is storing the information it has just retrieved over the network, but the connection itself is not active until you click on a menu choice, at which point Gopher goes to the link specified for the menu item you have chosen.

The method for FTP, then, is to look first in the directory I specify in this book. If you can't find the file you need, go back to the root directory and look for a help file. Retrieve that help file and read it off-line. Then return to the site, armed with your knowledge of how the site is constructed, and find the file you need. Many sites, especially popular archival sites like **sumex-aim.-stanford.edu** or **oak.oakland.edu**, maintain listings of all the files available; these are frequently updated, and you can download them as readily as you can download the other help files. Use these materials, as they can untangle even the most intricate FTP situation. There is one FTP site out there with more than 1,500 subdirectories branching off its root directory; you wouldn't want to count on luck to find what you need at a site like that!

Don't forget, either, that client programs are in a state of constant development. The exciting pace of change in this field means that the file I mention called **pmail122.zip** might, by the time you read this, be found as **pmail201.-zip**, or some other combination of numbers indicating which version is available. Generally, the latest version will be the one that is posted; if earlier versions are available as well, you will be able to find them by comparing numbers—the larger numbers always indicate later versions. Version 1.02 is a later product than version 1.01, while version 2.01 is later than both.

Finally, be aware of the limitations of FTP access. In sharp distinction to commercial on-line services, most FTP sites are not maintained as businesses. The people who run these sites do so out of their own interest and their willingness to help the Internet community. You should expect no technical support from the people at an FTP site, and you should exercise basic courtesy when working with an FTP connection. The most important etiquette consideration is to use the site after business hours at its location. Many, if not most, FTP sites are also in use by the organization running them; overloading these computers with file transfer requests during business hours is not the way to express your thanks for their availability.

> **Note:** It can be a difficult proposition getting into some FTP sites. When you attempt to log in and nothing happens, or a message appears telling you that too many people are now using the system for you to log in, don't be surprised. Given the rapid growth in Internet connections, many sites and services are simply being overwhelmed with requests. The thing to do in such a case is to wait a few minutes and try again; if that doesn't work, try a little later in the day. I can think of several popular archival sites where it took me days to get in, an unusual situation, to be sure, but one that occasionally occurs. Patience will eventually pay off.
>
> You should also consider obtaining a list of *mirror* sites. A mirror is simply a duplicate collection of the files found at a particular location; the files are duplicated and synchronized automatically through the mirror facility. The most popular archival collections tend to be mirrored at many places around the Internet. For example, **sumex-aim.stanford.edu**, which is one of the most popular Macintosh sites, is mirrored by some 30 computers around the world. You can obtain a complete list at the site itself; you can then use the mirrors to obtain the same software, but without taxing the overburdened central site.

If You Are Using a Commercial On-Line Service

The distinction between the Internet and the commercial on-line services like CompuServe or America Online has begun to blur somewhat, with the arrival of, first, mail gateways and, later, USENET access from these services. Today, CompuServe provides mail, USENET, and FTP, and is rapidly moving toward Telnet access as well. DELPHI already provides all of these, along with Gopher and World Wide Web capabilities; and America Online is moving aggressively into Internet regions with limited USENET access, mail, Gopher, and the clear intention of expanding in some fashion into the World Wide Web environment.

This means that there are many users out there whose first taste of the Internet has come through one of the big commercial services, and who are now thinking of getting an account with a full-service Internet provider. A person in this situation will want to retrieve Trumpet Winsock to run his or her pending SLIP/PPP connection, but without existing Internet access, it will be necessary to find the software on the commercial service. Fortunately, this is no longer a problem. CompuServe maintains a File Finder for both IBM-compatible equipment and Macintoshes; you can search under keywords for the software you need. Inserting an appropriate name or keyword will quickly tell you in which forum library to search.

America Online also provides easy search capability; I've found most of the programs described in this book there. Of course, the main issue is to get the SLIP/PPP connection enabled, and that means finding either Trumpet Winsock for the Microsoft Windows environment or InterSLIP for the Mac; both are available on-line. Once they are loaded according to the instructions provided in this book, you can exercise your new SLIP/PPP connection by retrieving the other software at FTP sites. The key point is, no matter what kind of connectivity you currently possess, and even if you are limited to a commercial on-line service for your Internet access at present, you can retrieve the necessary software to expand your capabilities. But at some point you are going to have to set up a SLIP/PPP connection with an Internet provider.

How Addresses Are Specified

In my previous books, I have always broken addresses down by specifying an FTP site and following it with directory and file information. The method was accurate but space-consuming. I might, for example, have specified a file this way:

> Site: **ftp.utas.edu.au**
> Directory: */pc/trumpet/winsock*
> File: twsk20a.zip

And, as mentioned previously, when you went to the site to retrieve the file, it was always possible that the directory had changed.

In this book, I have decided to change all addresses to the new, precise URL method. URL stands for Uniform Resource Locator. Using URLs, I can state exactly the address and the resource in one line. In the preceding example, I could state the entire address this way as a URL:

ftp://ftp.utas.edu.au/pc/trumpet/winsock/twsk20a.zip

I have managed the entire statement in a single line, saving space. Notice that the name of the service, FTP, is shown at the far left, followed by double slashes and then the address of the computer at the site. This is followed by the entire directory tree, until the URL reaches its terminus in the actual name of the file. Because filenames do change so frequently, I will make it a habit in these pages to show the entire directory tree, followed by a note as to what the filename is as I write.

In later chapters, you will see URLs used quite a bit. World Wide Web browsers like Cello, Mosaic, and Netscape use URLs to pinpoint resources. Not only FTP sites can be so specified, but also Gopher, Telnet, and other types of services. It seems likely that Internet documentation will gradually move over to the URL method for any kind of address specification. This would be a welcome change from the diversity that characterizes Internet publishing today. After all, our great need when dealing with this farflung network is to be able to point to what we want. The URL method makes that process much easier.

Ready to begin? The first thing to do is to master Chapter 2, which explains how the Internet works, and how your SLIP/PPP connection functions within its broad context. After that, I will show you how to install a TCP/IP stack on a Microsoft Windows-based machine, as well as, in Chapter 4, a Macintosh. After that, we move out into the broad avenue of software development. I can't show you every client program out there because of space constraints, but I think I've found most of the best. In any case, there's nothing wrong with trying one and, if it doesn't suit you, moving on to another. On the Internet, diversity is bliss.

2

SLIP/PPP and the Structure of the Internet

Well-chosen names contain definitions. Thus the word "Internet" contains the essential elements that make the concept work—*inter*linked *net*working, in which multiple networks manage to exchange data between themselves. CompuServe is accessed over a single network, so is America Online. The Internet is made up of thousands of networks—more than 40,000 at the time of this writing—exchanging information. Whereas each separate network is maintained by a central organization somewhere, the Internet itself has no central office or control center. It is a collaborative effort that proceeds through the efforts of system administrators at thousands upon thousands of sites. And it works because its constituent networks make use of a common methodology called TCP/IP.

TCP/IP: The Definition of a Protocol

Protocols are working parameters that allow computers to exchange messages or other data. We need such rules because of the formidable challenge posed by internetworking. After all, the world of digital data is not made up of a single type of computer; out there on the network we run into Macintoshes and Unix workstations, Digital Equipment Corp.'s VAX computers and IBM mainframes, Windows-based Intel platforms and Amigas. If we want to allow all of these platforms to coexist and to share their resources, we need to establish common rules. And if one rule is a protocol, a set of such protocols is called a *suite.* TCP/IP, then, is a suite of protocols that establish working parameters for the worldwide Internet.

We can think of protocols in terms of *stacks* (envision a stack of pancakes). Each layer of the network stack is designed to perform a specific function, and the work of each is determined by a protocol particular to that layer. Application programs are at the top of the stack, in the *application layer;* when they have processed the data, they pass it down to the next layer, the *transport layer,* which is in charge of breaking that data into pieces that can be provided with addresses by the next lower layer, the *network layer.* This network layer is in charge of routing the resulting *datagrams,* which it passes down to the *data link layer* and the *physical layers;* these assume the role of actually transmitting the data out onto the broader Internet.

 Note: The stack concept is a fruitful one, and not just because it allows us to visualize what is going on in a complex network connection. Because stacks isolate the basic processes involved in internetworking, they allow programmers to focus on specific aspects of the data transaction. Everything that goes on in the layer in question must conform to accepted standards. Imagine how difficult it would be to try to accomplish in a single software package every single function necessary to make diverse computers communicate, coping with every possible hardware architecture. So, just as programmers break computer code into manageable units, network gurus divide the tasks their networks accomplish into distinct and understandable layers.

TCP/IP is actually made up of two distinct protocols. The first is Transmission Control Protocol. TCP is used in the Internet's transport layer; it is given the responsibility of ensuring that data is delivered. To do so, it assembles that data into packets. These *datagrams* are then routed by the Internet Protocol, or IP. This is what is meant by the term data *packet*—it is data prepared in a particular format for routing through the network by IP. When I send you a message, my message will be assembled into such packets, each of which will be addressed and routed, and each of which will take whatever route to destination is determined by the network. The same message may contain data packets that take entirely different routes to the recipient. Upon arrival, TCP on the destination computer is in charge of reassembling these packets in the correct order.

Data packets can be up to 1,500 characters long. Naturally, much of the traffic we would like to send over the network is longer than 1,500 characters, which is precisely why we need Transmission Control Protocol, to break larger messages into smaller pieces and to provide the necessary information to ensure they can be rebuilt at the other end. TCP is also a *reliable* protocol, meaning that it can verify that the information it sent has been received. It does so by waiting for a confirmation from the destination computer that the message has indeed made its journey and been reassembled.

You may also run across reference to a transport layer protocol called User Datagram Protocol, or UDP. Unlike TCP, UDP does not have the ability to confirm that a message has been received; on the positive side, it is very sparing in its use of network resources. Both UDP and TCP exist in the Internet's transport layer. UDP is technically referred to as connectionless, meaning that it communicates without a direct physical connection and the exchange of control information. The protocol is mostly used in programs that send only short messages, in which it is not necessary to break the message into multiple packets with their corresponding ordering information.

In the next two chapters, you will see that, before you can run any of the interesting client programs to take full advantage of the Internet, you have to acquire a TCP/IP stack for your computer. The software that handles data packet management is available for both Microsoft Windows-based PCs and Macintoshes, and I'll show you how to get it. You'll also have to retrieve software to manage the connection between your computer and the network it's contacting. Using a SLIP/PPP connection, that link takes place over the telephone line; you therefore need a dialer to make the call, along with the necessary SLIP/PPP software to make the connection work. The next two chapters will tell you how to find this software. But first, let's take a closer look at packet switching.

How Packet Switching Works

The general term for the entire procedure of Internet data management is *packet switching;* the Internet can be said to be a packet switching network. Each data packet is complete in itself; it contains all necessary address information to ensure its safe delivery. The packets flow out onto the network through a *router,* a computer that takes over the task of directing messages through the system; in Internet parlance, we commonly speak of *IP routers.* Despite its name, a router is just a computer that has been put to work at a particular task, although dedicated routers contain specific connections necessary to link Local Area Networks (LANs) to the Internet. You've heard a little about routers if you follow the stock market. Cisco Systems, a company specializing in creating routers, has been a darling of Wall Street in recent years.

What does a router do? It examines the destination of each data packet and makes a decision about how to get that packet delivered. Think of the journey as proceeding in a series of bursts, from one router to another, until the packet finally arrives. The computer at the destination site must reassemble the data packets to retrieve the entire message. And, significantly, if that computer finds that one or more of the packets was damaged or lost along the way, it will request retransmission from the computer that sent them.

Notice what happens in the following scenario. Perhaps I want to send a message to a friend of mine in Hong Kong. I write the message and tell my mail program to send it. The message is broken into data packets, which flow out onto the Internet. These packets proceed through routers along the way until they arrive and are reassembled. My friend gets my message and can respond to it, but note a key fact: at no time along the way were our two computers directly linked. This is a major difference between a packet switching network like the Internet and what is known as a *circuit switching* network, like the telephone system.

Circuit switching involves creating a single circuit between the two telephones involved in a call. If I decide to call my friend in Hong Kong, our two telephones become connected through the work of the telephone companies' switches. For the duration of our call, we have a direct connection, which is broken when we hang up. By not requiring a direct connection between computers to send data, the Internet boosts efficiency. Everyone can use the network's resources by sharing them; the workload tends to be distributed across the computing capabilities of the net. As far as the end user is concerned, it doesn't matter how the packets of a message are divided or where they are routed; the result is the same when they arrive.

We know that packet switching works because the Internet handles our message traffic every day. But how did it originate? The answer is, the Department of Defense (through its Advanced Research Projects Agency) saw in packet switching the solution to a key problem faced by the military during the Cold War. In the event of a nuclear strike against the United States, major computer installations were sure to be knocked out. A way needed to be found to allow traffic to reroute itself automatically around such sites, and packet switching was the solution. If it seems ironic that a technology spawned in the era of nuclear blackmail should now power the world's largest information network, it isn't the first time that military expertise has resulted in gains for the civilian sector. We have air traffic control radar today because in the early days of World War II, British scientists had to find a way to track incoming Luftwaffe bombers.

The Client/Server Model

You now know a little about how the Internet manages its flow of data, so let's try to place the three types of modem connectivity discussed in Chapter 1 into perspective. When you have a shell account, no data packets pass between your service provider's machine and your own. Instead, the packets flow between the Internet and your service provider; what you receive is simply the ability to use your service provider's tools to manipulate the data that you can generate with those tools. The same is true of an account with a commercial on-line service, in which the actual Internet packets are dealt with at the service's central site. You enjoy the fruits of that site's labors, but you exchange no data packets over the network.

Using SLIP/PPP, the model changes utterly. Now the data packets flow directly to you, to be managed by the TCP/IP software you have installed on your machine. Your computer may be said to have its own IP address, which becomes activated when you sign on. The first task you will complete in this book is to set up the necessary software to allow you to use SLIP/PPP. You must load a TCP/IP stack on your machine, and various commercial implementations are out there that allow you to do this. In this book, we'll look at a fine shareware package called Trumpet Winsock, for Windows-based computers, and one called MacTCP for Macintosh users. We'll also examine the distinction between SLIP and PPP to help you decide which to use.

But the TCP/IP stack and SLIP/PPP software is only the beginning. You'll also need programs that you can run on your computer to take advantage of your newfound network power. If you have been using the Internet for a while with a straight shell account, I think you will be amazed to see how many programs are out there, and how diverse are the jobs they can perform. Indeed, one of the frustrations of my own early days on the Internet was reading in USENET newsgroups about programs that greatly simplified network use, and knowing that even if I retrieved them by FTP, I couldn't run them over my existing network connection. SLIP/PPP opens up that whole world of software development for you.

To understand how such programs work over a network, we need to examine the client/server model. A *client* is a program you use to contact other computers that make information services available. A *server* is a program that runs on a remote computer and dispenses information to the client. The nature of networking is to distribute computing resources, and this is exactly what the client/server model does. In Internet terms, data is placed upon server computers, and the tools to access that data are placed upon the computers of the users. The division of tasks means that the server can be reserved for the maintenance of the actual data. The jobs of displaying and manipulating that data are off-loaded to the client programs on remote computers throughout the Internet.

This is where the processing power of your computer becomes critical. As described earlier, a terminal emulation routine presumes that your computer lacks processing muscle; it is dependent upon what the server computer can send it. This limits both the display you see on the screen and the functionality of the programs you can run. When your computer is recognized as having its own processing capabilities, then it can use client programs to interact with the server to display information in more intuitive ways and to increase the flexibility of your management of that information. In addition, by distributing the burden of client program chores to separate computers, the server is freed from applying its own processing power to the data it provides; instead, it lets that data flow to clients that will tap the information flow.

The tools we will look at in this book are all examples of the client/server model in action. Run Gopher, for example, on your own computer over a SLIP/PPP connection and you will activate one of several possible client implementations of Gopher. Your client software will go out over the network to contact a server, retrieving the Gopher menus from whichever site you have chosen to reach. It is your client program, not the server, that will determine how these menus look on-screen. The client, in addition, may provide you with a variety of tools that also use your computer's power to do things like maintain file folders of interesting information or provide various links to other software on your system to display graphical images or play sound files. Good client programs are being written all the time, and older ones are being updated. Keeping up with them is one of the pleasures of network use.

Bandwidth and the Digital Speed Limit

Bandwidth refers to the amount of data that can flow through a given connection in a fixed amount of time. A major network site, such as a university or a research laboratory, might use several high-speed links, usually T-1 connections; T-1 refers to a telephone trunk line made up of two twisted pair copper cables that can transfer data at 1.544 megabits per second (Mbps). Such T-1 lines form much of the infrastructure for the Internet on the regional level. Much excitement attended the implementation of T-3 speeds on the National Science Foundation's backbone network several years ago, and for good reason; T-3 allows data to flow at 45 Mbps.

As you use the Internet, you will realize that bandwidth is a key constraint everywhere. The fact that you can hook into a high-speed network doesn't mean that you can move data to your own computer at the same speeds that the network can transfer data between its nodes. Your transfer rate will be dependent upon your modem. I will discuss modem issues later in this chapter.

The future of the so-called "information superhighway" will be determined by how the telecommunications infrastructure can be modified to meet the need for ever greater bandwidth. Video and audio, for example, take up considerably more bandwidth than plain text. You can get a glimpse of this if you simply examine the difference between file sizes of an ASCII text file and a photograph in GIF or JPEG format (two of the most widely used methods of storing such information). A GIF image of a text file, for example, would be significantly larger than its ASCII equivalent. An audio file that takes 10 minutes to transfer across a SLIP connection might take a mere 20 seconds to play. Obviously, with interest in multimedia and real-time video connectivity growing, our telecommunications infrastructure will require a massive expansion of current bandwidth.

But let's pause for a moment on the speed issue, from the perspective of today's networking and a Local Area Network standard called *Ethernet*. Developed at Xerox Corporation's Palo Alto Research Center, where so many things we take for granted—mice, graphical interfaces, pull-down menus—were pioneered, Ethernet was worked into a network specification by Digital Equipment Corp., Intel Corp., and Xerox Corp. Ethernet connects computers in the office environment, providing transfer rates of 10 megabits per second (10 Mbps).

Now consider the speeds involved. When I say that SLIP/PPP allows your computer to act as if it were hooked into your service provider's local area network, I mean that it provides the ability to run network programs on that computer. But these programs are limited by the nature of the SLIP/PPP transaction over the telephone line. An Ethernet may run at 10 Mbps, while a high-speed dedicated T-1 line runs at 1.5 Mbps. A low-speed digital line to your house is going to top out at 56 kilobits per second (56 Kbps), while your new modem may set a limit of 14.4 Kbps, which is less than 2 percent of the speed Ethernet is capable of reaching.

We must also consider the delays that occur as data is moved through the network. In packet switching networks, we call this delay *latency;* it refers to the fact that data must travel through a series of routers as it moves toward its destination. The round trip time may be negligible for most things—I'm always amazed when I send e-mail to Australia, for example, and receive a reply almost immediately; the message actually arrives there in seconds. But for some applications, like real-time video, this latency makes packet switching a less than effective transport mechanism. With SLIP/PPP, we must add in the fact that the data is moving over a slow line to begin with. Screens are going to take a moment to redraw, while generating files like graphics and audio over Gopher or Mosaic can be time-consuming even with a fast modem.

The digital speed limit is thus built into what we do with SLIP/PPP. Moving past it will require not only faster modems, but also better telephone connections to home and business. We are at the end of the era of copper wire into the home; the next advance will surely be fiber optic or coaxial cable and high-bandwidth digital telephony. This revolution in how we use communications will one day make high-speed, full network connections available just about anywhere, but until it occurs, we must use the tools in today's market to join the network. In any case, SLIP/PPP must be weighed against the cost of high-speed dedicated lines, at which point its benefits become obvious and its disadvantages excusable.

Network Addressing: The Domain Name System

When I first became acquainted with the Internet, I was baffled by the arcane addressing schemes that were used. When I sent a message to a person, I used an address with an @ symbol tucked inside, on the order of **roliver@mercury.interpath.net**. Most of these addresses took the same general form, with the @ symbol enclosed, but others did not. I ran into addresses like **ftp.ncsa.uiuc.edu**, which also used periods to separate names, but which left out the @.

Note: It's possible to envision a day when the client/server model becomes so widespread that it alters what you maintain on your own hard disk. When I began writing about the Internet several years ago, I kept huge numbers of text files, culled from my travels on the network, on my hard disk, and used them for reference. The more I traversed the network, the more it seemed pointless to do this. I was using up hard disk space at my office, while the files were located in places that I could reach quickly with my FTP client program whenever I needed them.

Now imagine a future when networking has expanded through broader data pipes to home and business. As you use your word processor, for example, you may want to run a spell check against a database of correctly spelled words. This function currently takes up the necessary space on your hard disk. Will we reach a point where such dictionary resources are made accessible through servers, so that your spell checker goes out seamlessly over the Internet and runs your query against such a database? Certainly the current state of the net argues against this kind of use because of performance considerations, but it is possible that as we broaden bandwidth, we will also broaden the connectivity between our everyday programs, our word processors, and spreadsheets with databases and other research tools that exist on server computers on the Internet.

Later I learned that periods in Internet names are referred to as "dots," so that the above address would be voiced "ftp dot ncsa dot uiuc dot edu." And then there were those numbered addresses, like **199.72.4.57**. How did they relate to the others?

The situation seemed confusing, but in reality, the Internet's name and addressing schemes are remorselessly logical, once you get past the hurdle of relating them to the underlying network architecture. Numbered addresses are called *IP addresses;* they're used to give the network the information it needs to deliver a given data packet. You will never have to decipher such numbers, but it helps to know that the network reads them from left to right. On the left are the numbers with the broadest significance; they tell routers to which network they should send the packet. On the far right are numbers that actually specify a given computer, or host; this is the destination of the data packet. Although there are over 4.8 million host computers on the Internet, each has a unique address that can be specified by using this scheme.

Computers work well with numbers, but most people do not. The key argument against nine-digit zip codes is that while people can hold five numbers in their memory, even seven (think of phone numbers), nine moves past some primal barrier that forces us to look such information up to verify that we have it right. For instance, if I want to tell you where to go to download a particular software package, I would rather say "try wuarchive.wustl.edu" (even if it sounds bizarre) than try to rattle off a string of digits of the same length. Out of such common sense concerns was the Domain Name System born. Computers thus gained names, which is why your e-mail address sounds as peculiar as it does.

One address I maintain is **gilster@mercury.interpath.net**. Note the managing principle here: it is the reverse of the IP address. With the latter, we began at the left and worked from lesser to greater specificity. The Domain Name System begins with greater specificity on the left and proceeds to the general. The above address can be broken down thus: "gilster" is my user name; "mercury" is the name of the computer on which my account resides, the machine I dial into when I activate my account; "interpath" is the name of the service provider whose network I use to move onto the Internet. And "net" is the designation for the type of service Interpath is, a network.

Each of the names separated by a dot is called a domain. The top-level domains, those of the most general significance, are as follows:

com   A commercial operation. The number of these is growing faster than any other domain.

edu   A university, college, or other educational institution.

gov   A government organization.

mil   A military site.

org   Any organization that does not fit into any of the preceding.

net   A network.

These domain names were the original ones, but there are now two-letter domains that denote individual countries, a tribute to the fact that the Internet has rapidly become an international network, with more than 130 countries boasting some kind of connectivity. Thus we run into designations like these:

at   Austria

gt   Guatemala

ve   Venezuela

zw   Zimbabwe

Thus you will encounter addresses like **rubens.anu.edu.au**, where the final **.au** tells you this is a site in Australia. Some 300 country codes now exist, many for countries that are not yet on the Internet.

Names help us remember and refer to Internet sites. But it's obvious that the computers that route network traffic have to be able to translate these names back into the IP addresses (numbers only) that they use in their work.

This lookup procedure works through *nameservers,* computers that can turn domain names into IP addresses. The process is known as *resolving* a domain name (picking up on the original Latin meaning of *resolvere*—to untie, or unsort). The Domain Name Service, or DNS, is actually a software program that runs on the computers that do this work. Every domain in the Internet maintains a server that keeps information about how to deliver a message within that particular domain. When a router doesn't know how to deliver a message within a domain, it contacts the server for that domain to procure the relevant information.

The Domain Name System is a remarkably useful way of structuring Internet addresses. Not only does it provide for easy-to-remember computer names, it also ensures that these names will not overlap in a way that will be confusing for the network. It is one thing to register names when the network you're dealing with is small, but quite another to try to keep names individual and thus recognizable when thousands of new networks and millions of new users are signing on every year. For mail to work, after all, each computer has to have a unique address. How long could it be before names began to repeat?

The Domain Name System gets around this problem nicely. When a computer is untangling a DNS name, it turns to a nameserver, beginning with the most general part of the address. Ponder sending mail to my address **gilster@mercury.interpath.net**. Perhaps there is a **mercury.patagonia.net** out there somewhere (presumably in Tierra del Fuego); the fact that two computers named "mercury" thus exist presents no problem, because to reach each machine requires that a message be routed along an entirely different path. The message goes first to "patagonia" and only then up the address chain to "mercury"; a message addressed to me goes first through "interpath" and then on to "mercury". As far as the DNS is concerned, the two addresses are absolutely distinct.

Think of a telephone directory. The operator trying to reach my publisher, John Wiley & Sons, has a listing for the Wiley switchboard, but no information on the phone numbers of individual employees. When you call the switchboard, you can retrieve the number for the specific person you want to reach. Finally,

Note: Hang around the Internet for a while and you're bound to hear about the "hosts" file. This was a list, maintained by the Network Information Center, of names and addresses on the Internet; it was distributed on a regular basis throughout the net. When your computer needed to resolve a name, it would simply consult this file and be on its way. The Domain Name System grew out of the pressures placed upon the old hosts file method, but there are still some computers that use the hosts file. On such a system, a needed address might have to be added manually, which demonstrates the superiority of the DNS.

you can be put through to that person. In Internet terms, of course, the process of moving through these levels of nested directories takes mere seconds.

In this book, you will use this background information about the Domain Name System as you install and configure the software needed to make your SLIP/PPP connection. Doing so requires entering the correct information in appropriate fields, and rather than simply inserting numbers given to you by your service provider, I want you to understand what those numbers refer to, and why a mistake in any of them can cause your connection to be disabled. The Internet is complex and fascinating, but it needn't be overly intimidating if you understand the rationale behind its workings. And—a bit of good news for the less technically inclined—once you've set up the SLIP/PPP connection, you won't have to tinker with it again, other than to occasionally tweak it in the event, for example, that you buy a new modem or change service providers.

Note: Here's another problem that the Domain Name System neatly solves for system administrators. Let's say you decide to move a particular computer to a new location. Because that computer's host name remains the same, the move becomes transparent to network users. The only thing the system administrator has to worry about is changing the link between the host name and the physical IP address that underlies it.

SLIP versus PPP

I hope you now have a feel for how the Internet moves its traffic. You should be considering at this point how and where to set up your account with a local service provider. And as you begin this process, you will need to determine the kinds of services your provider makes available. SLIP is being offered inexpensively in most cities, with prices dropping as low as $20 per month for a certain number of hours of access. But PPP is beginning to spread as well. The next question to ask, then, is which of the two is better, and why? Your service provider may have his or her own thoughts on this, and you should certainly determine which is the more likely to be supported at that site. Although either SLIP or PPP will get you up and running, the digital tea leaves do favor PPP, for reasons having to do with SLIP's limitations. You'll see why in a moment.

A Hard Look at SLIP

Serial Line Internet Protocol is not an official standard; indeed, it was more or less thrown together as an expedient means of accessing the net over a telephone line. We can date this solution to the year 1984, when Rick Adams set up a form of the protocol to run on Sun Microsystems workstations. SLIP met

Note: On the Internet, there is a central place to look for technical information. Requests for Comments, or RFCs, are standards documents that shape the development of network research. All of the standards for TCP/IP are found in the RFCs, as are the various other protocols that make up the network's primary tools. The RFC system is managed by the Internet Architecture Board, which is, in turn, a part of the Internet Society. The documents are maintained at the Information Sciences Institute of the University of Southern California, and are mirrored at numerous network sites.

For SLIP users with a hankering for all the details, two RFCs will do the trick. The title of RFC 1055 describes SLIP perfectly: "A Nonstandard for Transmission of IP Datagrams over Serial Lines: SLIP"; the protocol is described as "a de facto standard, commonly used for point-to-point serial connections running TCP/IP. It is not an Internet standard." RFC 1144 is called "Compressing TCP/IP Headers for Low-Speed Serial Links"; it describes a form of SLIP known as Compressed SLIP, or CSLIP, which improves performance over low-speed lines.

PPP users who want to go to the source can start with the following RFCs:

- RFC 1134 The Point-to-Point Protocol; A Proposal for Multi-Protocol Transmission of Datagrams Over Point-to-Point Links
- RFC 1172 The Point-to-Point Protocol (PPP) Initial Configuration Options
- RFC 1334 PPP Authentication Protocols
- RFC 1548 The Point-to-Point Protocol (PPP)
- RFC 1663 PPP Reliable Transmission

an obvious need; researchers, academics, and other users needed a way to dial in to their business or university's computers when they were out of the office to gain network access.

The compelling nature of this need caused SLIP to spread quickly, a fact that led to its widespread adoption as a method of running TCP/IP over serial lines. A measure of SLIP's popularity is the fact that it comes with Berkeley Unix and several other Unix implementations. It is also widely circulated in various TCP/IP solutions for personal computers. But the system was not officially documented until 1988, and has never been proposed as an Internet standard because of its numerous limitations.

SLIP does not, for example, provide for error detection on noisy telephone lines; nor does it provide diagnostic features—if something goes wrong with a

SLIP connection, weeding out where the problem lies can be a difficult chore. Network administrators must worry about such issues, and about the fact that SLIP does not allow for host computers to communicate addressing information with each other, which means that for correct routing to occur, both computers involved in the SLIP connection must know each other's IP address. SLIP is also limited to using a single protocol, IP, meaning that companies with complex networking needs cannot support simultaneous use of IP and any other protocol. A final limitation: SLIP in its original form does not allow for data compression. This is the reason for the development of the revised form of SLIP called CSLIP, which compresses header information and thus speeds up overall performance.

PPP on the Fast Track

Point-to-Point Protocol emerged as a way of coping with the problems that using SLIP had revealed. It is, therefore, a more feature-laden protocol and, in the eyes of many users, a faster one. The protocol first appeared in 1989, with implementations by Russ Hobby of the University of California at San Diego and Drew Perkins of Carnegie-Mellon University; most versions of PPP available today derive from these implementations. Unlike SLIP, then, PPP is a product of more or less official channels. The Internet Engineering Task Force, which coordinates engineering projects for the Internet in the United States, set up a Point-to-Point Working Group, and PPP can be seen as a logical development of research into this connection issue. PPP is considered the more robust of the two protocols, with self-contained error detection; PPP also offers data compression, which is automatically negotiated as the connection to the network is made. And in terms of future use, PPP is under active development, whereas SLIP's era seems to have passed.

Thus, while SLIP may be easier to implement than PPP, users wanting to keep up with the latest in serial line technology may opt for PPP when they are given the choice. And that, of course, is the problem. In my area, for example, SLIP came first and remains the most widely available option. However, in recent times, service providers have begun to offer PPP. My advice would be to opt for PPP; if it is not a possibility, SLIP will still provide perfectly sufficient connectivity for most home and small business users. Talk to your service provider to get the opinion of experienced network administrators in your area before making a final decision. With more startup service providers coming on-line every month, it is likely that PPP will soon spread into your area. The wave of the future is TCP/IP in some fashion over telephone lines into home and business; we can surely expect development of PPP to continue and accelerate.

The programs I discuss in this book can run over either a SLIP or a PPP connection. Thus, to save unnecessary verbiage, I will simply speak of SLIP/

Note: As interest in the Internet mushroomed in the past two years, major software vendors began to take note. One of the more interesting developments is the inclusion of Internet connectivity in the operating systems that run our computers. Microsoft plans to include both SLIP and PPP in both Windows NT and Windows 95, the successor to version 3.1. It is interesting to note that the company will include PPP, but not SLIP, server capability in Windows NT, an indication of the continuing rise of PPP (SLIP, however, will be supported for client workstations for those who already have SLIP servers). IBM, meanwhile, has included Internet connectivity in its new version of OS/2 called Warp; SLIP and TCP/IP are built into the product, as are graphical browsing tools to help newcomers explore the net.

Thus we see two trends of development among the commercial providers. On the one hand, there is growth in the area of one-stop solutions, tools like Spry's Internet In A Box or Ventana Press' Internet Membership Kit. On the other, the inclusion of the basic software into operating systems may reach a new generation of users, people who wouldn't have thought to explore SLIP/PPP on their own, but who will activate a menu option that leads them to easy connectivity; IBM's Warp, for example, is said to make signing up to the Internet a matter of clicking a few buttons, to enable an account through Big Blue's own service. The key question for service providers: how big is this audience, and how many users will companies like Microsoft and IBM be able to appropriate from the ranks of newcomers?

PPP as if they were interchangeable, except in the following two chapters, when you perform the actual SLIP or PPP software installation.

Equipment Needs for SLIP/PPP

Getting SLIP/PPP up and running at your site doesn't call for a lot of horsepower. But running some of the necessary client programs can consume lots of resources, depending upon which clients you use the most. If you're an IBM-compatible computer owner, virtually any PC will do, provided you have at least an 80386 processor (a 486 is preferable). You'll also need a hard disk drive, preferably as large as possible, because your journeys onto the Internet will result in numerous finds—software programs, images, and documents that you'll want to squirrel away. If you're a Microsoft Windows user, you should be using version 3.1 or later.

If you drive a Macintosh, you'll also need a hard drive and a minimum of 4 MB of RAM (I recommend 8), along with System 7 or better.

Note: If you become a frequent SLIP/PPP user, it may make sense to invest in a second telephone line, to avoid tying up your house or office phone for long stretches of time. Alternatively, you can look into answering options offered by your telephone carrier; it's usually possible to bypass a busy signal so that callers can leave a message when you're on-line.

Getting the Right Modem

So much for the easy part. Your modem is the critical link in the SLIP/PPP transaction, and it should be as fast a modem as possible. It will only take one attempt at running Mosaic over a 2400 bps modem to convince you that higher-speed modems pay for themselves over and over again in terms of easing your frustration and making your network sessions more productive. A V.32 9600 bps modem is the bare minimum for this kind of work, while a 14.4 Kbps V.32bis/V.42bis modem is even better. The next step up, a 28.8 Kbps modem, is now becoming a feasible alternative, particularly with the appearance of the V.34 standard that makes questions of compatibility moot. Aim at the highest speed your service provider can support, and if you choose 28.8, make sure your modem is V.34 compatible. The older V.FC and V.FAST modems are now giving way to the new standard.

Note: Modem speeds are deceptive. You go to the store to buy a 28.8 Kbps modem only to find its manufacturer claiming transfer rates of 115,200 bits per second. And with a 14.4 Kbps modem, you will see speeds of 57,600 bps quoted. If you look closely, you will see that these speeds are in each case a multiple of 4 over the base speed. What is happening is that the new high-speed modems are using data compression to squeeze out much higher transfer rates than would otherwise be possible.

These speeds sound astonishing over a telephone link; indeed, in many respects they are more mirage than actuality. Data compression won't do much for you, for example, if you are trying to retrieve a file that is already compressed. That file can't hope to come in at any speed faster than the base rate of the modem. Thus, a 28.8 Kbps modem could theoretically retrieve the file at 28,800 bits per second, *except* that telephone line conditions are rarely clean enough to allow that transfer rate, causing the modem to drop back to a lower speed level. Yes, you will achieve faster transfer speeds with a faster modem, but perhaps not those suggested by the manufacturers.

The cryptic terminology of the various modem protocols is confusing. Here's a quick look at the terms that are most significant for today's high-speed modems:

V.32	A standard for 9600 bps modems, adopted by the CCITT (International Telegraph and Telephone Consultative Committee) in 1984. V.32 has been largely replaced now by V.32bis.
V.32bis	The standard for 14,400 bps modems, backward compatible to V.32.
V.34	The current standard for 28,800 bps modems.
V.FC	A de facto standard established by Rockwell. This standard is now superceded by V.34, and modem manufacturers are supplying upgrade chips to make the conversion.
V.FAST	A proprietary implementation used by some vendors to enable 28,800 bps speeds.
V.42	A standard for error control established by the CCITT. Error control allows modems to maintain communications under poor line conditions. Both V.42 and MNP2-4 (see below) retransmit data as necessary to cope with noisy lines.
V.42bis	A standard for data compression that uses V.42 error correction. Compression ratios of 4:1 are theoretically possible but rarely achieved.
MNP4	An error control protocol developed by Microcom (MNP stands for Microcom Networking Protocol). MNP2 to MNP4 are used for error correction.
MNP5	A data compression protocol developed by Microcom. Modems that support V.42bis include MNP5 in their list of features.

Finding the Right Cable

Two devices that are exchanging information need some way to control the flow of data between them. One such method is called *software handshaking*, which occurs when control codes are used to regulate this flow. In XON/XOFF software handshaking, a Ctrl-S is used to pause the stream of transmission; a Ctrl-Q resumes it. This technique will probably be familiar to anyone with some experience with on-line services from the days when everything was character-based. (You used Ctrl-S, for example, to pause the scrolling of a long document on CompuServe, and Ctrl-Q to resume it.)

Hardware handshaking, by contrast, employs a control wire to signal the other device when there is to be a change in the data flow. Of the two methods, hardware handshaking is the fastest and most efficient, but whether you use a Macintosh or a PC running Microsoft Windows, you will need to establish hardware handshaking, both by setting it up in your software and by choosing the right kind of modem cable. Read on.

If you are a Macintosh user, you will need a special kind of modem cable to make hardware handshaking work. A standard 8-pin to 25-pin cable won't do the trick; you can find out quickly enough if this is what you have by going into your standard communications software package (ZTerm, Microphone, or the like), and clicking on the hardware handshaking option. If your modem won't accept this setting, you need a new cable.

The problem is where to find one. Many computer stores aren't yet up to speed on fast modems, and either don't carry the right kind of cable, or don't know the difference between the two. Specify that you need a cable that does hardware handshaking; these are sometimes labeled "high-speed modem cables," or something similar. You won't be able to draw the full power out of that new modem if you don't have such a cable.

IBM-compatible PC users using standard 25-pin to 25-pin cables don't have this problem; their cable should enable hardware handshaking. To be technical about it, a hardware handshaking cable should include wires for pins 4 (RTS) and 5 (CTS) on the 25-pin side of the connection; anything less won't work. To be sure, try to change the setting in your comm software and see what happens, but get a new cable if necessary.

Configuring the Windows Communications Port

Using Windows creates several additional issues that you have to deal with. First, you will want to configure the Windows comm port to handle hardware handshaking. This can be done by going into the Main program group and choosing the Control Panel. There, click on the Ports icon, then choose Settings. You will call up the box shown in Figure 2.1.

Notice in the figure that I have set the Flow Control field to the Hardware setting; I have also chosen 19200 as the baud rate (this is the maximum setting that the Windows dialog box allows). The baud rate entered here is not the critical factor; the baud rate value entered in your communications software is actually what your computer will use (the baud rate in the comm port box is established for the benefit of serial pointing devices, printers, and other serial devices). In a moment, I will show you how you can transcend the Windows comm port settings to achieve much higher speeds.

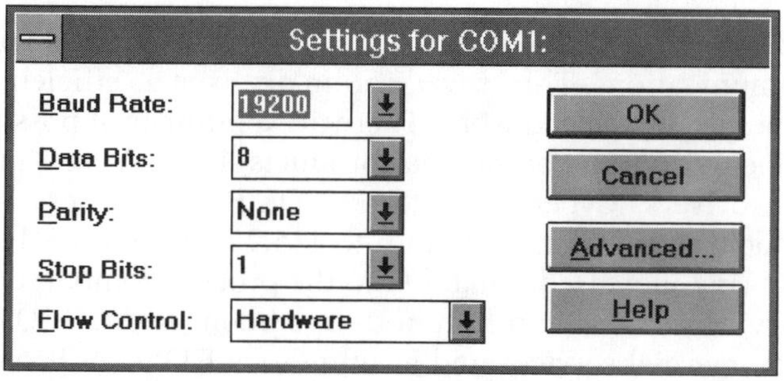

Figure 2.1   Setting hardware handshaking in Windows comm port.

Setting Up Hardware Handshaking in Your Software

Hardware handshaking must also be enabled in your modem. Most high-speed modems come with hardware handshaking on as part of the factory default settings, so this should not be an issue. A command of **AT&F1** will restore the modem to its factory defaults, which in most cases will work with your communications software. As you'll see, you'll also turn hardware handshaking on in the communications stack you use to work with the Internet.

The All Important UART

The third issue involves yet another acronym—UART, or Universal Asynchronous Receiver/Transmitter. A UART is a chip inside your computer that renders its data stream suitable for transmission in the serial environment used in data communications. We call such communications *asynchronous* when the data bits are sent one after another, using a start bit at the beginning and a stop bit at the end to mark the boundaries of the data unit. The UART aids us by turning the computer's parallel data stream into a serial data stream.

And therein lies the problem. Older computers may have an 8250 or a 16450 UART chip, neither of which is able to communicate as efficiently as we would like it to in a high-speed environment. Speed and reliability are enhanced when using a 16550A UART. The 16550A buffers a larger number of characters as data comes in, allowing the computer's processor time to read the data and act upon it. The older chips can run into problems in losing data.

To find out which kind of UART you are using, exit Windows and run the MSD.EXE utility that Microsoft includes with Windows (be sure to run MSD in DOS before launching Windows, as the program can misidentify the UART when run in a DOS window inside Windows). If you have one of the older UARTs, look into replacing it, perhaps through a new communications card.

Using the Best Communications Driver

The final Windows-related issue involves the driver that Windows uses to manage serial communications. This driver, comm.drv, isn't as efficient as it might be when it comes to high-speed work. There are a number of possible replacements for it, including the commercial products TurboCom, KingCom, and two shareware drivers, Cybercom and CHCOMB.EXE. These new drivers allow your modem to transfer data at up to 115,200 KB with a 16550A serial port chip, and bring increased reliability to the process compared to the Windows comm.drv driver. You can find both Cybercom and CHCOMB.EXE on most major commercial services and at numerous FTP sites around the net. Here is contact information for the commercial products:

KingCom

E Ware
145 West 28th St., 12th Fl.
New York, NY 10001-6114
Voice: 800/892-9950
Fax: 714/236-1390

Provides a useful high-speed driver that not only allows you to get the most out of a high-speed connection, but also to use multiple programs while sharing the same communications port. Supports the 16550 UART. $49.95.

TurboCom/2

Pacific CommWare
180 Beacon Hill Ln.
Ashland, OR 97520
Voice: 800-856-3818, 503-482-2744
Fax: 503-482-2627
E-mail: 71521.760@compuserve.com

Dependable throughput up to 115.2 kilobits per second; supports the 16550 UART. TurboCom's port monitoring functions are unique and valuable. $49.95.

I recommend that you buy TurboCom. After working with it for the past several months, I have become convinced that it is the best communications driver on the market. In addition to providing you with the ability to monitor your communications ports through a separate window, TurboCom lets you configure and control Windows communications to a level of detail that no other software can match. On each port, for example, you can specify a setting that sets the data rate used by the UART to a multiple of what is set in your communications software. Thus, if your communications program tops out at 57600, you can set a multiple of 2. Your high-speed modem using data compression at a ratio of 4 to 1 can then, theoretically, obtain transfer rates for uncompressed files of 115,200 bps.

SLIP/PPP Software Options

A year ago, getting started with SLIP/PPP meant contacting your service provider and working through the installation process, with one hand on the keyboard and the other clutched around the telephone. Today, SLIP software is increasingly being offered within Internet access packages of various kinds, and the number of new tools from developers is rapidly multiplying. In the next two chapters, we will proceed to install SLIP software in both a Microsoft Windows-based PC and a Macintosh. The software in both cases is shareware or freeware.

This raises an interesting question. Is shareware for network access really up to the challenge, or should you opt from the start for a commercial prod-

Note: If you want to explore the arcana of serial port communications, you may want to get a document called "The Serial Port," by Christian Blum, which goes into all these matters in great detail. You can retrieve this document by sending mail to the following address:

et11hks4@etcip9.ee.uni-sb.de

In the Subject: line, put the word **help**. You will be sent instructions for how to retrieve the document.

I also highly recommend an excellent Frequently Asked Questions (FAQ) document called "The 16550A UART & TurboCom Drivers," by Bob Niland. I have found it posted in the following newsgroups:

comp.dcom.modems
comp.sys.ibm.pc.hardware.comm
comp.answers
news.answers

The comp.dcom.modems newsgroup, in particular, is a major source of up-to-date information about Windows communications issues.

uct? Having worked with both, my answer is that the shareware/freeware alternative for Internet work is vibrant. Excellent client programs exist in both arenas, but you can establish a complete complement of network tools by keeping up with FTP sites where the latest shareware is distributed. As for the SLIP/PPP software itself, there is no better method for Microsoft Windows-based access than Trumpet International's Winsock, a shareware product. In the Macintosh universe, MacTCP, which provides the basic TCP/IP protocol stack, is now shipping with System 7.5 on all new Macintoshes; users of older Macs can get it by upgrading to System 7.5. InterSLIP, which makes the actual SLIP connection for the Macintosh, is freeware; both work effectively.

You should think of the Internet as a continuously evolving medium, one that demands that you live on the edge of development. In some cases, this is a frustrating experience; you load your software correctly, make the connection, and find that the site is inaccessible, or that its directories have changed, or that it is simply overloaded with users and you can't get in. In other cases, you are happily examining a network site when your computer locks up, through some inexplicable mystery, and you must reboot to get started again. All of this will happen to you as you wend your way through the net, and you should not be surprised when it does.

But along with the occasional frustration comes the excitement of downloading an upgraded version of an old favorite. Perhaps the new program is more stable than the old, and contains new features that make network use far more enjoyable. Shareware and freeware products offer the excitement of participating in this ongoing development with your comments and suggestions. I have found over the years that nothing creates better software than the efforts of programmers working from within the Internet community out of their own sense of commitment. The Internet has always maintained this great spirit of cooperation that makes advancement possible, and it is a spirit that has not died. Using the network's freely available tools as well as its shareware is part of this.

My recommendation, then, is that you begin with these tools before moving on to any commercial products. Evaluate your own needs and take a good look at the kind of uses to which you put the network. Then, and only then, will you be in a position to decide whether there are commercial alternatives that provide significant additions to the programs you already use. Don't forget, too, that shareware is not free. Most shareware programs include a screen explaining their terms of use and where to send your registration fee. Your part in the ongoing development of Internet software is to help to compensate the people who have spent so much time working on the programs we all use every day to gain access to the net.

3

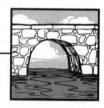

Running SLIP/PPP under Microsoft Windows

Thanks to ongoing software development and the rising interest in the Internet among home and small business users, it's now possible to find packages that will let you set up a SLIP/PPP account on almost any kind of computer. This chapter examines the issues and problems related to doing so under Microsoft Windows; the next chapter focuses on setting up SLIP/PPP on a Macintosh. Each machine poses its own questions, and requires a degree of fine-tuning to achieve the best results. But make no mistake about it—you can achieve SLIP/PPP access to the Internet on either of these platforms. I use both a Macintosh and a 486 in my office on a daily basis, and run client software of all descriptions on each.

Perhaps because of its background in the academic community, where so much good Internet software was written, the Macintosh boasts some advantages over Windows; the client programs written for it occasionally display an elegance lacking in their IBM-compatible cousins—a fact that shows up particularly in newsreaders—but there is no question that the arrival of Windows 95 has kindled the interest of developers, and that Windows-based software is now becoming more widely available and diverse.

Check out any good FTP site where client programs are made available and you will see how quickly this trend is accelerating. Two years ago, some Windows clients were downright primitive; today, existing programs are being refined and turbocharged with new features, while the number of programs for each area of Internet activity is rapidly expanding, something that can't be said about the Macintosh. If it's sheer diversity that appeals to you, you'll find no end of pleasure in rooting through the myriad clients for Windows.

From the standpoint of the SLIP/PPP connection itself, Windows boasts some excellent TCP/IP software, and one product in particular, Trumpet Winsock, which is both shareware and world class. Trumpet Winsock is now in version 2.0, and the hard efforts put into its development by Tasmania's Peter Tattam show. While this chapter will examine the nature of the SLIP/PPP connection through Windows in a broad sense, it will also demonstrate how Trumpet Winsock is installed, my thinking being that you need to see an actual installation to be able to generalize about how TCP/IP runs on your computer. Your choice of software depends upon your own preferences, so I will also present a variety of other options for making the connection.

Making Windows Connect

Before 1993, trying to connect a Windows-based computer to the Internet was a challenge. The programs available were commercial in nature, and proprietary; choose your TCP/IP stack and you were establishing an environment incompatible with any other vendor's offerings. Proprietary software usually means expensive software, for there is no genuine competition when each product is in essence its own computing environment. This situation contrasted sharply with Unix, whose open design ensured the availability of robust programs; the Macintosh, too, boasted fine programs, though not as many. Yet Windows, the operating system, was growing in popularity. Something had to give.

You can relate this situation to what happened in the early and mid-1980s, as we watched the evolution of the personal computer. The IBM PC offered an operating system, MS-DOS, which took off thanks to the fact that the hardware was open—any manufacturer could study how PCs were made and attempt to clone them. The Macintosh, by contrast, was kept deliberately closed, a decision on Apple Computer's part that was intended to retain control over the operating system that made their machine so different from the IBM-compatible PC in terms of its user interface. The results, so striking today, suggest that closing an architecture drives software developers away; you have only to examine the shelves of your local software house to see which system has attracted the greatest number of programmers.

In the Internet world, then, what Windows needed was some way to open it up in the networking sense, so that a client program from one vendor would be compatible with the networking products of any other. The solution was called Winsock. Winsock is an applications programming interface that makes such compatibility possible. It is no exaggeration to say that the wave of Windows-based client programs we see today would never have occurred were it not for the creation of the Winsock standard. Today, you can leaf through any network-oriented magazine to see how numerous are the providers of Windows-based solutions, and the shareware scene is equally active.

Winsock Defined

Windows, of course, is ideally suited for Internet use, at least in terms of its interface—it brings the graphical touch to the widest-selling computer platform. Thus the importance of Windows versions of programs like Mosaic, which explicitly use a graphical interface to make Internet information-browsing productive. But don't think purely in terms of Mosaic; brilliant as it is, we can also look to Windows implementations of all the major Internet protocols, from Gopher to Telnet, from FTP to WAIS. In each case, laid over the Internet's complexity is a graphical system that helps us perform our tasks, and requires not so much that we know how to master networking per se, but that we be able to define what it is we need to do.

Winsock works its magic by inserting itself between the client program you are running and the TCP/IP software that makes your network connection possible. To be precise, we must refer to Winsock as the Windows Sockets Application Programming Interface, and therein hangs a tale. A *socket* is the combination of an IP address and a port address. Widely used Internet tools like Gopher run on a standard port (it happens to be 70); we can assume when we use them that, unless directed otherwise, that port will be the default. But an individual program running on a particular computer may require that you enter the socket to reach it. Thus, to reach a particular database of geographical information, I need to provide the socket:

telnet://telnet martini.eecs.umich.edu:3000

Here, I am using Telnet to access a remote computer whose address is **martini.eecs.umich.edu**, and am specifying that I need to access the program at port 3000 on that machine. The entire statement, address plus port, comprises the socket.

But notice the rest of Winsock's official name. It is called an *application programming interface*, otherwise known as an API. An API is a shared subroutine that performs a basic function that is common across various operations. For example, the task of displaying text on your screen is something that any Windows program you use must be able to do; similarly, any Windows application must be able to produce a window on the screen. An API can be used by the various Windows applications to perform a needed function. The application program issues a call for the API, which then performs the task in conjunction with the operating system of the computer.

Tying it all together, then, the Windows Sockets Application Programming Interface contains the information that Windows itself needs to work with TCP/IP to perform Internet tasks. Once you have Winsock working, you can then run client programs like Eudora, WinVN, or Mosaic, and communicate with the Internet through your SLIP/PPP connection. The basic model for this operation comes from a variant of Unix called Berkeley Unix, named after the university where it was created. Berkeley Unix (sometimes referred to as BSD,

Note: One way to visualize the relationship between ports and addresses is to compare them to what you might see on a business envelope. You place an address in the center of the envelope, specifying the company and place where the enclosed letter is to go. In the bottom right corner, you create an ATTN field; in it you place the name of a particular person. The address gets your letter to the right building; the ATTN field gets it to the person you need to reach inside that building. In computer terms, the address gets you to the right machine; the port gets you to the right process.

And just as some areas within a company may be standardized, so are ports standardized around common processes. For example, you might send a letter to Morse, Inc., 3212 Templeton St., Bramley, MI. Your ATTN note might read ATTN: Claims Dept.; the letter would be routed to the appropriate destination. When you use Gopher at a particular site, the port has similarly been standardized; unless you specify otherwise, port 70 will be used. Telnet normally defaults to port 23.

for Berkeley Software Distribution) was a major player in the growth of the Internet, for it included TCP/IP as a built-in protocol. The distribution of Berkeley Unix to universities throughout the U.S. was a key driver for the growth of the Internet into the academic community. Berkeley Unix used the basic sockets API model that is developed in Winsock for communications between programs.

Winsock as an Open Standard

How does a particular program work with Winsock? Suppose I want to use WinVN, a newsreader program I frequently tap for my USENET work. When I click on the WinVN icon, the program looks to a file called winsock.dll. The latter is the file that contains the procedures Windows will use in linking with TCP/IP. Once WinVN has found the winsock.dll file (and I make sure that it can by adjusting the path statement in my autoexec.bat file accordingly), the program can run as if my computer were using a dedicated network connection to the Internet. At this point, the nature of the connection doesn't matter; the only criterion is that the data packets to and from the Internet flow.

But let's look more closely at that winsock.dll file. There is no single, correct version of the winsock.dll file; in fact, a different winsock.dll exists for every TCP/IP implementation. Think of the situation this way: each vendor of a TCP/IP stack works up a version of winsock.dll that will hook into his or her stack. TCP/IP stacks differ, and on the TCP/IP side of the winsock.dll file, the stack must be adapted to fit the Winsock model. Once fitted, the two have established a common interface that can be hooked into by any client program.

On the client side, the Winsock standard thus allows any client program to work with any vendor's winsock.dll. This has huge ramifications for the developers of clients. They know that any program they write will be able to work with any TCP/IP stack, thus freeing them from writing for proprietary environments. Winsock therefore separates the two sides of software development. A developer who wants to create a client that will manage USENET news need not worry about developing a separate TCP/IP stack of his or her own; instead, he or she can concentrate on creating the best client program possible, while letting winsock.dll handle the interface to TCP/IP functions.

Thus, whenever you examine a particular vendor's TCP/IP implementation, you will find a winsock.dll file included. This can have some interesting ramifications if you are the sort of person who enjoys trying out different varieties of TCP/IP management. If you have set up a package like the Chameleon Sampler, a widely available TCP/IP stack with accompanying client software, and have included it in your path statement in the autoexec.bat file, you can cause conflicts if you then try to load a different vendor's TCP/IP stack. Loading Trumpet Winsock on my machine, I forgot to delete the Chameleon path from my autoexec.bat file, with the result that the Trumpet stack looked to the wrong winsock.dll and refused to run. Make sure, then, that your system points to the correct winsock.dll.

Installing SLIP/PPP in Windows: A User's Tale

Anyone who has attempted to get SLIP/PPP up and running under any environment has already learned an obvious fact: configuring the software is an exasperating and nonstandardized procedure, made more difficult by the fact that so many service providers are appearing in such numbers that technical support is often lacking in the rush to get people on-line. It would be wonderful to be able to offer a short course that showed how to install every implementation of SLIP/PPP on every Windows-based computer, but that, alas, is hardly possible. What I can do here is provide you with a look at how I installed one TCP/IP stack, Trumpet Winsock, on my machine, and provide you with a framework you can use to apply to your own situation.

No two vendors' implementations are going to be the same. It will be necessary, then, to persevere. Your first point of contact has to be your service provider, who in most cases will give you whatever software he or she has chosen to use for SLIP/PPP customers. If you've chosen your provider with care, you will have found one who offers a 24-hour help desk. Follow the directions in your provider's startup materials and be ready to call the help number if and when you run into trouble. The first step is always to get a connection made; later, you can explore other software options. You may decide to change your TCP/IP stack at some point in the future, and perhaps this chapter will give you some pointers about how to do that.

Before we get into Trumpet Winsock, let me pass along my own experience with setting up a SLIP/PPP connection under Microsoft Windows. My provider, Interpath, offered NetManage Chameleon Sampler, a software kit that includes the basic TCP/IP stack, called Newt, along with a SLIP dialer and a variety of client programs. Interpath also provided me with a book that explained how to load the Chameleon software, and a sheet listing all the technical materials I would need to properly configure it. Installation, at least on the surface, looked cut and dried, and I proceeded to load and open the software.

Configuration, however, was another problem. SLIP/PPP accounts may require that you enter such information as your IP address, or the address of the nameserver at your provider's site. You will need information about the news server at that site if you want to read USENET newsgroups, and further names and addresses that will enable you to set up electronic mail. You will also have an account number and a password. Depending on the software, you may be asked to fill in blanks associated with fields like Subnet Mask: and Gateway Address: or similar terms. Make a mistake in any of these and your SLIP/PPP operations are likely to come to grief. Frustratingly, no help screen pops up to tell you that the IP address you have entered was the wrong one, or that you have forgotten to set the right comm port, or perhaps have entered the wrong initialization string for your modem. And what do you do if you need to enter information in a particular field and that field is dimmed and disabled?

Four telephone calls to Interpath's help desk got these problems, and others, straightened out, and I finally connected. From talking to other users at various sites, such a progression of events seems relatively normal. Configuring SLIP/PPP is not trivial, and you should expect some bumps along the way. There is also the issue of stability. The Microsoft Windows environment is notoriously finicky anyway; TCP/IP makes it even more so. I quickly found that it was easy to crash using the NetManage software; I crashed out of various client programs, some of them provided by NetManage, some of them independent.

So make this a hard and fast rule: when you are setting up SLIP/PPP, *close your other applications*. I can't stress this enough. Working on a feature story for a magazine, I had Microsoft Word 6.0 open but iconized; in it was a draft of my story. Having set the program up to save my work automatically every ten minutes, I wasn't worried about losing data. But when Mosaic crashed during my first attempts to set it up, it took Newt with it, and thus TCP/IP. That froze my system, so that I had to reboot. Which should have been OK, except that when I went back to Microsoft Word, my file was cleaned out. I have no idea what caused this, nor am I likely to figure it out. Fortunately, I maintain regular backups, and so should you. But I also learned that TCP/IP can be unstable on a PC, and that you want to do anything you can to minimize the dangers. Microsoft Word, in particular, eats plenty of system resources; closing it when you load your SLIP/PPP software can help. Properly closed files are generally not at risk.

Above all, don't be surprised when you run into trouble. It's not just the Windows platform; I've crashed and burned many a time with my Power

Mac, using MacTCP and InterSLIP and a variety of client programs. The Internet itself is only twenty-five years old; connecting home and small business users to it is in the nature of an experiment sitting atop a test drive within a controlled crash. The up side of pushing the network envelope is that you are participating in this experiment; you are trying out ideas and programs as they are developed. Some of them don't work well; others, like Mosaic, are under constant development, and getting better all the time, even though they're still not what anyone would call fully stable. That's the price of envelope pushing, and if you're patient, you will find that it's worth the effort. The rewards are great.

I am now going to show you Trumpet Winsock, a shareware TCP/IP implementation that has become my standard SLIP/PPP tool for Microsoft Windows. I chose it because of all the software I have looked at, Trumpet Winsock is the sturdiest and provides the best performance. Installation has its own quirks, but I think I can talk you through the real trouble spots. Whether or not you want to use Trumpet Winsock, read through this material, because much of what I present here is generic—all TCP/IP stacks need your IP address, for example, your port settings, your modem speed, and a series of related information. But even if you use a different stack, I suspect that sooner or later, you'll want to give Trumpet Winsock a try. Read on to learn how to find and download it.

Trumpet Winsock

Trumpet Winsock provides you with the basic tools you need to get a SLIP/PPP account running. It consists of the TCP/IP stack that manages the flow of data packets to and from your computer, and contains all SLIP/PPP functions built in. There are several ways for you to get a copy:

Through FTP

If you already have a shell account with an Internet service provider, you can use it to make an FTP connection to one of several sites where Trumpet Winsock is found. Here are some sites where the software is currently available; I begin with Trumpet's home site. But remember that popular programs like Trumpet Winsock appear in a variety of places, so you needn't feel confined to these locations.

ftp://ftp.utas.edu.au/pc/trumpet/winsock/

ftp://ftp.trumpet.com.au/ftp/pub/winsock/

ftp://ftp.cica.indiana.edu/pub/pc/win3/winsock/

At the time of this writing, the filename was twsk20a.zip.

Pick up one more file while you're retrieving Trumpet Winsock. The file is:

ftp://ftp.utas.edu.au/pc/trumpet/winsock/apps/winapps2.zip

This file contains a program called pingw.exe, which is a quick way to check your Trumpet Winsock installation. When you use the ping utility, you are checking to see if the computer whose address you have entered is reachable on the network. We'll put this to work after we load Trumpet Winsock.

The CICA site mentioned has numerous mirrors as possible alternatives. Try any of the following URLs. In the United States:

ftp://wuarchive.wustl.edu/

ftp://mrcnext.cso.uiuc.edu/

ftp://archive.orst.edu/

ftp://gatekeeper.dec.com/

ftp://ftp.cdrom.com/

ftp://polecat.law.indiana.edu/

ftp://ftp.marcam.com/

In Europe and Asia:

ftp://ftp.monash.edu.au/ (Australia)

ftp://ftp.funet.fi/ (Finland)

ftp://ftp.uni-paderborn.de/ (Germany)

ftp://ftp.iij.ad.jp/ (Japan)

ftp://src.doc.ic.ac.uk/ (United Kingdom)

ftp://ftp.nectec.or.th/ (Thailand)

ftp://ftp.technion.ac.il/ (Israel)

ftp://nic.switch.ch/ (Switzerland)

ftp://ntu.ac.sg/ (Singapore)

ftp://nctuccca.edu.tw/ (Taiwan)

ftp://ftp.cyf-kr.edu.pl (Poland)

Because directory structures can vary site to site, you may need to do some digging to uncover the files you need if you choose one of these mirrors. Look for README or INDEX files that contain information about available files. And, as always, look for possible changes in filenames as new versions are released.

Through a Commercial On-Line Service

You can find Trumpet Winsock in any of the major on-line services. Old hands at such services know that each contains numerous file libraries, usually corresponding to the various forums or special interest groups where members exchange messages about particular topics. Because of the large number of such forums and the diversity of people managing each, it is more than likely that a particular file will be found in more than one forum. My suggestion, then, is that you use your service's search capabilities wherever possible.

On CompuServe, for example, you can use the IBM File Finder, reachable through the command **go ibmff**. This command will create a menu that gives you the chance to search by keyword, filename, or a number of other criteria. Use a keyword search, since you won't know at this point what the latest filename is. For Trumpet Winsock, searching under the terms trumpet and winsock should do the trick. Running this search, I find copies of the program in several forums, although none would have suggested themselves at first glance (several are devoted to European access to CompuServe, for example). This is why a search facility is helpful on a commercial service; you find things stuffed in crannies that you didn't realize existed. As the listings will have changed by the time you read this, the best thing to do is to use IBMFF yourself to locate the most recent copy of Trumpet on CompuServe.

America Online provides the same kind of search facility. Choose Computing from the top menu and proceed to the Software Center by clicking on its icon. You can then search the various file libraries with a keyword-driven search. I found several listings of the Trumpet Winsock file this way. DELPHI offers extensive file libraries; check into the Internet SIG to search them. Comparable libraries are available on both BIX and GEnie.

A Shareware Reminder

The amount of programming, and thus time and energy, that went into Trumpet Winsock is enormous. If you run the program and use it, you have an obligation to repay these efforts by registering your copy. The documentation for the program includes a registration form that allows you to register your copy and enclose the appropriate fee. For the single user, the fee is $25, making Trumpet Winsock a major bargain. Multiuser site licenses are also available;

the pricing structure for these is provided with the documentation. You can contact Trumpet Winsock's developers at:

Trumpet Software International Pty Ltd.
GPO Box 1649
Hobart, Tasmania
Australia 7001

Unpacking Trumpet Winsock

What follows is a general outline to installation of Trumpet Winsock. I present it for two reasons, the first being that it provides an overview of how a Winsock installation proceeds, and the issues that it raises. The second is that I highly recommend the Trumpet Winsock product for your own use; even if you choose to move on to a commercial product, I think examining Trumpet's offering will provide you with a standard to measure other products against (and I doubt you'll find any that match it). Be aware that later versions of the program may contain slightly different file information from what is presented here.

Having retrieved the Trumpet Winsock file from one of the above sources, you can now proceed to unpack it. As are many software tools on the Internet, Trumpet Winsock is compressed using PKware's PKZIP utility program, which allows system administrators to save disk space by storing files in as small a space as possible. To unzip it, you need a copy of the PKUNZIP program that complements PKZIP. Both are so widely distributed over the Internet and by the commercial on-line services that, if you don't already have PKUNZIP, it will be a quick exercise to track down the program. The FTP archival sites listed above offer copies, as do all the commercial services, where you can use the same search tools to find them. The complete PKZIP package is shareware, and contains the information necessary for you to run the program. There is also a Windows-based version of PKZIP called WinZip, likewise widely distributed on the net.

Note: Can't find PKZIP or WinZip? If you use a commercial on-line service, search its file libraries under the keywords pkzip or winzip to locate a copy. If you're already on the Internet in some fashion, major FTP sites have the software available. Try the following:

ftp:/oak.oakland.edu/pub/msdos/zip/pkz204g.exe

For the Windows-based WinZip, try this:

ftp://ftp.winzip.com/winzip/winzip56.exe

Or try WinZip's World Wide Web page:

http://www.winzip.com/winzip/

Be sure to put the directory your decompression program is in into the path statement of your autoexec.bat file so that you can call it from anyplace on your hard disk. I keep my copy in a directory called *utility* and have added that to my PATH. My PATH statement, for illustration purposes, now reads:

PATH C:\DOS;C:\WINDOWS;C:\NDW;C:\WINWORD;C:\UTILITY;C:\TRUMPET

with the c:\trumpet statement added to the end. You can make the change to the PATH statement in any text editor. Windows provides a program called Sysedit which offers a convenient way to edit all of the basic system files. You could also use the DOS program EDIT from the DOS command line to do the same thing. Your command from the DOS prompt would be:

cd
edit autoexec.bat

As for Trumpet Winsock itself, you need to set up a directory in which it will reside. I have created a *trumpet* directory on my hard disk and have added it to my PATH statement as well. To proceed with the installation, you will need to set up a comparable directory and place your twsk20a.zip file there. From the DOS prompt, the command to create a *trumpet* directory is this:

cd
mkdir trumpet

PKUNZIP requires the DOS environment to run, so to proceed, you need to enter Windows' DOS shell or else run the program from the DOS command line with Windows closed. Then follow these steps:

1. Move the compressed winsock file to your *trumpet* directory.
2. Unpack the Trumpet Winsock file by using the **pkunzip twsk20a.zip** command. If the filename has changed in the interval since this book was published, substitute whatever the current filename is for the one given here.

This command will work as long as PKUNZIP is in your path statement; it will also work if PKUNZIP is in the same directory as the file you are decompressing, even if the program is not in the path statement.

When PKUNZIP goes to work, it will unpack the files inside twsk20a.zip. Here are the most significant ones. Note that Trumpet Winsock can also be used by computers on a Local Area Network (LAN), so the package also contains files necessary for such installations:

hosts   A list of host names, along with the IP addresses to which they correspond. A *host* is simply a computer that is directly connected to the Internet, whether it is a workstation, a personal computer, or a huge mainframe. Think of a host as a computer that runs the Internet protocols.

Note: Why offer a hosts file in the first place? The Domain Name System (DNS), after all, is set up expressly to provide the necessary translation service between IP address and domain name. But not all networks provide Domain Name System support. If you are administering a site, you have to keep a record of which host computer is linked to which IP address; this is what a hosts file allows you to do. That way, if you move a particular computer to a new location, you can make a simple change to the hosts file to reflect the fact, while the host domain name remains constant. As a SLIP/PPP user, you are doubtless working with a provider who offers DNS support, automatically allocating DNS addresses to your machine. You won't, therefore, have to make any additions to the hosts file. Entering the basic configuration information in Trumpet Winsock will provide you will full connectivity to the Internet.

install.doc	A Word for Windows file that contains installation instructions and registration information for Trumpet Winsock.
install.txt	The same file in ASCII text format.
protocol	A list of Internet protocols.
sendreg.exe	The registration program, which allows you to register your copy of Trumpet Winsock as a shareware product.
services	A list of Internet services and port assignments, from Telnet to FTP to whois.
tcpman.exe	The basic Winsock executable program.
winsock.dll	The *dynamic link library* needed to run TCP/IP on your computer.
winpkt.com	A packet driver interface for those using Trumpet Winsock over a Local Area Network. The packet driver provides an interface between the network card and the TCP program itself. SLIP/PPP users will not need to use this driver.

Once you have unpacked all these files in your \trumpet directory, you will be able to proceed.

Creating a Trumpet Winsock Program Group

A change to your path statement doesn't take effect until your computer is rebooted. Reboot now, making sure you have closed all your other files so you don't lose data. When the computer has rebooted, you can restart Windows.

Your next step will be to create a program group for Trumpet Winsock. To do so, follow these steps:

1. Pull down the File menu from Program Manager and select New. The New Program Object box should appear, giving you the option of creating a new program group or a new program item.

2. Assuming you would like Trumpet Winsock to appear in its own group, click on the Program Group button, if it is not already activated.

3. Click OK.

4. A Program Group Properties box will now appear. Here, enter Trumpet Winsock in the description field.

5. Click on OK.

6. A program group called Trumpet Winsock will now appear. To add the TCP/IP program to this box, repeat the above procedure, only this time click on Program Item, if it isn't already selected. You can now fill in the Program Item Properties box with the correct information for Trumpet Winsock, including path and executable filename.

7. Click on OK.

You can see this process in action in Figure 3.1. When you click on OK, the Trumpet Winsock icon will appear in your program group. Clicking on this icon will run the program.

Configuring Trumpet Winsock

Go ahead and double-click on the Trumpet Winsock icon. This will run tcp-man.exe and cause the setup screen to appear. We will need to fill in various values on this screen and discuss their meaning. Examine the screen shown in Figure 3.2 with care. Notice that some of the fields are darker than others; the ones that are greyed out cannot be filled in. As you'll see, there are some values you do not need to fill in for a SLIP/PPP connection, others that you do. To begin your installation, then, take the following step: Click on either SLIP or Internal PPP, depending upon which protocol you are using. This has the helpful effect of making those fields that are now irrelevant to your installation inaccessible. We can now proceed to enter the necessary values for the other fields.

When you set up your SLIP/PPP account with your service provider, you will have been given a document that provides the necessary information to enable your network connection. The numbers should look familiar; they're IP addresses for the most part, numbers divided by periods. Be sure as you proceed through the Trumpet Winsock installation that you have this information at hand. Ninety-five percent of the trouble people encounter with SLIP/PPP is in the initial configuration stages, and it usually involves entering the wrong values in the setup screen. Let's begin at the top left of the Network Configuration dialog box. I will only discuss those fields that you need to change; the others can remain at their default settings.

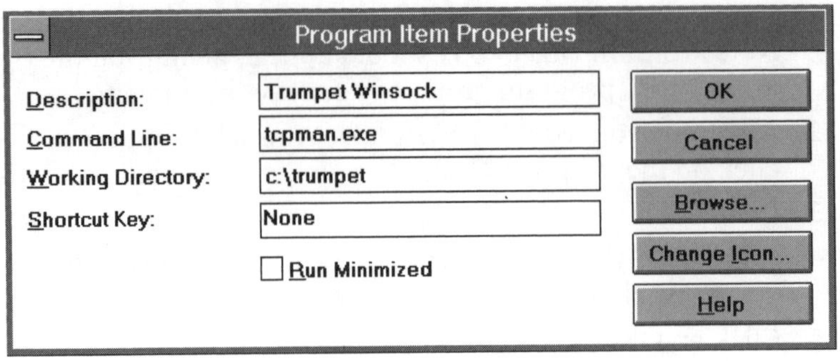

Figure 3.1 Creating a Program Group for Trumpet Winsock.

IP Address

Recall from Chapter 2 that an IP address is a unique number that is used to identify the location of a computer on the Internet. Normally, we work within the Domain Name System when referring to computers; it's easier to remember a name like **oak.oakland.edu** than the string of numbers that corresponds to this name. But for our purposes in configuring Trumpet Winsock, we need to enter a numerical value.

But which one? Examine the information sheet given you by your service provider. Somewhere on it should be a field giving your Internet address information. You are looking for the address that specifies your computer and

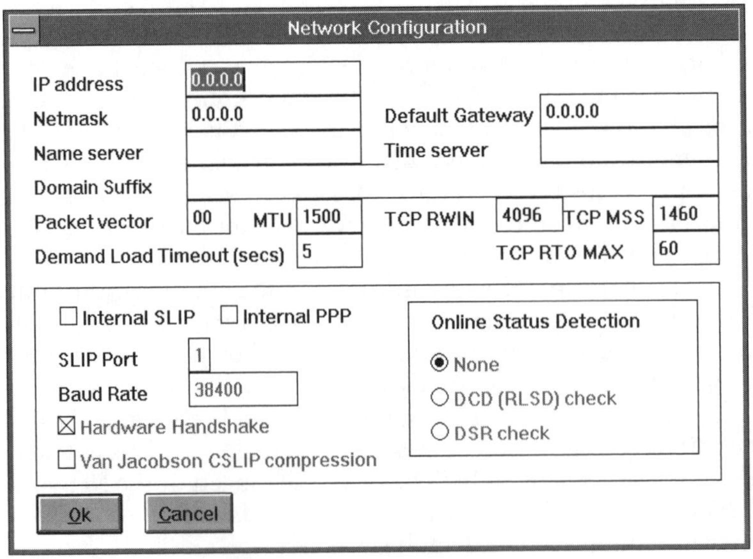

Figure 3.2 Trumpet Winsock's Setup screen.

yours alone. Remember that a SLIP/PPP account has this significant difference from a shell account: with SLIP/PPP, your computer actually acquires an IP address. This is the address you need to enter here.

Nameserver

A name server is a computer that translates IP addresses, with their arcane numbering, into the Domain Name System which allows us to use words to define computers. Your service provider will have one or more computers explicitly dedicated to this task. In this field, you are specifying the address of that computer. Look in the information provided you when you established your account for the IP address to enter here.

Time Server

You can leave this field blank, as it is at present unused.

Domain Suffix

SLIP/PPP users need not fill in this field; it is established to allow users on Local Area Networks to communicate quickly with other machines on the same network. If I were to fill in **mercury.interpath.net** in this field, I could then send a message to someone named Johann Bach, whose address was **jbach@mercury.interpath.net**, simply by entering his user ID, jbach; the software would fill in the rest of the address for me. DNS is not employed for a domain name entered here.

MTU

MTU stands for maximum transmission unit. We already know that packet switching networks break data into discrete units, sometimes called datagrams; MTU is a measure of the size of those units. Trumpet Winsock's default MTU, 1500 bytes, is established for Ethernet connections (to be absolutely precise, the 1500 refers to *octets* rather than bytes—these are data units that are 8 bits in length; the reason for the distinction is that some Internet-connected computers use data units larger than 8 bits). There are, however, no absolutely established standards for MTU size. If a particular network can't handle the size of the packets it is receiving, it breaks them into smaller units through a process called *fragmentation*. Each new datagram, of course, is given its own header, with routing and destination information included.

A SLIP/PPP account is best established with whatever MTU your service provider suggests. To get up and running, you can start with a value of 256. Later, you may want to experiment to see which values produce the best result. Be sure to check with technical support at your provider's site to find the number they recommend (and see the upcoming note for some suggestions by Trumpet Winsock's author, Peter Tattam).

TCP RWIN

This value marks the size of the TCP Receive Window. The value will be determined by the size of the following field (TCP MSS); Trumpet Winsock's documentation recommends that you use three to four times the value inserted there. Check with your service provider, or start with an initial value of 848, which can be adjusted later.

TCP MSS

TCP Maximum Segment Size. Try a value of 212 to start with, as recommended by the Trumpet Winsock documentation.

SLIP Port

This field should contain the communications port your computer uses—COM1, COM2, and so forth.

Baud Rate

Here you are at the mercy of your modem. The value can be set as high as 115200, but what you enter will depend upon what speed your modem can communicate at, and what your provider supports. I use 115200 at the recommendation of my provider.

Here are the highest speeds supported by various modems:

	Without V.42bis or MNP-5	With V.42bis or MNP-5
V.32	9600	38400
V.32bis	14400	57600
V.34	28800	115200

Hardware Handshake

Handshaking is the means by which two devices control the flow of communications between themselves. Hardware handshaking uses a wire as the control signal to advise when one or the other component is ready to receive data. Software handshaking requires control codes; the most common form found today uses the Ctrl-S character to pause transmission, and the Ctrl-Q character to resume it. If you are using a high-speed modem, you need to enable hardware handshaking, which is the most efficient way to exchange data quickly. Clicking on this box will do the trick.

Van Jacobson CSLIP Compression

CSLIP is a way of compressing datagram headers which can make for speedier transmission. Many service providers now make this option available; check with yours to see whether you should check this box.

Click on OK to cause Trumpet Winsock to accept the new settings. To allow your new settings to take effect, you now need to exit Trumpet Winsock and then restart the program.

> **Note:** Determining precisely which settings are the most effective in some of the preceding fields is tricky. I have given you the settings recommended in the Trumpet Winsock documentation, but on newsgroups like **alt.winsock**, the issue has been kicking around for some time. Here are some further thoughts from Peter Tattam, Trumpet Winsock's creator:
>
> - If your service provider allows header compression, set MSS= 212, RWIN=848.
> - If you are using standard SLIP or PPP, set MSS=512, RWIN= 2048 (Tattam notes that, as a rule of thumb, you should use a value for RWIN that is four times that of MSS)
> - Set MTU=1500 if your service provider will accept that value, or else use the maximum allowable.

Logging In to a SLIP/PPP Account

Setting up a manual login with Trumpet Winsock requires that you start the program and pull down the Dialer menu. You will encounter the screen shown in Figure 3.3; I have already pulled down the relevant menu. Clicking on Manual login will allow you to place the call.

But before you do, make sure you have all your ducks in a row. First, do you have the correct telephone number from your SLIP/PPP provider? Make sure, too, that you have your password and your user ID available. At this point, you're ready to check the modem and make sure you are communicating with it. Entering an **ATZ** command followed by a Return should result in an OK message being sent by the modem. If you do not receive such a message, you will need to double-check that you have your communications port set correctly. Assuming you have been using other kinds of communications software before now, however, you should have no problem assigning the correct port.

You can now initialize the modem. The following command returns the modem to factory defaults for hardware handshaking:

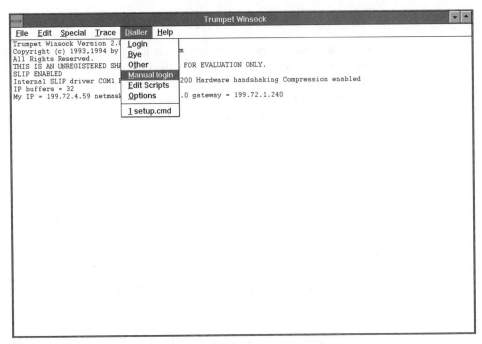

Figure 3.3   Preparing for a manual login with Trumpet Winsock.

AT&F1

Again, you should see an OK returned on the screen. You are now ready to tell Trumpet Winsock to dial the telephone. To do so, enter the following command:

ATDT *number*

where *number* stands for the telephone number given you by your service provider.

When the modem at the other end of the line answers, the two modems will perform their handshaking ritual and you should see a login query, asking you for a user ID and a password.

1. Enter your user ID, followed by a Return.

2. Enter your password, followed by a Return.

3. Press the Esc key.

Using the Esc key tells Trumpet Winsock to go into SLIP/PPP mode. The complete dialog for this transaction, as it will appear on the Trumpet Winsock screen, is as follows (you will, of course, need to substitute the number of your own service provider; the login information is fictitious). I have shown the text the user enters in bold.

Manually dialing.
AFTER LOGGING IN, TYPE THE <ESC> KEY TO RETURN TO NORMAL
SLIP PROCESSING.
SLIP DISABLED
atz
OK
at&f1
OK
atdt 832-7284
CONNECT 28800/ARQ/VFC/LAPM/V42BIS

Welcome to Interpath's Raleigh Point of Presence

stargazer login: X9493445
Password:

Welcome to the Internet through Interpath!

Packet mode enabled
SLIP ENABLED

In this dialog, I have first issued an **atz** command, which checks to see that the modem is on-line. Next comes the **at&f1** command, which resets the device to factory defaults for hardware compression. Finally, the **atdt** command dials the telephone. As you can see, I am prompted for login and password. Following the statement "Packet mode enabled," I have pressed the Esc key (this doesn't show up on the screen), with the result that Trumpet Winsock goes into SLIP mode.

Contrast this sequence with what happens when you use your modem to dial in to a regular commercial on-line service or, for that matter, into a shell account on the Internet. Normally, you would be taken either to a menu of some sort, or to a command prompt, from which you would issue commands to perform your work. In the case of SLIP/PPP, you simply see the SLIP ENABLED statement and there is no other prompt. But the statement is enough. It tells you that you have now established your own presence on the net, and that data packets can travel between your computer and the service provider's site.

This is the point at which you will want to minimize Trumpet Winsock into an icon (press the Minimize button in the top right side of the window) and proceed to activate your applications. Any of the Windows-based applications discussed in this book can be run once this initial step is taken. By clicking on their icons, you start them in the SLIP environment, allowing them to become full-fledged network tools.

Let's check to see that the connection is actually working. To do so, we can use the pingw.exe program we downloaded earlier (in the winapps2.zip file).

If you run this program, either by using the Run command in Program Manager or by creating an icon for it in the Trumpet Winsock program group and clicking, you should be able to check to see whether a particular computer is active on the net. Pick a well-known host, or one in your local area that you know to be working. Then enter the IP address and try it. *Remember: this or any other client will not function unless you have first activated your SLIP/PPP connection!*

Figure 3.4 shows the ping process in action. I have enabled my SLIP connection and have then minimized Trumpet Winsock to an icon by clicking on the Minimize button in the right-hand corner of its screen. I have then run pingw.exe. The program is basic; all it wants is a host address, which I have entered. Immediately, I am given information on the round-trip time to the site (rtt). I can press the Esc key to exit pingw, having demonstrated that my connection is live.

The joy of a SLIP/PPP connection is that there are so many fine tools you can use to explore the Internet. We proceed in Chapter 5 to activate the first of these tools, an FTP client. We will then use FTP to travel to a variety of sites around the globe, looking for new software to evaluate. But first, let's examine the other options for setting up a SLIP/PPP connection through Windows.

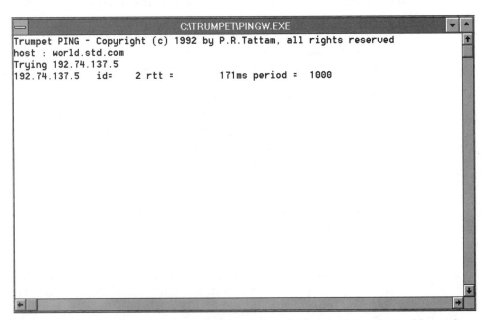

Figure 3.4 The pingw screen. I am checking to see whether the host whose address I have entered is on-line.

Setting Up a Dialing Script

We used manual dial-up to make our initial connection for two reasons: first, to ensure that any problems that occur are not the result of a faulty script; and, second, to check the necessary steps used in making the connection. My service provider, for example, asks me two questions in a specific format:

stargazer login:
Password:

The word "stargazer" is simply the name of the machine handling this transaction, and the login is its request for my user ID. You've seen above how the actual dial-in transaction occurs.

While typing in this information is not a particularly onerous task, it would be nice to be able to automate the process. Trumpet Winsock provides scripting functions that allow you to do this, and includes a description of its scripting language in the documentation. To translate the process into a script, I need to use the Trumpet scripting language. If you will examine the following script, you will see one way to handle this. Because most logins are not complex, this script should give you some basic ideas on how to set up your own automated login. Note that I can use the numeric symbol # to lead off any line that I don't want Trumpet to recognize. This way I can insert my own comments about the script.

```
# Winsock Script for Interpath
#
# Send signal to modem to verify it's on-line, followed by
# carriage return
#
output atz\r
#
# Wait for the OK message from the modem
#
input 10 OK
#
# Set modem factory defaults for hardware handshaking, followed by a
# carriage return
#
output at&f1\r
#
# Wait for the OK signal from the modem
#
input 10 OK
#
```

```
# Send telephone number and carriage return
#
output atdt 832-7284\r
#
# Connection now takes place. Wait up to thirty seconds for the login query.
#
input 30 login:
#
# Send login and carriage return
#
output login\r
#
# Wait for Password: statement
#
input 20 Password:
#
# Send password and carriage return
#
output password\r
#
# Wait for login to be completed
#
input 30 Interpath!
#
# Go into SLIP mode
#
output slip\r
#
# SLIP connection should now be up and running
```

The script I have just demonstrated is utterly basic; it does no more than log in and set up the SLIP session (you would substitute, of course, your own login and password information), and it makes no attempt to correct for possible errors during this process. I show it to you simply for purposes of illustration. Trumpet Winsock comes with a more complex script called login.cmd, which can be edited by pulling down the Dialer menu and choosing the Edit Scripts option. You will need to enter values for your service provider's telephone number, your user name, login, and so on.

The important point is this: if you want to use a particular script as your login script, it must be located in the same directory in which you have placed Trumpet Winsock, and you will need to name it login.cmd. To run it, simply pull down the Dialer menu and choose the Login option. You will also notice that there are other scripts listed on the menu. A Bye script, for example, logs you off from the service provider. Each script is run from the Dialer menu.

Note: You may have noticed the numerical values following certain fields in the above script. For example, at one point as we wait for the script to be completed, I have inserted the following statement:

input 30 Interpath!

The line tells Trumpet to wait up to 30 seconds for the response, which should be the string Interpath! on-screen.

We use time commands like this one because it's important that the script doesn't get too far ahead of what is actually happening with the modem and the device to which it connects. If the script were to insert the password before the remote computer asked for it, the connection process would abort. The 30-second delay simply ensures that script and login move in tandem.

Keeping Up with Trumpet Winsock

There are two excellent sources of information about Trumpet Winsock. The first is a mailing list that you can subscribe to through electronic mail. To do so, send mail to the following address:

listproc@petros.psychol.utas.edu.au

In the body of the message, enter the following:

subscribe trumpet-user *your_name*

Leave the subject field of the message blank, and replace the *your_name* field with your actual full name; for example, **subscribe trumpet-user Ernest Hemingway**.

The other good source of Trumpet Winsock news and tips is a USENET newsgroup, **alt.winsock**. In this group, issues relating to the SLIP/PPP environment, the various client programs, alternative TCP/IP stacks, and more are discussed. The list is active and interesting; at the time of this writing, it was about to split into several subgroups. You may also want to examine your service provider's other USENET offerings; there are several newsgroups dedicated to Trumpet products, but many sites do not carry them. The **alt.winsock** group is probably your best bet.

Whether you use Trumpet Winsock or one of the commercial TCP/IP products discussed next, it's a good idea to read at least **alt.winsock** to keep an eye on new client programs and to follow discussions about the field. You may also want to sign on to another newsgroup for still more discussion. The group is

comp.protocols.tcp-ip.ibmpc, and it maintains a FAQ list that is quite detailed, providing as much technical information as you are ever likely to need about the inside workings of the protocols.

Commercial TCP/IP Stacks for Microsoft Windows

A variety of commercial applications exist to get your Windows computer connected to the net through a SLIP/PPP account. This is inevitable given the nature of Winsock itself. Residing between the TCP/IP stack itself and the layer that connects to the various client programs, Winsock is becoming a de facto standard for running TCP/IP on a Windows-based system. Not all the TCP/IP products mentioned here support Winsock, but we can expect more and more of them to do so as its popularity spreads. No vendor will want to ignore the opportunity Winsock presents to standardize access for so large a market.

Some of the products listed in this section are specifically optimized for communication within an existing Local Area Network; others (and this is true of most) can be used either on such a network or through SLIP/PPP access from a stand-alone computer. With the increasing interest in developing TCP/IP products, all of these companies remain interesting resources for future development and SLIP/PPP connectivity. Each, of course, will provide its own user interface and thus set up its own configuration requirements, although the basic information necessary will parallel what you saw in the installation of Trumpet Winsock. Don't forget as well that in any SLIP/PPP installation, a critical factor is your relationship with your service provider. The provider will need to give you the information necessary to fill in the various setup fields, and likewise will need to be available for questions should problems arise. Choose your provider with attention to this fact.

Here are some of the commercial vendors whose products you may want to look for. The prices listed should be regarded as approximate; in many cases, multiple pricing is necessary across a diverse product line, and there are discounts for multiple purchases.

BW-TCP

Beame & Whiteside Software, Inc.
706 Hillsborough Street
Raleigh, NC 27603-1655
Voice: 919-831-8989
Fax: 919-831-8990
E-mail: **sales@bws.com**

A highly regarded firm with TCP/IP stack, Windows-based applications, and SLIP support. $245.

Chameleon

NetManage, Inc.
20823 Stevens Creek Blvd.
Cupertino, CA 95014
Voice: 408-973-7171
Fax: 408-257-6405
E-mail: **support@netmanage.com**

This is perhaps the most widely known of the SLIP/PPP packages, given its distribution in numerous Internet books and what seems to be a determined campaign to
corner the home user market. The product contains various clients, including
Gopher, Telnet, FTP, Finger, Whois, and a mail program. $199.

Distinct TCP

Distinct Corp.
14082 Loma Rio Drive
Saratoga, CA 95070
Voice: 408-741-0781
Fax: 408-741-0795
E-mail: **mktg@distinct.com**

With SLIP, compressed SLIP (CSLIP), and PPP support, Distinct offers Telnet, FTP,
and a variety of other clients. $395.

Fusion

Pacific Softworks Co.
4000 Via Pescador
Camarillo, CA 93012-5049
Voice: 800-541-9508
Fax: 805-484-3929
E-mail: **sales@nrc.com**

Supports MS-DOS 3.x and better, Windows 3.1. FTP, Telnet, and other clients. $349.

Internet In A Box, AIR for Windows

Spry, Inc.
316 Occidental Ave. South
Seattle, WA 98104
Voice: 206-447-0300
Fax: 206-447-9008
E-mail: **sales@spry.com**

Spry offers a comprehensive solution through its Internet In A Box package, which
contains all the software necessary for setting up a PPP connection to the Internet. Its AIR series also contains, in a variety of packaging options, a set of client
programs for the Internet environment. The basic AIR package is $299; Internet
In A Box sells for $149.

Internet Membership Kit

Ventana Press
P. O. Box 2468
Chapel Hill, NC 27514
Voice: 919-942-0220
Fax: 919-942-1140
E-mail: **info@vmedia.com**

An all-in-one package that contains the software you need to connect to the net. Includes client programs and TCP/IP stack from NetManage, along with documentation such as Harley Hahn and Rick Stout's *The Internet Yellow Pages* (Osborne McGraw-Hill). $69.95.

Lantastic with TCP/IP

Artisoft, Inc.
691 E. River Rd.
Tucson, AZ 85704
Voice: 602-293-6363
E-mail: N/A

Supports MS-DOS 5.0 with a variety of client programs. $199.

LAN Workplace

Novell, Inc.
122 East 1700 South
Provo, UT 84606
Voice: 800-772-UNIX
Fax: 408-473-8990
E-mail: **sales@novell.com**

Supports SLIP and PPP, with Telnet, FTP, and numerous other services. $399.

Pathway Access

The Wollongong Group, Inc.
1129 San Antonio Rd.
Palo Alto, CA 94303
Voice: 415-962-7202
Fax: 415-962-0286
E-mail: **sales@twg.com**

Telnet, FTP, mail, newsreader. Support for SLIP and PPP. The Wollongong Group also provides an OS/2 product called Pathway Access for OS/2. $350/multiple copies; call for information.

PC/TCP

FTP Software, Inc.
2 High Street
North Andover, MA 01845
Voice: 508-685-4000

Fax: 508-794-4477 (sales)
E-mail: **info@ftp.com**

Supports MS-DOS 5.x and Windows 3.1 as well as OS/2 2.0. Telnet, FTP, ping, e-mail, finger, whois, and other clients. Support for SLIP and PPP. $400.

Piper/IP for DOS & Windows; Piper/IP for OS/2

IPswitch, Inc.
333 North Ave.
Wakefield, MA 01880
Voice: 617-942-0621
Fax: 617-246-2975
E-mail: **bob@ipswitch.com**

Wide variety of application programs. $375.

Reflection Series

Walker, Richer & Quinn, Inc.
2815 Eastlake Ave. East
Seattle, WA 98102

or

Buitenhof 47
2513 AH Den Haag
The Netherlands
Voice: 800-926-3896 (US); +31 70 375 1100 (Europe)
Fax: 206-322-8151 (US); +31 70 376 1244 (Europe)
E-mail: N/A

Supports MS-DOS and Windows 3.x. FTP and Telnet clients.

SunSelect

PC-NFS
2 Elizabeth Dr.
Chelmsford, MA 01824
Voice: 800-24-SELECT
Fax: 508-250-5068
E-mail: N/A

Supports both MS-DOS 5.0 and Windows 3.x, with Telnet, ping and other clients, and support for SLIP. $365.

Super-TCP/NFS for Windows / Superhighway Access for Windows

Frontier Technologies Corporation
10201 N. Port Washington Rd.
Mequon, WI 53092
Voice: 414-241-4555
Fax: 414-241-7084
E-mail: **tcp@frontiertech.com**

Super-TCP provides support for MS-DOS 3.3 and above, as well as Windows 3.x. SLIP and PPP support. Super-TCP supports a Windows mail product that handles the MIME binary file attachments that allow you to send graphics and other files through electronic mail. $395. Superhighway Access for Windows integrates Web tools and provides preconfigured access choices for a variety of Internet providers. Contains a utility program that helps you to organize material you find on the net. $149.

TCP/Connect II

InterCon Systems Corporation
950 Herndon Parkway
Herndon, VA 22070
Voice: 703-709-5500
Fax: 703-709-5555
E-mail: **sales@intercon.com**

Basic Internet applications, available in both Macintosh and Windows versions. Supports both SLIP and PPP. The freeware InterSLIP and InterPPP allow MacTCP to work over the telephone lines. A variety of client programs are included. $495.

TCP/IP for DOS; TCP/IP for OS/2

IBM
Department G90
P. O. Box 12195
Research Triangle Park, NC 27709
Voice: 1-800-IBM-CALL
Fax: 404-238-1054
E-mail: N/A

The TCP/IP for DOS product handles MS-DOS 3.3 and above, along with Windows 3.1, with various clients available, including Telnet, FTP, finger, and ping. Support for SLIP. $230.

TCPOpen

Lanera Corporation
516 Valley Way
Milpitas, CA 95035
Voice: 408-956-8344
Fax: 408-956-8343
E-mail: **lanera@netcom.com**

Supports MS-DOS and Windows 3.x, with FTP, Telnet, finger, whois, and SLIP support.

TTCP

Turbosoft Pte Ltd.
248 Johnston St.
Annandale, NSW
Australia 2038
E-mail: **info@abccomp.oz.au**

No SLIP/PPP support as yet, but this is a company you may want to query as to future plans.

TUN

ESKER
1181 Chess Dr.
Suite C
Foster City, CA 94404
Voice: 415-341-9065
E-mail: N/A

Winsock support and various clients.

WinGopher and WinGopher Complete

Notis Systems Inc.
1007 Church St.
Evanston, IL 60201
Voice: 800-556-6487
Fax: 708-866-4970
E-mail: N/A

A superb Gopher implementation that ships, in the WinGopher Complete version, with Distinct TCP/IP network drivers. $69.95. WinGopher Complete sells for $129.

To keep up to date with the release and development of new TCP/IP stacks, both shareware and commercial, you will want to check out the following URL:

http://www.rtd.com/pcnfsfaq/faq.html

This is the PC-Mac TCP/IP & NFS FAQ List, which is an acronym-filled way of saying that this is a list of questions and answers about TCP/IP and Network File System (the latter allows users to work with files and directories on remote systems as if they were available locally). Maintained by Rawn Shah at RTD Systems & Networking, Inc. and prepared by an impressive list of contributors, this FAQ is a treasure trove of information about current products and the background issues related to TCP/IP. It will be a good idea to add its URL to your Mosaic, Netscape, or Cello hotlist, a task we'll set about handling in Chapter 11.

4

SLIP/PPP
on a Macintosh

The Macintosh places fewer demands upon the prospective SLIP/PPP user than Microsoft Windows. Whereas we needed to consider a variety of possible TCP/IP implementations for Windows, the Macintosh is relatively straightforward. The common stack is MacTCP, which is available through Apple Computer, and is, indeed, provided as part of the operating system in all new Macintoshes sold. There are a variety of SLIP/PPP applications available, but the most common, InterSLIP and InterPPP, are provided by Intercon Systems Corporation as freeware. Getting the Mac up and running ought to be a snap.

But as is the case with most SLIP/PPP issues, things are not always as simple as they seem. Equipment issues continue to raise their heads, especially with regard to your modem and the cable necessary to connect it to your computer. The configuration of MacTCP, InterSLIP, and InterPPP is not intuitive, causing many a frustrating delay as you try new options and ponder why your connection isn't going through. Again, a good relationship with your service provider is well nigh critical; this company is the one responsible for answering your questions and guiding you through the login process. Be prepared to use its expertise, and choose your provider not only on price, but on the quality of its technical support.

In this chapter, we examine a typical Macintosh setup and illustrate the steps necessary for getting on-line. Once the connection is sound, we will be able to proceed in later chapters to using the various client programs for the Macintosh. Because of its background in the academic community, the Mac has spawned a set of Internet applications such as Fetch, from Dartmouth University, and Newswatcher, developed at Northwestern, that are not only powerful but easy to use and, in comparison to some (but certainly not all) of their Windows counterparts, more stable in the SLIP/PPP environment.

Macintosh Equipment Requirements

To get SLIP/PPP up and running on your Macintosh, you need the following by way of equipment and software:

- *A Macintosh with a hard disk drive:* Your hard disk should be as large as possible to handle not only the client programs you'll be picking up as we go through this book, but also the other network finds you're bound to make as you explore Internet sites.

- *At least 4MB of RAM:* As is true of Microsoft Windows, the Mac will perform best in the Internet environment if you load it with as much memory as you can afford, and 8MB is preferable; you will find that big programs like Mosaic require a good chunk of RAM just to run.

- *System 7 or later:* Actually, you can get by with System 6 as your operating system, as long as you use the most recent version, but the latest client programs take advantage of System 7 and later, so you should definitely consider the upgrade. The necessary MacTCP software now comes with System 7.5, so the upgrade is worth the expense.

- *A high-speed modem:* High-speed in this context means 28.8Kbps. I know many people who use a 14.4Kbps modem to do network chores, but it's frustratingly slow to run a graphically oriented tool like Mosaic at such speeds. Even 28.8 can seem to crawl when you're dealing with a big image file, so it makes sense to go for the fastest modem possible. As explained in Chapter 2, a V.34 modem is now the tool of choice for 28.8Kbps work; the earlier V.FC and V.FAST modems were not a worldwide standard. V.34 is. Your V.34 modem will also have V.32bis, V.42, V.42bis, and other inscrutable combinations of letters and numbers. These are the protocols that allow data compression and other modem magic to pump information over the telephone lines at high speed.

- *A modem cable that does hardware handshaking:* Hardware handshaking refers to the way two electronic devices control the flow of information between them. This can be managed through software or hardware, and hardware is preferable when you're dealing with high-speed modems. Standard Macintosh modem cables simply won't work; when you try to enable hardware handshaking with them, the communications program you're using won't accept the setting and will probably fall back to software handshaking. Hardware handshaking cables are found with labels stating "high-speed modem cable" or some such, and if your computer dealer doesn't know what they are, you need to find a dealer who does.

The Macintosh TCP/IP Stack

MacTCP is the basic Macintosh TCP/IP stack. As with any TCP/IP implementation, MacTCP is the software engine that lets your computer exchange data packets with the Internet. Again, we distinguish between the two kinds of software needed to run SLIP/PPP. The TCP/IP stack, whatever kind you use, is necessary whether you run SLIP/PPP or a full network connection; IP, remember, is what breaks the data into packets that are then sent out onto the network. The SLIP/PPP software is a separate program that is expressly designed to make the necessary modem connection. You do not, obviously, need SLIP/PPP software if you already use a full network connection, but you do need MacTCP.

Where to Get MacTCP

If you already own a Macintosh running System 7.5, you have MacTCP built into your operating system; it's in the System Folder. The software used to be sold separately, and it is a measure of the growing popularity of the Internet that it's now available as an integral part of your computer's operations. In the IBM-compatible PC world, much the same thing has happened, with both Microsoft and IBM building network links into new versions of their Windows and OS/2 products respectively. The day will doubtless come when Internet access is simply a matter of clicking on an icon and logging in; indeed, the new OS/2 Warp comes close to achieving this kind of seamless connectivity.

If you don't already own MacTCP, you can get a copy direct from Apple Computer by upgrading to System 7.5. At the time of this writing, the version in use was 2.0.4, with 2.0.6 about to be released. You can also contact the Apple Programmers & Developers Association (APDA) at 800-282-2732 to order MacTCP; in addition, many mail-order dealers sell the product.

Because Apple is the major supplier for the MacTCP product, and thus for the TCP/IP software that makes SLIP/PPP possible on the Mac, all Macintosh applications for the Internet will work with it. If you run into a problem with a particular piece of software, it probably relates to the version of MacTCP in use rather than to any fundamental incompatibility between MacTCP and the program. All of the client programs we will examine in this book work comfortably with version 2.0 releases of MacTCP.

Configuring MacTCP

Before doing anything else, turn off any anti-virus software you may have running. MacTCP will need to install two files, MacTCP DNR and MacTCP Prep, in the System Folder, and it is possible that anti-virus software might identify these new files as viruses. When you have eliminated this possibility, you are ready to proceed.

If you already have MacTCP on your hard disk as part of your operating system, you will find its icon in the Control Panel Folder within the System

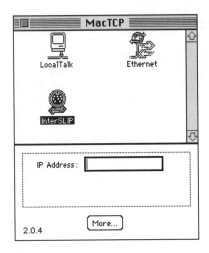

Figure 4.1 The initial MacTCP screen.

Folder on your Mac. Double-click on the MacTCP icon to call up the initial screen, as shown in Figure 4.1.

The first time you do this, you won't see the InterSLIP icon in the MacTCP dialog box. This, or its PPP equivalent, will appear later, when you set up Inter-SLIP or InterPPP for network use. For now, leave the IP Address: field blank.

Alternatively, if you are installing MacTCP from a diskette, follow these steps:

1. Drag the MacTCP Control Panel file to the System Folder icon.
2. Drag the Hosts file to the System Folder icon.

MacTCP will then be moved into the Control Panel Folder, while the Hosts file will remain in the System Folder. You can now restart your Macintosh to begin the configuration of MacTCP; double-click on the MacTCP icon to initiate this process.

You must fill in the information MacTCP needs to make a proper network connection. To do so, click on the More box in MacTCP's initial screen. The main MacTCP screen will now appear, as shown in Figure 4.2. Configuring MacTCP is a matter of filling in the appropriate fields. Provided that you have obtained the necessary information from your service provider, the process is relatively simple. Be sure that you have contacted the technical support staff at your service provider's site; entering inappropriate values in these fields can cause network problems and will certainly result in a failure to launch your SLIP/PPP connection successfully.

Let's now go through the MacTCP fields to enter the proper values.

Obtain Address

There are three options for telling your computer how it will obtain an IP address. The IP address specifies the location of your computer on the service

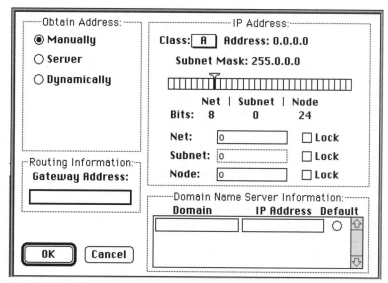

Figure 4.2 The main MacTCP screen, ready for configuration.

provider's network which, in turn, connects you to the Internet. Your service provider will tell you which option to choose. Most likely, the choice will be Manually. This is the item to click on when you are using a permanent, or static, address.

Most service providers will set up your account with a static IP address, but it is possible to have IP addresses dynamically assigned, which means that the server assigns you an address each time you connect (this occurs when networks have more nodes than addresses available to them; addresses are assigned on the fly to those computers that request them). If this is how your service provider functions, you will need to choose the Server option on the MacTCP dialog box.

Class

Network class can be set manually or you can let MacTCP figure it out automatically. Any network with an IP number beginning 1 to 127 is Class A; Class B uses 128–191; Class C uses 191–254. You can change this setting by clicking on the Class: field and moving the marker to the correct class. Check with your service provider to ensure that you have the correct information.

Subnet Mask

Your service provider will have given you correct class information with the materials you received when you opened your SLIP/PPP account. Be sure to follow your provider's instructions with regard to network class and subnet mask. The settings are standardized at 255.0.0.0 (Class A), 255.255.0.0 (Class B) and 255.255.255.0 (Class C).

How does a subnet mask work? A *netmask,* often called an *address mask,* is frequently used in large networks to help the organization in question divide its various internal networks according to its own needs. To do so, the organization must modify its IP address structure. An IP address identifies both network and host computer addresses; a subnet modifies the network and host portions of this address to create additional networks within that structure. Considering the fact that most service providers are running relatively large operations, subnetting is fairly common (a subnet mask is only necessary if there is more than one physical network at the site that uses the same address). The subnet mask is applied to the IP address to define the particular subnet on a given network to which a machine is assigned.

The creation of subnets can ease administrative chores for the people administering a large network; subnets are also frequently used to work around the physical constraints created by network cabling, which can limit how widely dispersed a network can be at a particular site. The subnet itself, however, is of concern only to the local network. Machines that exist within the various subnets at a given provider's site all appear, to the Internet at large, to be on a single network.

Gateway Address

The Gateway Address: field contains the IP address of the default gateway; this is where MacTCP sends data packets that are addressed to other networks (notice that the data is entered under the general rubric "Routing Information"). In many installations, you can leave this field set to 0.0.0.0; MacTCP will then locate the remote gateway through a tool called Routing Information Protocol. But you will need to enter an address here if your network doesn't implement RIP. In that case, use the information provided by your service provider to enter the correct address.

Domain

This is where you enter the address for the domain name server, the computer that converts domain names into numerical IP addresses. Your provider may offer two name servers, a primary and an alternate; in this case, enter both values here. You can choose which of the two you want to use as your default.

IP Address

This is the IP address for the domain name server(s) just specified.

Entering Your Own IP Address

You must now leave the configuration screen and enter your own IP address in the initial MacTCP box. Click on OK and you will return to this box, where you can enter the IP address your provider has assigned you in the IP Address:

field. Click on More once again to double-check that the IP address you entered has not caused any of the values on the configuration screen to change. Pay particular attention to network class, which must correspond to the numerical values you entered in the IP Address: field.

MacTCP should now be configured for your use. You can exit the MacTCP screen by clicking on the button at the top left. Now, restart your Macintosh so that the values you have entered in your MacTCP configuration can take effect. Having done so, you are now ready to move on to the second half of the Macintosh SLIP/PPP installation. You need the software that makes it possible to move your TCP/IP data out onto the network over a modem.

SLIP Software for the Macintosh

While MacTCP contains everything necessary to run TCP/IP networking over a full network connection, you need a SLIP/PPP software tool to make the connection with your modem. For SLIP, the first option is in the freeware arena. InterCon Systems Corporation, a Reston, Virginia-based developer, provides a free product called InterSLIP. You can retrieve InterSLIP at the following URL:

ftp://ftp.intercon.com/pub/sales/InterSLIP/

At the time of this writing, the filename was InterSLIPInstaller1.0.1.hqx. Don't expect technical support for InterSLIP. InterCon Systems Corporation is the developer of a number of commercial products that I'll discuss shortly, including InterPPP and TCP/Connect II, and it would be too much to ask that it actively support a product that it has generously made available for free.

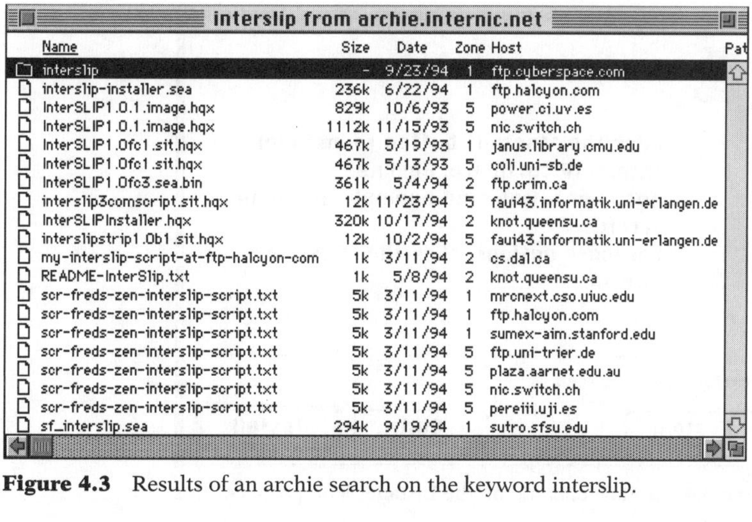

Name	Size	Date	Zone	Host	Pat
interslip	-	9/23/94	1	ftp.cyberspace.com	
interslip-installer.sea	236k	6/22/94	1	ftp.halcyon.com	
InterSLIP1.0.1.image.hqx	829k	10/6/93	5	power.ci.uv.es	
InterSLIP1.0.1.image.hqx	1112k	11/15/93	5	nic.switch.ch	
InterSLIP1.0fc1.sit.hqx	467k	5/19/93	1	janus.library.cmu.edu	
InterSLIP1.0fc1.sit.hqx	467k	5/13/93	5	coli.uni-sb.de	
InterSLIP1.0fc3.sea.bin	361k	5/4/94	2	ftp.crim.ca	
interslip3comscript.sit.hqx	12k	11/23/94	5	faui43.informatik.uni-erlangen.de	
InterSLIPInstaller.hqx	320k	10/17/94	2	knot.queensu.ca	
interslipstrip1.0b1.sit.hqx	12k	10/2/94	5	faui43.informatik.uni-erlangen.de	
my-interslip-script-at-ftp-halcyon-com	1k	3/11/94	2	cs.dal.ca	
README-InterSlip.txt	1k	5/8/94	2	knot.queensu.ca	
scr-freds-zen-interslip-script.txt	5k	3/11/94	1	mrcnext.cso.uiuc.edu	
scr-freds-zen-interslip-script.txt	5k	3/11/94	1	ftp.halcyon.com	
scr-freds-zen-interslip-script.txt	5k	3/11/94	1	sumex-aim.stanford.edu	
scr-freds-zen-interslip-script.txt	5k	3/11/94	5	ftp.uni-trier.de	
scr-freds-zen-interslip-script.txt	5k	3/11/94	5	plaza.aarnet.edu.au	
scr-freds-zen-interslip-script.txt	5k	3/11/94	5	nic.switch.ch	
scr-freds-zen-interslip-script.txt	5k	3/11/94	5	pereiii.uji.es	
sf_interslip.sea	294k	9/19/94	1	sutro.sfsu.edu	

Window title: **interslip from archie.internic.net**

Figure 4.3 Results of an archie search on the keyword interslip.

You can also find the InterSLIP product in the file libraries of the various on-line services, like CompuServe, America Online, and DELPHI. These are your best bet if you are starting on the Internet from scratch; use the file search options these services make available to search under the keyword interslip. If you already have a shell account, simply use FTP to reach the InterCon site, bearing in mind the usual consideration about not using FTP during working hours at the site (these computers have other uses than anonymous FTP!). Or you can try a different FTP site. Figure 4.3 shows the results of an archie search I ran on the term interslip from a particular archie site.

As you can see, there are a variety of options here (we'll learn all about archie and how to run searches using it in Chapter 5). Configuring the software depends upon changing settings in a control panel. We'll now go through the InterSLIP configuration, and then I'll give a brief rundown on PPP possibilities for the Macintosh.

Installing and Configuring InterSLIP

The InterSLIP Installer application is what you use to set up InterSLIP on your Macintosh. When you double-click on the Installer icon, you will see the screen shown in Figure 4.4.

Simply follow the prompts to load InterSLIP on your system. You will receive a reminder that your Macintosh needs to be restarted after installation, followed by a message that the installation was successful. Restart your Mac to begin working with InterSLIP. Double-clicking on the InterSLIP Setup icon will call up the screen shown in Figure 4.5. This is the InterSLIP connection window. Using it, you can connect to and disconnect from your service

Figure 4.4 Double-clicking on the Installer icon produces this dialog box.

Figure 4.5 The basic InterSLIP screen.

provider. To do so, you have to set up a configuration that InterSLIP will use to make the connection.

Setting Up an InterSLIP Configuration

To create your InterSLIP configuration, choose New from the File menu. You will be prompted for the name of your configuration. Enter the name of your service provider at the prompt. The name you have chosen will then appear in the InterSLIP box beneath the Connect button.

Now you need to fill in the necessary information for your configuration. To do so, double-click on the configuration name. The basic InterSLIP configuration screen will appear. This screen is illustrated in Figure 4.6. While the screen itself may seem unfamiliar, the information it is asking you to enter is relatively simple. Let's go through the necessary fields one at a time.

Serial Port

The port used for sending and receiving data to and from your modem. Choose Modem Port, which is the default.

Baud Rate

Choose baud rate depending upon the speed of the modem you have available. Assuming you are using a high-speed modem that handles data compression, choose the highest value possible, which is 57600.

Data Bits

Asynchronous data transmission, which simply means sending data bits one after another rather than in parallel, creates a problem. The computer needs to be able to determine which set of bits make up a byte, the basic unit of mea-

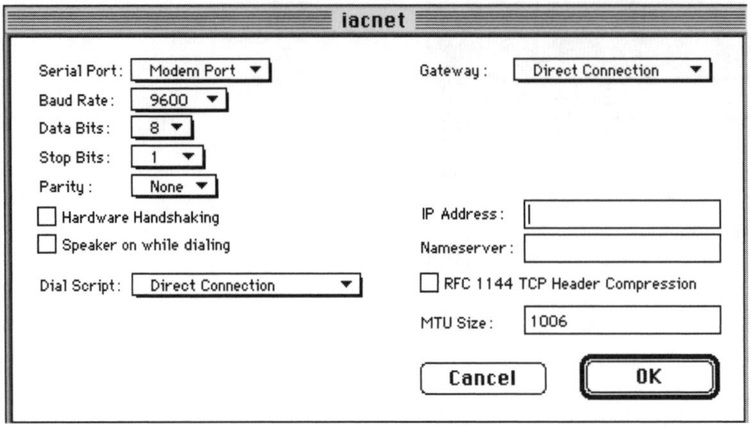

Figure 4.6 The InterSLIP configuration screen.

surement for computers (each byte stores the equivalent of one character). Normally, bytes are "framed" by start and stop bits, which denote where the byte stops and starts. Your serial port adds these bits to bytes as it converts them into serial format, and also strips away the start and stop bits from incoming bytes.

For your purposes, setting the data bits to 8 is the right choice; SLIP connections require 8 bits to run properly. Choosing 7 would allow the system to use parity checking, which sets up basic error detection. Many commercial on-line services require 7 data bits, but using InterSLIP through an Internet service provider does not.

Stop Bits

Choose 1 as your stop bit setting; other settings are obsolete.

Parity

This refers to a technique for error detection that can be set to values of None, Even, or Odd. When you set up InterSLIP to work with 8 data bits, you should set Parity at None.

Hardware Handshaking

A means of controlling the flow of serial communications using a signal line in the modem cable. Assuming you have installed a high-speed modem cable that handles hardware handshaking, you should check this box. If it is not checked, you will have to turn off data compression in your modem, thus losing the major benefit of its high-speed capabilities.

Speaker on while dialing

It's up to you, but I always leave the speaker on so I can follow the progress of the call. Too many things can go wrong when using a modem, and I don't want to assume I am connected and start launching client programs when I'm actually off-line.

Dial Script

In almost all cases, choose the Hayes-Compatible Modem selection, which works with virtually every modem on the market. When you choose this setting, three new fields will appear immediately below this box (not shown in Figure 4.6).

Dial.   Choose Tone or Pulse as required by your telephone system. The default is Tone.

Phone No.   Enter the telephone number given you by your service provider in this field.

Modem Init.   This is the command string that is sent to your modem before it dials the telephone. The commands to enter here will vary depending upon the modem being used. In most cases, simply entering AT&F will work; this tells the modem to reestablish factory default settings before it places the call. If you choose to add other parameters to control your modem, you will need to consult the manual for the modem itself. It would also be a good idea, if you are having difficulty in selecting the right initialization string, to speak to your service provider.

 The modem I have connected to my PowerMac, a Microcom DeskPorte ES 28.8, uses the following initialization string:

AT&F&C1

The AT command gets the attention of the modem, while the &F resets it to factory defaults. The &C1 tells the modem's Data Carrier Detect signal to track the condition of the remote modem, so that the CD modem light is on only when the modem detects the presence of a carrier signal from the other modem.

Gateway

Though not shown in Figure 4.6, pull down the Gateway menu and choose Simple Unix/Telebit. This is the selection to be used with a system that prompts you for a Login and Password. When you choose this item, 2 additional fields will open up immediately below the Gateway: field, as follows.

User Name.   Enter the User Name given you by your service provider here. Be sure that you enter the name exactly, minding the difference between capital and lowercase letters.

Prompt for password at connect time.   Click this box if you want to enter your password manually every time you log on. If you leave this box unchecked, InterSLIP will supply the password automatically.

Password.   Enter the password given you by your service provider here.

IP Address

Enter your IP address here. If your provider assigns IP addresses dynamically, leave this field blank.

Nameserver

Enter the IP address of the Domain Name Server as given to you by your service provider.

RFC 1144 TCP Header Compression

Header compression can improve response time, but you need to make sure that your provider supports CSLIP. If so, check this box.

MTU Size

The default value for Maximum Transmission Unit is 1006. Double check with your provider to see what setting is suggested. MTU denotes the maximum size of the data packet that can be used on the network. Messages larger than the MTU are broken into separate packets.

Click OK to save the configuration.

Making the SLIP Connection with InterSLIP

To run InterSLIP, double-click on the InterSLIP Setup icon. Make sure that the configuration you have just established is highlighted, and then click on Connect. The progress of your call can be tracked in the upper right corner of the InterSLIP window, and if you have left the speaker on to follow your call, you will be able to hear the connection as it is made.

Once InterSLIP has made the connection, you are now SLIP-enabled, and can proceed to run whatever client programs you choose. The balance of this book will discuss various options in client programs that you can download and run under the SLIP/PPP environment. The method throughout will be the same: you will launch your SLIP connection and, once it is established, double-click on the client program that you want to run.

To disconnect from your SLIP session, click on Disconnect. If you are not using hardware handshaking, InterSLIP will hang up the telephone. If you do have hardware handshaking enabled, the modem may not automatically hang up when InterSLIP disconnects. In that case, you may have no choice but to cycle the modem by turning the power switch off and then back on again. Once you are more familiar with InterSLIP, you may choose to create a dialing script that contains hangup commands.

Note: InterSLIP makes using your client programs a snap. When you double-click on a client program's icon, that program will attempt to open MacTCP. Even if you're not already connected, InterSLIP will then make the necessary connection, using the most recently selected configuration. On my desktop, for example, I have set up aliases of my most frequently used Internet applications. All I need to do to connect to them is to double-click on any one of them. The InterSLIP connection then takes place automatically.

Installing PPP on the Macintosh

MacPPP is a freeware program that is also available at various FTP sites and through the commercial on-line services. I retrieved my copy from the following URL:

ftp://ftp.merit.edu/internet.tools/ppp/mac/

At the time of this writing, the filename was macppp2.0.1.hqx. It is also available at numerous FTP sites, as an archie search will show. MacPPP was developed at the Michigan-based Merit Network and at the University of Michigan itself, based on public domain code written by William Allen Simpson.

In Figure 4.7, you can see the contents of the MacPPP folder I downloaded from **ftp.merit.edu**. Notice that the icons show a configuration routine, the PPP implementation itself, and two text files, one containing installation instructions, the other release information about the particular version of MacPPP I am using.

The actual installation proceeds as follows:

1. Drag the Config PPP icon to the Control Panels folder (this is located inside the System Folder).
2. Drag the PPP icon to the Extensions folder (also found inside the System Folder).
3. Restart your Macintosh to allow the changes to take effect.

Configuring MacPPP

Next, we will configure MacPPP for your account.

1. Select the PPP icon in the MacTCP control panel.
2. Select the Config PPP icon in the Control Panel folder.
3. Double-click on the Config PPP icon.

Setting the correct information in the Config PPP control panel will allow MacPPP to create a file called PPP Preferences, which will appear in the Preferences folder (inside the System Folder). Figure 4.8 shows the Config PPP screen.

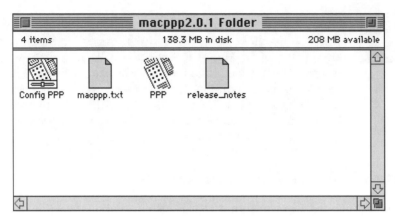

Figure 4.7   Contents of the MacPPP folder.

There is nothing particularly difficult about this screen; the tricky side of MacPPP installation is, as with InterSLIP, the actual configuration. Several settings must be added to the preceding control panel. Let's go through them one at a time.

PPP Up/Down

This icon indicates the current status of network traffic on your computer. When it registers down, PPP is not ready to accept data packets; when it registers up, it is activated.

Open/Close

When MacPPP has been configured, you will click on the Open button to begin a session, while the Close button will end it.

Stats

Although you may not need to use it, the Stats button opens a dialog box that shows the current state of MacPPP and its operations.

Port Name

Although the modem port is your default, this setting allows you to choose the printer port or any other serial connection for MacPPP's use. Modem users will, of course, choose the modem port default.

Idle Timeout (minutes)

You can use this setting to change the way MacPPP monitors an ongoing connection. In its default state of None, MacPPP will not select a timeout interval. But if you choose to set such an interval, MacPPP will alert you when the ses-

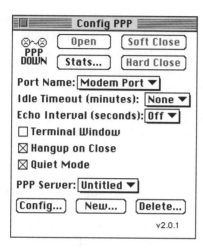

Figure 4.8   The configuration screen for MacPPP.

sion has remained idle for the specified period of time. This can be a handy tool to know about, because when you get busy working between an ongoing PPP session and other work on your Mac's desktop, you can easily forget that the PPP session is still open. With a PPP connection through a commercial service provider, that can lead to steadily accumulating bills.

The menu here allows you to set the timeout at anything from 5 to 120 minutes. I set mine high, because I often need to remain on-line for extended periods of time. But it would probably be wise for a newcomer to set this value at, say, ten minutes. If the alerts come too frequently for your taste, you can always change the timeout setting to a higher value.

Echo Interval (seconds)

This setting determines whether MacPPP will query the server to which it is connected to check on the status of the connection. The default is Off, meaning that MacPPP will not send out such a request. You can use the menu available in this field to set intervals from two to twenty seconds if you do want these queries to be made. The query itself is in the form of a packet called a Line Control Protocol echo request. MacPPP will assume that the connection is not operational if it gets no response after three successive requests.

Terminal Window

The Terminal Window is MacPPP's terminal emulation box. When this box is checked, the emulation window will appear when you make the connection, and it can be used to put the server you are connecting to into PPP mode. When you have entered the appropriate commands, you can click on the OK button to launch the PPP session. When the Terminal Window box is checked, MacPPP will ignore the telephone number and the modem initialization information that you have entered in the Config field (we will add these values in a moment). It will also ignore any scripts you have created for automatic login.

Why would you want to use a terminal emulator with MacPPP? In most cases, you won't need to, and can safely leave the box unchecked. But there may be times when the emulator is useful. Nothing can be quite so frustrating as to write a script for automatic login, only to find that the script keeps stumbling over some unexpected sequence in the login process. Using the terminal emulator, you can walk through the login step by step as a way to debug your script. Having learned where the problem lies, you can then modify the script and use it to handle your logins in the future.

Hangup on Close

This box determines what MacPPP will do when you end your PPP session. Modem users should check it so that MacPPP will send a hangup string to the modem. You may recall that InterSLIP, when used with a hardware handshaking cable, will not hang up the telephone after the SLIP connection is broken. Having to cycle your modem every time you go off-line gets old fast, so you'll want to be sure this box is checked.

Quiet Mode

When checked, disable notification for "Idle Timeout" conditions.

PPP Server

This is the computer that you connect to for your PPP service. To activate this field, you will need to fill in the Config options, discussed next.

Config

These options allow you to enter the server information that MacPPP needs to make the connection. When you click on this item, the dialog box shown in Figure 4.9 will appear. Here we have a set of additional fields.

PPP Server Name.   Enter the name of the server computer you will be connecting to here. You will have received this information from your service provider when you signed up for PPP access. MacPPP allows you to set up multiple servers and choose the one you want to use from a pop-up menu. The New button allows you to add new server names.

Port Speed.   This field should contain the baud rate for the serial port you are using for your PPP connection. Assuming you are using a high-speed modem of the kind recommended in this book, you should set the baud rate at the highest value of 57600.

Flow Control.   Flow control is the way modems talk to each other to negotiate the transfer of data. Choose the CTS & RTS setting to enable hardware handshaking; this will enable your modem's data compression capabilities to

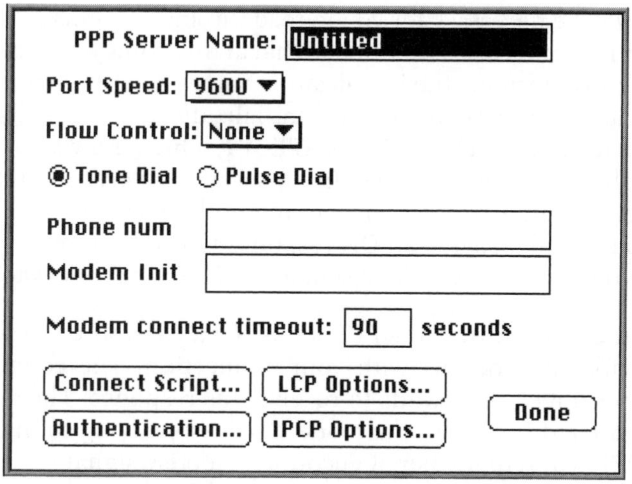

Figure 4.9 Entering connection information in MacPPP.

function, which, in turn, means higher speeds (you will, however, need a high-speed modem cable to make this possible). MacPPP will not work with modems that are using XON/XOFF software flow control. If your modem uses XON/XOFF by default, you will need to check the documentation to select an initialization string that will disable it. This initialization information will be placed in the Modem Init field we will discuss shortly.

Phone num.   Enter the telephone number your service provider has assigned you here.

Modem Init.   Modem initialization strings are sent to the modem before it places a call. In many cases, the factory defaults for your modem will do the job, and you will not need to enter any special values here. But, as just mentioned, an initialization string can be valuable if you need to disable XON/XOFF flow control, or enable the CTS (Clear to Send) and RTS (Request to Send) capabilities of your modem.

How do you know which initialization string to enter? A few simple rules apply. First, all modem initialization strings are preceded by the AT command which is common to Hayes modems, and which have become standardized throughout the industry. Second, it is best to try your modem's defaults first to see if they work. The best way to do this is to enter the following string in the Modem Init field:

AT&F

This command resets the modem to factory defaults. If you use this as your initialization string and your sessions connect normally, then entering any other values is unnecessary. If this initialization string does not produce the desired results, then it will be necessary for you to read through the documentation that came with your modem. I also recommend that at this point you check with your service provider to determine the initialization values he or she recommends.

MacPPP, incidentally, sends a small initialization string of its own each time it dials the telephone. This string is ATE0V1, which is a way of putting the modem in verbose response mode. In this sense, "verbose" refers to the modem's responding in words rather than in numbers when it receives a command. The modem will provide an OK response to this command. Any initialization string you have added will be sent after the string that MacPPP sends.

Modem connect timeout. MacPPP looks for a CONNECT response from the modem before it proceeds with your connection. The connect timeout value determines how long it waits to receive this response. The default value is 90 seconds; after this period, the modem will stop trying to make the connection. MacPPP will redial when it encounters a busy signal.

At this point, you have given MacPPP everything it needs to make a connection. But there are several optional fields we also need to discuss that can streamline operations.

Connect Script. Scripts are sequences of commands and responses that you can use to log on to a server automatically. MacPPP makes it easy to construct a script for such a connection by providing a field that you can fill in with the appropriate values. You can see this dialog box in Figure 4.10. As you can see, I have inserted values for the connection that will be appropriate for a hypothetical service provider.

Examine the script with care. It follows the normal sign-on procedures that you would use with a service provider. In the case of Trumpet Winsock, we saw that such a script could be constructed by inserting the correct values into

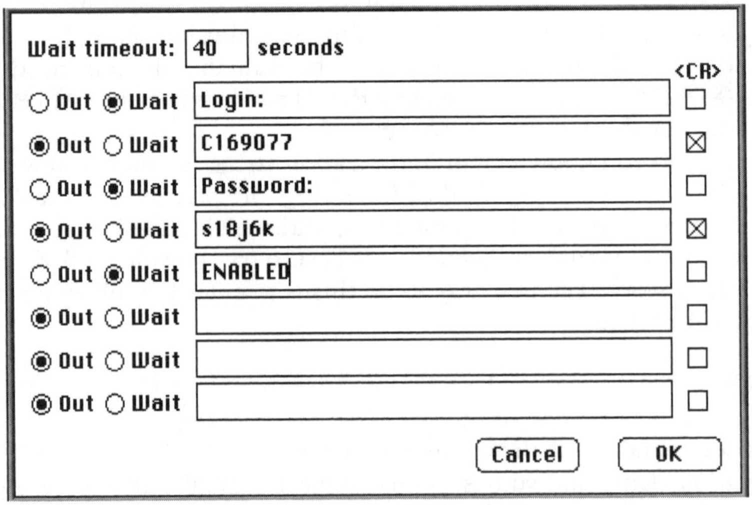

Figure 4.10 Setting up a login script in MacPPP.

a matrix of fields that we ourselves constructed, using the Trumpet Winsock command language. With MacPPP, the hardest part of the job has been done for us. All we need to do is to determine what our provider wants in terms of sign-on procedures, and then to insert those values as required.

The method is straightforward. When you click on the Wait button, the value you insert in the following field will be the one the modem waits for before proceeding with the login. When you click on the Out button, the following value will be send to the server. You can choose to follow that statement with a carriage return by clicking on the appropriate <CR> box. So in the case of the script given, I have automated the following process:

- Wait for the string Login:
- When the string is received, send the string C169077, followed by a carriage return.
- Wait for the string Password:
- When the password is received, send the string s18j6k, followed by a carriage return.
- Wait for the string ENABLED.

The ENABLED statement is an indication from this hypothetical provider that the PPP session has begun. Notice the Wait timeout: field at the top of the script box. This tells us that MacPPP will wait 40 seconds for the wait string to be received. If this time expires, the session will end. At this point, you will be asked if you want to retry the script or quit MacPPP.

Authentication.   The authentication box, shown in Figure 4.11, allows you to enter a login ID and password. You will not need to fill in this information if you have already completed a connect script as per the instructions just given.

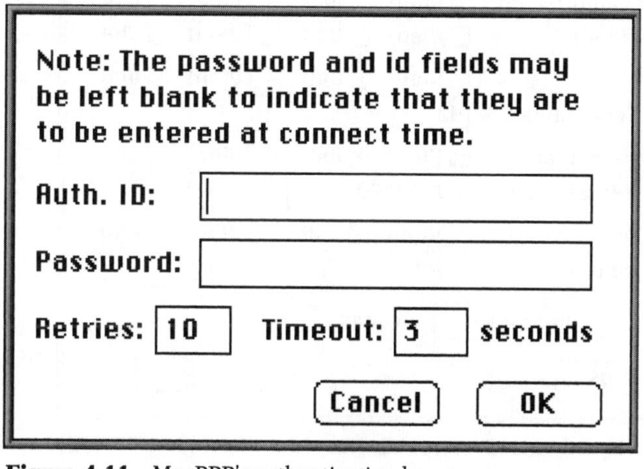

Figure 4.11   MacPPP's authentication box.

Notice that MacPPP provides a box to specify how many times it should attempt to resend the ID and password information; the default is 10, after which the connection will be aborted. A timeout value is also provided, to specify the number of seconds MacPPP will wait for the server to respond to this information. The default timeout is three seconds.

LCP and IPCP Options. The LCP, or Line Control Protocol, box is shown in Figure 4.12. It allows you to configure the method MacPPP uses to negotiate with the server. The default values are generally sound and can remain as they are.

You will, however need to change the IPCP, or IP Control Protocol, box to enter your own IP address, provided you are using a preassigned IP address. If your address is being provided by the server, you will not need to change the defaults. Ask your service provider if you're unsure what to enter here. The dialog box is shown in Figure 4.13.

Connecting with MacPPP

To initiate a PPP session with MacPPP, double-click on the Config PPP icon in the Control Panel. Click on Open to establish the connection; the script you have completed for the login will now be executed. When the connection has been made, you can close the MacPPP dialog box and proceed to use whatever client programs you have elected to run. As with SLIP, PPP is transparent to the end user once the connection has been established. Your Macintosh is now Internet-ready.

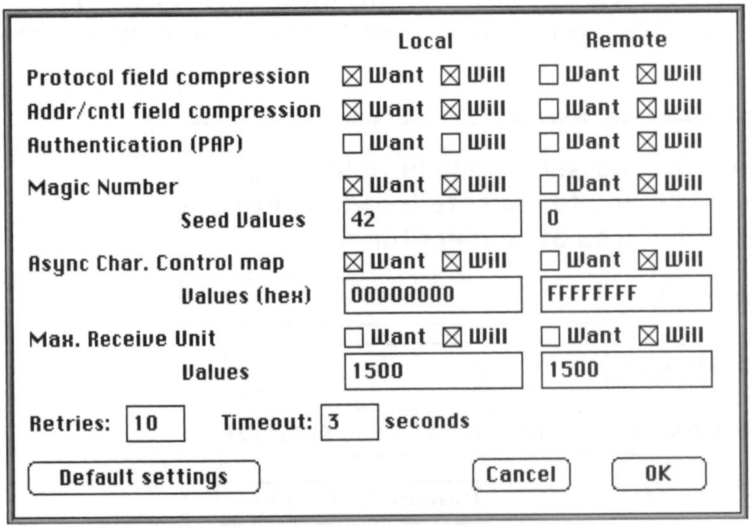

	Local		Remote	
Protocol field compression	⊠ Want	⊠ Will	☐ Want	⊠ Will
Addr/cntl field compression	⊠ Want	⊠ Will	☐ Want	⊠ Will
Authentication (PAP)	☐ Want	☐ Will	☐ Want	⊠ Will
Magic Number	⊠ Want	⊠ Will	☐ Want	⊠ Will
Seed Values	42		0	
Async Char. Control map	⊠ Want	⊠ Will	☐ Want	⊠ Will
Values (hex)	00000000		FFFFFFFF	
Max. Receive Unit	☐ Want	⊠ Will	☐ Want	⊠ Will
Values	1500		1500	

Retries: 10   Timeout: 3   seconds

[Default settings]   [Cancel]   [OK]

Figure 4.12 The Line Control Protocol box lets you configure how MacPPP negotiates with the server.

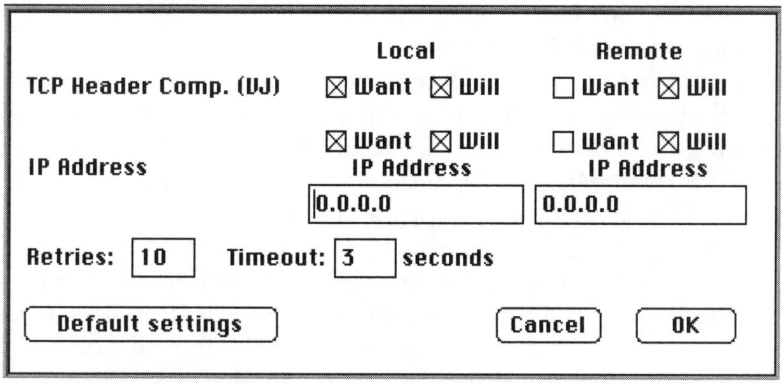

Figure 4.13   MacPPP's IP Control Protocol box.

To close a MacPPP session, you have two options. Clicking on Soft Close will close the IP session itself, allowing you to use your serial port to run a non-PPP communications program. Clicking on Hard Close will end PPP entirely.

SLIP on the Mac: A User's Tale

My Power Macintosh is basically a network tool; I do all of my other work on a 486. But frequently, while I'm writing, I keep the Mac connected to the net with a SLIP account. Its screen sits to my right, so that access to whatever network tool I need is quick and easy. My friends in the academic world have the luxury of full-time network connectivity; my e-mail to them is often answered immediately because they're working on a networked machine that informs them as soon as new mail arrives. Cost issues keep us SLIP/PPP users from staying connected round the clock, but for at least a good portion of every day, I'm able to stay connected and use the network as my database.

When I set about configuring my Mac for Internet use, I already had MacTCP loaded as part of System 7.5, the operating system for the computer. I retrieved InterSLIP from an FTP site and assumed I was ready to go; after all, I already had a SLIP connection up and running with Interpath on my 486. That's when the configuration problems began to appear. My copy of MacTCP wouldn't let me load the relevant IP address, my own. I knew which number to use from loading the information into Trumpet Winsock, but MacTCP simply didn't make that field available to me. Thus began the first of many phone calls to my provider.

The problem was, as such problems usually are in retrospect, a simple one. MacTCP specifies three ways to obtain an Internet address: manually, through the server, and dynamically. Click on the Server or Dynamically buttons on its Setup screen and the IP Address field is unavailable. And for good reason; some service providers allocate IP addresses "on the fly," meaning that your IP address might actually change between one on-line session and the next. But my provider doesn't handle things this way; I had to click on the Manually button to open up the IP Address field.

Having done that, I faced the inscrutable question of Network Class. I could call up my service provider and get a "connected" statement on-screen, but nothing else would happen. By setting Class: equal to C in MacTCP, I could adjust the Subnet Mask: field to the appropriate value: 255.255.255.0. At this point, MacTCP seemed to be happy and I could proceed.

Except that InterSLIP didn't want to work. About halfway through my sign-up process, I had upgraded to a new 28.8 modem. Now I needed to establish hardware handshaking as the default; InterSLIP makes a field available for this if you click on the appropriate box. But thus clicked on, the software refused to make the connection to my provider. Left unclicked, I was able to go straight through. Without hardware handshaking, of course, but at least the connection was made. The problem? As just specified, I needed a hardware handshaking modem cable.

With a new cable in place, I was able to use InterSLIP to log on and run my client software. All seemed well until I attempted to hang up the telephone. Although I could click on InterSLIP's Disconnect button, the modem refused to go off-line. It was necessary to recycle it every time I made the connection to my service provider. I could have gotten around this by incorporating the hangup command in an InterSLIP script, but until my script was ready, I simply powered off the modem to disconnect.

All of these issues were readily solvable once I understood what the problem was. But I have great sympathy for those who tell me they find the SLIP/PPP process utterly mysterious. As the net expands into home and small business use, surely we can't expect the average user to know, or care about, the differences between the various classes of network, or the definition of a subnet mask, or the workings of dynamic IP address allocation or any of the rest of it. An intuitive approach to SLIP/PPP software installation through truly intelligent setup screens would seem to offer software developers a golden opportunity to get rich. Surely someone, somewhere, is working on it?

Commercial SLIP/PPP Possibilities for the Macintosh

While not as prolific as commercial implementations for Microsoft Windows, several excellent Macintosh-specific SLIP/PPP packages do exist. Let's examine these now.

Internet In A Box for the Macintosh

Spry, Inc.
316 Occidental Ave. South
Seattle, WA 98104
Voice: 206-447-0300

Fax: 206-447-9008
E-mail: **sales@spry.com**

Spry offers a comprehensive solution through its Internet In A Box package, which
contains all the software necessary for setting up a PPP connection to the Internet. $149.

Internet Membership Kit

Ventana Press
P. O. Box 2468
Chapel Hill, NC 27514
Voice: 919-942-0220
Fax: 919-942-1140
E-mail: **info@vmedia.com**

An all-in-one package that contains the software you need to connect to the net.
Includes client programs and TCP/IP stack from NetManage, along with docu-
mentation such as Harley Hahn and Rick Stout's *The Internet Yellow Pages*
(Osborne McGraw-Hill). $69.95.

LAN Workplace

Novell, Inc.
122 East 1700 South
Provo, UT 84606
Voice: 800-772-8649
Fax: 408-473-8990
E-mail: **sales@novell.com**

Includes support for both SLIP and PPP along with Ethernet and Token-Ring.
Includes Telnet, ping, finger, whois. $399.

Pathway Access for Macintosh

The Wollongong Group, Inc.
1129 San Antonio Rd.
Palo Alto, CA 94303
Voice: 415-962-7202
Fax: 415-962-0286
E-mail: **sales@twg.com**

Provides Telnet, FTP, mail, newsreader. Supports both SLIP and PPP. $295.

TCP/Connect II

InterCon Systems Corporation
950 Herndon Parkway
Herndon, VA 22070
Voice: 703-709-5500
Fax: 703-709-5555
E-mail: **sales@intercon.com**

Supports both TCP/IP and AppleTalk protocols using PPP. Provides extensive logging and monitoring features. $495; discounts for volume purchases. Includes

e-mail, news, FTP, and Telnet. InterCon also provides InterPPP as a stand-alone product for $99.95.

VersaTerm/Versatilities

Synergy Software
2457 Perkiomen Avenue
Reading, PA 19606
Voice: 215-779-0522
Fax: 215-370-0548
E-mail: **maxwell@sales.synergy.com**

The VersaTerm terminal emulation package includes Versatilities, a set of Internet utilities. The Synergy Software offering includes the necessary TCP/IP stack and SLIP support, along with Internet tools like Telnet and FTP. $145.

5

Downloading Files with FTP

Using the Internet effectively involves three major functions. First, you need the ability to transfer data from one computer site to another. Second, you must be able to log on and use the resources available at a remote computer site. And third, you need to be able to send electronic mail over the network to communicate with other users, and to tap the various resources available through mail server computers. I'll begin with file transfer because it is a tool you will be able to use throughout this book to retrieve interesting software.

Downloading files on the Internet makes use of a protocol called FTP, or File Transfer Protocol. Using FTP, you can log on to a remote computer site and examine the files available there. When you find something you would like to retrieve, you can issue the appropriate command and move the file over the Internet to your own computer. Unlike a shell account, in which you would be required to download the file first to your service provider's computer and then to your own, a SLIP/PPP account allows you to download the file directly to your machine.

The SLIP/PPP environment takes the burden out of FTP transfers by bringing graphical features to the process. Good FTP tools are available both for Microsoft Windows and the Macintosh; we'll examine examples of each in this chapter. We'll also examine a file finder tool called archie that allows us to go out over the Internet and search for particular files, or files fitting a broad description. Coupling these tools allows us to search the Internet and to treat its vast holdings as a software library.

How FTP Works

We have system administrators at computer sites all over the world to thank for the current FTP largesse. Although the specifics of what happens at a particular site will vary, the general procedure is the same. A system administrator decides to dedicate part or all of a particular computer's storage capabilities to publicly available data. This data might be in the form of text files, graphics, software programs, or a combination of all three. Having made the decision to make this material accessible to the public, the administrator then establishes FTP procedures that will allow users to log on and retrieve the data.

We call these procedures *anonymous FTP*. They allow anyone to log on and, by using **anonymous** as their login and their e-mail address as their password, to tap publicly available resources. Remember that the computers at these sites are often doing things other than anonymous FTP. Perhaps there are company files at a given location that the administrator would like to make available to employees but to no one else.

Anonymous FTP allows him or her to separate public files from private ones; employees would need an appropriate password to log on, which would give them access to the full range of these files. The anonymous FTP user would only need to use an e-mail address as password, as long as he or she has specified **anonymous** as the login. But, unlike the employee, the anonymous FTP user would have access only to the public area of the server.

A Sample FTP Session

Let's run a quick FTP session using a shell account to illustrate what happens during the sign-on and file transfer process. We'll then carry the discussion into the SLIP/PPP environment and install programs to run FTP under Microsoft Windows and the Macintosh. What you see here is the sequence of events as I sign on to **funet.fi**, a site in Finland.

```
% ftp funet.fi
C onnected to funet.fi.
220 etana FTP server (SunOS 4.1) ready.
Name (funet.fi:gilster): anonymous
331 Guest login ok, send ident as password.
Password:
230 Guest login ok, access restrictions apply.
ftp>
```

The commands I have given are shown in bold. As you can see, from my service provider's command prompt, I have entered the **ftp** command followed by the address of the computer I am trying to reach. When prompted for a name,

I have entered **anonymous**. The password is not printed on the screen for security reasons, but I have entered it in the appropriate space; as stated above, I have used my e-mail address as my password. At this point, the computer has accepted my login and has placed me at the ftp> prompt. From this point, I can examine the directory structure of the remote machine and decide where I need to go. A **dir** command provides a listing of directories and files:

```
ftp> dir
200 PORT command successful.
150 ASCII data connection for /bin/ls (199.72.1.1,2317) (0 bytes).
total 149
-rw-r--r-- 3 0        1      234 Sep 5 1993 This is not FTP.FUNET.FI
-rw-r--r-- 3 0        1      234 Sep 5 1993 see file: README.funet.fi
-rw-r--r-- 1 2105     1      530 Mar 24 1993 Index
-rw-r--r-- 1 2105     2      585 Jan 30 18:00 Logo
-rw-r--r-- 3 0        1      234 Sep 5 1993 README.funet.fi
drwxr-xr-x 5 2105     60     512 Apr 16 1990 archive-server
drwxr-xr-x 2 0        0      512 Dec 2 1987 bin
drwxr-xr-x 2 108      60     512 Sep 13 1991 dev
drwxr-xr-x 2 2105     60     512 Oct 14 1991 docs
drwxrwxr-x 2 0        60     1024 Feb 10 1994 documents
drwxr-xr-x 2 0        1      512 Oct 26 1990 etc
d--------- 2 40       1      1536 Jan 12 21:18 in.coming drwxrwxr-x 2 2105
-rw-r--r-- 1 108      1      45877 Sep 6 19:50 ls-1R.Z
drwxrwxr-x 3 2105     60     512 Feb 4 1991 misc
drwxr-xr-x 2 40       1      512 Jul 4 1993 moa
drwxrwxr-x 7 0        60     1024 Jan 30 13:43 netinfo
drwxrwxr-x 18 2105    60     1024 Oct 23 00:00 networking
drwxrwxr-x 2 2105     60     24576 Jan 30 00:00 rfc
drwxrwx--x 2 0        1      512 Sep 20 1993 secret
drwxrwxr-x 2 2105     1      512 Jan 25 15:15 tmp
drwxr-xr-x 3 0        1      512 Oct 26 1990 usr
226 ASCII Transfer complete.
1424 bytes received in 12 seconds (0.12 Kbytes/s)
ftp>
```

Those items beginning with the letter d are directories; I can change between them with the **cd** command, followed by the directory of choice. To retrieve a file, I can use the **get** command, followed by the name of the file I would like to retrieve. In this case, I am about to give the command to download the Index file, which contains a list of what is available at the site. Many FTP sites provide some kind of index in the directory to which you first log in; it will save you time to retrieve this file and read it off-line to give direction to your explorations. This also reduces the amount of time you spend connected to the remote site, which is a factor given the strain placed upon these sites by numerous login requests. Here is my command:

```
ftp> get Index
200 PORT command successful.
150 ASCII data connection for Index (199.72.1.1,1926) (530 bytes).
226 ASCII Transfer complete.
local: Index remote: Index
550 bytes received in 0.4 seconds (1.3 Kbytes/s)
ftp> bye
221 Goodbye.
%
```

Notice that I have also added the **bye** command to log out from this site. I am then returned to the command prompt on my system.

I show this to you to illustrate that moving files between two computers is not particularly difficult, and to point out what is actually happening behind the scenes as you make the file transfer. When you move into the SLIP/PPP environment, the transfer process will be masked by the graphical overlay of your client program. Although this makes FTP easier to use, in some cases, it makes it harder to understand how the protocol works. The **get** command is an example. Because the file I just transferred was an ASCII text file, I could use the command with no modification; FTP works under the assumption that you are moving ASCII data when you transfer files. If I needed to transfer a binary file, I would have needed to give the **binary** command first, followed by the **get** command.

Some FTP programs, like Fetch on the Macintosh, render this process automatic; they know the type of file they are looking at and transfer it appropriately. Thus the new user moves the file to his or her machine, but the underlying negotiation is hidden. If you're the kind of person who lifts the hood of your car now and again, or opens up your PC just to see how it's put together, seeing the shell variant of FTP may satisfy your curiosity. Having seen it, you can now move forward in the knowledge that the SLIP/PPP environment will keep it hidden.

Running FTP under SLIP/PPP

Now take a look at the same session as run through SLIP/PPP. Here, I am using the client program I will recommend you use with Microsoft Windows (we'll download it in a moment). Figure 5.1 shows the directory listing at the site in Finland. It also shows a lot more; in fact, it may take a few seconds of study to translate between the shell session I just ran and the graphical program you are now looking at.

Notice that along the bottom of the screen a series of buttons provides point-and-click capability for using the basic commands. Here we can close the connection, use the help file, or perform a variety of other tasks we'll examine shortly when we set the program up. Buttons also run along the right side of the screen, allowing us, for example, to change directories, or to view files

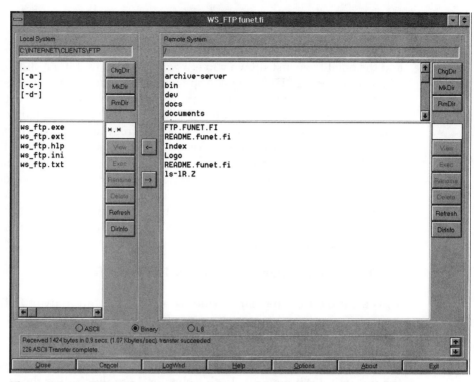

Figure 5.1   An FTP session as seen through a graphical interface.

on-line (not a recommended practice, in my book, since it ties up the site; the correct procedure is to download what you need and read it off-line). The directory and file information is, as you see, broken into two windows, with directories at the top and files at the bottom. You highlight what you want to do and use the buttons to activate your commands. No more need to memorize command sequences or parameters.

Note: The reason I keep harping on connect time is that FTP is a different environment than Gopher or Mosaic. With the latter two programs, you move out onto the net to retrieve what you need and the program then disconnects, waiting for your next command. Only then does it return to the site to retrieve further information. An FTP session, on the other hand, remains connected the entire time you use it. Slip away to make a cup of coffee with an FTP session running and you are tying up system resources that are already crowded to the breaking point.

WS_FTP: Windows-Based File Transfer

To work the graphical wonders of SLIP/PPP, you need a good client program, and the one I have just shown you is a gem. Created by John A. Junod, WS_FTP (Windows Sockets FTP Client Application) is made available free for non-commercial use; commercial users will need to contact Ipswitch Inc. at **info@ipswitch.com**, or else call 617-246-1150. By now it should be becoming apparent that the quality level of Internet freeware and shareware can be remarkably high. I would not be recommending programs like WS_FTP and the Macintosh Fetch and Anarchie programs if they weren't full-featured and powerful; I would also have a hard time coming up with commercial equivalents that are significantly easier to use than these.

Running an archie search, as I will teach you how to do later in this chapter, I found WS_FTP at sites all over the Internet. But the program's documentation suggests looking first at the following URL:

ftp://ftp.usma.edu/pub/msdos/winsock.files/ws_ftp.zip

You can also check the major Windows site at the University of Indiana:

ftp://ftp.cica.indiana.edu/pub/pc/win3/winsock/ws_ftp.zip

A 32-bit version of the program is also available for users of Windows NT and the upcoming Windows 95. In this chapter, I am illustrating the standard, 16-bit version of WS_FTP.

Installing and Running WS_FTP

Few programs are as easy to install as WS_FTP. When you download the compressed file containing it, you will have to unpack it with the PKUNZIP program from PKware, Inc. (available at sites all over the Internet, and through the major commercial on-line services like CompuServe and America Online). Follow this sequence:

1. Create a directory for WS_FTP; its name is up to you.
2. Move the compressed ws_ftp.zip file to the new directory.
3. Unpack the ws_ftp.zip file.

You should find the following files within ws_ftp.zip:

ws_ftp.exe	The executable program
ws_ftp.ini	The initialization file
ws_ftp.hlp	The help file
ws_ftp.txt	The documentation

Note: Sites like the one at the University of Indiana are heavily traveled, and getting logged on by anonymous FTP is often difficult. But throughout the Internet exist so-called mirror sites that contain updated collections of the same material found at the primary site. You will often be given a list of such mirror sites when you attempt a login that cannot be completed because of the number of users already on-line. Here, for example, is what you might see if you tried to log in to the Indiana site and it was too busy to use.

Name (ftp.cica.indiana.edu:gilster): **anonymous**
530-Sorry! We have reached maximum number of connections (45).
530-Please retry again later, or connect to a mirror site:
530-** USA Sites: wuarchive.wustl.edu (MO); archive.orst.edu

(OR);

530- gatekeeper.dec.com; ftp.cdrom.com (CA); ftp.marcam.com;
530- mrcnext.cso.uiuc.edu (IL); ftp.dataplex.net [or 199.183.109.245] (TX)
530-** Non-USA Sites: ftp.monash.edu.au (Australia); ftp.funet.fi (Finland);
530- ftp.uni-paderborn.de, ftp.uni-stuttgart.de, ftp.uni-koeln.de, and
530- ftp.uni-regensburg.de (Germany); ftp.iij.ad.jp (Tokyo); ftp.nectec.or.th
530- (Thailand); ftp.technion.ac.il (Israel); nic.switch.ch (Zurich);
530- src.doc.ic.ac.uk (London); ntu.ac.sg (Singapore); nctuccca.edu.tw
530- (Taiwan); ftp.cyf-kr.edu.pl (Cracow, Poland); cuinfo.netserv.chula.ac.th
530- (Bangkok, Thailand) and info.nic.surfnet.nl (Netherlands, after 8/26/94).
530 User anonymous access denied.

As you can see, FTP sites place limitations on the number of users who can log in to the computer simultaneously. But you are given a listing of sites throughout the world that contain the same files at this one. Choose a site geographically close to you to minimize the load on the network.

ws_ftp.ext	A set of file extensions which **WS_FTP** will use to determine whether to download a file in binary or ASCII format.

Once you have unpacked these files, you can create an icon for the program in whichever program group you would like it to appear; I maintain a group called **SLIP/PPP Clients**, where I place all new programs I am evaluating. You can use File Manager to do this, by dragging the program into a program group, or you can use Program Manager, pulling down the File menu and choosing the New option. In either case, you will now have the WS_FTP icon in a program group ready for use.

Note: For WS_FTP to work properly, you must have the ws_ftp.-hlp and ws_ftp.ini files in your working directory, or else in your *windows* directory.

Once you have established your SLIP/PPP connection with Trumpet Winsock or whichever TCP/IP stack and SLIP/PPP program you are using, you will be able to activate WS_FTP. Double-click its icon to call up the program. The first thing you see will be the box shown in Figure 5.2. This is housekeeping work. WS_FTP needs to know your e-mail address so it can insert this value automatically when it logs on; remember that your e-mail address is used as your password in anonymous FTP logins.

After you have given this information, WS_FTP shows you two screens. The first is the primary screen from which you give commands about what you want to do, shown in Figure 5.3. Notice the major division of this screen between the local system (i.e., your own) and the remote system, the computer you will connect to during the FTP session. Notice, too, that the upper half of the window on each side contains directory information, while the lower half specifies files. Buttons along the bottom of the screen provide help and con-

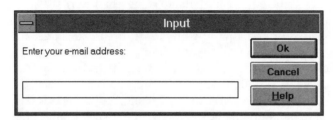

Figure 5.2 Your first step in configuring WS_FTP is to enter your e-mail address for anonymous FTP login purposes.

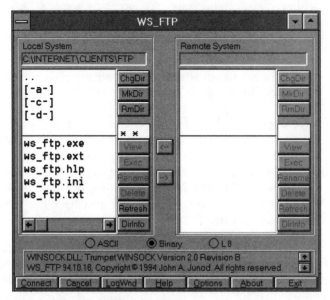

Figure 5.3 WS_FTP's main screen.

figuration options. Buttons to the right of each box provide capabilities for moving about in the directories of the remote computer.

A Sample Connection

Before going into the WS_FTP command possibilities, let's take the program out for a spin on the net; this will illustrate how easy it makes the FTP process. To do so, simply click on the Connect button at the bottom of the WS_FTP box. The Session Profile screen shown in Figure 5.4 appears. This is the screen on which you enter the basic connection information. To set up a session, click on the New button.

The Profile Name: field will clear; there, you can enter a short identifier for the session you plan to run; in this case, I will simply enter **eudora** (the reason for declaring a session name will be made clear shortly). Notice the field marked Host Name. Here you can enter either a domain name or an IP address for the site you want to contact. I will enter a domain name: **ftp.qualcomm.-com**. Click on the Anonymous Login box; you will see that the program then supplies the information I gave it about my e-mail address. I can set the Remote Host directory to whatever I choose; in this case, I will simply opt for the root directory by using the conventional Unix / symbol. My completed Session Profile form, then, should look like the one in Figure 5.5. I can now proceed with the connection by clicking on the Connect button from the main screen. WS_FTP will negotiate the connection and soon the file and directory information at the remote site will appear, as in Figure 5.6.

If I want to download a file, all I have to do is to highlight it in the remote host file list and then click on the left-pointing arrow that indicates I want to

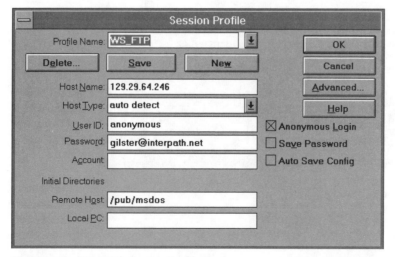

Figure 5.4 WS_FTP's Session Profile is where you enter information about the connection you want to make.

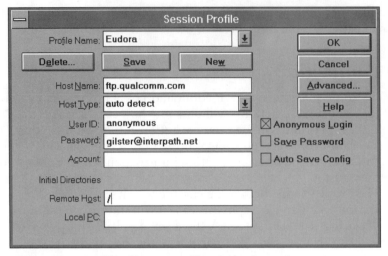

Figure 5.5 A completed session profile, ready to be used.

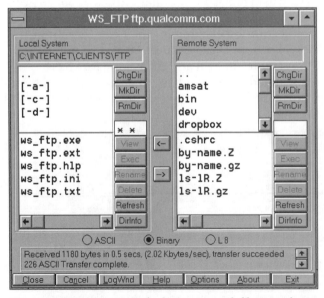

Figure 5.6 A remote site's directories and files, as shown through WS_FTP.

move it to my own computer. A box will pop up showing the status of the transfer, and the file will be moved.

WS_FTP Command Possibilities

WS_FTP provides command buttons from its primary screen that let us do a number of tasks. Let's look at the major ones now:

ChgDir   Use this button to change directories. Highlight the name of the directory to which you want to move and press this button to make the change. If you have not highlighted a directory to change to, the program will prompt you for one.

MkDir   Use this button to create a directory on a remote system. This is not an option that will be useful for anonymous FTP users; it is designed for authorized users logging on to proprietary sites to conduct their work.

RmDir   Use this button to remove a directory. Again, this is not an option for anonymous FTP users.

View   Use this button to view an ASCII text file on-screen.

Exec   Use this button to execute a file on the local system. If you specify a file on the remote computer and click on Exec, the file will be downloaded to the Windows temporary directory in binary mode. It will then be executed, just as if it were run from the Windows File Manager.

Delete   Use this button to delete files. You would only do this if you were an authorized user on a remote system; it is not an option for anonymous FTP users.

WS_FTP File Transfers

You have seen that transferring a file is simply a matter of highlighting it and then clicking on the left-pointing arrow to move it to your own computer. You can also simply double-click on the file you want and WS_FTP will download it. Nothing could be simpler than clicking on a single arrow button or filename to transfer a file; it certainly beats entering the **get** command followed by a filename, and the transfer is visually explicit so that you're unlikely to make a mistake. But what if you want to download multiple files at once? WS_FTP provides for this by allowing you to highlight several files for downloading. To do this, simply highlight the first of the files you want to transfer; to add files, hold down the Ctrl key and click on each file. Having selected the files you need, you can click on the transfer button to move them.

You will notice on the main WS_FTP screen that the program provides ASCII and Binary buttons. When you are transferring an ASCII file, you will need to click this button; binary files, set up as the default, are downloaded with the Binary button clicked. In general, you will use Binary mode most of the time; only use ASCII if you know the file contains nothing but text. The L8 button is used when you are dealing with VMS systems and transferring binary files; in most cases, you won't have to worry about it.

Look back at Figure 5.5 for a moment. This screen is the Session Profile you must fill out to make the connection. There, you will notice a field called Host Type: in which the default is set at auto detect. When auto detect is selected, all files will be transferred in binary mode unless a particular extension is found in the ws_ftp.ext file. For example, if ws_ftp.ext contains the extension .txt, the program will automatically download any files with the .txt extension in ASCII format. You can specify any ending characters in a filename in the ws_ftp.ext file to make switching into ASCII mode automatic. Such a setup would be useful for files with the right extensions, though in the case of the Index file we transferred previously, you would need to manually set the system for an ASCII transfer.

Customizing WS_FTP

Good software lets us tailor it for our own use. In this regard, WS_FTP is a rich environment. We don't want to enter the same connection information every time we log on to a familiar site, so WS_FTP lets us store session profiles that we can choose from a pull-down menu. Notice the Session Profile screen as shown in Figure 5.7, where I have pulled down the Profile Name menu to show you the various options that come already set up in the program.

By highlighting any one of these options, I can automatically insert correct connection information into the program; when I make the actual connection, this information is sent, customized for each site that I routinely visit.

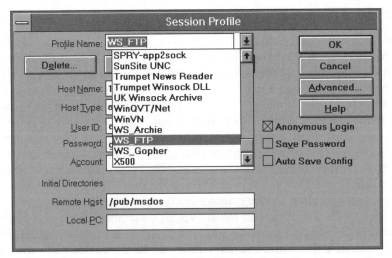

Figure 5.7 Choosing a session profile. WS_FTP makes logging on to frequently accessed sites easy through predefined profiles.

To set up a profile of your own, simply click on the New button on the Session Profile window. You can then insert a profile name and fill in the appropriate values. For seldom visited sites, it may not be worth your while to establish a profile, but for the frequently accessed sites you use for downloading, this method saves time and simplifies the process.

Program Options

WS_FTP provides other options for customization as well. These are accessed by clicking the Options button at the bottom of the main WS_FTP screen. Here, you are given a variety of possible changes to the program's operations, including modifications to the program's defaults, the way WS_FTP handles individual sessions and the extensions it uses when downloading data. In Figure 5.8, I have clicked on the Options button on the main screen to produce the screen shown there. Notice that in the center of the screen are two defaults—the e-mail address WS_FTP uses when it logs in to a remote site, and the text viewer the program uses for ASCII files. Notice also the Double Click box to the bottom right of the figure. When set on Transfer, as is the default, the program downloads any file that you double-click on. And, as you can see, you also have vari-

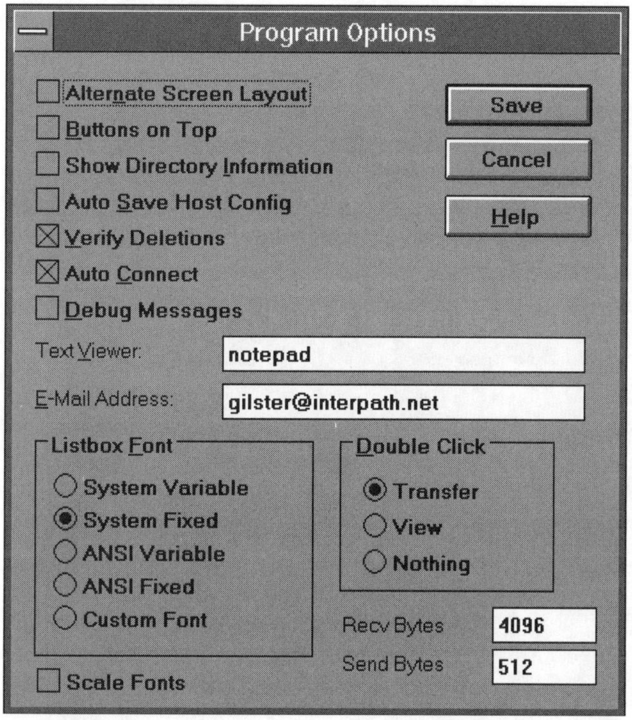

Figure 5.8 Looking at the various program options available in WS_FTP.

ous options regarding the program's appearance on the screen. You can choose to control the display of buttons on-screen or choose the amount of directory information that WS_FTP routinely shows, depending upon the capabilities of the server to which you are connecting in a particular session.

Two other values need mentioning:

Recv Bytes   Controls how many bytes the program reads at a time from the network. This value can be set from 80 to 4096, but best results appear when 4096 is left as the default.

Send Bytes   Controls how many bytes are sent to the network at a time. Again, the possible values range from 80 to 4096. For SLIP/PPP connections, setting this to Maximum Transmission Unit size is recommended.

Session Options

WS_FTP session options can also be controlled by clicking on the Options button from the main program screen. The Session Options dialog box is shown in Figure 5.9. In most cases, the default settings function well, and there is no need to change them. But there are three settings that may prove useful.

Prompt for Destination   When clicked, this option causes the program to prompt you for a destination filename when you download a file. You can then change the proposed name or directory.

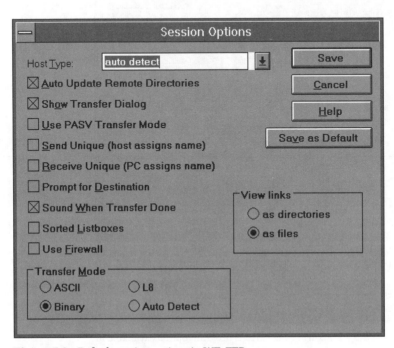

Figure 5.9 Default session options in WF_FTP.

This is useful if you want to have more control over the placement and naming of downloaded materials.

Sorted Listboxes Automatically sorts the files listed on the remote computer. This is a valuable option in helping you find a particular file.

Transfer Mode Determines the kind of transfer WS_FTP will make as its default. Shell account users know that FTP systems normally default to ASCII transfers, and that you must give a **binary** command before initiating the download of a program file. This setting allows you to use binary transfers as your default.

Associations

Here's a handy WS_FTP trick. The Extensions button, available by clicking the Options button from the main WS_FTP screen, lets you set up links between WS_FTP itself and external programs. Why would you want to do such a thing? Consider the kinds of files you may encounter at a remote site. An ASCII text file can be read immediately by clicking on View once you have highlighted its name in the remote computer's file listing. But what if you have found, for example, an archive of graphics files and want to see one as soon as it's downloaded?

To do this, you could use the Extensions setting. Clicking on this button calls up the screen shown in Figure 5.10. I can place an extension in this dialog box and then associate it with an external program. In the case of images, for example, I could place the .gif extension, as you can see I have done in Figure 5.10, in the Files with Extension: box. I then enter a pathname and a program name for the extension.

This means that when I highlight a file on the remote computer and then click the Exec button, WS_FTP will first transfer that file to my computer, and then display it in the external program I have chosen. The external program will appear in its own window, displaying the file I have just found. In this way,

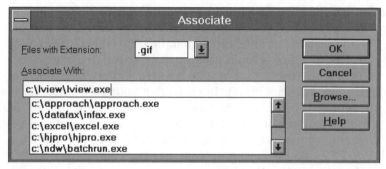

Figure 5.10 Setting extensions in WS_FTP tells the program how to process certain kinds of files.

WS_FTP simplifies transfer and display of graphics files, and can be used to associate other types of files with external viewer programs. We'll see this same principle at work as we move into the various World Wide Web browsers we'll examine in Chapter 11.

Finding Files with Wsarchie

Examine WS_FTP's Session Profile screen and you will see that the program already includes a number of session profiles for various computer sites. Each points to either a major archive of Internet programs and data, or the home site for a particular client program. It's handy to have these sites already listed, and you now know that it's a fairly simple matter to include session profiles of your own as you discover new sources for files. But there are thousands upon thousands of FTP sites on the Internet today, which poses a huge problem.

Unlike a commercial on-line service, which can house its files at a central site and make a universal directory available for use (CompuServe does this, as does America Online), the Internet is composed of independent computer networks linking their computers voluntarily to exchange information. There is no common methodology, no accepted standard directory, no universal file naming strategy in place. This means that the file you may be looking for could be found at a number of different sites, in different directories at those sites, and under different names. Finding such files is a herculean task, and we have yet to discover a satisfactory solution to the problems thus posed. But a program called Wsarchie can help.

Drawing on the archie program originally developed at the McGill University School of Computer Science in Montreal, the archie system depends upon computers called archie servers. At specified intervals, archie connects to the FTP sites it includes in its data sweep and downloads a listing of all publicly available files, which are then stored in a database (be aware, then, that the archie database is not an index of *all* FTP sites on the Internet, but of those selected for the purpose—it is a huge database, but not a comprehensive one).

Your job is to tell archie what you are looking for. The system then searches its database and provides you with an FTP site name and the complete directory path to the program you have specified. At that point, you can use FTP to reach the site and download the file. Using a shell account, this process involved running a Unix archie client, specifying particular parameters for your search (these you would have to either remember, or else enter through consultation with a printed guide); your FTP connection would likewise be handled from the command prompt, leaving you to navigate through the remote site to the specified directory to find the file you needed.

Wsarchie allows us to leave the command line world behind, just as we did with WS_FTP, and invoke a graphical interface that makes the search process easier. Let's now use WS_FTP to reach out over the Internet to retrieve Wsarchie.

Downloading Wsarchie

WS_FTP includes among its session profiles a profile for Wsarchie that you can use to download the program. Click on the Connect button from the main WS_FTP screen to call up the Session Profile screen; there, pull down the Profile Name: window and highlight Wsarchie. The profile will allow you to make the connection when you click on the Connect button.

Alternatively, you can enter the correct FTP information yourself. Wsarchie is the work of David Woakes, who makes it available at the following site:

ftp://ftp.demon.co.uk/pub/ibmpc/winsock/apps/

As of this writing, the current filename was wsarch07.zip. As always, remember that filenames change as programs are updated, so you may have to explore the directory structure at a particular site to find what you need if the administrators there have made any changes. Fortunately, the tool we are about to implement is itself handy in minimizing file-finding problems for the future.

The Wsarchie Installation

The Wsarchie zip file should be moved to its own directory once you have downloaded it. There you can unzip the file using PKware's PKUNZIP utility. You will find the following files within the archival package:

dispmsg.exe   A program that can be run at the same time as Wsarchie to provide information about the progress of searches.

wsarchie.exe   The Wsarchie program.

wsarchie.hlp   The Wsarchie help file.

wsarchie.ini   The Wsarchie initialization file, with user settings as appropriate, and a list of archie servers.

wsarch07.txt   A text file that provides basic installation information.

Having unpacked these files in the directory of your choice, you can now proceed with the installation.

- From File Manager, drag the wsarchie.exe file to the desired program group.

Or:

- Use Program Manager to create a new item in the program group of your choice.

The Wsarchie icon should now appear in the chosen program group. You are ready to begin using the program.

Configuring Wsarchie

When you click on the Wsarchie icon, you should see the main Wsarchie screen, as shown in Figure 5.11. Your first task is to set up Wsarchie to handle FTP sessions. The program does so by calling an external program, in this case, WS_FTP. Pull down the Options menu and click on FTP Setup to call up the setup screen, as shown in Figure 5.12. First of all, be sure that you enter the correct path to your WS_FTP program; otherwise, Wsarchie won't be able to find it. If you keep WS_FTP in a directory called FTP, you would specify c:\ftp\ws_ftp in the Command field.

The other fields you will need to fill in are the Password field, where you need to insert your own e-mail address, and the Directory field, where you will insert the default directory you want to use for any files you retrieve through WS_FTP. This is an important point, for if you do not specify a valid directory for your downloads, WS_FTP will simply abort the file transfer, and you will wonder why the program is not able to function with Wsarchie. I have set my program up to download files to my root directory by inserting a slash (/) symbol. Clicking on OK establishes the values you have entered as the new defaults.

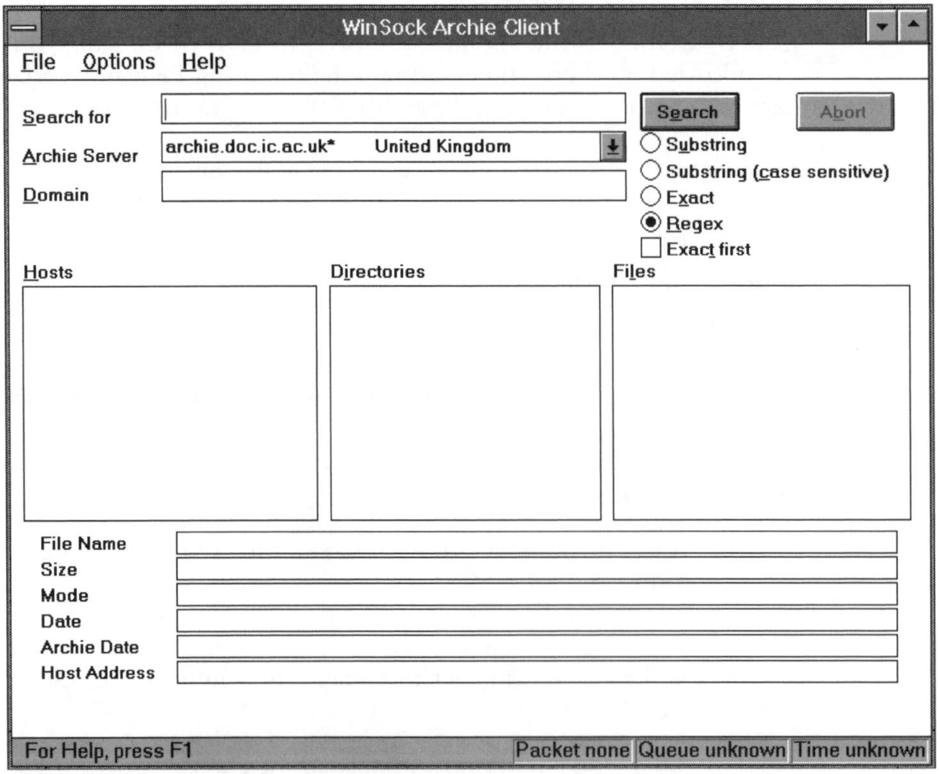

Figure 5.11   The primary Wsarchie screen.

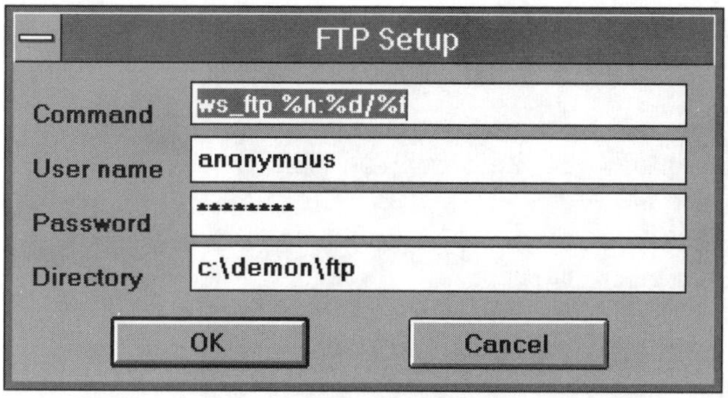

FTP Setup

Command	ws_ftp %h:%d/%f
User name	anonymous
Password	********
Directory	c:\demon\ftp

OK   Cancel

Figure 5.12 Setting up an FTP client for Wsarchie to use.

As you would imagine, linking archie and an FTP client makes great sense. In a shell environment, you would have to run an archie search by using a Telnet connection to an archie server, or else by running an archie client on your service provider's machine. Once you had found the file you wanted to use, you would then need to use FTP to connect to the site and retrieve the file. Combining the two operations by linking archie with an external FTP program greatly simplifies the retrieval task. We'll run such a search and retrieval in a moment, but first, we need to finish configuring the program.

The Options menu also contains a User Preferences item. Click on this to call up the screen in Figure 5.13. The key field here is the Default Archie Server entry, which you should change to reflect your own location. In general, choose an archie server relatively near where you are, so as to minimize the load placed upon the network by your searches. Table 5.1 provides a list of archie servers.

Examine the Wsarchie User Preferences screen, and you'll see that the default is set up for Imperial College, London, the site that makes sense for the program's developer, David Woakes, who lives in the United Kingdom. You will find a list of some, but not all, of the archie servers listed above in Wsarchie itself; pull down the menu in the Default Archie Server field by clicking on the arrow to see it.

Note: With reference to this list and the one above, you will want to establish whichever server is closest to you as the default for Wsarchie. You should also be on the lookout for new archie servers when they become available, and always try to take advantage of geographical proximity, as well as trying to avoid contacting your server during local business hours when usage may be peaking.

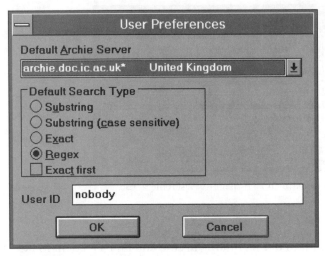

Figure 5.13 The User Preferences screen in Wsarchie.

Running an archie Search

Using Wsarchie proves to be a simple matter. The basic search is established by entering keywords in the Search for field, and then clicking on the Search button. Let's assume, for example, that I am interested in finding a new communications driver for Microsoft Windows. I've heard that the comm.drv driver that comes with the program is not very robust, and there are several shareware programs that are much more effective at handling high-speed data transmissions. One of these is called Cybercom. archie can search throughout the world for this program, if I provide it with the appropriate keyword.

Theoretically, an archie search on any server should pull up the same list of hits, as the system is designed to contain the same information, routinely updated to reflect additions to the various sites. In reality, the methods used to retrieve and collate database information can sometimes cause disparities to arise, most of which are smoothed out as updated information is retrieved. So whichever archie server I choose to make my search (and I'll use archie.internic.net), I should be able to track down the Cybercom driver I need.

I'll enter cybercom as my keyword in the Search for field and click on the Search button. Wsarchie displays three things on its status bar as it searches: the number of packets received, the position of my search in the queue at the archie server site, and the time archie thinks it will take to process my query (an often inaccurate estimate). What I get in return is shown in Figure 5.14.

The screen shows a host computer's address: **ftp.cisi.unige.it**, a computer in Italy. The directory is also specified: */PC/serial*. And Wsarchie has found two files with the keyword—cybercom—in their name: cybercom.drv and cybercom.txt. I would like to retrieve the cybercom.drv file. To do so, all I need to do next is double-click on the filename. Wsarchie will call WS_FTP and insert

Table 5.1 Archie Servers Worldwide

Address	Location	Country
archie.internic.net	South Plainfield, NJ	USA
archie.sura.net	SURAnet, Baltimore, MD	USA
archie.unl.edu	University of Nebraska, Lincoln	USA
archie.rutgers.edu	Rutgers University, NJ	USA
archie.ans.net	Advanced Network & Services, Inc.; Elmsford, NY	USA
archie.au	University of Melbourne	Australia
archie.univie.ac.at	University of Vienna	Austria
archie.edvz.uni-linz.ac.at	Johannes Kepler University, Linz	Austria
archie.uqam.ca	University of Quebec	Canada
archie.doc.ic.ac.uk	Imperial College, London	United Kingdom
archie.funet.fi	Finnish University and Research Network	Finland
archie.th-darmstadt.de	Technische Hochschule, Darmstadt	Germany
archie.ac.il	Hebrew University of Jerusalem	Israel
archie.unipi.it	University of Pisa	Italy
archie.kuis.kyuoto-u.ac.jp	University of Kyoto	Japan
archie.wide.ad.jp	WIDE Project, Tokyo	Japan
archie.sogang.ac.kr	Sogang University	South Korea
archie.kr	Telecom Research Center, Seoul	South Korea
archie.nz	Victoria University, Wellington	New Zealand
archie.rediris.es	RedIRIS, Madrid	Spain
archie.luth.se	University of Lulea	Sweden
archie.switch.ch	SWITCH, Zurich	Switzerland
archie.ncu.edu.tw	National Central University, Chung-li	Taiwan

the correct host, directory, and file information into that program, causing it to download the file. If you try to download a file this way and WS_FTP does not appear, the fault probably lies in your FTP setup information. Go back to the Options menu and double-check that you have correctly entered your e-mail address as your password and that you have specified the correct path to WS_FTP.

Figure 5.14   Results of a search for the Cybercom driver with Wsarchie.

A Broadened archie Search

People often use archie to look for specific files, but sometimes forget that the program is also helpful when they are trying to identify collections of information. For example, I had much to say in Chapter 2 about Winsock, and have configured Trumpet Winsock for use as our TCP/IP stack. Given its importance, there are probably lots of directories at computers around the world that are filled with Winsock programs and information. We can find these directories by entering winsock as our keyword in an archie search. Doing so produces the screen shown in Figure 5.15.

Notice, because we have multiple hits, that a whole list of host computers is presented; we don't even see all of it here, but would have to scroll through the list using the scroll bar to its right to examine all the names. When we highlight a particular host, the directory and file information at that host is then presented in the appropriate boxes. We know that when we double-click on a file, it will be downloaded through WS_FTP. When we double-click on a directory, it will be expanded. Thus we could double-click on the winsock directory shown in Figure 5.15 and then retrieve a list of the files in that directory. If we

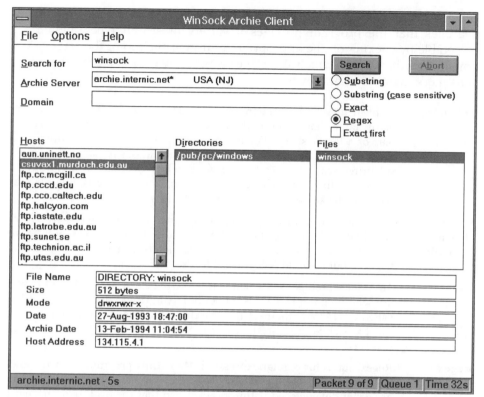

Figure 5.15 Results of a Wsarchie search using the keyword winsock.

found a particular file that seemed interesting, we could double-click on it in turn to download it with WS_FTP.

> **Note:** You may have noticed in Figure 5.15 that directly under the Archie Server field, Wsarchie provides a field called Domain. You can use this if you want to restrict your search to a particular site or domain. Thus, placing **interpath.net** into this field, I could restrict my search to any hits within that domain. I could also use this feature to search for files only found within a particular country. Entering it in this field, for example, would pull up only those hits that were found in Italy.

archie Search Types

As you explore the archie system, you'll find it useful in uncovering sources for the kind of information you need, and the shareware and freeware files and documents you want to download. You will have noticed as we ran our searches that the program provides a variety of search types, which are selectable by clicking on the appropriate button at the top of the screen. You can control the ways in which Wsarchie searches by your choice of these buttons. Let's examine what they do.

Substring   A substring search is one in which Wsarchie searches for any directory or filename that contains the keyword, even if that keyword exists as part of a larger string. For example, suppose we were searching for a program called Telix, a shareware communications package. If we ran a substring search using the keyword telix, Wsarchie would retrieve telix.exe, telix10.exe, telix.doc, and so on; in other words, any file that contains the keyword telix as part or all of its name.

Substring (case-sensitive)   A case-sensitive substring search is one that follows case exactly as you specify it in the keyword field. If you specify Telix as your search term, then, the case-sensitive search would not find a hit on telix.exe or telix.txt, but it would recognize Telix.exe, and so on.

Exact   An exact search is used when you know the exact name of the file you are searching for. If there is no doubt in your mind that you need a file called chx14a.zip, then set the search on the Exact setting and go. An exact search is the fastest way to use archie, provided you know what you need.

Regex   Regex stands for regular expression. Many Unix programs provide powerful searching features based on Regex statements. These statements are generally enclosed within brackets, so that the expression tr[aeio]l would pull up any of the following hits: tral, trel, tril, and trol. Without brackets, a regex search proceeds largely as a substring search. Searching with the keyword aviation, for example, pulls up files with the name foodwine or files containing that string in their name.

Exact first   Wsarchie allows you to check this option, which runs an exact search first and, if nothing is found, then turns the search to whichever of the search type buttons is enabled.

We now come to the critical question. Which search type is the best one to use? There is no single answer to this question, although the fact that Wsarchie defaults to regex is not an indication that you should use regex in all your searches. Let's run through the possibilities:

- Use a substring search for most of your routine searching. It will pull up any file or directory name containing your string; in most cases, this is all you need to do.

- Use a case-sensitive substring search only if you are reasonably sure of at least a part of the name of the file you are trying to locate. By making the search case-sensitive, you are locking out a good number of possible hits.

Note: Regular expressions are an enormously complicated subject, and one that repays careful study for those interested in working the archie system to its limits. It's useful to know, for example, that regex statements can include various wildcard strategies. All regular expressions assume a * wildcard statement at beginning and end. Thus the keyword stat is functionally equivalent to the keyword *stat*, meaning that archie would retrieve any hits with the string stat found anywhere in the searched filenames. The only time that the wildcard is not assumed is when special characters are shown. A ^ anchors the string to the beginning of the statement; thus the keyword ^stat would find only those files whose name *began* with the stat string. Similarly, a $ anchors the string to the end of the statement; the keyword stat$, then, isolates those filenames with the string stat at the end of the name.

Numerous other options are available, too many to list here. If you get caught up in such Unix arcana, I recommend that you get a copy of Harley Hahn's *Unix Unbound* (Osborne McGraw-Hill, 1995), which is not only a comprehensive guide to all matters pertaining to Unix, but also a fine demonstration of just how good technical writing can be. I have also found a book called *Unix in Plain English* very useful; it is the work of Kevin Reichard and Eric F. Johnson (MIS Press, 1994).

- Use an exact search only when you are absolutely sure of the filename. Remember that files often have names other than what you would expect. You might know, for example, that Trumpet Winsock is a widely used TCP/IP stack, but you wouldn't want to run an exact search for it under the keyword trumpet because the filename is usually compacted to something like twsk20a.zip. Remember, archie searches for filenames; the complete name of the compressed files inside a particular archive is of no significance to archie.

- Use a regex search if you want to fine-tune your search with wildcards or other variables. Regex allows you superb control over your search strategy, but formulating the keyword can be complex. In simple cases, a regex search will be equivalent to running a substring search, but in cases like that, you might as well be using substrings anyway.

- Check the Exact first box if you think you know the name of your file but aren't absolutely sure. archie will run a quick exact search and, if it doesn't find what you're looking for, it will then revert to a substring search, or whatever search type you have previously selected. In general, I keep the Exact first button unselected, only using it in particular cases.

Note: archie servers can be exasperating. One day you run a search on your favorite server and the results come right back to you. The next day you can't log on. The day after that you get no hits when you're absolutely sure of the filename you listed and, in fact, when you try later in the day, you find exactly what you're looking for by using the same keyword.

The key to archie searches is patience. If the server you're trying to use doesn't seem to be functioning, move on to another. A good archie client program makes this easy to do. You always have to think on your feet when you're trying to find things on the Internet, whether archie or some other search engine is your tool of choice.

FTP on the Macintosh

Several excellent programs for FTP and archie use are found in the Macintosh world. I'm particularly fond of Anarchie, a program that combines FTP and archie capabilities more efficiently than the WS_FTP/Wsarchie combination. But another program of considerable standing is Fetch, which brings a graphical interface of surprising agility to the process, along with a charming animated icon that goes into motion as your file retrieval is made. Both programs make it easy to find and retrieve what you need, and provide the necessary options to take maximum advantage of FTP sites worldwide.

Retrieving Files with Fetch

Developed at Dartmouth College, Fetch is a must for any Macintosh user. The program requires a Mac 512K and System 4.1 or better at minimum. It is free for use in educational and nonprofit organizations, and users in government and commercial enterprises may obtain a license by sending $25 to the following address:

Software Sales
Dartmouth College
6028 Kiewit Computation Center
Hanover, NH 03755-3523
E-mail: **fetch@dartmouth.edu**

To retrieve Fetch, look at the following URL:

ftp://dartmouth.edu/pub/mac/

At the time of this writing, the filename was Fetch_2.1.2.sit.hqx.

As you begin exploring the Internet's FTP resources with Fetch, you will encounter a wide range of Macintosh-specific file extensions. The preceding file, for example, contains both the .sit and .hqx extensions. The following may help in understanding how these strange extensions relate to the file compression programs that created them.

bin   A binary file.

cpt   A file that has been compressed by Compact Pro.

hqx   A file that is in BinHex format. The BinHex standard allows files to be accessed regardless of the type of computer involved.

ps   A PostScript file, which can be printed on any PostScript-compatible output device.

sea   A self-extracting archive created by any of a variety of programs.

sit   A file that has been compressed by Aladdin's StuffIt utility, or the related StuffIt Lite or StuffIt Deluxe programs.

txt   An ASCII text file, which can be read in any text editor.

You will need a Macintosh utility program to decode some of these formats. I recommend StuffIt Expander, from Aladdin Systems, Inc., which handles a wide range of file types; you can find the shareware version of StuffIt available at Macintosh archival sites on the net, like **ftp://sumex-aim.-stanford.edu/** and **ftp://mac.archive.umich.edu/**. To unpack a compressed file, you simply drag the file onto the StuffIt icon and let the decompression program do its work.

Installing and Configuring Fetch

To begin to use Fetch, simply double-click on the Fetch icon. You will be presented with a Connection dialog box that allows you to insert an address for an FTP connection. For now, don't use this box, as it's first necessary to set software preferences for Fetch to use the program effectively. Therefore, click on the Cancel button in the Connection box.

Now pull down the Customize menu and choose the Preferences item. You will see the dialog box shown in Figure 5.16. The field you need to change is the one holding your default password. Traditional anonymous FTP practice calls for you to enter your e-mail address as your password. Enter it into this field. Then click on OK to accept the new password.

There are a number of other configuration options, all of which can be found by pulling down the Topic: menu and moving through its fields. I've used Fetch for some time now with the default settings and have found no major items that need changing, but you will want to go through this list to determine whether there is any detail you'd like to tweak.

Now pull down the File menu and choose the Open Shortcut item. You will see the menu shown in Figure 5.17. Shortcuts are preconfigured FTP sessions, designed to allow you to log on to particular sites simply by clicking on them. If you find that you return to a site often, you will want to add it to the Short-

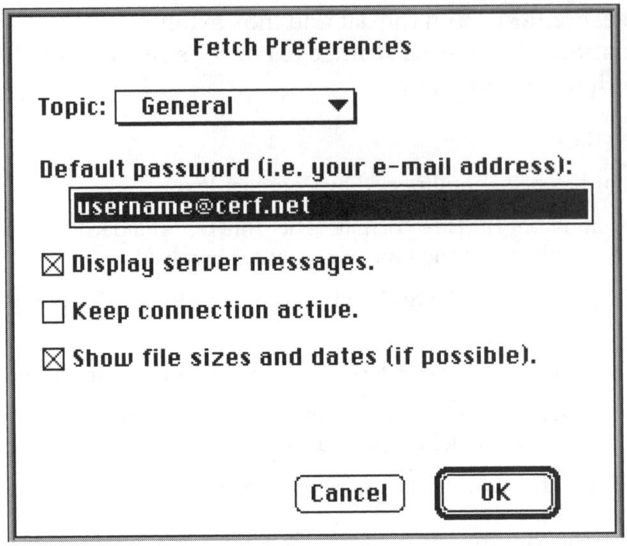

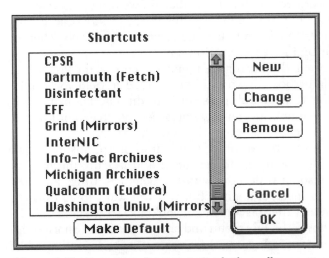

Figure 5.16   Setting preferences when configuring Fetch.

cuts list. You can do so at any time by going back to the Customize menu and choosing the Edit Shortcuts item. As configured, Fetch provides you with links to such servers as Dartmouth, the home of Fetch; you'll also see the InterNIC, the big Macintosh archives at **ftp://mac.archive.umich.edu** and **ftp://sumex-aim.stanford.edu**, and other interesting sites. You can choose any one of these to be the default.

Figure 5.17   Examining shortcuts in Fetch; these allow you to log on to frequently visited remote sites with a mouse click.

Running an FTP Session with Fetch

To make an FTP connection, pull down Fetch's File menu and take the Open Connection option. In Figure 5.18, I have just called up this dialog box and entered the appropriate information to connect to a NASA file archive; its address is **ftp://explorer.arc.nasa.gov**. As you can see, Fetch has entered the configuration information I just gave it. All I need to do, having entered the host address, is to click on **OK** to travel to the site.

When you connect, Fetch will produce a display of the directories and files at the remote site. To move about in the remote site's file directories, double-click on the folder symbol of the directory to which you want to go. In Figure 5.19, I have moved to the */pub/SPACE/GIF* directory using this method, and Fetch has presented me with a list of files, most of them images from various NASA missions.

To retrieve a file, all I need to do is to highlight the file I am interested in and click on the Get File button (the alternative is to double-click on the file in question; either method will work). Fetch will begin the file transfer and show information about the status of the file transfer at the lower right of the screen. In Figure 5.20, I have chosen a file called gaspra2.gif; it's a collage of two images of the asteroid 951 Gaspra taken by the Galileo spacecraft from approximately 3,000 miles away in October 1991.

You will notice that text files, with their .txt extension, are also scattered through the file listing. These explain what the particular images are. A text file can be viewed on-screen by pulling down the Remote menu and choosing the View File option. This eliminates the necessity of downloading a file you're merely curious about, but it should be used sparingly, as the more time you spend connected to an FTP site, the more you are tying up a resource that

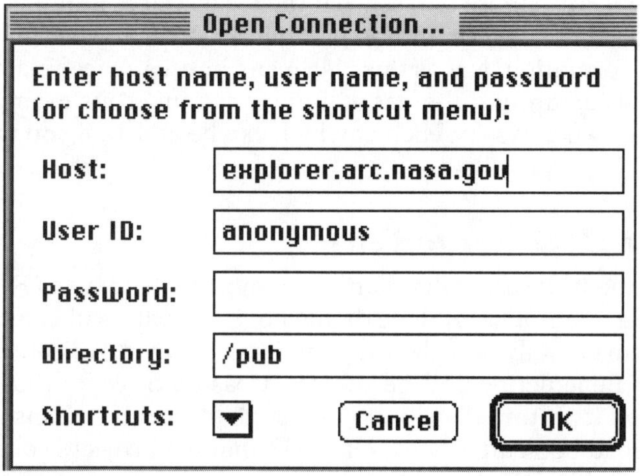

Figure 5.18   Setting up an FTP connection with Fetch.

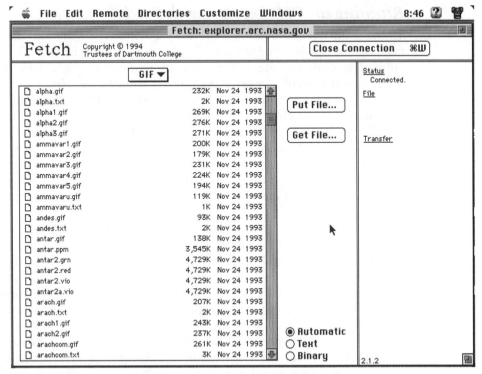

Figure 5.19   Directories and files at a remote site as viewed through Fetch.

many other people are trying to use. Many FTP sites maintain restrictions on the number of people who can use the site at any one time.

The Gaspra image is shown in Figure 5.21. By now, you realize that the Internet's FTP sites are more or less what the local system administrators have decided to make them. It's a common practice for a site to specialize in particular kinds of information, just as this NASA site houses space-related material. Your own browsing around the net will uncover numerous examples of sites that pique your own curiosity, each of which can be added, if you wish, to your Shortcut list.

Adding an FTP Server to Fetch

Let's now add the FTP server that handles Project Gutenberg to Fetch. Project Gutenberg is an attempt to produce digital copies of works of classic literature and spread them globally over the Internet; it is managed by Professor Michael Hart at Illinois Benedictine College, and is a treasure trove for those interested in literature and its future distribution through electronic means. At this site, you can download book after book, all works that the Project's volunteers have scanned or typed into ASCII text form.

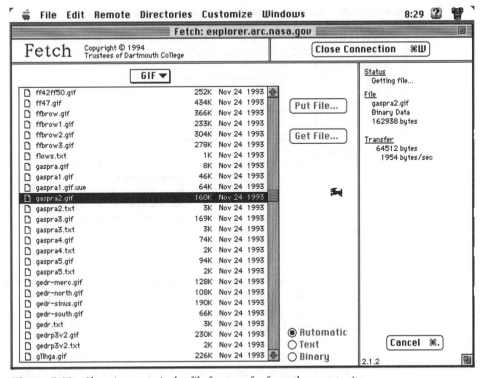

Figure 5.20   Choosing a particular file for transfer from the remote site.

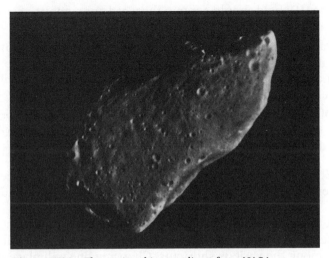

Figure 5.21   The retrieved image, direct from NASA.

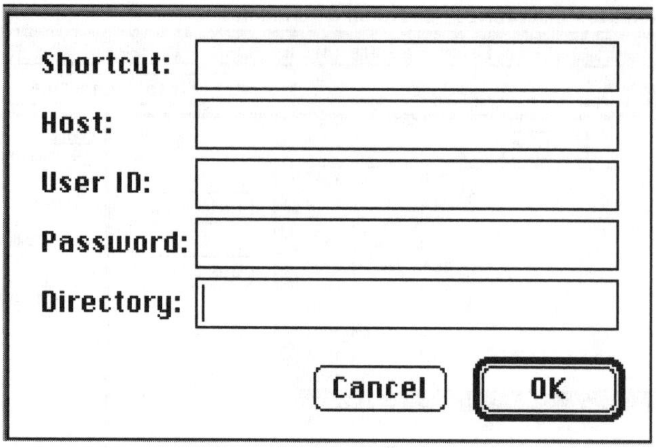

Figure 5.22   Creating a new shortcut for Fetch involves filling in this dialog box.

The site address is **ftp://mrcnext.cso.uiuc.edu**. To add it to Fetch's list of shortcuts, pull down the Customize menu and choose Edit Shortcuts. Click on the New button to produce the dialog box shown in Figure 5.22. You can now fill in this box with the correct information. The fields work as follows:

- The Shortcut: field contains whatever name you want to assign this server. This is the name that will appear when you pull down the list of Shortcuts. It is not the site address.

- The Host: field contains the address of the site you are establishing as a shortcut. In the case of Project Gutenberg, then, enter the address **mrcnext.cso.uiuc.edu**.

- The User ID: field should contain the word anonymous, to allow you to perform an anonymous FTP login at the site.

- The Password: field should contain your e-mail address. But since you have already entered it when you configured Fetch, you don't need to add it again. Fetch will use the value you entered on the original Preferences screen.

- The Directory: field allows you to specify which directory you want to log in to at the site. In most cases, you can leave this blank or else use a / as the root directory symbol.

In Figure 5.23, you see the completed dialog box. Click on OK to accept the values you have entered. The Project Gutenberg shortcut will now be added to the list.

To use the shortcut, simply pull down the File menu and choose the Open Connection item. By selecting the Shortcuts: pop-up menu, you will be able to choose from among the various shortcuts. Choosing one will place its address information into the relevant fields in Fetch's Open Connection box. You can

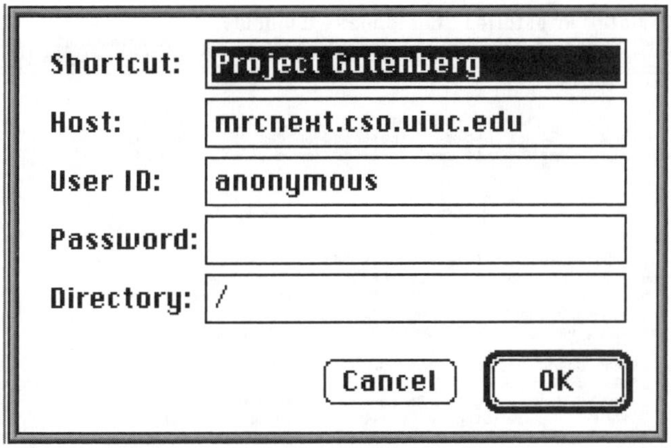

Figure 5.23 The completed shortcut entry.

then click on the OK button to initiate your session with the site. In Figure 5.24, you see one of Project Gutenberg's index files, viewed on-line with Fetch. All of these titles are currently available at the Gutenberg site.

Download Specifics

Fetch goes a long way toward simplifying the downloading process because of its user-friendly features. These are the kind of things we expect from graphical clients; they remove the need to memorize or look up complicated commands and let us proceed with much of the work taking place transparently to us.

You may have noticed, for example, that Fetch's main screen contains information about how file transfers should proceed. Normally, FTP servers are set up to facilitate ASCII file transfers. If you were running an FTP session and wanted to download a binary file, you would specify that by giving the **binary** command at the ftp> prompt. Some clients, like WS_FTP in the Microsoft Windows environment, can be customized to use either binary or ASCII as the default file setting. With Fetch, you can get around the problem entirely, because when the program is set on Automatic, it will recognize the type of file being transferred and adjust the session accordingly. This saves you from determining the file type by examining file extensions and then giving the right command.

Fetch also helps out by handling the unpacking procedure for file transfers. The program can handle files compressed with the standard Macintosh utilities, including the StuffIt series from Aladdin Systems and Compact Pro from Cyclos Software. To configure Fetch to handle decompression chores, you will need to have the appropriate decompression utility on your hard disk. If you do, pull down the Customize menu, choosing the Post-Processing option. You will see the dialog box shown in Figure 5.25. If you have not pre-

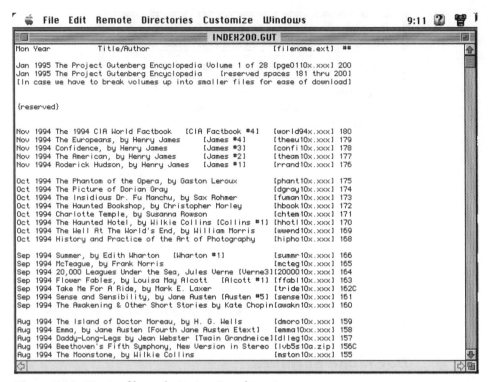

Figure 5.24 Viewing files at the Project Gutenberg site.

viously configured this box, all of the items will be shown in gray rather than black, indicating they are not yet enabled. Here is how to proceed:

1. Highlight any of these items and then click on the Change button to open a dialog box that allows you to choose the external application you want to use for decompression or file viewing (Fetch can also link to a GIF file viewer, for example).

2. Choose the folder containing the appropriate application.

3. Click on OK.

4. Click the Enable button in the Post-Processing Configuration dialog box. The item you have just changed will now appear in black type rather than gray, indicating it is now enabled.

5. Click on OK to save your changes.

Figure 5.26 shows the screen that appears when I choose GIF Files as my file type and click on the Change button to configure Fetch to handle such files. I can now click on Choose Application to establish the location of my GIF file viewer.

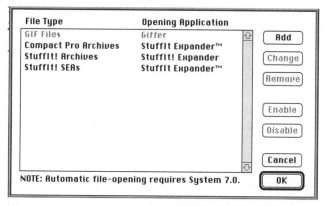

Figure 5.25 Setting up post-processing options in Fetch.

From now on, when you download a file, Fetch will act upon it when it meets one of the file types you have just configured. Compressed files will be unpacked, and if you have chosen a GIF file viewer, any GIF image that you download will be displayed as soon as it is retrieved. By doing this kind of chore for us, Fetch saves us time and makes exploring FTP sites more productive.

Finding and Downloading Files with Anarchie

When you begin working with a SLIP/PPP environment, you quickly realize that gathering the best software tools will become a preoccupation. My own desktop, for example, is littered with icons for the various programs I run on the Internet. And while I enjoy the sheer diversity of this software, it's sometimes daunting to see how many programs I've accumulated. Finding one that

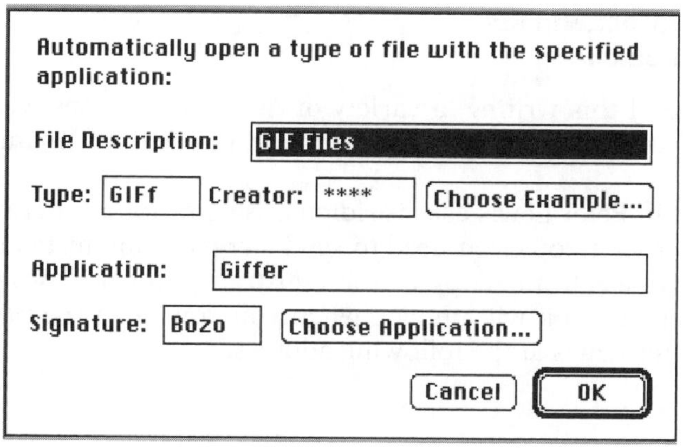

Figure 5.26 Telling Fetch how to handle GIF files.

can combine several key functions is therefore a pleasant surprise, especially when that software functions as smoothly as Anarchie.

Anarchie is a shareware program that deftly combines the functions of FTP and archie. When you insert a keyword, Anarchie will go out over the network and consult whichever archie server you have designated for the file or directory in question. When it locates it, Anarchie will then become an FTP engine; click on that file and the session will be initiated. This is extremely useful for a variety of reasons. When you get a list of hits from archie, for example, you always have to contend with the fact that many of these hits are located at sites that labor under a heavy traffic load; these can be very difficult to get into and are best avoided where possible.

With Anarchie, I simply scan the list of hits, looking for sites that are not as well traveled. Best, perhaps, to find a file on a computer at a seldom visited university site than to try to get into one of the big archives, like **ftp://sumex-aim.stanford.edu** or **ftp://mac.archive.umich.edu**. The latter can consume literally hours of your time with repeated attempts to connect. And by making the entire FTP process a simple matter of clicking on that site, Anarchie allows me to relax. The program goes into the site, logs me in for anonymous FTP, supplies my password, and navigates directly to the directory where my file is located. It then issues the appropriate commands and downloads the file. What could be easier?

Finding and Retrieving Anarchie

Anarchie is a shareware program written by Peter N. Lewis. It is available at Macintosh-related software sites all over the Internet. When I ran an archie search for Anarchie using the program itself as my search tool, I found numerous hits. Among them are the following URLs, which you may want to try in your search for the program:

> **ftp://mrcnext.cso.uiuc.edu/**
> **ftp://casbah.acns.nwu.edu/**
> **ftp://plaza.aarnet.edu.au/**
> **ftp://ftp.switch.ch/**

At the time of this writing, a variety of Anarchie versions were available over the Internet. The one I am using is found under the filename anarchie-121.hqx.

The $10 tariff Peter Lewis asks is ridiculously low for a program this valuable. To register your copy, you need to send a registration form and payment to its author; an electronic copy of the registration form is provided in the Anarchie folder that you will unpack when you download the program. You can contact Peter Lewis at the following address:

Peter N. Lewis
10 Earlston Way
Booragoon WA 6154

Australia
E-mail: **peter.lewis@info.curtin.edu.au**

Site licensing is also available; contact Lewis for further information.

Configuring Anarchie

Once you have unpacked the Anarchie folder, you can open it and double-click on the Anarchie icon to launch the program. The first step is to pull down the Edit menu and choose the Preferences item, which will allow you to set the program up for your own use. When you do this, you will see the dialog box shown in Figure 5.27.

Fill in your e-mail address in the field at the top. In the Country Code field, make sure your country is listed correctly. Anarchie will use this information to list hosts in the most appropriate order. Anarchie is now configured for your use.

Running a Search with Anarchie

Let's run a search for Netscape, the fine new World Wide Web browser from Netscape Communications Corp. As with any archie search, we must first remember a key principle: archie is literal-minded; we would need an exact file-name if we hoped to find the file immediately, or else a partial filename that we could use with a substring search. But archie also searches directories, which can be a big help when we're looking for a program but don't know how its file-name would appear. We can always use it to find directories containing our file.

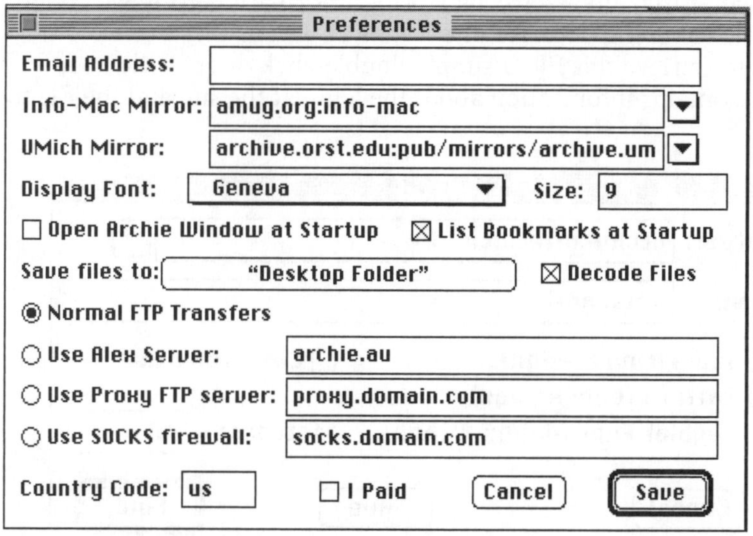

Figure 5.27 Setting up Anarchie's preferences during initial configuration requires filling in this dialog box.

To launch the search, pull down the File menu and take the Archie option. You will see the screen shown in Figure 5.28. As you can see, I am currently using the archie server at **archie.internic.net**. I have inserted the keyword netscape into the Find: field, and have left the search on the default setting of Sub-string. When I click on Find, Anarchie searches the server and finally pulls up the screen of hits shown in Figure 5.29.

Notice that we have several files here, but most of our entries seem to be directories (you can tell by examining the icon to the left of each entry). It's likely that any one of these directories will contain the Netscape program we're after.

 Note: Anarchie provides the usual tools for file searching. Its keyword screen allows you to choose between the default substring search, wildcard searches, and regex, with the option of turning case-sensitivity on or off (the default is off). Notice, also, that you can set the number of matches. Setting this number lower than the default of 40 will make for faster searches, and 20 hits is usually more than sufficient.

By picking a directory and clicking on it (I chose the one at *bitsy.mit.edu*), I tell Anarchie to home in on the site and show me a listing of what is in that directory. You can see that listing in Figure 5.30. I have highlighted a particular file, which was the most recent version at the time of this writing—version 1.0 has since appeared. The filename is mosaic-netscape-B09.sea.hqx. It's clear we wouldn't have known to search for that exact filename when we ran the archie search unless we had prior information. But we found it by using archie's ability to look for directories as well as files.

To retrieve this file, I simply double-click on it. A file transfer box appears that contains information about the login at the site and the file transfer itself.

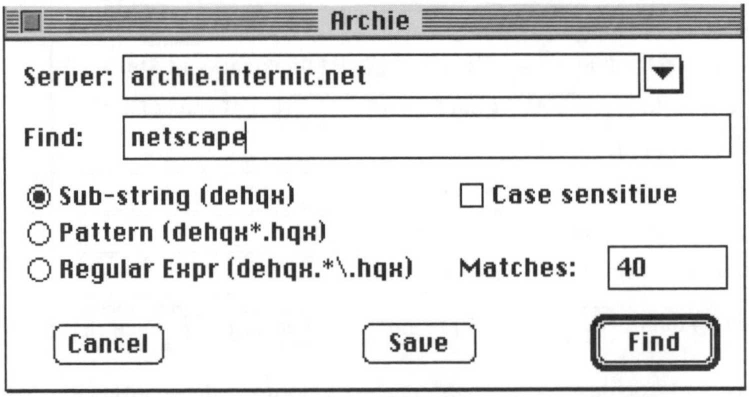

Archie

Server: archie.internic.net ▼

Find: netscape|

● Sub-string (dehqx)   ☐ Case sensitive
○ Pattern (dehqx*.hqx)
○ Regular Expr (dehqx.*\.hqx)   Matches: 40

[Cancel]   [Save]   [Find]

Figure 5.28   The search screen as filled in for a search for Netscape.

Name	Size	Date	Zone	Host	Pat
▯ mosaic-netscape-b09.sea.hqx	739k	10/17/94	5	chalmers.se	
▯ mosaic-netscape-b09.sea.hqx	1k	10/17/94	5	chalmers.se	
▯ mosaic-netscape-b09.sea.hqx	0k	10/17/94	5	chalmers.se	
▯ netscape	2186k	12/7/94	1	sunsite.unc.edu	
▱ netscape	–	12/12/94	1	ftp.cme.nist.gov	
▱ netscape		12/2/94	1	serv1.cl.msu.edu	
▱ netscape	–	11/19/94	1	ftp.uoknor.edu	
▱ Netscape	–	12/7/94	1	ftp.isri.unlv.edu	
▱ netscape	–	11/17/94	1	bitsy.mit.edu	
▱ netscape	–	12/13/94	1	ftp.cyberspace.com	
▱ netscape	–	12/8/94	2	ftp.cc.umanitoba.ca	
▱ netscape	–	12/16/94	5	alf.uib.no	
▱ netscape	–	10/18/94	5	ajk.tele.fi	
▯ netscape	1k	11/20/94	5	ftp.luth.se	
▱ netscape	–	10/20/94	5	ftp.umu.se	
▱ netscape	–	12/7/94	5	lut.fi	
▱ netscape	–	10/19/94	5	ftp.umu.se	
▯ netscape	1k	10/20/94	5	ftp.umu.se	
▱ netscape	–	11/18/94	5	ftp.umu.se	
▱ netscape	–	11/20/94	5	ftp.luth.se	
▯ netscape	1k	10/19/94	5	ftp.umu.se	
▯ netscape	1k	10/20/94	5	ftp.umu.se	
▯ netscape	1k	10/20/94	5	ftp.umu.se	
▯ netscape	1k	10/19/94	5	ftp.umu.se	
▱ netscape	–	10/20/94	5	ftp.umu.se	
▯ netscape	1k	10/20/94	5	ftp.umu.se	
▯ Netscape	1k	10/25/94	5	ftp.sunet.se	
▱ Netscape	–	11/6/94	5	ftp.eunet.no	
▯ netscape	1k	10/20/94	5	ftp.umu.se	
▯ Netscape	1k	10/16/94	5	ftp.sunet.se	
▯ netscape	1k	10/19/94	5	ftp.umu.se	
▱ Netscape	–	10/16/94	5	ftp.sunet.se	
▯ netscape-09b.hqx	704k	11/5/94	1	ftp.uoknor.edu	

Figure 5.29 A screen full of hits from Anarchie.

Note: How did we know that the version of Netscape we chose to transfer was the one for the Macintosh? There are, after all, versions for other computer platforms. The answer is in the file extensions. In this case, a file with the .sea and .hqx extensions is one that is specific to the Macintosh. If we were dealing with a file for Microsoft Windows, we'd be more likely to look for files with the .zip extension, or perhaps the .exe extension that marks a self-extracting file. Always examine filenames with care to make sure you get the right one.

Name	Size	Date	Zone	Host	Path
mosaic-netscape-B09.sea.hqx	739k	10/17/94	1	uoselx.sdsu.edu	/pub/mac/mosaic-netscape-B09.sea.h
mosaic-netscape-B09.sea.hqx	728k	11/29/94	1	gargoyle.uchicago.edu	/pub/users/fasciano/mozilla/mosaic-
mosaic-netscape-B09.sea.hqx	728k	12/7/94	1	bitsy.mit.edu	/pub/mac/alpha-beta/web/mosaic-net
mosaic-netscape-B09.sea.hqx	739k	10/13/94	1	sunsite.unc.edu	/pub/packages/infosystems/WWW/cli
mosaic-netscape-B09.sea.hqx	739k	10/20/94	1	ftp.cyberspace.com	/pub/ppp/Mac/www/mosaic-netscape
mosaic-netscape-B09.sea.hqx	739k	11/8/94	2	owl.nstn.ns.ca	/pub/mac-stuff/mosaic-netscape-B09
mosaic-netscape-B09.sea.hqx	739k	10/12/94	5	ftp.bhp.com.au	/internet/www/clients/netscape/mac
mosaic-netscape-B09.sea.hqx	728k	11/21/94	5	pippin.cc.flinders.edu.au	/pub/mac/Network/netscape/mosaic-
mosaic-netscape-B09.sea.hqx	248k	10/28/94	5	telva.ccu.uniovi.es	/pub/Mac/Netscape/mosaic-netscape-
mosaic-netscape-B09.sea.hqx	739k	11/17/94	5	power.ci.uv.es	/pub/mac/network/Netscape/mosaic-
mosaic-netscape-B09.sea.hqx	739k	10/13/94	5	ftp.mi.cnr.it	/pub/Mac/mosaic-netscape-B09.sea.h
mosaic-netscape-B09.sea.hqx	739k	10/11/94	5	unix.hensa.ac.uk	/pub/uunet/networking/info-service/
netscape.alpha-dec-osf2.0.B09.tar.Z	2254k	10/13/94	1	sunsite.unc.edu	/pub/packages/infosystems/WWW/cli
netscape.alpha-dec-osf2.0.B09.tar.Z	2254k	11/17/94	5	power.ci.uv.es	/pub/unix/Netscape/netscape.alpha-de
netscape.alpha-dec-osf2.0.B09.tar.Z	2254k	10/11/94	5	unix.hensa.ac.uk	/pub/mosaic.comm.corp/unix/netscap
netscape.hppa1.1-hp-hpux.B09.tar.Z	1804k	10/13/94	1	sunsite.unc.edu	/pub/packages/infosystems/WWW/cli
netscape.hppa1.1-hp-hpux.B09.tar.Z	1804k	10/11/94	5	sun.rediris.es	/infoiris/web/netscape/unix/netscape
netscape.mips-sgi-irix5.2.B09-inst.tar	640k	10/13/94	1	sunsite.unc.edu	/pub/packages/infosystems/WWW/cli
netscape.mips-sgi-irix5.2.B09-inst.tar	640k	11/17/94	5	power.ci.uv.es	/pub/unix/Netscape/netscape.mips-sg
netscape.mips-sgi-irix5.2.B09-inst.tar	640k	10/11/94	5	sun.rediris.es	/infoiris/web/netscape/unix/netscape
netscape.mips-sgi-irix5.2.B09-inst.tar	640k	10/11/94	5	unix.hensa.ac.uk	/pub/mosaic.comm.corp/unix/netscap
netscape.mips-sgi-irix5.2.B09.tar.Z	630k	10/13/94	1	sunsite.unc.edu	/pub/packages/infosystems/WWW/cli
netscape.mips-sgi-irix5.2.B09.tar.Z	630k	10/11/94	5	sun.rediris.es	/infoiris/web/netscape/unix/netscape
netscape.mips-sgi-irix5.2.B09.tar.Z	630k	10/11/94	5	unix.hensa.ac.uk	/pub/uunet/networking/info-service/
netscape.rs6000-ibm-aix3.2.B09.tar.Z	683k	10/13/94	1	sunsite.unc.edu	/pub/packages/infosystems/WWW/cli
netscape.rs6000-ibm-aix3.2.B09.tar.Z	683k	10/11/94	5	teseo.unipg.it	/pub/unix/aix/aix6000/netscape.rs6
netscape.rs6000-ibm-aix3.2.B09.tar.Z	683k	10/11/94	5	unix.hensa.ac.uk	/pub/mosaic.comm.corp/unix/netscap

Figure 5.30 Examining a remote site through Anarchie.

You can see that the transfer rate is logged and the time left in the transfer is displayed, just as progress in the download is shown by the bar at the bottom of the box. When the transfer is complete, I will have the Netscape folder on my desktop, ready for installation.

Getting the Most Out of Anarchie

Anarchie arrives with a set of bookmarks which make connecting to various sites easy. You can see this bookmark list in Figure 5.31 (it is accessed by pulling down the File menu and choosing the List Bookmarks item).

The idea here is that the sites you visit often, or that hold established archives, are ones you want to be able to return to quickly. Double-click on any of these and you can go right to the site. Once there, Anarchie lets you browse for files (remember, Anarchie is as much FTP client as archie client).

Naturally, a bookmark feature is doubly useful if you can add to it, and Anarchie makes this a simple matter.

1. Select the item you want to set as a bookmark.
2. Choose Save Bookmark from the File menu.

Anarchie will then bring up a dialog box that allows you to name the bookmark and place it in the appropriate folder.

Bookmarks can be handy indeed when you're dealing with a site that is frequently busy. Because major archive sites like **sumex-aim.stanford.edu**

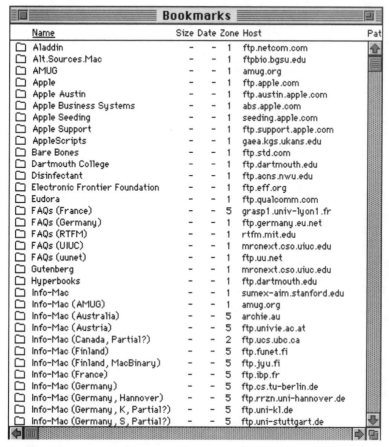

Name	Size	Date	Zone	Host	Pat
Aladdin	–	–	1	ftp.netcom.com	
Alt.Sources.Mac	–	–	1	ftpbio.bgsu.edu	
AMUG	–	–	1	amug.org	
Apple	–	–	1	ftp.apple.com	
Apple Austin	–	–	1	ftp.austin.apple.com	
Apple Business Systems	–	–	1	abs.apple.com	
Apple Seeding	–	–	1	seeding.apple.com	
Apple Support	–	–	1	ftp.support.apple.com	
AppleScripts	–	–	1	gaea.kgs.ukans.edu	
Bare Bones	–	–	1	ftp.std.com	
Dartmouth College	–	–	1	ftp.dartmouth.edu	
Disinfectant	–	–	1	ftp.acns.nwu.edu	
Electronic Frontier Foundation	–	–	1	ftp.eff.org	
Eudora	–	–	1	ftp.qualcomm.com	
FAQs (France)	–	–	5	grasp1.univ-lyon1.fr	
FAQs (Germany)	–	–	1	ftp.germany.eu.net	
FAQs (RTFM)	–	–	1	rtfm.mit.edu	
FAQs (UIUC)	–	–	1	mrcnext.cso.uiuc.edu	
FAQs (uunet)	–	–	1	ftp.uu.net	
Gutenberg	–	–	1	mrcnext.cso.uiuc.edu	
Hyperbooks	–	–	1	ftp.dartmouth.edu	
Info-Mac	–	–	1	sumex-aim.stanford.edu	
Info-Mac (AMUG)	–	–	1	amug.org	
Info-Mac (Australia)	–	–	5	archie.au	
Info-Mac (Austria)	–	–	5	ftp.univie.ac.at	
Info-Mac (Canada, Partial?)	–	–	2	ftp.ucs.ubc.ca	
Info-Mac (Finland)	–	–	5	ftp.funet.fi	
Info-Mac (Finland, MacBinary)	–	–	5	ftp.jyu.fi	
Info-Mac (France)	–	–	5	ftp.ibp.fr	
Info-Mac (Germany)	–	–	5	ftp.cs.tu-berlin.de	
Info-Mac (Germany, Hannover)	–	–	5	ftp.rrzn.uni-hannover.de	
Info-Mac (Germany, K, Partial?)	–	–	5	ftp.uni-kl.de	
Info-Mac (Germany, S, Partial?)	–	–	5	ftp.uni-stuttgart.de	

Figure 5.31 Anarchie's bookmark list functions like similar session profiles in WS_FTP and Fetch.

are subject to a huge flow of traffic, mirror sites have been set up to handle the overflow. Anarchie's bookmark page contains numerous mirrors of the most popular sites. When you try to connect to a site and can't get in, simply call up the Bookmarks list and choose one of these mirrors. You should be able to point-and-click your way to an open connection faster this way than by using conventional techniques, and Anarchie has certainly saved you some keystrokes.

Anarchie comes with an Anarchie Guide that helps you use the program and provides convenient shortcuts. You should consult the guide and the documentation to learn about other tips and techniques that I don't have time to go into here. Suffice it to say that Anarchie is a rich and rewarding program, one that any Macintosh user with a serious interest in the Internet cannot afford to be without. Don't forget to register it!

6

Managing Electronic Mail with SLIP/PPP

If there is a single, critical tool for Internet users to master, it is surely electronic mail. Most newcomers learn e-mail procedures first and, until recently, many did little else than send messages. (The advent of stable Internet browsing tools is changing all this, but more about that in Chapter 11.) Although old Internet hands sometimes become jaded enough to take e-mail for granted, even the most venerable networker occasionally feels the twinge of excitement associated with receiving a message from halfway around the world. It's not so much the distance that message has traveled, or the exotic nature of its origin, as the ease with which it appears. Above all else, electronic mail makes communication simple.

Because I write Internet books, I tend to receive unsolicited mail from readers, a fact which, more than anything else, has demonstrated to me how widely the Internet has grown. I've talked to a schoolteacher in the Peruvian Andes and an accountant in Moscow, a translator in Italy, and a winegrower in South Africa. Electronic mail makes these conversations easy by simplifying the process of response. Any e-mail program lets me hit a key to initiate an answer to the message I am reading, including, if I wish, a quotation from that message followed by my own thoughts. To send my response, it's only necessary to give the proper keystroke and, within seconds, my mail has traversed the Internet to a distant computer, where it will reside until my recipient examines his or her mailbox.

Electronic mail, like postal mail, accumulates in a mailbox until it is read, but it's surprising how often you get responses to your mail on the same day you sent it. I've engaged in single-day, multiple-message conversations on numerous occasions, a testament to the fact that many users either check their mail frequently through the course of a day, or else, if they use full network connections at work, monitor it as it arrives and respond. SLIP/PPP users don't have the latter luxury; their mailbox chores involve placing a telephone call with their modems and launching the necessary applications to read mail, but a routine check every morning and afternoon keeps them up on their correspondents' news and lets them read the postings of any mailing lists to which they may have subscribed.

The key factor in all this is the mail reader program you use. Any mail program lets you do certain things; even the most basic reader, like Unix mail, lets you reply quickly, view your mail by subject and sender, and insert not only quotations from the received mail into your response, but also external files, such as prepared text or encoded binary files. More sophisticated Unix tools like pine or elm add a variety of features, including basic help systems that provide the most important commands at the bottom of the screen as you proceed.

Among the Unix tools, pine is the most full-featured in terms of its interface, as the screen in Figure 6.1 reveals. By moving the on-screen highlight bar and pressing a return, I can choose basic functions such as composing a message, looking at an index of messages in my mailbox, or moving between folders, which are storage areas for messages that can be customized as needed.

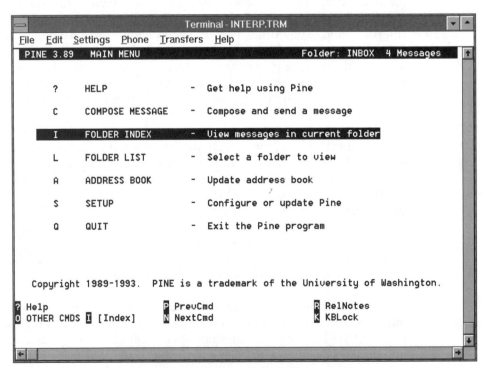

Figure 6.1 The pine mail program as used in a Unix shell account.

Notice that there is also a built-in help system, accessible by highlighting the ? key and pressing a return.

Given all of this, and a host of features that we haven't examined, what can SLIP/PPP provide by way of mail functions that programs like pine don't already give us? The answer is revealed in the title of this chapter—"Managing Electronic Mail." The better SLIP/PPP clients provide excellent mail management capabilities. Perhaps you'd like to sort your mail by sender or by date. A good client lets you do this with a mouse click or two. Or it could be that you would like to filter incoming mail, sending certain messages to particular folders, while retaining the rest in a high-priority area for quick response. A SLIP/PPP client can manage this, if you choose your client wisely, and in the process bring a measure of control to an otherwise ungovernable jumble of received mail.

And then there are the times when you want to send binary information over the net. Because the Internet works with 7-bit ASCII text files, your binary file isn't going to fly as a mail enclosure unless you code it into ASCII, a process which can be performed by *uuencoding*. With a shell account, you would need to handle this chore separately, from your service provider's system prompt, using whatever tools the provider made available on his or her machine; you would then give your mail program a separate command to include the coded file in your message. A good SLIP/PPP client should be able to include this chore in its bag of tricks, adding it as one of the menu options it provides through an easy-to-use, mouse-driven interface.

We'll examine such a program in a moment, but first, let me put in a word for the much maligned Unix mail tools. The movement toward SLIP/PPP has created a rather uncritical acceptance of the notion that character-based interfaces are always inferior to their graphical cousins. In fact, both elm and pine in their individual ways provide most of the functionality of the SLIP/PPP clients, although using them does require more digging to turn up the appropriate commands. Those who find Unix fascinating, and I am in their camp, continue to use such tools along with their graphical counterparts, which is not to say that you have to do so, but that good software is very much a matter of personal preference. I will admit that on more than a few occasions, when I simply want to dash off a quick note, I simply use Unix mail. But for managing those big mailing lists, I turn to the program I am about to discuss.

Mail Issues over the Network

To make sense out of Internet mail, we need to run through several acronyms that you will see in your network use. First, a reminder about the layers of a network stack. You may recall from Chapter 2 that we divide network functions into *layers* because of the need to simplify the complex tasks of communications between different computers. Thus we can differentiate between a *transport* layer that deals with moving data, an *applications* layer that copes with end-user applications, a *physical* layer that describes wire and fiber-optic connections, and so forth. In the standard Open Systems Interconnection Reference Model, there are seven such layers.

Let's focus now on the upper layers of the network stack, which is where the standards used by applications programs are found. The protocols we think of as being key to Internet use—FTP, Telnet, electronic mail—are found with their various counterparts in this area (TCP/IP is not involved in the lower two layers of the standard OSI model; it begins in the Network layer, which contains the Internet Protocol, and the Transport layer above it, which contains the Transmission Control Protocol). The key protocol I focus on in this chapter is called Simple Mail Transfer Protocol. When I say that e-mail is one of the big three Internet protocols, along with FTP and Telnet, I am really referring to SMTP.

Simple Mail Transfer Protocol

SMTP is the protocol by which electronic mail messages are transferred; it has become a worldwide standard for e-mail messages, one that is comprehended by non-Internet networks as well as the multitudinous computers of the Internet itself. This acceptance of SMTP as the lingua franca of electronic mail provides us with an unprecedented global messaging environment, one in which it is as easy to send e-mail down the street as it is to dispatch that same message across an ocean. The basics behind SMTP are described in two Request for Comments documents, RFC821, "Simple Mail Transfer Protocol," and RFC822, "Standard for the Format of ARPA Internet Text Messages." The RFC is dated August 13, 1982.

When you activated your SLIP/PPP account, you received a data sheet with the information necessary to configure your software. We have already used this information to configure Trumpet Winsock for Microsoft Windows and both InterSLIP and MacPPP for the Macintosh, thus enabling the SLIP/PPP link so you can run the client programs we have been examining. You should examine this data again to find the information needed to work with electronic mail. Look for the name and IP address of your provider's SMTP server, which you will need to insert into the appropriate field as we configure Eudora, a superb e-mail program from QUALCOMM.

The SMTP protocol establishes the format by which electronic mail will move over the Internet in the form of ASCII text. In this regard, the date on RFC822 is telling; it's now over 12 years old, and was written before the advent of today's extensive multimedia capabilities. As we've seen, including a binary file in a message you want to send over the Internet involves encoding it in ASCII format, and decoding it at the other end, a cumbersome process without sophisticated software tools. Another key issue is privacy: Can the ASCII mail format conceived for a much smaller and far less inclusive network provide sufficient security features in today's Internet, which is being increasingly developed by commercial interests? To handle these issues, a set of new protocols have been created which provide extended capabilities. Let's examine them now.

Multipurpose Internet Mail Extensions

MIME is a new mail protocol that was designed to incorporate multimedia features into standard Internet mail. By multimedia, I simply refer to the ability to include graphics, sound, and video into a message, adding onto the base already established by ASCII text. The beauty of a good mail program is that it can handle messages with MIME capabilities.

Why would you want to add these capabilities? Perhaps sending photographs over the network isn't an attraction, but the ability to move word processing files in their native format and spreadsheets ready to be loaded on your recipient's machine should make MIME more intriguing. And you certainly don't want to have to go manually through the cumbersome coding and decoding process that standard electronic mail requires on the Internet. In a MIME-compliant system, the different media in a particular message—text, graphics, audio, and so on—are interpreted by the mail package and reassembled correctly. Take MIME to its logical conclusion and you enable multinational character sets to be used, effectively transcending the limitations of ASCII for languages like Russian and Japanese. There are also theoretical applications for voice mail interactivity, for MIME can define sets of e-mail audio that would be compatible with telephone messaging systems.

Privacy Enhanced Mail and E-Mail Security

Privacy Enhanced Mail, or PEM, is all about encryption, the idea being to code messages in such a way that no one but the intended recipient of the text can read it. Recently approved by the Internet Engineering Task Force, PEM addresses a critical issue in the evolution of the Internet. We have, for example, no way to authenticate the sender of a particular message. If you receive e-mail from a particular account at a given site, there is no guarantee that the message actually originated with that person. It is too easy for a determined prankster to obtain a login and password, after which he or she can use the computer resources available to the legitimate user without detection.

Privacy issues pose a likewise telling problem. Even if you are religious about keeping your password to yourself, software exists that can record what you write, and system administrators at your site can examine whatever you store in your home directory if they choose. For that matter, postings you make in various mailing lists or USENET newsgroups are frequently archived, and thus made available to a wider audience than you perhaps intended. On a larger scale, remember that any message you send may pass through dozens of

Note: MIME raises some intriguing issues about Internet mail. The SMTP protocol is, as we've seen, limited to the ASCII character set. This works well for speakers of English, but what happens if you work with a language that uses letters not found within the ASCII set? For that matter, what do you do when you want to use special characters for text formatting and the like? The regular ASCII set cannot help you here.

MIME gets around the ASCII limitation by using encoding methods that can represent special characters or nontextual data. Its "quoted-printable" encoding is used for textual data that contains special characters. The text looks normal enough until a special character appears, at which time the special character is itself replaced by an "=" and two more characters that represent the special character code are inserted. Such encoding methods can also allow mail to use lines longer than the 76-character limit demanded by quoted-printable formatting. Such lines are broken but relinked with the addition of more encoding after the end of the first broken segment, to indicate to the mail reader that the two lines should be joined.

Quoted-printable encoding allows you to send text in a foreign language through normal Internet mail channels, with all the special characters appearing in proper form on the receiving end. As it made its way through the mail system, the message would look bizarre, stuffed with the variously encoded special character codes that tell the mail reader at the other end how to handle the text. But your recipient would be able to call it up in his or her mail reader and read it in its natural form.

Eudora uses quoted-printable encoding automatically when your mail contains any special characters; it also employs quoted-printable techniques in any plain text document you attach to a message. All of which works fine provided that your recipients also use a mail program with MIME capabilities. If they do not, the addition of quoted-printable characters may, depending on the type of material you are sending, make your file attachment difficult to read. You can turn off quoted-printable encoding by using the QP button on the message icon bar.

MIME also uses an encoding method called Base64, which is how nontextual data moves. Between quoted-printable encoding and Base64 encoding, MIME can therefore handle everything from standard U.S. ASCII documents to text documents in a variety of foreign alphabets and, using Base64 encoding, it can work with pictures, sound, and moving video within an Internet message. Several different kinds of data, as we have seen, can coexist within the same message, making MIME a remarkably effective way of surmounting the straight ASCII limitation of RFC822.

packet-switching nodes on its way to its destination; anyone who has access to any site along the way can get into your information.

The issue of encryption is a charged one, particularly in a time when government security agencies have raised concerns about allowing encryption to fall into the hands of terrorist organizations, drug traffickers, and other unsavory groups. But it is clear that interest in the technology is rising, particularly as electronic commerce grows on the net. A retailer, for example, needs to be able to make credit card transactions available, yet anyone conversant with Internet security will question whether sending such information over the net is a safe idea. Large financial institutions can't begin to examine the Internet for business activity unless the integrity of their data can be assured. And private users are latching onto the issue with surprising speed, as determined by the rising number of users of Pretty Good Privacy (PGP), an encryption system made available over the Internet.

The establishment of PEM as an Internet standard should begin the process of validating its use worldwide; it has already been implemented on a variety of computer platforms, including DOS, Macintosh, and Unix. Riordan's Internet Privacy Enhanced Mail (RIPEM) is a freeware implementation of PEM developed by Mark Riordan of Michigan State University in East Lansing, while a shareware package called TIS/PEM is available from Trusted Information Systems Inc. (Glenwood, Maryland), which also produces a commercial product called Trusted Mail. AT&T, Computer Associates, and Novell Inc. have announced that they will support a PEM-compatible encryption scheme. We should soon see the adoption of the PEM standard by commercial e-mail vendors and its appearance in new products as a standard feature.

 Note: If you're interested in getting into the details of various Internet protocols like SMTP, you will want to access the various RFC documents that describe them. Numerous FTP sites exist that house these documents, but perhaps the easiest way to reach them is through the InterNIC, a collection of three organizations that provide information, directory and database services, and registration for the network in the United States. A complete, searchable listing of RFCs, for example, is provided by the InterNIC's Gopher (**gopher://gopher.internic.net**). As we'll see, there are other access options as well, including logging on through a World Wide Web browser (**http://www.internic.net**). More on these as we consider each type of client program.

Post Office Protocol

SLIP/PPP accounts require a particular kind of mail handling. After all, when you do not maintain a continuous network presence, you need to have a mail system that recognizes when you log on and sends you the messages that arrived while you were absent from the network. Post Office Protocol is the name of the Internet standard that handles this operation.

Let's consider the routing of your electronic mail. When you receive a message from the Internet, your mail arrives at the Post Office Protocol server that has been set up for your use by your service provider. There it will remain until your mail program downloads it to your computer, using Post Office Protocol version 3, commonly called POP3. The mail you send out onto the Internet goes from your mail program via SMTP to your service provider's SMTP server. That computer sends the mail to your recipient using the SMTP protocol.

As you can see, your Internet mail isn't moving in real-time, in the sense that, say, an FTP session works in real-time. With FTP, you actually log on to a remote site and the connection between your machine and the remote computer is active as long as you are connected to the site. When you download a file, the file is sent automatically; when you move through file directories, you see the results immediately (with only a slight lag depending upon the speed of your connection and the nature of the FTP server's access to the Internet).

Electronic mail can't move in real-time with a SLIP/PPP connection because if it did, your computer would be forced to make contact with each of your recipient's computers to deliver the mail one message at a time. Your service provider's SMTP server will hold your outgoing mail until it can be sent through the network, allowing you to upload multiple messages in a single burst of traffic. Incoming mail works the same way. You wouldn't want to keep your SLIP/PPP connection up and running 24 hours per day because of the costs involved, not to mention the fact that you may have other uses intended for your computer. By holding your mail for you, your provider's POP server allows your mail program to pick up your mail at a time of your convenience, and move it to your own computer. There you can answer it at your leisure and upload your responses when ready.

When you activate your electronic mail program, then, you can read and reply to messages that have just arrived and upload your answers onto the network. Because POP moves your mail to your computer, you aren't limited to using the software available at your service provider's site, but can instead use whatever client program you find most efficient. And efficiency is precisely what a good client delivers, as is made abundantly clear when we turn to our first e-mail package, Eudora.

 Note: The protocol used in electronic mail transfer depends upon the direction of its routing. When you retrieve messages from your service provider, you are using Post Office Protocol, which allows you to pick up mail at a time of your choosing. When you send mail from your computer to your service provider, you are using Simple Mail Transfer Protocol; your service provider's server also uses SMTP to send mail out onto the Internet. We use two different protocols because of the nature of the connection. SMTP works best when the two computers using it are continuously available for mail processing. POP works best when mail processing and delivery occurs in queued fashion, as is necessary with a SLIP/PPP connection.

Eudora: Electronic Mail through Windows

A variety of good e-mail programs are now on the scene, but Eudora has established a commanding position thanks to its versatility and power. Originally crafted for the Macintosh, and still considered the best mail program for that platform, Eudora is available both as a commercial product and as Internet freeware. It simplifies incorporating binary files into messages and allows you to receive images and sound files as part of incoming traffic. The commercial package provides more bells and whistles—its message filtering, in particular, is excellent—but the freeware package allows you to examine Eudora's capabilities and get your feet wet with SLIP/PPP mail management. Learning to use it will be time well spent.

We have the University of Illinois at Urbana-Champaign to thank for the development of Eudora. That remarkable site (also the home of NCSA Telnet, as we'll see in Chapter 7) is a hotbed of software development. Research programmer Steve Dorner, in the university's Computing Services Office, went to work on the problem of finding a good e-mail package for campus use. But in the late 1980s, when his search began, the commercial software tended to use proprietary servers. Dorner opted to create a program of his own, called Eudora after a short story by Eudora Welty ("Why I Live at the P.O."—a sparkling tale for those who favor Welty's brand of fiction. Look in her collection *A Curtain of Green*).

Interested in developing Eudora further, Dorner joined QUALCOMM, a San Diego-based wireless communication systems provider, in 1992, from which the commercial versions of Eudora emanate. The first commercial product shipped in 1993, and a fully functional but less feature-laden freeware version continues to be made available. Even though the Microsoft Windows version of Eudora was a later development of the original Macintosh product, both platforms can use Eudora to their advantage, as is shown by the widespread popularity of this tool on the Internet. Look for future versions of the program to support increased data security and transaction features.

Where to Find Eudora

To retrieve the latest freeware version of Eudora, go to the following URL:

ftp://ftp.qualcomm.com/quest/eudora/windows/1.4

At the time of this writing, the filename was eudor144.exe. This is a self-extracting archive. You will also want to download the Eudora user's manual, which is found at the same site but in a different directory, as follows:

ftp://ftp.qualcomm.com/quest/eudora/windows/documentation

At the time of this writing, the filename was 14manual.exe, a self-extracting file.

Or, if you're in an adventurous frame of mind, you can retrieve the same materials by e-mail from QUALCOMM's list server. To do so, send a message to the following URL:

mailto://majordomo@qualcomm.com

The text should read **get freeware Win/Eudora.uu**, which will cause the server to send you a uuencoded file that must be decoded through a uudecode program. For more on uudecoding, see my book *The Internet Navigator, Second Edition* (Wiley 1994). The manual is also available in the same way, by using the message **get freeware Win/doc.uu** to the QUALCOMM server.

The freeware version of Eudora we are about to install is a powerful, full-featured mail program. It does, however, lack the useful mail filtering features that distinguish its commercial counterpart. To learn more, you can contact QUALCOMM at the following address:

QUALCOMM Inc.
6455 Lusk Blvd.
San Diego, CA 92121-2779
Voice: 619-597-5113
Fax: 619-597-5058
E-mail: **info@qualcomm.com**
ftp://ftp.qualcomm.com
http://www.qualcomm.com/quest/QuestMain.htm1

Installing and Configuring Eudora for Windows

You will need to create a directory on your PC for Eudora's files. You can do so by using the **mkdir** command from the DOS prompt or by pulling down the Windows File menu and choosing the Create Directory option. The directory name is up to you but it should be logical; *c:\eudora* works as well as anything. You can now proceed with the installation as follows:

1. Copy the Eudora executable file you have retrieved from the QUAL-COMM site into the new directory.

2. Run the executable file to unpack the Eudora software.

3. Open your autoexec.bat file in any text editor and add the following environment variable (if it does not already exist): SET TMP=C:\TMP. Here, you are setting a directory in which to store the temporary files that Eudora will create; you could give it any name you chose, but *\TMP* seems reasonable.

4. Add Eudora as a program item to a new or existing program group. Remember that you can do this in two ways: you can use Program Manager, pulling down the File menu and choosing the New option to

create a program group or add to an existing one; but the easier method is to highlight the Eudora executable file (weudora.exe) and drag it into the program group of your choice. The icon will be created automatically and you can proceed.

5. Reboot your computer, which will allow the change you made to the AUTOEXEC.BAT file to take effect.

You now need to configure Eudora for proper use. To do so, double-click on the Eudora icon to call up the program. From the Special menu, choose Configuration. You should see the screen shown in Figure 6.2.

Examine the following fields with care, as you need to modify them.

POP Account   Your electronic mail system makes use of a POP3 server, a computer that runs the Post Office Protocol discussed earlier. The POP account is where your e-mail messages go before they are transferred to your own computer. The information given you by your service provider should include a POP account address. The name should appear as a login name plus the full domain name of the computer in question; **jones@redstone.interpath.net** is an example. If you don't know what your POP Account address is, ask your service provider.

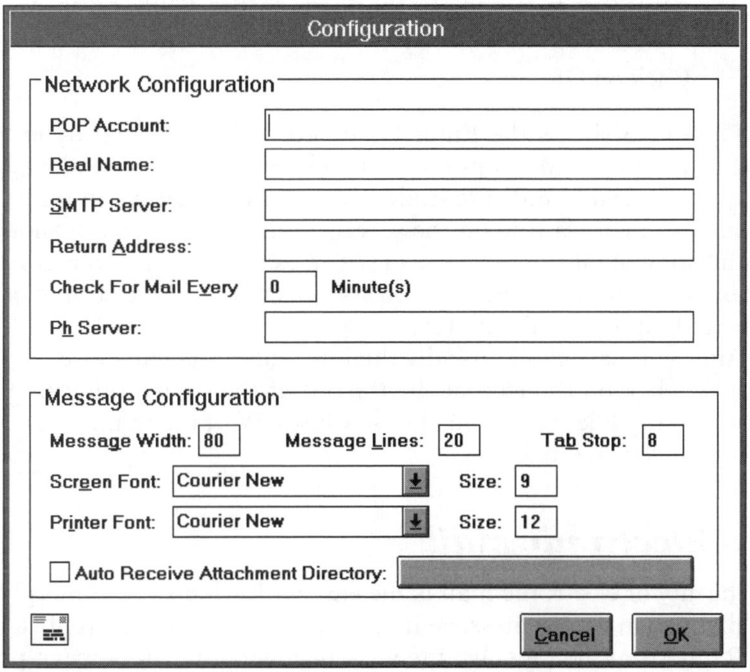

Figure 6.2   The Network Configuration menu in Eudora.

Real Name   Enter your full name in this space. It will appear in parentheses after your e-mail address in any mail you send.

SMTP Server   Enter the address of your SMTP server in this space. If your POP account appears on a computer that is also an SMTP server, this field may be left blank.

At this point, Eudora is configured for use. Click on OK.

Reading Your Mail

Remember the basic process that swings into play when you use Eudora. You are contacting a computer that runs the POP protocol (POP3 is now standard). Eudora will use the information you have just given it to log in to that server and request your mail be sent to you. It will then allow you to display a listing of your mail and read it. You can also take advantage of the program's ability to manage your incoming messages, and as you'll soon see, you have a variety of customization options.

To retrieve mail, perform the following steps:

1. Pull down the File menu and choose the Check Mail option.
2. Enter your e-mail password in the dialog box. If you don't know what your e-mail password is, contact your service provider. A password is necessary to complete the login to the POP server. And be careful about case; many passwords are case-sensitive.
3. Click on OK.

Figure 6.3 shows the Enter Password dialog box that appears when you click on the Check Mail option. You will see a Progress window appear at the top of the screen to indicate Eudora's success at logging on to the POP server. If you have mail waiting on the server, Eudora will then download it and display a listing of messages. You can see an example of this in Figure 6.4. To read a message, simply double-click on its subject line. An example of a displayed message is shown in Figure 6.5.

After you have read an individual message, you can close its window with a double-click on the icon at the top left of the screen (alternatively, you can pull down the File menu and choose Close). Working in this way, you can read through incoming mail.

Replying to Electronic Mail

The beauty of electronic mail is the ease with which you can reply to it. If you highlight a particular message in Eudora's inbox, you can reply to it by choosing Reply from the Message menu. A new window will appear, providing you with your own return address and the address of your recipient already set

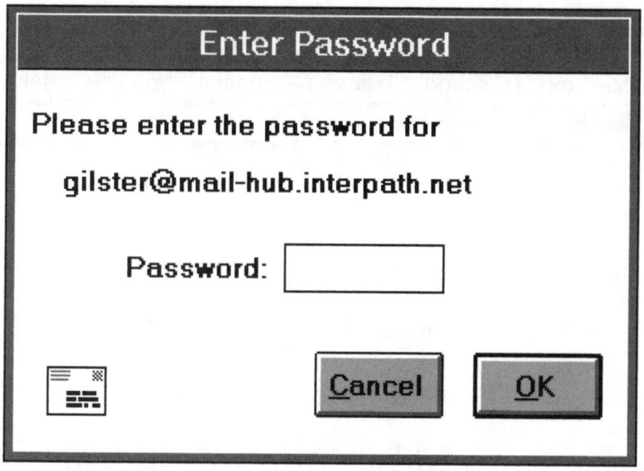

Figure 6.3 Eudora's Enter Password dialog box.

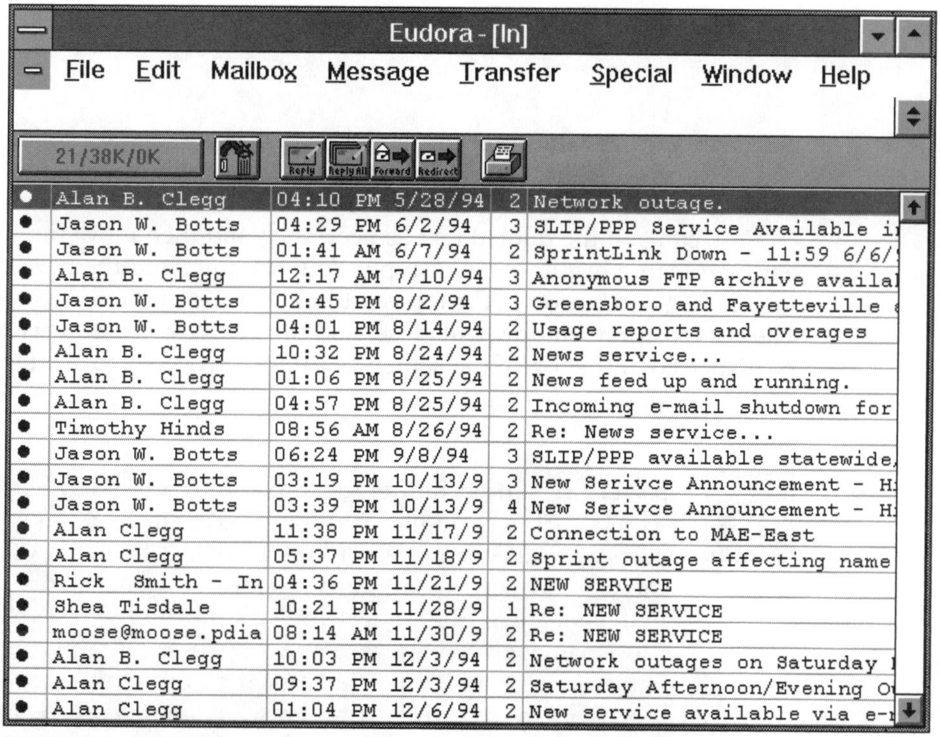

Figure 6.4 Eudora's In mailbox lists new messages by sender and subject.

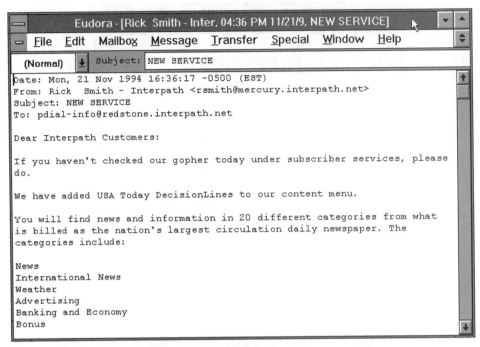

Figure 6.5 A new message being read in Eudora.

automatically into the appropriate fields. And as you can see in Figure 6.6, the text of the original message is inserted into your reply, prefixed by the > character at the beginning of each line to indicate that this is quoted text.

You can edit the quoted text as necessary, and then move the cursor to the end of it before beginning your reply. You can now send the message by clicking on the Send button in the top right-hand corner of the composition screen. The composition window will close, and the Progress window will once again be displayed at the top of the screen as Eudora proceeds to send the message.

Note: It is important to remember to be concise when using electronic mail. A good mail program makes it easy to quote from the message you have just received for clarity's sake, but in most cases, there is no need to quote the entire message before proceeding with your own. Eudora lets you edit the quoted text to choose just those passages that are germane for your reply. You can then insert your own response after the quoted material, thus making it clear what you are referring to, and also reducing your recipient's need to page through a lengthy text to find your response.

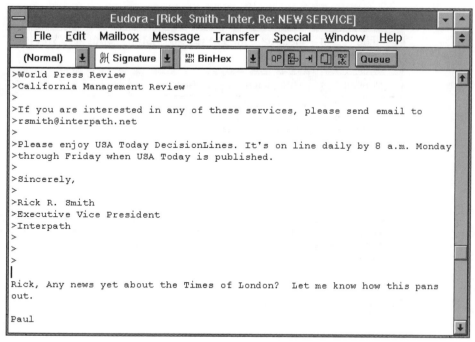

Figure 6.6   Eudora uses brackets to set off quoted text in your reply.

Creating New Messages

To write a new message, choose New Message from the Message menu. The composition window will appear, with the cursor already located in the To: field. You will also notice that your own e-mail address is automatically placed in the From: field. Type the address of the person you want to send mail to in the To: field. Then use the tab key to move the cursor into the Subject: field. Here, you can enter the subject of your message. When you move the cursor into the main composition area, you can proceed to enter your message. In Figure 6.7, you see a message in the process of composition. To send the message, simply click on the Send button. The composition window will close and the Progress window will display the sending operation.

All of this is extremely easy, but let's delve a little deeper into Eudora's bag of tricks. You will have doubtless noticed that below the Subject: field there are several other fields that we didn't use in sending this message. Each of them adds to our capabilities at sending and distributing mail. In addition, there are ways we can use the other fields that bear scrutiny. Let's talk about them one at a time.

To: We've already used this field to enter the e-mail address of the recipient. But Eudora doesn't limit us to a single person; multiple

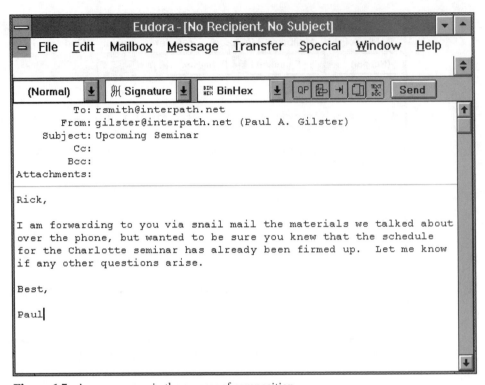

Figure 6.7 A new message in the process of composition.

addresses can be entered as long as they are separated by a comma. In addition, you can enter a nickname you have previously defined in this space. This simplifies address entry for people who are your regular correspondents. For more on nicknames, see below.

From: In most cases, this will be your POP account address followed by your real name, the information you entered when you configured Eudora. However, you can use a different return address if you choose. In my case, I maintain both a SLIP account and a Unix shell account. I get mail at both accounts, but I have found that the best way to manage my mail is to consolidate it in a single location. By adding a file called .forward to my Unix account, I am able to tell the system to forward all mail to my SLIP account. But by setting up my shell account's return address in the Return Address: field on the Configuration menu, I am able to continue to use the shell account address. This is important to me, because that's the address that goes out on the back cover of my books, and is thus more widely known.

Subject: This field contains a brief statement about the subject of your message. Unfortunately, many people fill in subject fields cursorily, leaving the reader no option but to call up the message to decide whether it is significant or not. Remember this: when you get involved in numerous electronic conversations and are subscribed to multiple mailing lists, your electronic mailbox will be frequently filled. There are times when the only way to work your way through a large block of mail (returning from a long vacation, for example) is to go through the headers and simply delete anything that does not look germane. An inscrutable subject field doesn't allow you to do this, which is why you should always be precise about what your message is about.

Cc: Enter the e-mail address of any person to whom you would like to send a copy of the outgoing message (cc = carbon copy). You can send multiple copies by entering e-mail addresses separated by commas. In most cases, this field is simply left blank.

Bcc: This field also allows you to send multiple copies of the outgoing message. But, unlike the Cc: field, any addresses that you enter into this field do not appear in the message header list of recipients. This is useful for those cases when you don't want each recipient to know who else received the message. As in the Cc: field, you can send to multiple addresses as long as they are separated by commas. This field can be left blank if you choose.

Attachments: This field lists the attachments you are sending along with the current message (see the upcoming section on attachments). You cannot enter information directly into this field; instead, you must add it through the Message menu, choosing the Attach Document option.

You will also have noticed the icon bar at the top of the new message screen. Three boxes and five buttons are provided; each of these icons provides you with the ability to control one aspect about your message. Let's go through the options now, starting from the far left side of the icon bar.

(Normal)   The Priority box allows you to indicate how important your message is. Eudora allows you to assign one of five priorities to a message, ranging from Highest Priority to Lowest Priority; you can see these if you click on the down arrow to the right of the priority box. The default is Normal. This priority information appears in the mailbox window when you receive mail from another Eudora user.

Signature   The Signature box lets you automatically attach a signature to any message you send (see the upcoming section on creating signatures). This is a useful box; many Unix mail readers, for example, allow you to automatically attach signatures, but there are times, as when contacting an automated LISTSERV, that you would prefer not to include a signature. Eudora gives you the option with each message you send.

BinHex   The Attachment type box lets you define which format you want to use for any attachments you will add to the current message. The Multipurpose Internet Mail Extensions setting is the one you will commonly use for attaching textual documents with unique formatting, or graphics, sound, or video files.

The Quoted-Printable encoding button allows you to use this feature when sending text documents that contain long lines or unique formatting (as with a foreign language). The default setting is to leave this button on.

The Word Wrap button causes text to be automatically wrapped to the following line, without your needing to insert a carriage return at the end of each line.

The Tabs in Body button allows you to control the actions created by pressing the tab key. When the button is on, hitting a tab will cause the cursor to move to the next tab stop. When off, hitting a tab will return the cursor to the To: field.

The Keep Copy button, when on, allows you to keep copies of all outgoing mail in the Out mailbox.

The Text as Document button, when on, sends attached text as a separate document. When off, any attached text will appear in the body of the message.

The Send button is used to send a message. It will appear when the Immediate Send option is turned on in the Switches dialog box.

The Queue button is used to send the message to the Out mailbox, from which it can be sent.

Using Eudora's Out Mailbox

Rather than sending your messages one at a time while you are on-line, it is frequently preferable to save them to a queue as you finish composing them. You can then send all the messages in a single burst of traffic. Those with direct network connections are less concerned about this issue than those with SLIP/PPP accounts, because their connection remains active at all times. But when you're dialing in to an account two or three times a day, you may find it easier to download your messages, read and answer them off-line, and then send your responses the next time you log in. With Eudora, this is easy.

The first step is to make a change to Eudora's configuration. As downloaded, the program is set to offer you an immediate send option for any message you compose; this is shown by the Send button that appears at the top of the composition screen. If you go to the Special menu and take the Switches option, you will be able to call up the screen shown in Figure 6.8.

Notice the Sending area within the dialog box; within it is a field marked Immediate Send, which contains an X. Click on this item to remove the X, which will disable the immediate send feature. Now, any message that you compose will contain a button marked Queue rather than one marked Send. By clicking on this button, you will be able to queue the message for later delivery. A queued message will appear with the letter Q next to it in the Out mailbox. You can call up the Out mailbox by choosing Out from the Mailbox menu. You will see a screen like the one in Figure 6.9. Here I am displaying two messages in the Out mailbox. Notice the Q next to the second one, which tells me that the message is in queue and ready for sending. To send queued messages, pull down the File menu and choose the Send Queued Messages option.

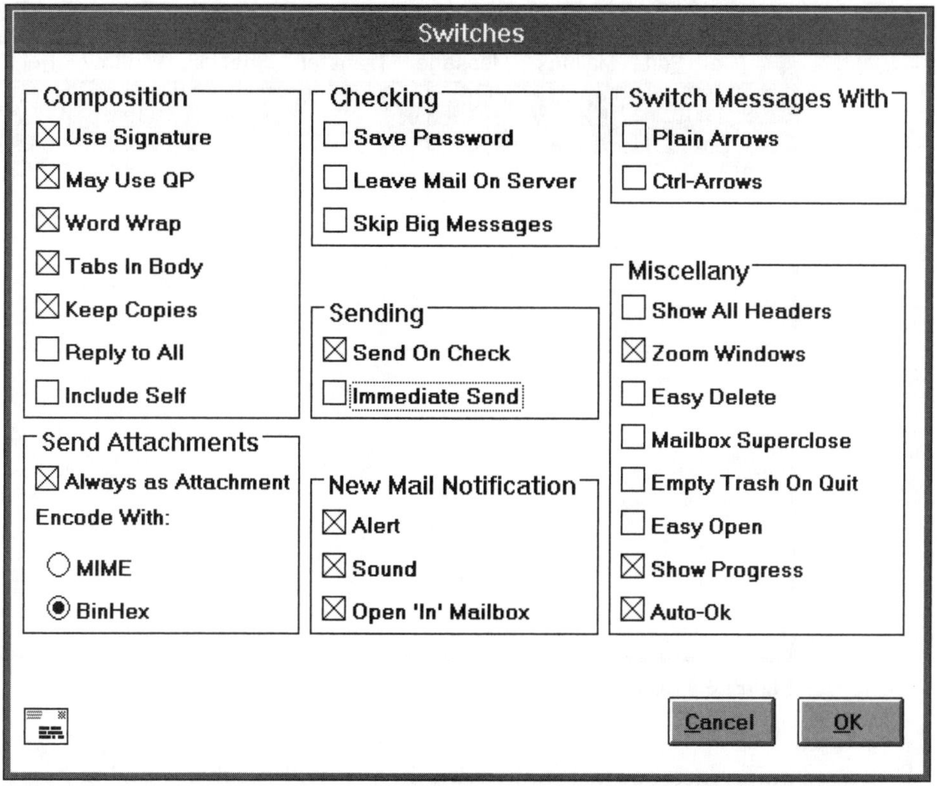

Figure 6.8 Eudora's Switches dialog box allows you to set many configuration options.

There is also a way to save messages for later editing even if you have Eudora's Immediate Send option enabled. To save mail to the Out mailbox, pull down the File menu and choose the Save option when you have finished composing. The message window will remain on-screen, but the current version of it will be stored in the Out mailbox. You have the option, then, of returning to it for subsequent editing. You can close the message by clicking on the close box at the top left of the window, or by choosing Close from the File menu.

In Figure 6.9, the first message in the Out mailbox has simply been saved (notice that it shows a bullet rather than a Q in the left-hand column). The bullet indicates that the message may be reopened before sending by calling up the Out mailbox and double-clicking on its subject field. The message can also be placed into the queue by highlighting it and choosing Queue for Delivery from the Message menu while in the Out mailbox.

All of these options may, at first, seem confusing, but you quickly get the hang of them as you work with Eudora; soon they become second nature, and I think you'll appreciate how much easier they make e-mail composition and retrieval. Eudora also keeps an eye on your work. If you try to close an out-

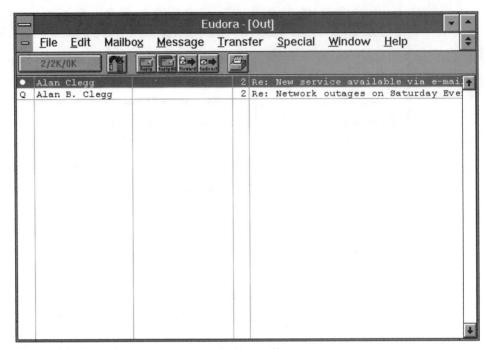

Figure 6.9   Queued messages appear in the Out mailbox.

going message without saving it, you will receive a dialog box asking if the message should be saved or discarded. Similarly, if you try to exit Eudora after queueing messages that you haven't yet sent, the program will show you a dialog box that allows you to send them before you exit. To my mind, these are the marks of an intelligently conceived mail reader, a program that assists you by anticipating your needs and preventing your mistakes.

Creating a Signature

In the network universe, a signature is an electronic text that appears at the end of any message you send. Normally, a signature takes up multiple lines, listing your name, your address, telephone number, and any other pertinent information, and perhaps a favorite quotation. The key to using a signature well is not to overdo it. Making a signature longer than five or six lines of text could be considered wasteful of bandwidth; after all, the signature is not, strictly speaking, necessary to getting the information in your message across. But it is helpful in letting people know who and where you are, and, if you so choose, in giving them some idea of your personality.

To set up a signature in Eudora, select Signature from the Window menu. A blank Signature window will appear, which you can fill in with the signature information of your choice. You can see an example of this window, with a signature inserted, in Figure 6.10.

When you close the Signature window, you will be asked whether you want to save the signature you have just created. Click on Save to do so. You now have the ability to add this signature to any outgoing mail you create. To do so, click on the Signature box on the Eudora icon bar at the top of the new message screen. You won't actually see the signature added to the message, but your recipients will receive it.

Using Nicknames with Eudora

A nickname is simply an alias, a short substitute for a perhaps lengthy e-mail address (the bane of e-mail is the length and complexity of the average address, which is why we need tools like Eudora to help make the process as transparent as possible). You can create a nickname by pulling down the Window menu and choosing the Nicknames option. Click on the New button in the Nicknames box that appears. You will see the dialog box shown in Figure 6.11.

In the New Nickname box, enter the nickname you would like to assign to a particular person. Thus, **cjhandy@mariner.syrtis.com** might be referenced by the person's first name—Carol. Click on OK. At this point, the new nick-

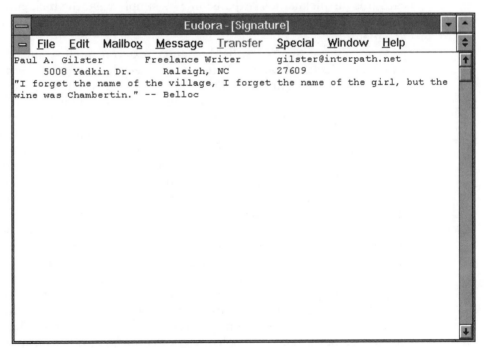

Figure 6.10 A signature window with new signature inserted.

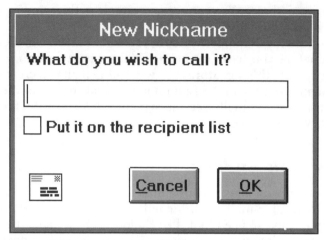

Figure 6.11 Creating a new nickname.

name will be inserted into the Nickname: field and the cursor will be placed in the Address(es): field of the Nicknames dialog box.

Enter the full address of the recipient in the Address(es) area; this will be the last time you have to remember it, at least while using Eudora. Eudora calls this the nickname's "expansion"; it's simply what the nickname refers to. Figure 6.12 shows a completed Nickname box with several nicknames already assigned.

You can use the Notes: field to enter text you might want to remember about a particular nickname. I often enter a telephone number for people I frequently talk to here, and sometimes a postal address. Whatever you choose to enter, the information will not appear in the final e-mail message.

To save the changes made in the Nicknames window, pull down the File menu and click on Save. You will find that your nicknames box soon begins to get crowded, because it is so much easier to type in a single name than an entire Internet address. But we haven't exhausted the capabilities of Eudora's nickname function quite yet. It is also possible to enter a series of e-mail addresses separated by returns in the Address(es): field. When you do so, all of these addresses are represented by a single nickname.

Here in North Carolina, for example, a journalists' group I belong to is increasingly held together by electronic mail. When it comes time for the monthly meeting, our chapter president sends e-mail to everyone in the group announcing the time and place of the gathering. All this is done by composing a single message and putting the appropriate nickname in the To: field of the outgoing message. The software then consults the nickname database and sends the message to everyone referenced by the nickname. Thus you have created a quick group mailing list; you can even enter other nicknames as part of this list.

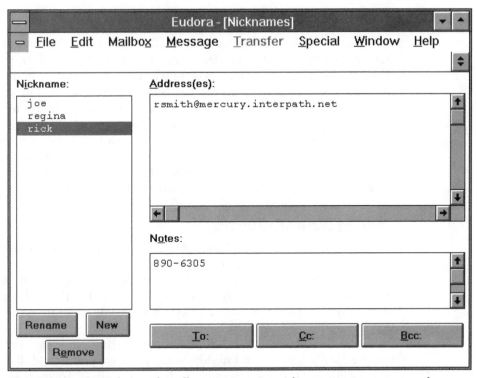

Figure 6.12 The Nicknames box allows you to assign nicknames to one or more people.

My own use of nicknames is heavily dependent upon my incoming mail. As I send more and more mail back and forth between myself and a particular correspondent, it becomes clear that making a nickname would save time in future messaging. A good way to do this is to highlight a message from the person for whom you want to make the nickname. When it is highlighted, choose Make Nickname from the Special menu. The new nickname dialog box is then displayed, allowing you to set up the nickname. If multiple messages are highlighted, the addresses from each will be put in the new nickname's expansion.

An even faster way to send messages using nicknames is to set up particular nicknames as part of the Message menu. Eudora lets you do this by double-clicking on a nickname on the Nicknames dialog box. When you do so, a check mark will appear next to the nickname you have selected, indicating it has been placed on the program's Quick Recipient list. From now on, you can move quickly to this nickname from the Message menu. Choose the New Message To option, for example, and a submenu will appear with the nicknames on your Quick Recipient list. Simply select a nickname from this list and it will appear in the outgoing message's To: field.

Mail Management

Now we come to the crux of the matter. All of the tools we've already examined allow us to create and read electronic mail with greater facility than ever before. But what we will find most powerful in Eudora are its management capabilities. We need, for example, not only to be able to read messages but to categorize them. In my own work, I receive mail about books and articles I have written, most of which I save in an archive. I would like to be able to distinguish this mail from incoming mailing list traffic. For that matter, getting onto several different mailing lists means that I receive mail on widely differing topics. I would also like to segregate this mail for later reference, particularly when I'm in a time crunch and can't read it immediately.

Creating New Mailboxes

If you're familiar with any of the Unix mail packages, even basic Unix mail, you know that each of these programs gives you the ability to group mail into different mailboxes. Eudora does the same thing, though with considerably greater versatility. By creating separate mailboxes for the different kinds of traffic you can expect, you will be able to bring some order to the chaos of your incoming mail.

The best way to do this is while reading existing mail. To do so, choose In from the Mailbox menu and highlight the message you would like to move to a new location. At this point, click on New from the Transfer menu. This will display a dialog box, as shown in Figure 6.13. You can now name the new mailbox whatever you choose. When you click on OK, the mailbox is created, and the message you have highlighted is automatically moved into it. From now on, when you pull down the Mailbox menu, the new mailbox will be one of its items; click on it to move to the mailbox.

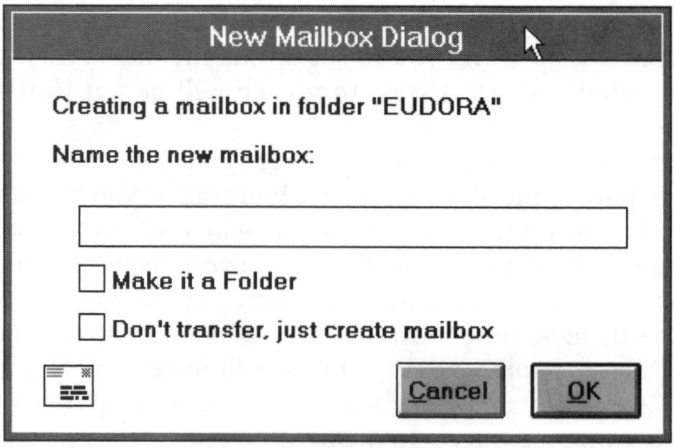

Figure 6.13   Creating a new mailbox.

To transfer messages from one mailbox to another, highlight the message you want to move and pull down the Transfer menu, which will give you the options for moving the message. A range of messages can be moved in the same way; click on the first message and use Shift-click on the last. If your selections are not continuous, you can use Control-click on specific messages. When you're ready to move the messages, select the recipient mailbox from the Transfer menu and click on it.

Creating Mail Folders

Eudora doesn't stop with the creation of new mailboxes. The program also lets you create folders within which you can store your information. A folder is a broader category than a mailbox; any folder can contain one or more mailboxes. For that matter, a single folder may hold mailboxes as well as other folders, which themselves hold mailboxes inside. Using Eudora's folders in combination with individual mailboxes, you can set up the kind of information categorization you need to keep track of multiple mailing lists and numerous correspondents.

Creating folders is simple. From the Mailbox menu, choose New, which will result in the appearance of the dialog box shown in Figure 6.13. This time, not only give the mailbox a name, but also click on the box marked Make it a Folder. Clicking on OK will then create that folder. The name of the new folder will now appear on both the Mailbox menu and the Transfer menu as another menu choice. In addition, you will see an arrow to the right of the name, which designates it as a folder rather than a mailbox. Messages can't be transferred into folders per se; they have to be sent to mailboxes within folders. You will, therefore, be prompted for a new mailbox to create within your new folder. Enter its name and click on OK.

In the future, as you choose to add new mailboxes to a particular folder, you can select that folder from the Mailbox menu and choose New from the ensuing submenu. The new mailbox dialog box will be displayed, allowing you to create the mailbox or nested folder of your choice.

Mailbox Management on the Fly

I am obsessed with the issue of organization. Indeed, anyone who gets involved with the Internet with the intention of tapping it as a learning experience can't help but focus on this issue. What the Internet does well is to offer massive amounts of information in every possible digital form. What it does poorly is to arrange and categorize that information so that it is possible to track it down or, once found, to tap it meaningfully—this is why we need all the help we can get in the form of good software. The ideal mail reader helps us bring order to incoming mail traffic, just as it makes it easy to weed out the material we really don't have time to consider.

My view of mailbox organization is that it should proceed on the fly. Sure, it's possible to start with an overarching structure that you impose on your mail habits, trying to fit everything into it as new messages arrive. But this method is ultimately unproductive; it assumes that your needs are static, and that you can anticipate what you will want to see in the future (a poor assumption, given the malleable nature of network activity). So I began with only one assumption: that I would need to keep up with my everyday mail traffic by answering incoming messages the same day they arrived. Everything else followed from that guiding principle.

It took only a few days before it became clear that I would need to separate personal messages from mailing list traffic. Like USENET newsgroups, of which there are over 11,000 at the time of this writing, mailing lists are discussions about particular topics, often extremely focused in content. The differences are several; mailing lists, because of their roots in the academic community through the university-oriented network called BITNET, are often attended primarily by specialists, which makes them a superb teaching tool for anyone interested in a digital, post-graduate seminar on virtually any subject under the sun (not all of them, it should be added, are academic). The other major difference between mailing lists and the USENET newsgroups is that mailing lists are distributed through e-mail. You receive message traffic in your mailbox.

Note: How do you sign up for a mailing list? By sending electronic mail to the mailing list address and requesting entrance onto the list. For example, I am a subscriber to the Anglo-Saxon mailing list, which is a discussion area for people interested in the early medieval period in England and, in particular, the Anglo-Saxon language, which preceded Middle English. To subscribe, I sent mail to this address:

ansaxnet-request@wvnvm.wvnet.edu

In my message, I simply requested that I be added to the list. I found the correct address by consulting Stephanie da Silva's Publicly Accessible Mailing Lists, which is regularly posted on the USENET newsgroups **news.answers**, **news.lists**, and **news.announce.newusers**. You should consult the da Silva list (it's a lengthy, multipart document) to get an idea for how many intriguing lists are out there, and how to contact them.

Now this can lead to considerable congestion, because some mailing lists are densely populated, producing hundreds of messages in a given week. My first job, then, was to create a category for my work in Anglo-Saxon language and literature. I therefore set up a folder called Anglo-Saxon, and within it created two mailboxes: Prose and Poetry. Most of the message traffic that came across the list was not material I planned to save, but I would occasionally find items I wanted to consider at greater length, and some I knew I would want to keep in an archive. So as these items appeared, I would save them to one of these two mailboxes, using the methods just described.

Organizing on the fly quickly brought more mailbox and folder choices. As an inveterate fan of movies—and in particular, old movies, from the late 1920s to the mid-1950s—I became caught up in discussions on the Cinema Discussion List. Using an automated server called a LISTSERV, the list was distributed to the mailboxes of subscribers in the same way as the Anglo-Saxon list. I therefore set up a Cinema mailbox to handle archive-worthy messages on Humphrey Bogart, Clark Gable, and other greats from the golden era of the screen. Note that I set this up as a mailbox, not a folder, the reason being that there were no subcategories branching off from it that required further choices.

And so it went. I soon added a Music folder, with branching mailboxes to cover a classical music mailing list, and a separate list that discussed musical form and function. A Science Fiction folder branched off to mailboxes on the latest books, Star Trek comments, and an electronically distributed magazine. And because the volume of incoming personal mail was growing, I set up separate categories for mail from readers, one for each of my books. This turned out to be a productive tool, since several sharp-eyed readers have become not only good on-line friends, but also excellent proofreaders, finding the various errata that need correction in future editions.

Deleting Messages

Of course, there always comes the time when you realize that your mailboxes are simply too stuffed with material that you'll probably not get around to reading again. To delete a message in Eudora is a two-step process. The software handles it this way for safety's sake; you'd hate to delete a message only to realize ten minutes later that it contained a valuable address or a comment you had intended to save. Thus, when you choose Delete from the Message menu, the current message is not actually deleted, but is sent to the Trash mailbox. You won't see it in the current mailbox, but if you need it back, you can switch to the Trash mailbox and handle it just as you would in any other mailbox. The difference is, when you delete the message from the Trash mailbox, it stays deleted. To do this, select Empty Trash from the Special menu. If you want to delete selected messages only from the Trash mailbox, use Delete from the Message menu. In either case, the message is now gone.

Renaming and Removing Mailboxes and Folders

Packrats like me are forever reorganizing, searching for the perfect solution to our information management problems. That means there comes a time when a particular mailbox just has to go, and another needs to be renamed. In the meantime, I'd like to throw away a particular folder and subsume its tasks within another one. How to achieve this result?

Renaming either mailboxes or folders is a simple matter. First, open the Mailboxes window by pulling down the Windows menu and clicking on Mailboxes. You can see the result in Figure 6.14. Here we have a mailbox and folder management window that allows us to perform the needed tasks quickly; my current folders and mailboxes are shown here. To rename a mailbox, for example, click on that mailbox to highlight it (you can click on it in either window; you don't need to click on both). Then click on the Rename button located below the list. This will produce a dialog box that allows you to enter the new name of your mailbox. Renaming folders is done in exactly the same way.

To remove a mailbox or folder, the same method is used. Pull down the Windows menu, choose Mailboxes, and highlight the folder or mailbox you want to delete. Then click on the Remove button that is located beneath the list. A dialog box will appear to confirm your decision to delete the selected item. Clicking on Remove It will cause the deletion to be effected. You can perform these actions on more than a single mailbox by holding down the Ctrl key while selecting the mailboxes and folders you want to delete. Eudora will then proceed through the items one at a time, asking you in each case whether you are sure you want to proceed. You will also have the option of removing all items without further prompts from the program.

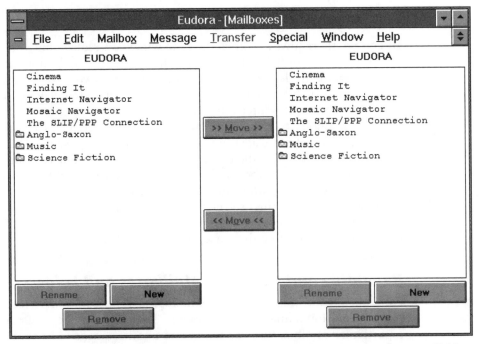

Figure 6.14 The Mailboxes window allows you to move, delete, or rename mailboxes and folders.

It's likely that you will have messages in one or more of the mailboxes you decide to delete, so be sure to move anything that you want to keep to a new site. But if you're sure that you've already salvaged everything you intend to, you can delete either folders or mailboxes along with all the messages inside them. Eudora will prompt you to confirm your decision. This can come in handy when you decide to obliterate an entire category of messages as, for instance, when you log off a mailing list, having decided that its messages weren't as interesting as you had hoped they would be. A single command can remove the entire folder and all mailboxes within it.

Moving Mailboxes within Folders

If you examine Figure 6.14 again, you'll see that it also contains provisions for moving your mailboxes from one folder to another. Suppose, for example, that I choose to move my mail from readers to a separate folder. As is, I have set up mailboxes for each of my books. I would like to create a folder called Books, and place all of the current book-related mailboxes into it. To do so, I first move to the In mailbox and pull down the Mailbox menu, choosing New to create a new folder. I enter the name, Books, and click on the Make it a Folder box. When I do so, as shown earlier, Eudora creates the folder and asks me to create at least one mailbox within it. I enter the name of that mailbox, The Internet Navigator, after the title of my first book. I then remove the mailbox called The Internet Navigator from my list, since I have already created another mailbox with that title in the Books folder.

Now I can go back to the Mailboxes window. By clicking on the Books folder to select it, I change the display to show the contents of that folder. I can then move to the list of mailboxes and folders on the right and select the mailboxes I want to move. I hold down the Ctrl key while selecting each. By clicking on the Move button, I send them into their new folder. You can see this process in action in Figure 6.15. Here, I have highlighted the mailboxes to be moved. The Move button with left-facing arrows is then darkened, indicating it is ready to be used. When I click on it, the mailboxes are moved to the new folder.

As I work through my mail, I can put these mailboxes to use, but always sparingly. Once you have organized your mail environment, the temptation is to begin shuffling e-mail right and left, saving far more than you really need. I have found in my own work that the best procedure is to work through my In mailbox a message at a time, replying as necessary, and discarding with a fairly ruthless regard for what is of lasting value. Only those messages with clear significance, such as mailing list postings with valuable background materials, go into a folder. I also save all comments about my books for future reference as I look to correct typos and update addresses. Even with this approach, my Eudora-driven database of e-mail messages is becoming a significant consumer of disk space.

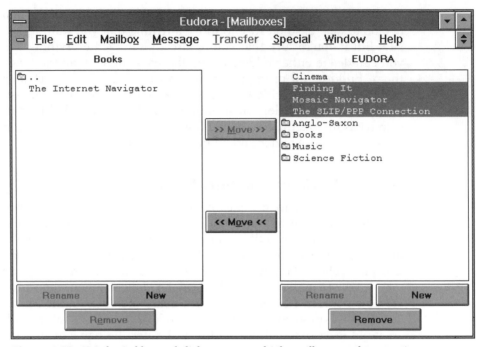

Figure 6.15   Use the Ctrl key and click to move multiple mailboxes at the same time.

Finding People with Ph and Finger

Ever inscrutable, the Internet offers up two means of finding information about people through Eudora: Ph and Finger. Ph, in fact, has an interesting history in this context: it was created by Steve Dorner, the talented author of Eudora itself. The program is useful for looking up a person at a particular location, a task at which it excels. Unfortunately, Ph is in this respect like most other Internet tools for finding people, in that it is functional only at a particular site. To use it well, therefore, you need to already know where the person you are looking for is likely to be found, and your mail server must, in any case, be equipped to handle a Ph search.

Finger is a Unix program that hunts down users and is, by comparison, wide-reaching. Here again, you are faced with a serious limitation; to use finger you must know the name of the host machine where your target person has an account. But if you possess this information, you can quickly check to see whether that person is on-line, and can call up whatever data that person has made available through the finger system. By creating files called .plan and .project, for example, a user can list information about current activities, office hours, or personal habits. And some sites, like **quake@geophys.washington.-edu**, produce information of a specialized nature on a variety of topics when fingered.

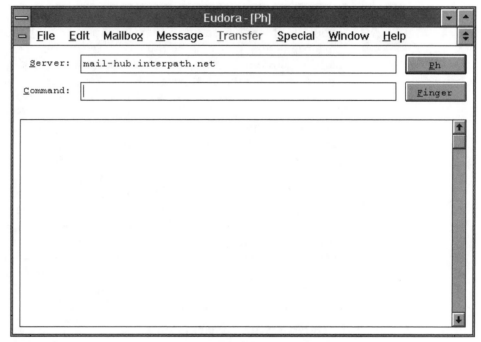

Figure 6.16 The Ph dialog box allows you to choose between finger and Ph searches.

To use either of these services, choose Ph from the Window menu. You will see the dialog box shown in Figure 6.16. As you can see, the dialog box includes buttons for both finger and Ph. The method here is to type the name of the server you want to consult in your search; the default entry is taken from the information you entered when you configured Eudora. The name of the person you are trying to find is then entered in the Command field. Click on Ph or finger to begin the search.

Let's suppose I want to see finger information for Jason Botts, who works at my service provider's site here in Raleigh. I know that his address is **bottsjw@mercury.interpath.net**. I set up the search according to the methods specified above, placing the server information (**mercury.interpath.net**) in the Server field, and the user name (bottsjw) in the Command field (yes, it is confusing to have this field called "Command"; "Query" might have been a better choice). Clicking on the finger button to begin the search, I soon receive the information shown in Figure 6.17.

As you can see, I retrieve a bit of information about Jason, such as when he last logged in, and the fact that he currently has no unread mail. I also see, in the Project field:, that his occupation is listed as Technical Support Manager for CIS/Interpath, my service provider. In the Plan: field, he has set up information about how to reach Interpath.

Note: For the insatiably curious, here's a little more information about ph. If you have a bit of Internet experience, chances are you have been using ph for some time, or at least have been in contact with it, without realizing it. That's because a ph server is also known as a CSO server. CSO stands for Computing Services Office, which is the organization at the University of Illinois at Urbana-Champaign that developed the tool. As mentioned, Steve Dorner was part of this development. Technically, the database itself is what is called the CSO. On the server, a program called qi handles information requests. The client program is ph; it, of course, is what you use to send requests to the server for data.

The CSO system has largely flourished in the academic environment, so that you will find most sites at universities. And because it has become so widespread, it is now available through a variety of client programs for the Windows-based PC as well as the Macintosh and other clients. Many of the programs now used to access the net, like Mosaic and Gopher, also contain ph capabilities, making it available to a broad number of users. You can get more information about ph at the following URLs:

ftp://ftp.wfu.edu/usenet/ph-FAQ

gopher://gopher.wfu.edu/Computer information/USENET News Information maintained by Wake Forest/ph-FAQ

http://www.wfu.edu/Computer-information/Usenet-News-information-maintained by Wake Forest/ph-FAQ

What you retrieve when you look at someone's finger information depends upon what they have decided to include in their files. Some people go to great length with the .plan and .project files, giving you several pages of information, for example, about their travel schedule over the coming year, and so forth. Others include whimsical quotations or comments about their work. Take a look at the finger information about Daniel Dern, a highly regarded author of Internet books and articles, shown in Figure 6.18. Daniel has included address and contact information in his Plan: field. He also adds a pointer to the area he maintains on the Gopher server at internet.com, where you can, he suggests, pick up your Internet learner's permit. The site is a good one to check, especially for newcomers to the net, as it's packed with good material. You'll want to explore it once you get a Gopher client up and running, as you will in Chapter 9.

While it has not been widely used as a source of broader information, finger is nonetheless in active service at some sites to provide specific data. After all, you can set up a server to send out any kind of information you choose with

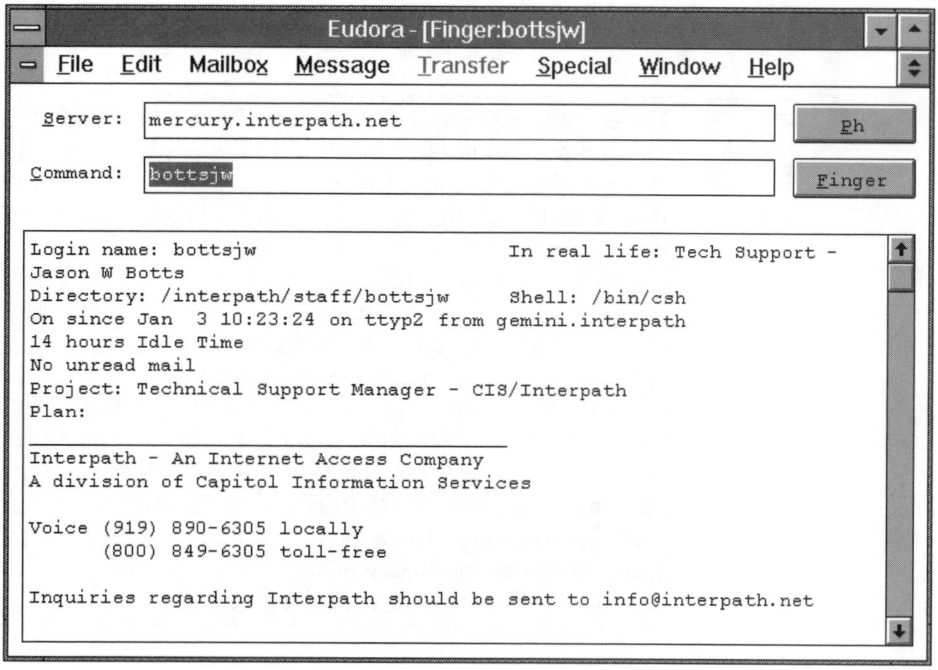

Figure 6.17 Results of a finger search with Eudora.

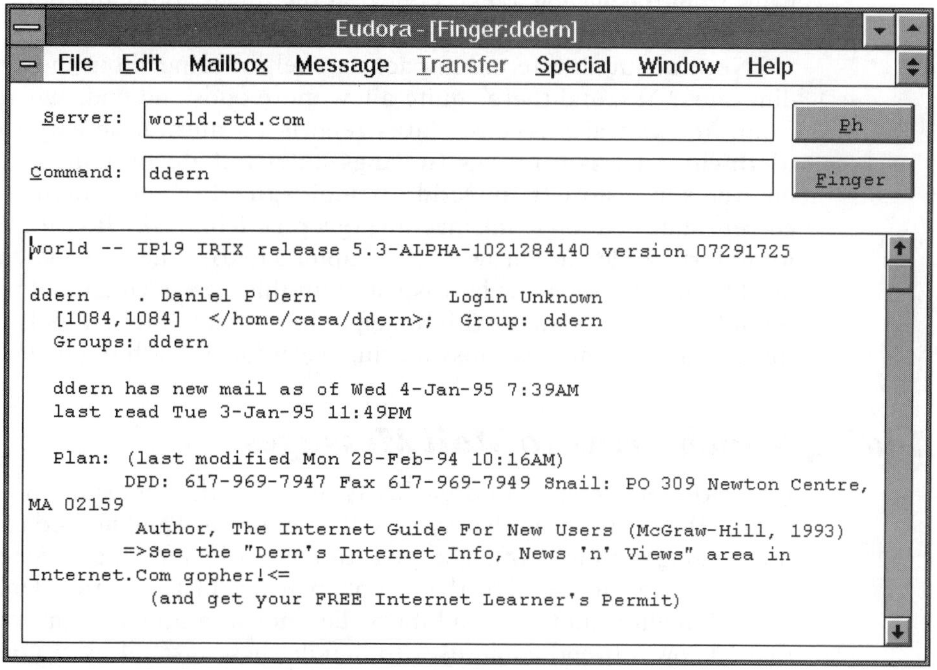

Figure 6.18 finger information can include background information about your work and anything else you want to add.

Note: As you can see, finger can be used to display information about a particular user. But what's the real value of this tool, given that you have to know the address and login of the person you are trying to finger in the first place? Clearly, finger isn't a search engine, but you may find yourself using it to puzzle out various anomalies in your Internet work. For example, suppose you have sent e-mail to a normally responsive contact for the last several days, and have received no reply. You'd like to know whether that person has actually received your messages. As you can see in Figure 6.18, finger can tell you whether a particular person has unread mail. And if your correspondent has been diligent about noting personal plans, you may also see a note telling you that he or she is currently out of the office until a certain date. Not a major Internet tool, it's true, but finger is surprisingly useful at those moments when no other method will work. And as you'll see shortly, it can also be used to retrieve other kinds of data.

this method. If, therefore, you are simply trying to make particular news available to anyone you choose, finger makes for a quick alternative to Telnet and FTP. In Figure 6.19, I have entered the name of a NASA server that provides news from the agency. When I click on the finger command button, I receive the result shown.

News about an asteroid impact that helped bring about the demise of the dinosaurs? Yes, and there's quite a few more odds and ends where this came from. You can also receive status reports on auroral activity (**aurora@xi.-uleth.ca**), television ratings (**normg@halcyon.halcyon.com**), daily updates on events in history (**copi@oddjob.uchicago.edu**), and even news about the current state of a soft drink machine (**graph@drink.csh.rit.edu**). When we get into World Wide Web browers in Chapter 11, you'll also see how they can be used to monitor a particular dispenser, in this case, a coffee pot whose image is continuously updated. With finger, as in so many Internet tools of the trade, there is an element of whimsy lurking never far beneath the surface.

Adding Attachments to Mail Messages

Let's close our look at Eudora for Windows with a consideration of attachments. How many times have you written a message and needed to send something along with it? I often work with editors by e-mail and need to write a cover message, followed by the text of an article I have written. On other occasions, I might want to send a binary file, such as a utility program I've located that I know a friend could use. To handle these tasks, I use Eudora's attachment capabilities.

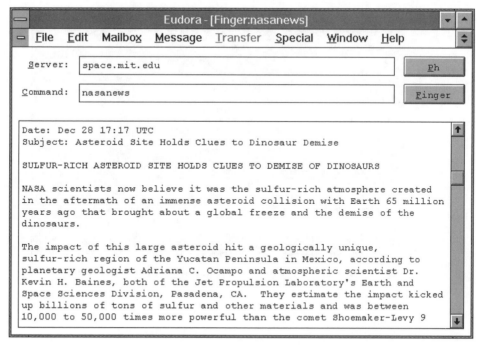

Figure 6.19 Using finger to tap into an information site provided by NASA.

Suppose I want to add a document from my hard disk to a new message. After writing the text I want to include in my initial message, I pull down the Message menu and click on Attach Document to proceed. Eudora then displays a dialog box that allows me to find the file in question. You can see this dialog box in Figure 6.20.

Find the file on your hard disk that you want to include and select it in the dialog box. When you do, its name will be inserted in the Attachments: field of your new message (if you attempt it, you will find that you cannot attach a document by editing the Attachments: line yourself; you must go through the insertion process as described). The attachment will be added to your message, and does not appear inside the message text you see on-screen. Multiple attachments can be sent in the same way. In Figure 6.21, you can see a message with attachment already inserted into the Attachments: field.

To send a binary file, click on the Attachment Type combo box at the top of the new message screen. When you add an ASCII document to a mail message, it is sent without any special encoding. But when you click on the Attachment Type box, you can choose between MIME and BinHex to select the format for outgoing messages. Choosing MIME allows you to use the Internet standard for encoding data through the electronic mail system.

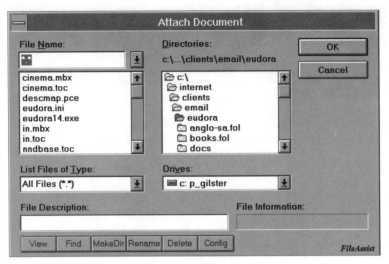

Figure 6.20   Choosing a document to attach to a Eudora mail message.

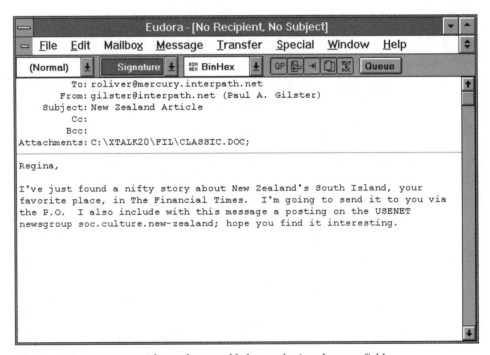

Figure 6.21   A message with attachment added; note the Attachments: field.

Including attachments in messages is a useful feature, to be sure, but Eudora is stuffed with so many helpful and time-saving devices that we haven't the time to go into them all. I strongly recommend this program to anyone in need of better mail management (and who isn't?). The commercial version's message filtering capabilities will probably tempt you as well; be sure to evaluate them in making a final decision about which program to use.

Pegasus Mail for Windows

The electronic mail world is an interesting one from the perspective of software, in that two excellent programs, Eudora and Pegasus Mail, are free (although Eudora also exists in a commercial version, as you've just seen). Pegasus Mail, written by David Harris, is a powerful e-mail program designed for use in both the Novell Netware and Winsock environments. You can find the latest version at the following URL:

ftp://risc.ua.edu/pub/network/pegasus/

At the time of this writing, the filename was pmail311.zip.

While Harris does not ask for money for Pegasus ("I give Pegasus Mail away for a number of reasons, very few of them logical," he writes in the documentation for his program), he does sell manuals to help offset development costs. You can reach him at the following address:

David Harris
P. O. Box 5451
Dunedin, New Zealand
Voice: +64 3 453 6880
Fax: +64 3 453 6612
E-mail: **david@pmail.gen.nz**

Among the program's innovative features is a user guide created with a program Harris created called David's Readme Compiler; it allows developers to take text files and compile them into a single executable file that can be used with the program. David's Readme Compiler is likewise free and available at the same site as Pegasus Mail.

Unpack the compressed Pegasus Mail file into a suitable directory. When you have done so, you can drag the winpmail.exe file to the program group of your choice, which will create the distinctive winged horse icon that denotes Pegasus. Double-click on the icon to call the program to the screen. Installation involves giving Pegasus Mail information about your system and its configuration. This will allow the program to manage the necessary files to store and manage your mail.

You will be prompted for a user name. Enter the name of your choice; the name is provided so that Pegasus Mail can identify your home mailbox. After entering the user name, you will be presented with the dialog box shown in Figure 6.22. Fill in these fields as follows:

Home mail path This is the path to the directory in which your home mail folder will be located. You can see that Pegasus Mail supplies a suggestion here, but you can select the directory of your choice. The ~8 statement stands for the first eight letters of your user name; Pegasus Mail inserts the proper value before it uses the path (allowing the program to separate mail from different users who are using the same machine).

Your user name The name you have chosen for Pegasus Mail to identify you. This name should not include spaces or special characters.

Save your user-name in WIN.INI If you are the only person using your computer for electronic mail (which is likely to be the case for SLIP/PPP users anyway), you can click on this option to insert your user name in the win.ini file that Windows uses to initialize itself. This will prevent Pegasus Mail from asking you for a user name every time you call up the program.

Pegasus Mail will now supply you with the mail screen, as shown in Figure 6.23. Your first step is to make sure that Pegasus knows it is working with Winsock. To ensure that it does, pull down the File menu and take the Preferences option. Choose Advanced Settings from the submenu. You will see a dialog box like the one in Figure 6.24. Note the field in the lower part of the screen

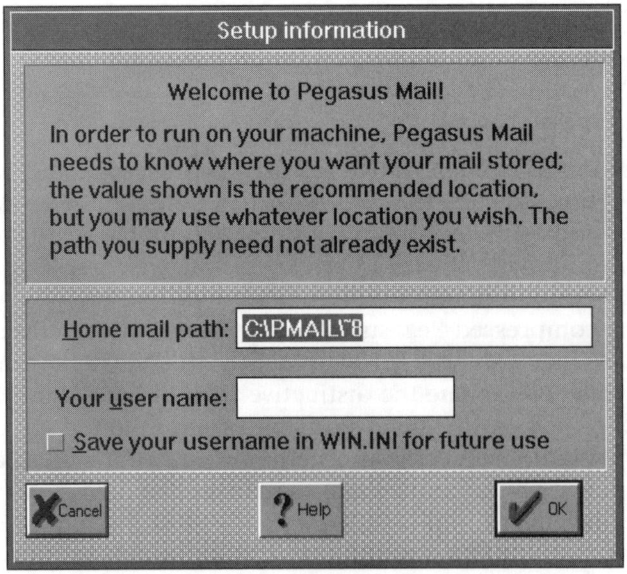

Figure 6.22 Configuring Pegasus Mail.

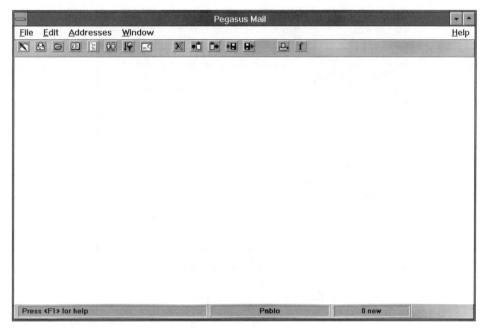

Figure 6.23 The main screen in Pegasus Mail.

marked "If WINSOCK.DLL is available, load it -," followed by several options. Be sure to click on the Always option. You should then click on OK and, finally, exit Pegasus Mail. Now double-click on the Pegasus icon once again. This time, when it loads, Pegasus will be configurable for a Winsock connection, with new menu items added within the File menu.

To configure it for Winsock, again pull down the File menu. Click on Network Configuration. You will see the screen shown in Figure 6.25. You must now fill in the appropriate fields. Here are the ones in which you need to insert values:

TCP/IP socket timeout value

This value determines how long Pegasus Mail will wait for a response before deciding that a problem has occurred. David Harris recommends setting this value higher than the default of 15; he suggests a value of 45. The default assumes a fast Ethernet connection, which operates at speeds far higher than those achieved by SLIP/PPP.

Relay host

This field should contain the address of your SMTP server. Remember, when using a SLIP/PPP connection, you send mail to the server via the SMTP protocol, while retrieving it via the POP protocol.

From field:

This is the address that will appear in the From: field of your outgoing messages.

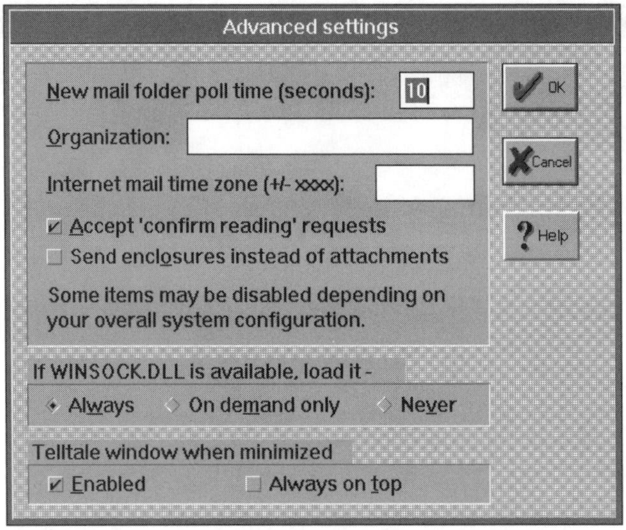

Figure 6.24   The Advanced Settings dialog box. Make sure the
Always option in the winsock.dll field is selected.

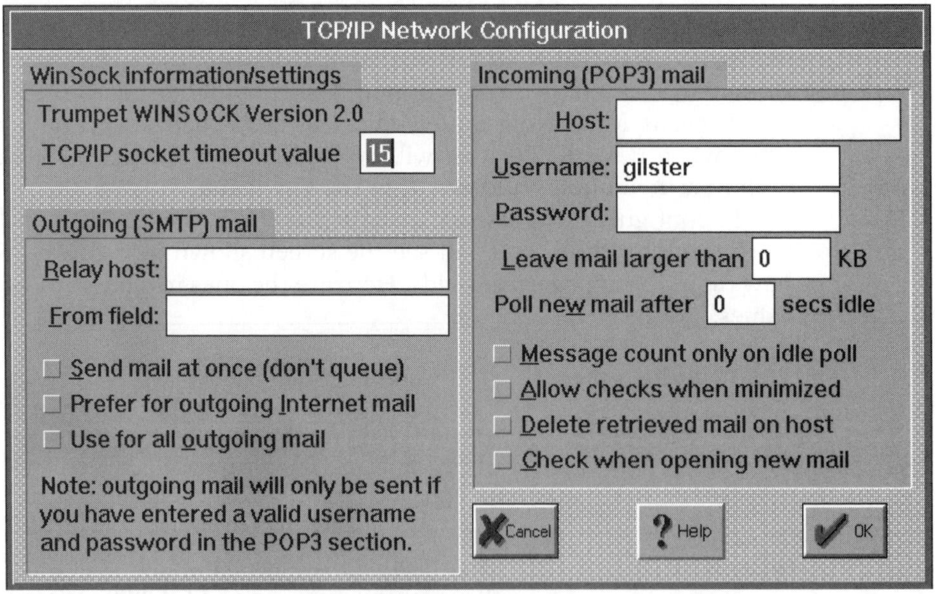

Figure 6.25   Configuring Pegasus Mail for your SLIP/PPP connection.

Send mail at once (don't queue)	When activated, this switch will cause mail to be sent as soon as you click the Send button in the message editor. When it is not activated, Pegasus Mail will queue your messages for delivery.
Use for all outgoing mail	When activated, this setting passes all outgoing mail to the SMTP server. SLIP/PPP users, who are likely to be the only ones using their machines, should check this box. Otherwise, Pegasus Mail will assume that any address entered without a domain portion is local to your machine.
Host:	This is the name of the POP account you access to retrieve your mail. If you have any doubts about what to enter here, ask your service provider.
Username:	This is the name of your POP account. Note that the username is already filled in when you call up this dialog box; it should contain the name you entered earlier in the configuration process.
Password:	The password for your account on the POP server. Both this and the username information should be in the materials given you by your service provider when you set up your account.
Delete mail retrieved on host	When checked, this setting will delete mail on your service provider's host computer after it has been successfully downloaded to your machine. If you leave the box unchecked, mail will remain on the server after you have downloaded it, and will appear every time you download mail.
Check when opening new mail	This setting, when activated, checks the host for new mail every time you click on the New Mail button from the button panel. If you do not activate it, you must check for new mail by clicking on the Check host for new mail item on the File menu.

Having filled in these settings, you have properly configured Pegasus Mail for use. But you still need to fill in several important preferences. To do so, pull down the File menu and click on the Preferences item; from the possibilities listed there, choose General Settings. You will see the dialog box shown in Figure 6.26. Most of the settings may be safely left in their default state. However, you do need to fill in one and possibly two of these fields:

Personal name	The name you enter here will be appended to your address when you send mail.
Default reply address	This address will be copied to the reply-to field of every outgoing message you send. In most cases, you can safely leave it blank. But if you often receive mail on a system different than the one you are using (unlikely for most SLIP/PPP users, but possible), then enter the address here.

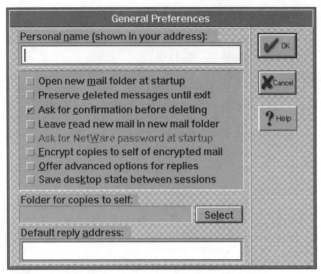

Figure 6.26 Finishing Pegasus Mail configuration with the General Settings dialog box.

Space simply doesn't permit going into Pegasus Mail as deeply as I would prefer. Suffice it to say that the program is a compelling alternative to Eudora; in fact, I would recommend that you evaluate both and make the decision based upon your own inclinations. In many ways, Pegasus is the more intuitive of the two programs. In Figure 6.27, for example, you can see a message being read in Pegasus Mail. What I like about this screen presentation is that the major tasks are conveniently assigned to easy-to-read buttons at the top of the screen. You will also notice how easy it is to move back and forth between retrieved messages by clicking on the Prev and Next buttons at the top right of the box.

Also outstanding in Pegasus Mail are built-in filtering options that allow you to perform a variety of actions upon incoming mail, such as automatic distribution to a particular mailbox or forwarding to another address. Pegasus Mail also sports a useful help system that makes most mail operations easy to figure out even without the user manual (although if you do become a Pegasus Mail regular, I recommend sending for the manual, as David Harris uses proceeds from it to fund his continuing development of the program).

E-Mail Alternatives for the PC

Both Eudora and Pegasus Mail provide full e-mail functionality, but development continues among both commercial and shareware companies interested in tapping this market. In particular, John Junod, the developer of the WS_FTP program we've already examined, has written a program called Imail (origi-

Figure 6.27   Reading a message in Pegasus Mail.

nally WS_Gmail), which is now a commercial product available through Ip-switch Inc. You can retrieve a demonstration version from the following URL:

ftp://ftp.ipswitch.com/pub/imail/

At the time of this writing, the filename was imail.zip, which represented version 1.07.24. The program provides MIME capability, but does not include BinHex or uuencode features.

Another option is RFD Mail, a program that contains interesting features for those whose modem use is not limited to SLIP/PPP connections. Using RFD Mail, you can log on to a wide variety of commercial networks and bulletin board systems through an extensive scripting capability. The program is shareware, and is available through the following URL:

ftp://ftp.std.com/customers/software/rfdmail/

At the time of this writing, the filename was rfdmail.zip, which represented version 1.23. While version 1.23 does not support either MIME or uudecoding, the upcoming version 2.0, which should be available by the time you read this, will handle both. What I like best about RFD Mail are its drag and drop capabilities, which simplify message distribution throughout your folder system (the commercial version of Eudora is also moving in this direction).

Electronic Mail on the Macintosh

What's this? Only a tiny section on electronic mail programs for the Mac? The reason is that the choice for Macintosh users is clear. Eudora is an even better program in the Macintosh environment than it is when running under Windows. And because most of the basic features of Eudora have already been discussed, I don't need to go into great detail with anything beyond the installation of the program. To retrieve the freeware version of the program, go to the following URL:

ftp://ftp.qualcomm.com/quest/mac/eudora/2.0/

At the time of this writing, the filename was eudora203.hqx; there is also a version for the Power Macintosh called eudora203.fat.hqx. Drag the file icon to the StuffIt Expander icon to decompress it. You can now begin your Eudora configuration by clicking on the Eudora icon. The menu we will focus on is the Special menu.

Eudora Configuration

When you choose the Configuration option from the Special menu, you will see the screen shown in Figure 6.28. Here are the fields you need to fill in to use the program:

POP Account	This is the name of your account on your service provider's POP3 mail server. It should be entered as a user name followed by a domain, as in **dwoskin@mail-hub.iac.net**.
Real Name	Your full name. The name you enter here will appear on all outgoing e-mail messages.
Connection Method	Click the MacTCP button to enable Eudora to use your SLIP/PPP account to the Internet.
SMTP Server	The name of your mail server. If you have any questions as to what this address is, consult your service provider. This information should have been provided when you first set up your account.
Return Address	Enter the e-mail address of your account here. Normally, this will be the same address as the one you entered in the POP account field, but it does not have to be; if you maintain multiple accounts, you can enter the name of your other account here if that is where you choose to receive mail.
Check for Mail Every	The value you enter here determines how frequently Eudora looks in your mailbox to retrieve mail. If you intend to retrieve mail manually, you should leave this box empty.

Ph Server   A Ph server can help you find user information about a particu-
                             lar person, as long as you already know where he or she is
                             located. But to use Ph facilities, your mail server must provide
                             that capability. If it does not, or if you are not sure, you can leave
                             this field blank.

Dialup Username   For SLIP/PPP work, leave this field blank.

The rest of the fields are optional, but provide useful tools if you are interested in customizing Eudora.

Message Window   Eudora uses a message width default of 80 characters, which
Width   should prove adequate for normal use.

Message Window   The default value for Eudora's message display is to show 20
Height   lines of text. You can change that value if you want to see
                             more or less text at a time.

Screen Font   The font you choose to view mail messages in can be set from
                             this pop-up menu.

Size   The font size for e-mail message display.

Print Font   The font used to print e-mail messages is selectable from this
                             pop-up menu.

Size   The font size for printing e-mail messages.

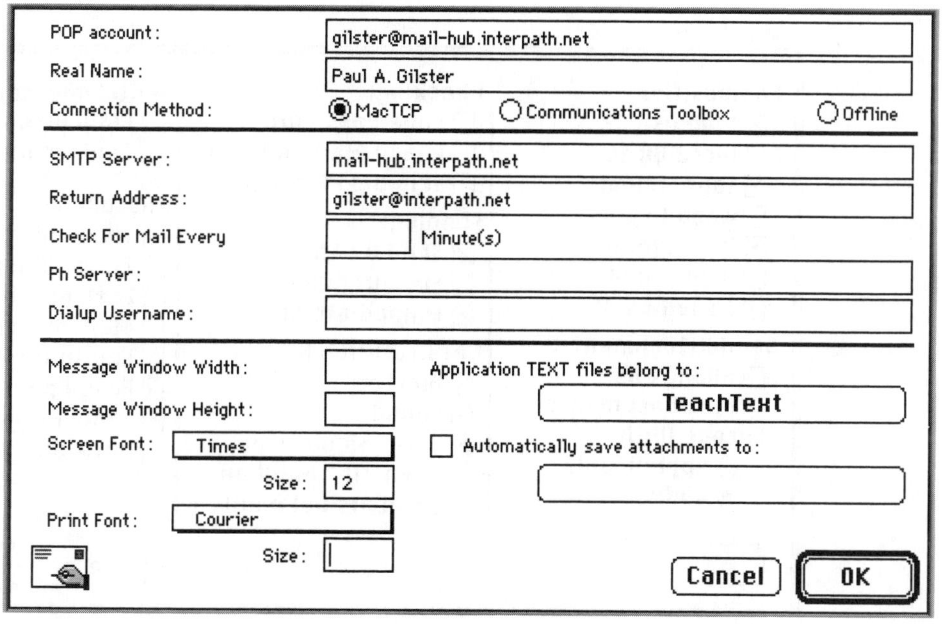

Figure 6.28   Configuring Eudora for the Macintosh.

Application TEXT files belong to   You can choose the software program you want to use to read and manipulate text files by clicking on this field. A dialog box will appear that allows you to choose whichever program you want.

Automatically save attachments to   You can also choose the location for any attached files that are sent to you. Clicking on this field produces a dialog box that allows you to make the choice.

Click on OK to complete the configuration process.

Customizing Eudora for the Macintosh

Both the Macintosh and Microsoft Windows versions of Eudora are fully customizable. By choosing the Switches item from the Special menu, you can further tailor Eudora to your preferences. The Switches dialog box is shown in Figure 6.29.

May Use QP   QP stands for quoted-printable encoding, a way of including special characters such as letters in a foreign alphabet in your messages. Eudora will use QP with any nonstandard characters it finds if this box is checked. The encoding method is also used in any textual attachment you include with a message.

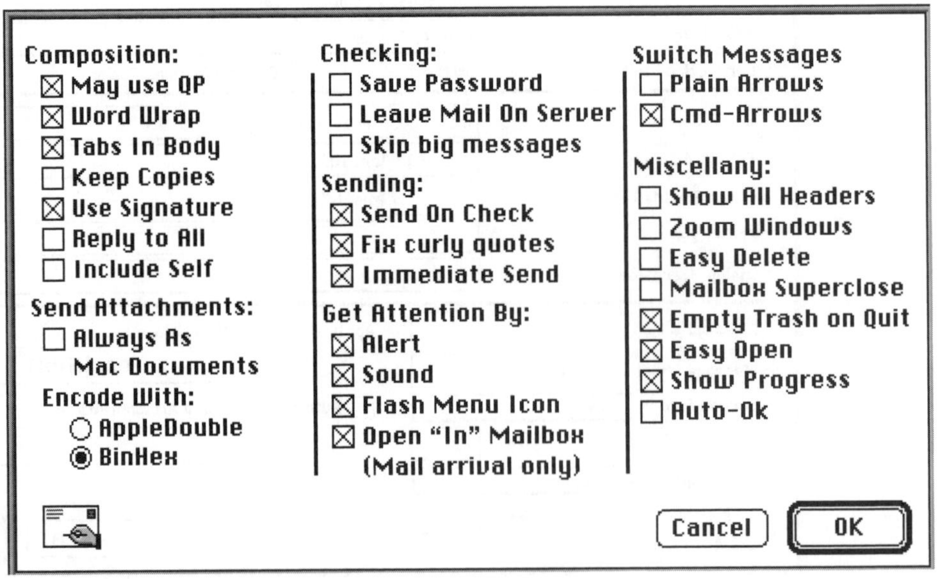

```
Composition:              Checking:                 Switch Messages
  ☒ May use QP              ☐ Save Password           ☐ Plain Arrows
  ☒ Word Wrap               ☐ Leave Mail On Server    ☒ Cmd-Arrows
  ☒ Tabs In Body            ☐ Skip big messages
  ☐ Keep Copies                                     Miscellany:
  ☒ Use Signature         Sending:                    ☐ Show All Headers
  ☐ Reply to All            ☒ Send On Check           ☐ Zoom Windows
  ☐ Include Self            ☒ Fix curly quotes        ☐ Easy Delete
                            ☒ Immediate Send          ☐ Mailbox Superclose
Send Attachments:                                     ☒ Empty Trash on Quit
  ☐ Always As             Get Attention By:           ☒ Easy Open
    Mac Documents           ☒ Alert                   ☒ Show Progress
Encode With:                ☒ Sound                   ☐ Auto-Ok
  ○ AppleDouble             ☒ Flash Menu Icon
  ● BinHex                  ☒ Open "In" Mailbox
                              (Mail arrival only)
                                                   [ Cancel ]  [  OK  ]
```

Figure 6.29   Using the Switches option to customize Eudora.

Word Wrap	Allows automatic line wrapping for all outgoing messages.
Tabs In Body	Controls whether the Tab key inserts space characters when pressed.
Keep Copies	Saves copies of your outgoing messages. These are stored in the Out mailbox.
Use Signature	Tells Eudora whether to use a signature file.
Reply to All	When checked, this box automatically sends your response to the sender of a message and all its recipients.
Include Self	Includes your own address in the reply message.
Always As Mac Documents	When checked, all documents included as attachments will be sent as Macintosh documents.
Encode With	Allows you to choose the format for encoding binary files. BinHex is the default.
Save Password	Saves your password between mail sessions.
Leave Mail On Server	Keeps your mail on the server even after you have downloaded it.
Skip big messages	Retrieves only the initial part of large mail messages.
Send On Check	Sends any messages that remain in your message queue when you check in for new mail.
Immediate Send	Sends outgoing messages immediately, without placing them in the queue. You will probably choose to leave this option off, since queueing your messages allows more efficient use of your SLIP/PPP account (see below).
Alert	Uses dialog boxes to get attention.
Sound	Uses sound.
Flash Menu Icon	Flashes the icon in the menu bar to get your attention.
Open "In" Mailbox	Opens your In mailbox whenever mail is received.
Plain Arrows	Allows you to use arrow keys to move through messages.
Cmd-Arrows	Uses command-arrow keys to move through messages.
Show All Headers	Displays complete message headers, including all routing information.
Zoom Windows	Opens new mailbox and messages windows to zoomed size.
Easy Delete	Deletes messages without showing the warning box.
Mailbox Superclose	Allows Eudora to close all messages from a mailbox when you close its mailbox window.
Empty Trash on Quit	Empties the trash mailbox each time you quit Eudora.
Easy Open	Opens the next message after you delete or transfer a message.

Show Progress	Shows the progress window as your network connection is being made.
Auto-OK	Dismisses network problem dialog boxes automatically.

Click on OK to accept your settings.

There is only one chore left before Eudora is ready to use—you need a signature file. To create one, choose the Signature command from the Special menu. A blank box will appear in which you can enter the signature of your choice. In Figure 6.30, I have filled in the Signature field. When I finish with my signature, I can click on the window's close box, at which time I will be prompted to save any changes I have made here. Click on Save to save the changes and your signature.

Working with Eudora on a Macintosh

Reading messages with Eudora is facilitated by the user-friendly interface designed into the product. When the program logs in at the POP3 server and discovers mail waiting for you there, for example, it shows you the box in Figure 6.31. Messages are read by choosing the Check Mail item on the File menu, which displays a password dialog box. Enter the password assigned by your service provider in this box and click OK. The program will display a progress window at the top of the screen as it logs on to the server and retrieves your mail.

To read mail, double-click on the subject line of the message you are interested in, and the message will soon be displayed. You can see such a message in Figure 6.32. To close a message, click in the close box at the top left corner

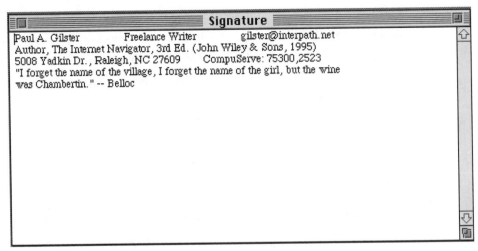

Figure 6.30   A filled-in signature file.

Figure 6.31   Eudora notifies you unmistakably when you have new mail.

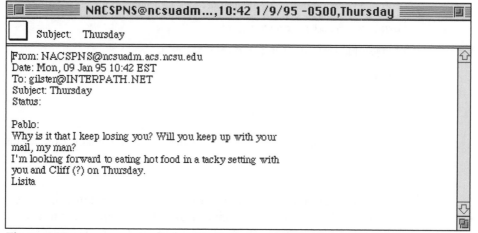

Figure 6.32   A new message displayed in Eudora.

of the message window. Your e-mail messages will remain in the inbox until you delete them or transfer them to another mailbox.

To reply to a message while reading it, pull down the Message menu and choose Reply. The new message composition window will appear; within it will be the text of the message you are replying to, with brackets preceding each line, as in Figure 6.33.

You can enter your own text after the quoted material. Quoting is useful because it helps the original sender remember what message you are responding to, and the parts of the message you have singled out for reply. It makes sense, then, not to quote entire messages, but to edit the quoted material to narrow your reply's focus. Eudora provides you with full editing capability of both your own message and the message you are responding to, so be as concise as possible by deleting extraneous material from the quoted message before proceeding with your response.

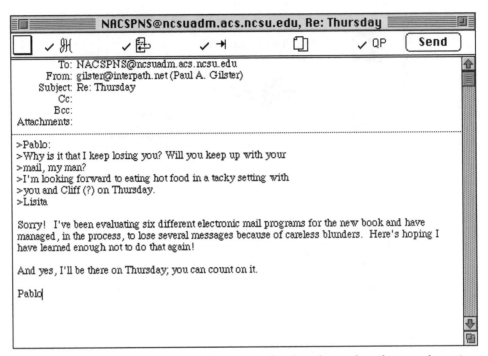

Figure 6.33 Responding to a message; notice the brackets that enclose the quoted, previous message.

Notice that in the top right of Figure 6.33, a Send button is available. Clicking on this button after you have finished the response will send the message immediately. Alternatively, if you have chosen not to use the immediate send option (this is configurable in the Switches window), you will see a Queue button rather than a Send button. When you click on Queue after finishing your response, the message is stored on your hard disk and is sent to the mail server when you choose the Send Queued Messages command on the File menu. Queueing your messages in this way makes sense for SLIP/PPP users, as it allows you to access the POP3 server, retrieve your mail and exit, compose your responses, and then log back in to send your replies.

Creating a new message is likewise simple. To do so, pull down the Message menu and select the New Message command. The new message window is shown in Figure 6.34. Notice that my e-mail address has already been inserted in the From: field, while the cursor has been placed in the To: field, waiting for me to enter an address. Once you have entered the address, you can press the Tab key to move to the Subject: field, where you can enter a short description of your message. Pressing the Tab key again then takes you through the various fields, allowing you to send messages to third parties if you choose. Both regular carbon copies and blind carbon copies (in which the addressee is not notified that a carbon has been sent to someone else) are

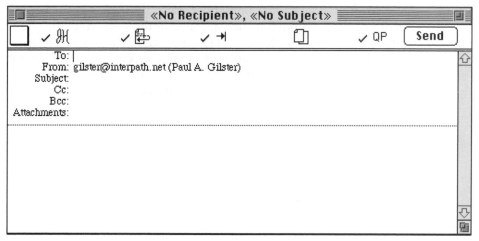

Figure 6.34   The new message composition screen.

available. Generally, blind carbon copies are best used for mailing lists to keep headers manageable. In the main text field, you can compose your message; when finished, send or queue it using the appropriate button. And, of course, you can add attachments to messages with BinHex.

Eudora provides the same key features for mail management, with full folder and mailbox creation and sorting capabilities, that it provides in the

Note: All computers understand ASCII, the format for plain text that is universally transferable. You would think, then, that to transfer a file from the Macintosh to another computer environment, we would simply use ASCII to do it. But the Macintosh imposes constraints upon how we transfer files because of the way it constructs files. We have to find some way to transfer not only the data within the file—the text, or the executable program code—but also the attributes and features of that file, such as its icon. BinHex is the format by which we do this; it is a way to convert both data and file resource information into a single text file. And, of course, BinHex can then be used in reverse to re-create the original file.

We have already seen that a good client program can handle the BinHex chores automatically. Eudora allows us to create attachments not only with MIME but also with BinHex, just as Fetch, the FTP client we looked at in Chapter 5, can un-BinHex a file on your Macintosh as it is downloaded. More and more client programs handle BinHex in this way; we'll see TurboGopher performing the same function for Gophers in Chapter 9.

Microsoft Windows environment. Especially if you have worked with Unix mail programs through a shell account in the past, you will be amazed at the difference a good graphical mail program can bring. The development of client software in the next few years will surely concentrate on information management as much as on information discovery. Eudora is a major contribution to that effort, and one that's sure to be continually improved as new versions are released.

7

Telnet Access to Remote Computers

The number of networks feeding into the Internet is growing so fast that cataloging, much less actually visiting, the more intriguing sites is a full-time occupation. We've already examined how File Transfer Protocol can get you into a collection of files, allowing you to browse between directories and download information and software programs. We've also tapped electronic mail, using helpful graphical client programs to manage the potentially massive amount of incoming messages. Now we turn to another kind of resource—programs available on computers around the world that can be reached and used via the Internet. Let's consider some examples.

- The National Institutes of Health Library Online Catalog contains numerous books of interest to scientists, researchers and health professionals. The catalog for this collection is made available over the Internet; logging in, you can search the system by keyword (**telnet://nih-library.ncrr.nih.gov**). Hundreds of university and college libraries around the world are likewise joining the net.

- Chess enthusiasts around the globe play interactive games by using Telnet to various sites, such as **telnet://lux.latrobe.edu.au 5000**, or **telnet://iris4.metiu.ucsb.edu 5000**. Others play the Japanese strategy game of Go at this site: **telnet://hellspark.wharton.upenn.edu 6969**.

- FedWorld is a taxpayer-funded service containing huge amounts of information about scientific and technical subjects, along with access to files covering a broad range of business and consumer issues. Rather than making these files available in an anonymous FTP site, the remote access capability (**telnet://fedworld.gov**) allows the developers to create a bulletin board style of presentation, guiding you through the system.

- At the Massachusetts Institute of Technology, simulated environments are made available, including a remarkably complex space station through which the user moves by entering commands and reading descriptions. Because such environments are created by a constantly growing base of participants, they take on a life of their own; sitting at your computer, you enter the persona of your on-line character as you push into unexplored digital terrain (**telnet://michael.ai.mit.edu**; log in as **guest**).

- The Victoria Free-Net is one of a growing number of community-centered networks springing up around the world. Focusing on issues significant in British Columbia, this Free-Net contains interesting materials on the environment and tracks local news and government. Free-Nets are created by local volunteers and provide free access to the Internet and other resources for people within their areas. You can also reach them over the Internet; the Victoria Free-Net's address is **telnet://freenet.victoria.bc.ca**; log in as **guest**.

As you can see, the one constant among these sources of information and adventure is Telnet, an Internet protocol that lets you gain access to a remote computer and manipulate its resources in real-time. The most common, although certainly not the only, reason for using Telnet is to gain access to a database, at which you can perform searches using keywords to locate targeted information. The database you connect to can be nearby or on the other side of the world; location becomes insignificant as you take advantage of whatever services the machine makes available to the terminals at its own site.

How Telnet Works

To illustrate Telnet functions, let's first look at a sample session as seen through a standard Unix shell account. I am going to log on to the catalog of the Library of Congress, which contains not only the records of millions of books published in the United States, but also government and copyright information. The address is **telnet://locis.loc.gov**. I enter the Telnet command as follows:

```
% telnet locis.loc.gov
Trying 140.147.254.3...
Connected to locis.loc.gov.
Escape character is '^]'.
```

As you can see, the connection is quickly made, and I am provided with an escape character, which would let me break the connection if I couldn't exit

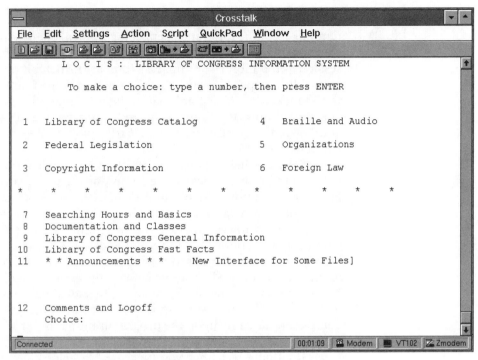

Figure 7.1   A Telnet connection to the Library of Congress.

normally. The Library of Congress main screen then appears, as shown in Figure 7.1.

To understand Telnet, you must realize that such a connection allows your computer to function as though it were a terminal on the remote machine. This is both an advantage and a limitation; the former in that it allows you to use computer resources that are widely dispersed, even on a global scale; the latter in that the remote computer isn't able to be terribly sophisticated by way of formatting when it sends its terminals information. The commands available to you once connected are those provided by the remote machine. In other words, if you are connected to a computer running Unix as its operating system, then the standard Unix commands are the ones you can use. Remember, with Telnet you're driving somebody else's computer, using your own machine as a window into that system.

Notice in the current example that I have available such choices as the catalog of the Library of Congress, federal legislation, copyright information, and other options. By entering the number of the area I wish to access, I can move quickly to it. It is this interactive capability that makes Telnet so valuable to us; coupling it with database search engines, as do the hundreds of libraries that now offer their catalogs to the network, renders Telnet invaluable for

Note: It's instructive to note the Telnet escape character, for it reminds us of the difference between graphical client software and command-driven access through a shell account. In the case of our session at the Library of Congress (and as the default on most systems), the escape character is a combination of the Control key and the] bracket key. The combination is written as ^], which means you should press the Control key and, while holding it down, the] key. You'll also see this written as Ctrl-], which refers to the same combination.

Were we using a shell account, the ^] escape character would help us out in a jam. Because we communicate with many different kinds of operating systems and deal with menu structures that aren't necessarily familiar to us when using Telnet, we sometimes find ourselves unable to exit the program. Pressing the escape character is, therefore, a shortcut; it ends our session and takes us back to the Telnet prompt. But when we use a graphical client program like the one we'll examine shortly, the escape function is built into the program's menus. Here again, the advantage of the graphical program is that we are released from the need to memorize commands, and rely upon the programming skills of the program's author to make the command process intuitive.

A final note. Whether you type the ^] escape character in the Unix environment or use a menu selection in our graphical client program, using this way out of a Telnet session should be regarded as a last resort. The best way to exit a program is to log out through the methods recommended at the site; these methods are almost always noted in the introductory screens you see when you log in. Leaving through the marked exit is always the preferable—and courteous—way to go.

researchers. The addition of a graphical user environment like the ones we examine in this chapter makes the researcher's job that much easier.

Telnet works because client and server software talk together to produce a standardized set of results. When you enter a Telnet session, your software creates a network connection with the remote computer, or server. The information you enter at the client end must be reformatted to a format the server can understand, just as the server's responses must be accepted by the client and then reformatted before being presented to you on-screen. This conversion process, which seems so cumbersome at first glance, is a necessity because a server has to be able to service a wide variety of different computer platforms. Whether you're using a Macintosh, a Windows-based PC, or some other computer, a client program that can run on your machine must be able to talk to the same server. Computer protocols are the rules that make this possible.

Ewan: A Telnet Solution for Microsoft Windows

A number of Telnet programs exist for Microsoft Windows, but I've found Ewan to be the most congenial. The work of Peter Zander, Ewan is freeware, although e-mail support is available for a fee. You can reach Zander at the following address:

ZanData
Peter Zander
Rydsvagen 258A:21
582 51 Linkoping
Sweden
E-mail: **zander@lysator.liu.se**

To retrieve Ewan, use anonymous FTP to the following site:

ftp://ftp.lysator.liu.se/pub/msdos/windows/

At the time of this writing, the filename was ewan105.zip.

You can also obtain information about the program with a World Wide Web browser from the following URL:

http://www.lysator.liu.se/~zander/ewan.html

This is a World Wide Web document. We will discuss how to view pages like it in Chapter 11.

Installing Ewan

Peter Zander has included an installation program with the Ewan package that greatly simplifies the process. Here is how to install the program:

1. Move the compressed file to a directory of your choice. The software itself suggests *c:\ewan*, but any directory will do as long as you specify it during the installation process.
2. Unpack the compressed file using PKware's PKUNZIP program or a decompression program like WinZip.
3. Return to Windows and run install.exe, the installation program file.

The installation program will take you through the process in a few short steps, creating a program group and icon for Ewan.

Starting the Program

To start Ewan, double-click on its icon. You will see the screen shown in Figure 7.2. This is the window within which Ewan stores site information. As with

WS_FTP, you will find that one of the major benefits of using a good client program is that it can store your frequently visited site information; the next time
you connect, you simply click on the desired site. Since this is the first time
you will have run the program, no sites will be listed.

To test the program, click the New button. The dialog box shown in Figure
7.3 will appear. We now need to fill in the information for a sample site. Let's
take a Telnet journey to the FedWorld site in Washington. To do so, enter Fed-
World in the Name field, placing the address, **fedworld.gov**, in the Network
address field. Leave the Service button set at the default, which is Telnet, and
the Configuration field blank. We'll discuss what Ewan's configuration options
are in a moment.

When you click on OK, the FedWorld site is placed into the site list. You
now need to click on it to highlight it in the Connect to site box; then click on
OK to make the actual connection. Ewan will then display a terminal screen
like the one in Figure 7.4.

When we make contact with the FedWorld site, we're asked for login information. Each Telnet site will have its own procedures; in this case, reading the
information on-screen tells us that we should enter NEW in the login field.

At FedWorld, once you enter NEW, you will be shown a screen like the one
in Figure 7.5. As you can see, the incoming information has scrolled down the
screen. FedWorld briefs us about its background as a function of the National
Technical Information Service, funded by Congress to disseminate scientific
and other information. At the bottom of the screen, we are prompted to hit a
Return to proceed through the rest of this introductory statement.

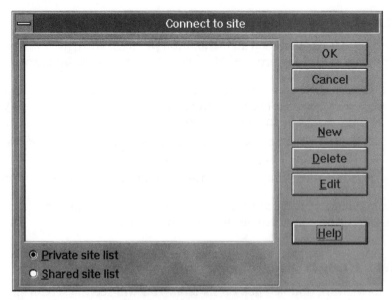

Figure 7.2 Ewan's connection screen.

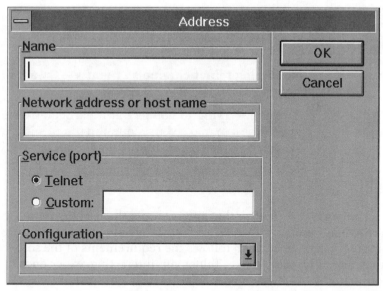

Figure 7.3 The new address dialog box in Ewan. Use it to fill in the information necessary to connect to a site.

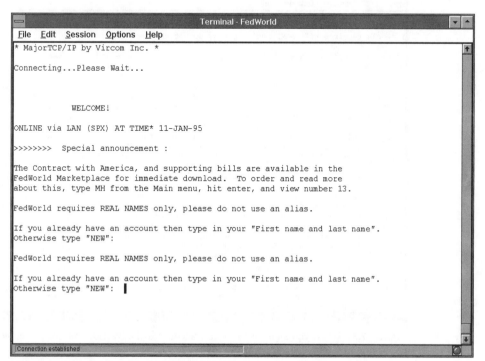

Figure 7.4 Logging on at the FedWorld site.

Note: It is always possible at a busy site that you will not be able to get in on the first try. At the FedWorld site, for example, you may receive a message like this one:

All incoming telnet channels are busy—Try again later.

If you do, simply wait a few minutes and try your request again. If you are trying to connect at a particularly busy time of day, it may be best to make your request in the evening, or the early morning. Traffic jams on the Internet are an increasingly common occurrence.

It's important to realize that the prompts themselves are not provided by Ewan. When we connect with a remote Telnet site, we are entering a separate computer system, one which follows the requirements of the software running at that site. This can make Telnet an interesting experience, for we will encounter numerous systems, many of which run software we have not previously encountered. The best course of action is to be an attentive reader. You

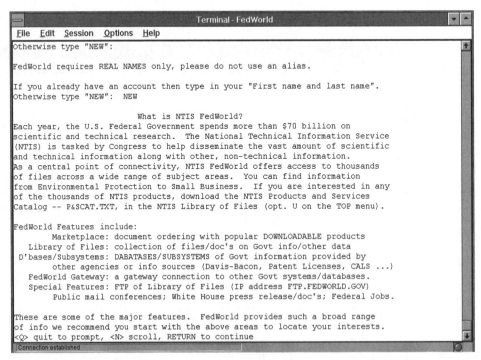

Figure 7.5 When you sign up for a new account at FedWorld, you are presented with background information about the site.

can see that FedWorld tells us at each step of the way what we need to do. Most systems do this, provided you read the fine print and keep an eye on the suggestions being provided on-screen. Remember especially to notice how to log off a system; this information is almost always provided on the initial screens, and you will always want to know how to exit when the time comes.

FedWorld is a full-featured database system and it's free to the public. But to use it, we're asked to provide some basic user information. As you page through the material here, you will be asked for your full name, a company name if applicable, address, and telephone number. You'll also be asked to choose a password, so that next time you log on at the site, you can dispense with the introductory material. FedWorld even includes a useful help file, which, it is suggested in a welcoming mail message that awaits you, is a good file to download. Certainly you will get more out of the system if you study this document.

Note: When you choose a password on a remote system, it's always a good idea to choose one that is different from the password with which you log on to your SLIP/PPP account. Although the odds are remote, someone could theoretically check the password database at the Telnet site and use your password to get into your SLIP/PPP account. Password security is something you should always take seriously.

When you've worked through the various introductory materials, you will finally reach the main FedWorld menu, as shown in Figure 7.6. Notice that we have now entered familiar terrain. If you have been a user of various on-line commercial services like CompuServe or America Online, this kind of menu structure will not seem unusual. It also reflects the kind of local bulletin board system we have become familiar with during the past decade's expansion of telecommunications services. You enter a number followed by a Return to move to the item you want to see. As you can see, the listings at FedWorld are extensive.

Note: When you are logged on at a Telnet site, you are directly connected to the computer there. Like FTP, then, Telnet demands a certain attention to on-line etiquette. Because your being on-line may affect other users who are trying to access the same site, be sure to keep your session short and to the point. Internet tools like Gopher and Mosaic won't require this, because they are connectionless, but Telnet demands that we keep in mind the nature of our shared resource.

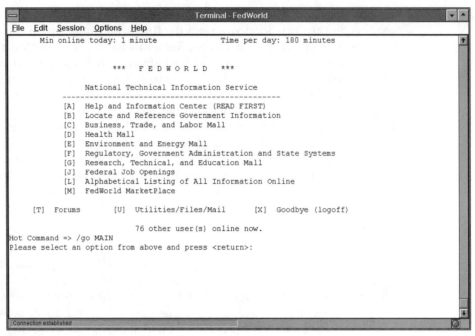

Figure 7.6 The main menu at FedWorld.

Using Ewan's Configurations

When I use the term "configuration" with Ewan, I must be careful in what sense the term is understood. We configure software to make it usable in our network environment; the process means entering the necessary settings so that the program can function. But Ewan also provides for separate configurations, or settings, that can be used for a particular Telnet site. We can create these, give each a name, and associate them with particular Telnet sessions.

Why would we need to make such arrangements? Because sites vary in terms of what they make available. In most cases, for example, we want to use VT-100 terminal emulation to govern how our computer responds to the information it receives from the Telnet site. But ANSI is also available from some sites, giving us greater flexibility in screen display (FedWorld, for example, offers ANSI graphics and color). If we had one site where ANSI was effective but the others used VT-100, it would make sense to create a separate configuration for the ANSI site, telling Ewan that when we logged in there, it should use ANSI as its method of terminal emulation. In a similar way, we can change the way Ewan shows us information by varying fonts, and we can tweak the way the program handles its keyboard mapping.

To create a configuration, pull down the Options menu and click on the Configuration command. You will see the dialog box shown in Figure 7.7. You can enter a new configuration name in the Name field and proceed to define it by selecting from the available buttons. Notice that you can choose from among a wide variety of screen options, and can manipulate emulation settings, keyboard mapping, the printer font used by the program, and more.

I quickly found, for example, that I wanted to change the screen font I was using with Ewan; what came up by default was far too tiny to read. By clicking on the Screen button in the Configuration dialog box and then choosing the Browse command, I called up the dialog box shown in Figure 7.8.

As you can see, Ewan gives me full choice over what font and size I'd like to deal with. Then, by clicking Emul. Options from the same Configuration dialog box, I was able to call up the dialog box you see in Figure 7.9. Here, I have the ability to manipulate screen colors; I can choose foreground and background settings, and determine how I want my system to handle bold and blinking text. And as you can see, I can do this for any of the terminal emulations I choose. This one happens to be VT-100, but I can return to the Configuration box to choose another for manipulation.

Having created a configuration, I can assign it to a particular Telnet site by pulling down the File menu and choosing the Open command, which will call up my site list. Highlighting the site of my choice, I can then click on the Edit button to call up site information. I place the name of the configuration I want to use in the Configuration field.

Building a Site List

Telnet is a useful tool, but my experience says that people don't tend to use it as much as they might. The reason, I think, is that with the kind of shell account access so many people have used until recently, putting Telnet to work

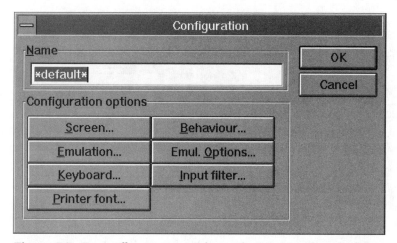

Figure 7.7 Ewan allows you to tinker with a variety of configuration options through the Configuration dialog box.

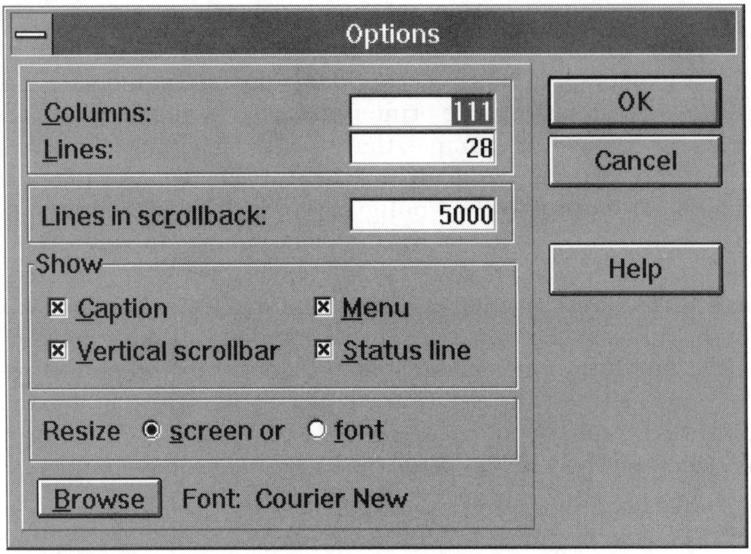

Figure 7.8 Setting screen options with Ewan.

always meant entering an address, often followed by a port number. As with FTP, this put a premium on their ability to remember or organize lists of addresses, while it tended to diminish their enthusiasm for finding new sites because of the need to keep all the addresses straight. If they made a single typing mistake, their Telnet session wouldn't connect.

Tools like Ewan help to simplify the process by giving you a point-and-click Telnet environment. Call up the list of Telnet sites and you have all the

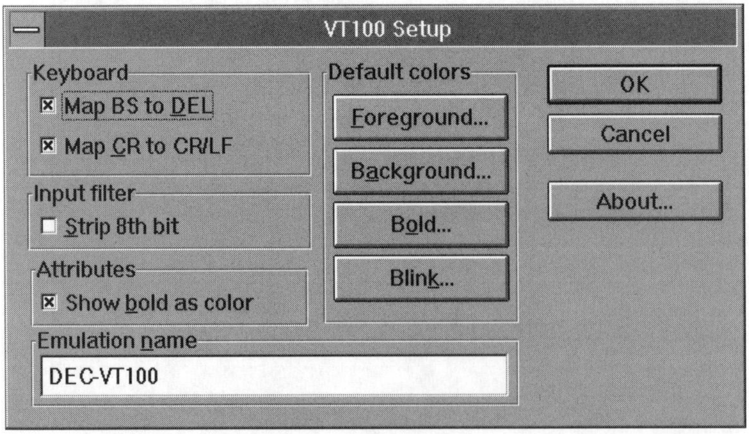

Figure 7.9 A variety of options are available from the Ewan Emul. Options screen. Notice your control over screen colors.

options spread out in front of you, and are more likely to return to that interesting database you located six months ago and would have otherwise forgotten. Your first task with Ewan, then, is to begin to build a good site list. The method is simple enough. From the File menu, choose Open, which will call up the site list. At this point, you should have just one site listed, FedWorld.

We can now expand the list. I know, for example, that the InterNIC, which provides network information and registration services, offers a wide variety of useful information about the Internet itself; the address is **rs.internic.net**. By clicking on the New button, I can call up an address box that allows me to enter the name of the site and its address. When I click on OK, this site is added to the list of sites. I can access it by clicking on the OK button, or by double-clicking on the entry.

> **Note:**   You don't have to add every Telnet site you visit to your permanent site list. If you simply want to try out an interesting new Telnet resource, pull down the File menu and click on New. This will pop up a dialog box that allows you to enter the necessary address information; you can press Alt-C to make the connection. If you do decide you want to add this entry to your site list, choose Save from the File menu.

But before we go to the site, let's add some other interesting possibilities. You might want to consider some of these:

European Commission Host Organization
telnet://echo.lu
Log in as **echo**.

NDLC—The National Distance Learning Center
telnet://ndlc.occ.uky.edu
Log in as **ndlc**.

NEWTON—Argonne National Laboratory Division of Educational
     Programs BBS
telnet://newton.dep.anl.gov
Log in as **bbs**.

HNSOURCE—The Central Information Server for Historians
telnet://ukanaix.cc.ukans.edu
Log in as **history**.

CARL—The Colorado Alliance of Research Libraries
telnet://pac.carl.org

Brotherton Collection of Manuscript Verse
telnet://bcmsv.leeds.ac.uk/
The login and password are the same: **bcmsv**.

Library of Congress Services
telnet://locis.loc.gov

Notice that some of these systems require login terms, while others do not. There is no rule about such things; the system administrators at a given site determine how they want to handle access, and whether they want to restrict it. In many cases, a login will be required, but you can find out what the login is by consulting lists of Internet information. I strongly recommend that you obtain Scott Yanoff's Special Internet Connections list, which is posted frequently in various USENET newsgroups. Try **news.answers**, **alt.internet.services**, **comp.misc**, or **alt.bbs.internet**. You can also retrieve the file by FTP from the following site:

ftp://csd4.csd.uwm.edu/pub/inet.services.txt

But the best way to use this file is with a World Wide Web browser, of the sort we will examine in Chapter 11. Because the Web provides hypertextual links between sites, you can browse the Yanoff list and then click on a site you'd like to visit. Your Web browser will handle all the underlying connections.

Note: Telnet addresses are constantly changing. The major sites, it's true, remain stable, but many interesting databases and other tools come and go, while others, having decided that the flow of incoming traffic is too high, institute new login procedures that require a password. If you run into such changes, the only thing to do is to move on to another site. Keeping up with the Yanoff list is the best way I know to verify that a site is on-line and that its login procedures haven't changed. I also recommend you keep up with the USENET newsgroup **comp.internet.net-happenings**, which monitors new sites.

Telnet Port Issues

Ponder for a moment the nature of servers. We tend to speak of servers as though they were computers; a "server" is often loosely used to mean a particular computer. Yet in reality, the word server denotes a software program that is running on a particular computer. And because computers fulfill many functions, it's not at all uncommon for several different software programs, or servers, to be running on the same machine. Software that communicates with this machine needs to be able to specify which particular service it is trying to access. This need is met by assigning a *port* number to each server. The server thus handles requests for different services on different ports.

When we use the term port, the implication is that we are referring to a hardware device, such as a serial or a parallel port, which protrudes from the back of a computer. But in reality, ports in this sense are pointers that are written into the software the computer is running. They simply allow the computer to differentiate between different kinds of requests, assigning each to the server it needs to connect to. Applications that are frequently used have standard port assignments. Gopher, for example, is standardized on port 70, while standard Telnet is given port 23. When the port is standardized, we don't have to refer to it explicitly. The client/server interaction will assume a standard port is in use unless we specifically tell it otherwise.

In most cases, then, the Telnet addresses we use will be in the form of a standard Internet address, as in the Library of Congress at **locis.loc.gov**. But when someone decides to create a specialized application at a site, it becomes necessary to assign nonstandard port numbers to the new server. In this way, a client program can log on to the server at the correct port. Such applications will have addresses followed by the nonstandard port number. Consider the following address:

telnet://camms2.caos.kun.nl:2034

Here we have a standard address followed by a nonstandard port assignment. To reach this site, we would need to enter not only the address itself but also the port assignment; otherwise, we would not connect to the server we anticipated reaching.

Let's contact this server. To show you how a different program handles a Telnet session, I am here using WinQVT, which includes a Telnet module as part of its Internet package (more on WinQVT shortly). You can see the result in Figure 7.10.

Other Telnet Solutions for Windows

A variety of Telnet clients for Windows exist, and you may want to browse to determine which is best for you. In general, Telnet software doesn't yet seem as advanced as, say, mail readers or newsreader programs, perhaps because the kind of sites accessible through Telnet are more individualized; many of them are of interest to specialists in a variety of fields, rather than being engineered for a broad audience. Moreover, the growth in SLIP/PPP connections has meant that many people who formerly would have accessed such tools as WAIS and archie through a Telnet connection are now doing so through client software on their own machines. This is no small change; it will eventually have the effect of reducing the amount of Telnet traffic to, we can hope, more manageable levels.

Here are several of the Telnet programs that are under active development. Each presents its own take on Telnet access, from a novel way to utilize your existing communications software to an all-in-one package that incorporates Telnet.

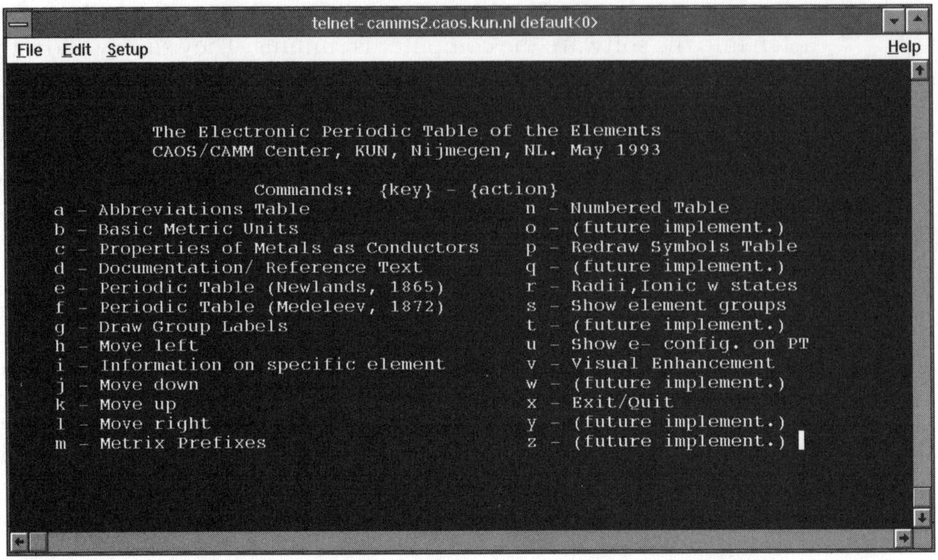

Figure 7.10   A Telnet session, using WinQVT, to access the Periodic Table of the Elements.

COMt: A Unique Telnet Solution

Created by David Yon, COMt offers an interesting solution for using Telnet. If many of the Telnet programs available on the net were rudimentary, why not develop a way to make use of communications software we already use to run Telnet sessions? After all, most of us have gotten familiar with one or more programs like Procomm Plus for Windows or Telix for Windows, using them to access local bulletin boards and commercial on-line services. If their familiar interface could be harnessed to manage a Telnet connection, the benefit would be palpable.

Yon's COMt does precisely this. By allowing your communications program to access the Internet in the Winsock environment, COMt gives you great flexibility and an abundance of features when compared to many of the stand-alone Telnet programs. You can get COMt at the following URL:

ftp://ftp.std.com/customers/software/rfdmail

At the time of this writing, the filename was comt.zip.

QWS3270: Support for IBM Mainframes

Available in both shareware and freeware packages, QWS3270 offers support for the IBM 3270 terminal emulation, about which a brief word. IBM's 3270 terminals were designed to provide many features that aren't available on standard terminals. While most Telnet applications function in line mode, sending characters one line at a time to your computer, 3270 applications manipulate the entire screen image. Such terminals make use of *programmed function,* or PF, keys, which often have particular commands linked to them. Making use of such an application requires a terminal emulator that can make your own computer act like a 3270 terminal. A special version of Telnet called tn3270 makes this conversion possible, and with the right client software, you can manage the process transparently.

QWS3270 supports such transactions, and provides a fully customizable keyboard, allowing you to configure your system for any remote computer you'll use frequently. You can get a copy of this program at the following URL:

ftp://ftp.cica.indiana.edu/pub/pc/win3/winsock/

At the time of this writing, the filename was qws3270.zip. Keep in mind that this Indiana site is heavily trafficked; you can also get the program from any of the numerous mirror sites where the same collection of software is maintained.

Written by Jim Rymerson at Queen's University in Kingston, Ontario, QWS3270 is a stable program that provides excellent service for users of 3270 systems. You can see an example of the program at work in Figure 7.11.

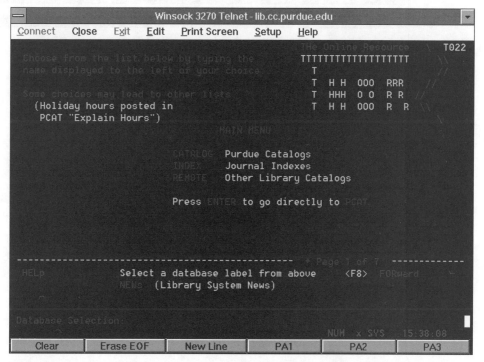

Figure 7.11 Using QWS3270 to contact an IBM mainframe at Purdue.

3270 terminal emulation makes you rethink the way you use the computer screen. Rather than proceeding one line at a time, the 3270 creates a model in which you move the cursor to screen areas and fill in the blank spaces. An IBM user at an actual 3270 terminal would use the PF keys to perform basic operations; the completed form would then be sent to the mainframe by hitting the Return key. Usually, but not always, primary program functions are found at the bottom of the screen; thus, the user knows what the various PF keys will do. A Clear key is used to redraw the screen as necessary.

All of this works well for IBM 3270 users, but what do we do if we're calling into a 3270 system and only emulating such a terminal? Our problem is that we don't have the right kind of keyboard; there are no PF keys on a standard PC or Macintosh keyboard, nor is there a Clear key. This means that the special keys of the 3270 emulation have to be mapped onto your keyboard; a PF key, for example, would have to be assigned to a function key, or a key combination involving a number and another key. Exactly how this keyboard mapping is done is handled by the client program you are using.

Take a look at Figure 7.12. If you look down this list of keyboard assignments, you will see that the PF keys have been assigned to the function keys on the PC. The Clear key is assigned to the plus (+) key on the keypad. And, as you

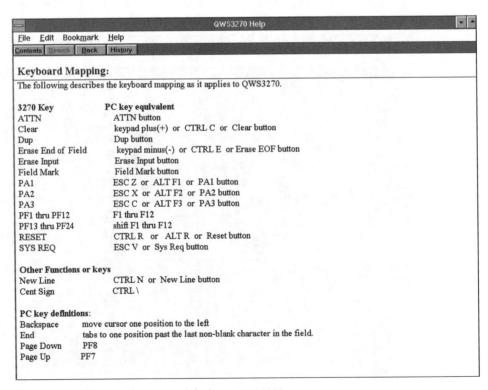

Figure 7.12   Keyboard mapping defaults in QWS3270.

can see, all the various keys available to the 3270 user are now accessible to anyone with a standard PC keyboard, allowing you to use full 3270 emulation with your connection.

Trumpet Telnet (Trumptel): A Sound, Basic Tool

From the developer of Trumpet Winsock and the Trumpet newsreader, this Telnet package is elementary, but provides basic capabilities for VT-100 emulation. You can find the program at the following URL:

ftp://ftp.trumpet.com.au/pub/beta/trmptel/

The filename at the time of this writing was ttel0_07.zip. Figure 7.13 illustrates Trumptel in action. Here, I've used Telnet to log on to The World, an Internet service provider in Massachusetts; I am accessing its Gopher.

WinQVT: An Internet Package Deal

WinQVT is a combination shareware package that offers a newsreader, FTP module, mail capabilities, and Telnet in an elegant and powerful package. I've found newsreaders I like better than WinQVT, but its Telnet features are well designed. You can find the program at the following URL:

ftp://biochemistry.cwru.edu/gopher/pub/qvtnet/

At the time of this writing, the filename was qvtws398.zip.

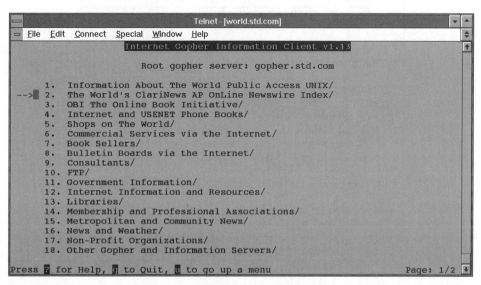

Figure 7.13   Using Trumptel to access a Gopher at The World.

Telnet on the Macintosh

To run Telnet sessions on a Macintosh, we can tap the archives of the National Center for Supercomputing Applications, in Urbana-Champaign, Illinois, for a freeware program called NCSA Telnet. You can retrieve the program at the following URL:

ftp://ftp.ncsa.uiuc.edu/Mac/Telnet/Telnet2.5/

At the time of this writing, the filename was Telnet2.5.sit.hqx (although version 2.6 was close to release). You will also want to retrieve the documentation, which is available at the same site in a file called Telnet2.5docs.sit.hqx.

When you unpack the NCSA Telnet file, you will find a file called config.tel, which can be opened with any text editor. Open this file now, and you will see the screen shown in Figure 7.14. The default settings here should work for you, but notice that I have changed the entry for domain to include my own domain; you should do the same. Save the file by using the Save command from the File menu, and you are ready to begin using NCSA Telnet (NCSA 2.6, incidentally, eliminates the need to edit the config.tel file).

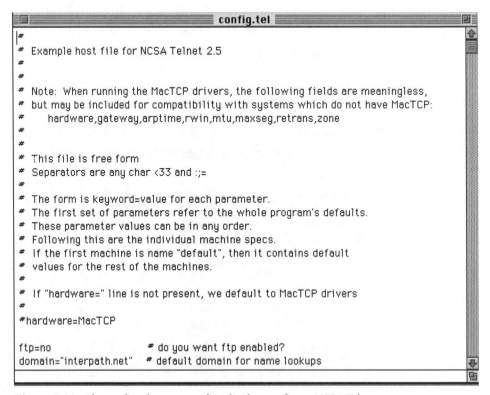

Figure 7.14   The config.tel screen can be edited to configure NCSA Telnet.

Let's take a sample Telnet journey. I would like to contact an on-line library, in this case the University of Wisconsin at Stout. The address is as follows:

telnet://lib.uwstout.edu/

The login is **library**. I have determined both the address and the login information from previous research.

To reach the site with NCSA Telnet, I pull down the File menu and click on Open Connection. The dialog box in Figure 7.15 appears. The session name, confusingly, refers to the address to which you want to connect. I enter **lib.-uwstout.edu** here. I can leave the Window field blank; it is of little value unless I am dealing with multiple connections open at the same time.

When I click on OK, NCSA Telnet establishes the connection. I'm first prompted for a login name, at which I enter **library**. At this point, the system needs to know what kind of terminal I'm using, and gives me several choices, from which I choose the standard VT-100 (NCSA Telnet emulates a VT102 as its default, so you are always safe in choosing VT-100). After pressing a Return, I am greeted with the screen shown in Figure 7.16.

This is an interesting screen. We have entered an information system which allows us to choose between various databases, including the listing of books and periodicals at Stout, as well as other articles, and index to periodicals not held at the university. The choice is made by typing in our selection at the bottom of the screen. When I enter INDEX in this field, I see the screen shown in Figure 7.17.

Here we have some, but not all, of the databases available at the site. Library database searching is useful to any researcher. We cannot actually search and retrieve text, but we can go through the titles available. You can see a sample search screen in Figure 7.18. As always, we are faced with the problem of mastering the remote system's command structure. But information is provided on-screen, and further help facilities are available.

| Session name | |
| Window Name | |

☐ FTP session (⌘F)
☐ Serial/SLIP (⌘S)

[Configure]   [OK]   [Cancel]

Figure 7.15   NCSA Telnet's Open Connection dialog box.

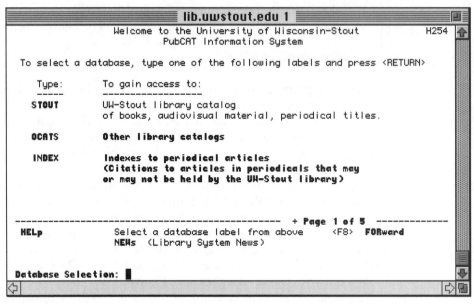

Figure 7.16   The introductory screen at the University of Wisconsin-Stout.

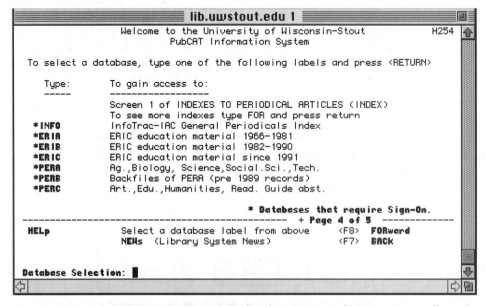

Figure 7.17   Entering INDEX as our command at the University of Wisconsin site calls up the databases available at the site.

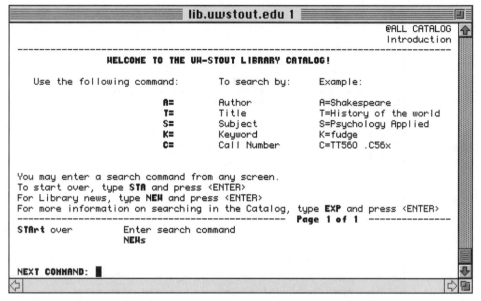

Figure 7.18   The library search screen allows us to search the library's holdings.

NCSA Telnet also provides us with a way of doubling up on our resources. Because the program can be used to make FTP connections as well as to log on to Telnet sites, we can run archie searches to locate files, and then switch into FTP mode to retrieve the files we find. In Figure 7.19, for example, I have logged in at the archie server at the following URL:

telnet://archie.rediris.es/

There, I can set up an archie search by using the find command.

For example, suppose I am trying to track down WAIS software, of the kind we will discuss in the following chapter. When I give the **find wais** command, I am instructing archie to run a substring search to locate any files that meet this keyword requirement. You can see one page of the results in Figure 7.20. I can choose from among my archie hits to pick the file I want to retrieve. Having done so, I can enter into an FTP session this way:

1. Click on NCSA Telnet's Open Connection command (from the File menu). This calls up the window we saw in Figure 7.15.

2. Enter the FTP address.

3. Click on the FTP box.

4. Click on OK to launch the session.

Figure 7.21 shows the FTP session in progress.

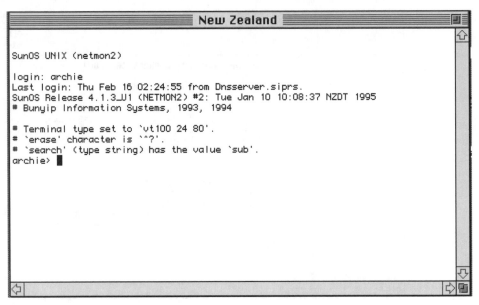

Figure 7.19   Using NCSA Telnet to log on to an archie site.

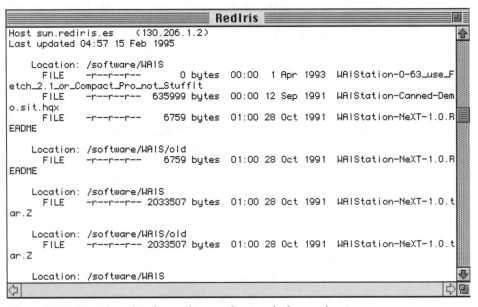

Figure 7.20   Partial results of an archie search using the keyword wais.

Note: Is Telnet on the eclipse? In a way, the answer is yes. In the early days of the Internet, Telnet was extensively used as a means of gaining access to the resources of remote computers. Today, we are seeing a migration of many services to other forms of connection. The proliferation of World Wide Web sites, for example, is changing the way we access network documents and files. And while many of us once used Telnet as our only access to archie servers and such tools as WAIS (Wide Area Information Servers, about which more in Chapter 8), we now use local clients to perform the same functions.

But Telnet is far from dead. It is particularly important in the library community where, as we have just seen, university and college libraries make their catalogs available on-line. Telnet remains useful for information delivery when you need to access a large, remote database of any kind, and it provides a host of other information, such as weather, court rulings, directory services, and more. While many of the Telnet sites now available are specialized in nature, the presence of such services will keep the protocol in active use. You'll be glad you acquired a Telnet client for those resources that are unavailable in any other way.

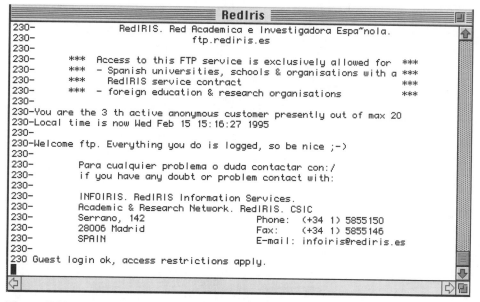

Figure 7.21 An FTP session as seen through NCSA Telnet.

Although the NCSA Telnet/FTP combination isn't as elegant as using Anarchie for the same purpose, it does point out that there are numerous ways of retrieving the same information on the Internet. This is a lesson to bear in mind as we move deeper into our set of network tools. We'll see that the World Wide Web browsers discussed in Chapter 11 can be used not only to access Web documents, but to perform other chores, such as connecting to FTP sites and downloading files, exploring Gopher menus, and reading USENET newsgroups.

8

Using WAIS as a Search Engine

Finding information on the Internet can be extraordinarily difficult. We examine several ways of doing that in this book; so far, we've used the archie system through several client programs to track down filenames at FTP sites, and later, we'll see how to use Veronica to search for titles on the system of menued information we call Gopher. But archie demonstrates a central problem with Internet search tools—what they find is often incomplete. How helpful is it to find a file called info.doc if we haven't the vaguest notion of what's in it? And how would we know to search for it in the first place with a title that is so uninformative?

Suppose we're looking for information about the works of Patrick O'Brian, that wonderful novelist who writes about the British Navy in the age of sail. Even if we know that info.doc is a file that contains background material on Lord Nelson's fleet, we're still faced with the necessity of finding it, downloading it, and printing or searching it on our own machines. Wouldn't it be nice if we could run a keyword-driven search that would check every word of the document in question, and a host of other, possibly related, documents as well, and then produce a list of the items that were most germane?

What we want, in other words, is a tool that will go beneath the surface of things, checking the contents of files on the Internet and helping us to locate the ones that count, without regard to their names, so that our searches are more productive. We'd miss our info.doc file in an archie search; who would think to search archie for so general a title, since it could refer to any of thousands of possible topics? But a textual retrieval system could pull that title out of thin air. And if it were built right, our text retrieval system would allow us to call up a list of related documents on-screen, compare them to each other in terms of their relevance to our needs, and retrieve the ones that were most likely to meet those needs. It would even let us redo the search with those hits as examples of the kind of thing we want to see.

WAIS—Wide Area Information Servers—is an attempt to fulfill this function. A number of client programs exist to manage our WAIS sessions, everything from a lean and cryptic Unix client to full-featured graphical programs for the Macintosh and the Windows-based PC. As we examine these tools, we'll see that WAIS is still in its infancy, and that it meets the information needs outlined in the previous paragraph only partly. WAIS cannot, for example, go out over the Internet and search wherever we point it. Instead, it functions by searching databases that are designed for the WAIS system. Like archie, then, WAIS works with a subset of Internet information, and that means we are reliant upon the quality of the subset as we determine whether we can find the data we need.

Note: Would you like to obtain a list of WAIS databases (in WAIS terminology, "sources"), to look over what's available? You can retrieve a list of sources known to Thinking Machines Corp. from the following URL:

> **ftp://quake.think.com/wais/wais-sources.tar.Z**

Or try the FTP server at WAIS, Inc:

> **ftp://ftp.wais.com/pub/directory-of-servers/wais-sources.tar.Z**

I think you'll find as you work with WAIS that the system holds great promise. Each database can be a collection of specialized information in any form; WAIS can just as easily be used to search a catalog of digitized photographs as a library of textual documents. And because WAIS is a networked database tool, it allows you to work with information no matter where it is physically stored on the network. This allows you to begin the process of building global, instantly accessible libraries, fully indexed and searchable, for any topics people have an interest in putting on the net. Ultimately, that means anyone can become a publisher of digital information; you or I could set up a WAIS server without too great a difficulty, using it to inform the world about subjects of particular interest.

Making Databases Communicate

The strength of databases, as well as their weakness, has always been that they are so specific. Let me illustrate this with reference to the kind of search I've often run in my own work. Suppose I would like to track down information about a British company that sells pharmaceuticals. I know there are countless business databases available through services like DIALOG and The

Knowledge Index: ABI/Inform, Trade & Industry Review, Business Dateline, Standard & Poor's Daily News, the Pharmaceutical News Index, Commerce Business Daily, the ICC British Company Directory, and so on. Having set up an account with one or more on-line services, I could search these databases, but given their fee structure, I must be careful in deciding which one. In making my choice, I sharply limit the range of possible responses to my query, and for all I know, I may miss the one article or abstract that precisely fits my needs.

The WAIS system gets around such limitations by allowing you to search one or more databases simultaneously. Each database is made available on a server somewhere on the Internet. To be usable, the database must be fully indexed; in the WAIS environment, that means making the whole text searchable (for text documents) or, for sounds or image files, making each file retrievable through the proper keywords. When you run a search with a WAIS client, the program on your computer contacts whichever databases, or *sources*, you have specified for the search; you can search through one database or many. The server returns a list of documents that meet your criteria, ranked according to which ones seem to fit your profile the closest (based upon the number of times your keywords appear within them). You can then choose what you want to see.

WAIS also includes a feature it calls *relevance feedback*. Suppose you find that, out of ten "hits" from your search, only three articles are really applicable. A good client will allow you to specify those three articles as the pattern for a revised search that will produce more articles like the first three. This is a significant feature, for the WAIS search engine remains relatively crude, and you will often find, mixed in with the useful hits, a number of articles that don't come close to fitting your description. This occurs because WAIS does not yet know how to differentiate between words in terms of their importance, making it imperative that you construct each query with care. Because WAIS will search for every word you enter, connector words like *and* or *not* should be avoided; WAIS will search for them as diligently as your primary keywords!

A Word about Interfaces

When you move to a SLIP/PPP account for Internet access, you significantly change the way you view networked information. As we've seen, all the major tools are available through command-driven interfaces and can be run from a Unix-based shell account. The same is true of WAIS. There is an interface called swais that is accessible by Telnet or usable as a local client for running WAIS searches, but its interface is challenging and at times confusing. While I often use a shell account to get my Internet work done, I find that the one place where I seldom resort to the Unix interface is with WAIS; it takes me longer to recall all the swais commands than it does to run the search and examine the results.

Note: WAIS has undergone development in many quarters. The project was first launched at Thinking Machines Corp., a company specializing in parallel processing technology and information retrieval. Under the guidance of Brewster Kahle, Thinking Machines entered into a working relationship with Apple Computer, Dow Jones and Company, and KPMG Peat Marwick. Out of this work came the groundwork for WAIS, as well as a freely distributable version of the software. As work in WAIS has advanced, Thinking Machines has given up its support for the free product, which is now in the hands of the Clearinghouse for Networked Information Discovery and Retrieval (CNIDR). You can learn more about CNIDR's work with WAIS at the following URL:

http://cnidr.org/welcome.html

We will examine how to access World Wide Web sites such as these in Chapter 11. A complete range of documentation is available here.

Brewster Kahle, meanwhile, remains active in WAIS work; he is the founder of WAIS, Inc., a company owned by many of the original developers of the WAIS concept. The company sells commercial WAIS servers and offers software with a range of additional features not found in the freeware version. Its FTP site is also a good place to look for text files about the background of WAIS and its current state of development. To reach the site, use this URL:

ftp://ftp.wais.com/pub/

If you do choose to run WAIS searches through a shell account, I recommend you use Gopher as your method. As we'll see in Chapter 9, Gopher was designed with ease of use in mind, which is why it is laid out as a series of nested menus; you point at the item you want and press the Return key. Many Gopher servers have links to WAIS-based information, in which case the search can be run through a standard Gopher interface. But again we face a drawback; while we can search a database using Gopher as our front end, we cannot search more than one database at a time. Because this significantly reduces the effectiveness of our search (and adds considerably to our overall search time), I recommend your sticking with a graphical client throughout. Nothing could drive home the power of your SLIP/PPP capability more than comparing swais or Gopher-based WAIS with any of the graphical WAIS clients.

WAIS for Microsoft Windows

To examine how WAIS works by example, we need to retrieve a WAIS client program through which we can run our first searches. The first of the programs we'll examine is EINet WinWAIS, a full-featured WAIS client that includes a graphics viewer program. The program, a creation of Microelectronics and Computer Technology Corporation, is distributed as freeware. You can retrieve this program from the following URL:

ftp://ftp.einet.net/einet/pc/

At the time of this writing, the filename was ewais204.zip. The program is also available as a self-extracting file called ewais204.exe; you can use either.

You can contact the developers at:

EINet
MCC
3500 West Balcones Center Drive
Austin, TX 78759-6509
E-mail: **license-info@einet.net**

Installation of the program is simple thanks to an automated install routine included by the developers. Here is all you need to do:

1. Place the compressed program file in a temporary directory for extraction. It should not be placed in the same directory in which you want to install it. Extract the ewais204.zip file with the PKUNZIP utility. Alternatively, if you are using the self-extracting ewais204.exe file, extract it by running the program; the included files will be decompressed automatically.

2. Run the setup.exe program from Windows Program Manager. Follow the instructions presented on the screen.

Running a WAIS Search with EINet WinWAIS

When you double-click on the WinWAIS icon, you will see the screen shown in Figure 8.1. We can now examine how WinWAIS, and by extension, the WAIS system, works to help us locate information. Notice first of all the Selected Sources: box in the upper center of the dialog box. A *source* is a WAIS database, of which there are now hundreds. Most databases focus on a particular subject, although there are also directories of servers that can help you find precisely the right database to perform your search.

To select from the available sources, pull down the Edit menu and click on the Select Sources command. You will see a screen like the one in Figure 8.2. As you can see, we are currently working with two sources; one is a server

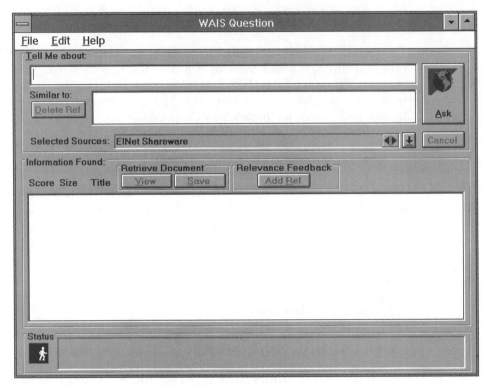

Figure 8.1   The initial EINet WinWAIS screen.

directory maintained by Thinking Machines Corp., where much of the early work on WAIS was performed. The other is a shareware database maintained at EINet. We know that a server directory can point us to hundreds of other sources on the Internet, so let's check into that source first.

To do so, highlight the Directory of Servers entry and click on Select. You will see that this server is added to the Selected Sources box on the right side of the dialog box. Now remove the EINet Shareware source by highlighting it in the Selected Sources box and clicking on the Remove button. The EINet Shareware source will disappear from the Selected Sources box. When you click on OK, you will see that the main query screen now shows only the Directory of Servers in its Selected Sources: field.

Choosing the Right Source

When you choose a source, you are deciding which database to use to perform a certain search and, as you have seen, you have the ability to choose more than a single source at a time. For this initial search, we will use the Directory of Servers to help us find the right database to use in our work. Let's decide,

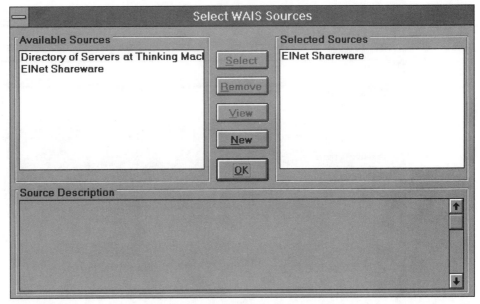

Figure 8.2 Selecting sources with WinWAIS. Use the Select and Remove buttons to manage the databases you will use in your searches.

first of all, what it is we'd like to find out about. I'm planning a trip to Peru, and would like to know more about the country before I make any arrangements. The Shining Path guerrillas have been a dangerous force in the Andes over the past decade. Can WAIS help me learn whether they are still a threat?

To find out, I will enter the keyword travel in the Tell Me About: field. I then click on the Ask button to set EINet WinWAIS searching. Soon I receive the results shown in Figure 8.3. Now this is an interesting screen, and it's one we need to focus on to understand what is happening with WAIS. Remember first of all that we are asking questions of the Directory of Servers. This means that the results we get will be WAIS databases that may be germane to our search. All the Directory of Servers does is to catalog the hundreds of WAIS databases that are out there, and help us locate the ones we want to use. We must then contact those particular databases to run our search.

Notice that the "hits" from this search are ranked with numerical values to the left. Those with 1,000 are the ones that WAIS thinks are the most germane; the system makes this distinction based on the number of times our keyword appears in the articles being referenced. As you can see, the first hit is the Directory of Servers itself, which makes sense, since that directory contains most of the WAIS servers that are out there, including those that have a specific travel connection. The second perfect score is a database called US-State-Department-Travel-Advisories.src. Here, the .src suffix tells us that we are dealing with a WAIS source, or database. You'll therefore encounter that suffix frequently as you work with WAIS.

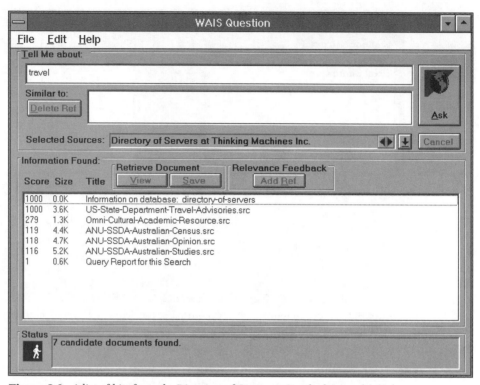

Figure 8.3   A list of hits from the Directory of Servers using the keyword travel.

Just what is WAIS searching as it goes through the Directory of Servers? It is looking through descriptions of various databases to check your keyword against what is in them. The descriptions are short but contain useful information. For example, let's look at the description of the travel advisories database. To do so, highlight the US-State-Department-Travel-Advisories.src item and click the View button under Retrieve document. This will generate a screen like the one in Figure 8.4.

Note: It is important that you understand the basic WAIS methodology. We are running two searches. The first is a search of a database directory, in this case, the Directory of Servers at Thinking Machines Corp. The second, once we have chosen the databases we think are most applicable, is a search of the servers we have thus uncovered. Later, as you discover particular WAIS databases that are useful in your work, you will be able to run searches without first running the broader search of the Directory of Servers. But it's always useful to check the directory just to see if new databases have been added that may be helpful.

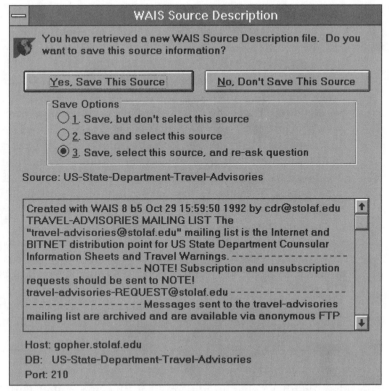

Figure 8.4 Examining a particular source in WinWAIS. The descriptive information provided helps you decide whether to use a particular source in your search.

Take a good look at this screen. The lower half of it contains a window with the database description within it. You can scroll through this description by using the scroll bar to the right of the text. Reading through it will provide you with information about what the database is for, who maintains it, and how you can obtain additional information.

Adding Sources for the Search

We can see from this description that we are dealing with a collection of information sheets and travel warnings from the U.S. State Department, which certainly seems helpful in our query. The next step, then, is to add this particular source to the list of sources we'd like to use in the second part of our search. To do so, I will click the button marked Save and select this source. I do this because I want to return to my list of hits from the Directory of Servers before running my query; it may be that there are other databases that could be helpful. I then click on the Yes button to save the source.

Note: How do you run a search of the Directory of Servers? As you can see, I have deliberately chosen a general search term, and this is the key to searching this broad database. If you make your search extremely specific, you are likely to fail. I could have asked the Directory of Servers to find all databases that fit the keyword peru, but chances are strong that I would have generated no hits whatsoever. That's because a travel-oriented database probably won't, in its file description, list every country it mentions within its holdings. But I do know that any database that focuses on travel is likely to have information on destinations throughout the world.

So think in broad terms as you query a server directory. If you want to find out where you can get an on-line version of Sophocles' Oedipus at Colonnus, don't use oedipus as your query—use literature, or perhaps classics. If you need to learn more about the planet Neptune, don't query for neptune; instead, look for databases using keywords like astronomy or planet. If you keep your search terms as broad as possible, you will be able to uncover resources that can then take you into very specific places. Once you move your search from a server directory to the specific databases that your first search has uncovered, you will be able to get more specific and target precisely what you need.

The other database that might apply is the one called Omni-Cultural-Academic-Resource.src. I don't know what's in this one, but by clicking the View button from the query screen, I can find out. I retrieve a description in the same dialog box as the one we saw in Figure 8.4. Here I learn that this database is a collection of information about various countries, one that is compiled from various USENET newsgroups, mailing lists, and other databases. The description, incidentally, also includes the keywords that are used to flag the database when we run our searches through the Directory of Servers. I like the looks of this database and save it for our search.

But what about the others? I learn that the final listings in our selection of hits are from Australian National University; one includes census information, one is stuffed with the findings of opinion polls in Australia, and the last is a collection of studies about Australia and New Zealand. None of these seem related to my travel plans in Peru so I choose not to select them. Returning to the query screen, I see that the two sources I did select are now listed in the Selected Sources: field, and I am ready to begin the second part of my search.

Searching the Selected Sources

My previous query to the Directory of Servers was the keyword travel; I wanted to find databases that would, in some way, deal with the subject. Now I can get

> **Note:**   While Australia and New Zealand are certainly interesting travel destinations, it's unusual to find a database of opinion poll information listed as one of the results of a search on the keyword travel. What's going on?
>
> The answer involves the way WAIS searches for data. All you can do when you search the Directory of Servers is to run a keyword check against the keywords listed in the various database descriptions. How accurately those descriptions fit the databases they describe is up to the people making up the keyword lists; some descriptions and keyword sets are more accurate than others. You should expect to retrieve far more hits than will actually be usable, as WAIS is building its list of hits on the basis of how many times your keyword appears in the descriptions. But we must also acknowledge that the Australian materials did receive a much lower score than the two databases that were our first choices. This indicates that, although WAIS found the keywords we wanted, it did not rank these databases high in terms of their possible relevance to our search. Items with a perfect score of 1,000 are those most likely, then, to meet our needs, while progressively smaller scores indicate less likelihood of relevance.

more specific. I will enter the keyword peru in the Tell Me about: field. When I click on Ask, EINet WinWAIS goes to work, producing the results shown in Figure 8.5.

Here we have quite a few hits, all entries in which WAIS has found our keyword of peru. As always, we begin by looking at those entries with the best scores. Notice that we have two; one seems to be a travel advisory, while the other is a Gopher item that seems to be from a network specializing in news from developing countries. I can look at any of these items by double-clicking on its entry, or by highlighting it and clicking on the View button. In Figure 8.6, for example, I have called up the travel advisory. And as you can see, I've obtained some interesting information. December may not be the time to travel in Peru, considering the news that the Shining Path guerrillas often mark the birthday of their leader with renewed activity.

Scrolling through the list of hits from my search, I see that they range from those with the 1,000 score to one with a paltry 39; WAIS is suggesting that the latter probably isn't of interest, but is showing it because it did contain my keyword. Now a word of caution. Although you should always check items with high scores first, it behooves you to work through the entire list of WAIS hits, because the system is imperfect, and often an item that WAIS thinks is not terribly interesting will be precisely the one you need. Remember, you are dealing with a document retrieval system that makes assumptions that are reasonable, but hardly infallible. Don't ever assume that you can ignore the items that turn up at the bottom of the list. I find, for example, a number of interesting docu-

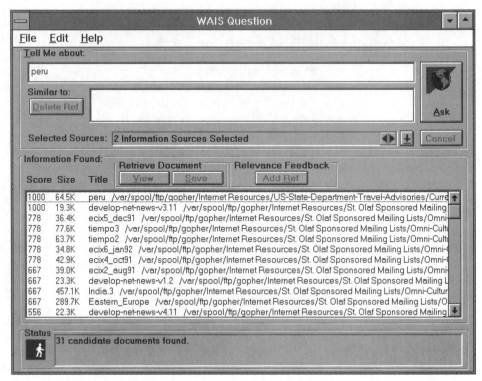

Figure 8.5   A targeted search using the keyword peru produces many hits.

ments about Peru, including others from the State Department, with scores below 500; several prove to be worth examining.

Using Relevance Feedback

As we've already seen, the list of hits WAIS generates is littered with inapplicable material. Some of it is relatively close to our information needs, while other sources seem bizarre. It's hard to see what a 457K document about India is doing on this list, and the same query might be made about a similar document on eastern Europe (all, of course, have multiple instances of our search term, but now we know that the mere appearance of a keyword doesn't mean that the articles work within our search parameters). We'd like to find some way to narrow our search to more relevant sites.

Relevance feedback is the technique by which WAIS accomplishes this. Let me show you how it's done before explaining the background; like many Internet tools, relevance feedback is easier to understand once you've seen it in action. In this case, I will compile a list of those items on my initial hit list that are most relevant. I will highlight each item on the list, and will then, one by

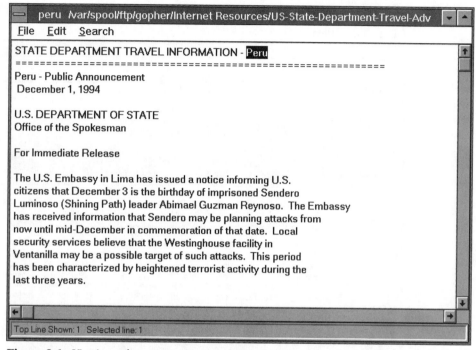

Figure 8.6 Viewing a document on-screen. This travel advisory tells me I might want to avoid Peru in certain months of the year.

one, click on the Add Ref button under the Relevance Feedback field on the query screen. Certainly I will add the top item on Peru, and also the other item with the perfect 1,000 score, the one on developing countries. I'll also click on something called tiempo (perhaps it's a newspaper article or a newsletter), and an item called peru-public-announcement, which appears well down on the list with a score of only 141. I choose it because it features Peru in the title and I know it may prove useful.

Once I have selected these references, they will appear, one by one, in the top screen window in the query screen. If you will examine Figure 8.7, you will understand at once what is happening here. We now have a multistage query. We are asking the selected WAIS databases to find information about Peru. But we are also telling them to run their list of hits about Peru past another filter; they should find documents that are similar to the ones we have just selected as particularly relevant. Running this new search by clicking on the Ask button will produce a new list of hits, one which is, theoretically, closer to what we need.

Now it's time for a word of caution and, perhaps, a reality check. Relevance feedback is a great idea; it allows us to gradually home in on what we need and produce search results that more closely approximate the kind of documents

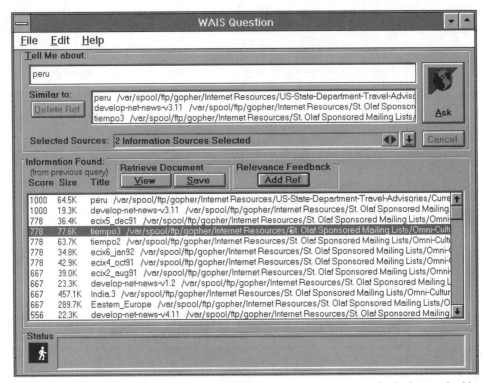

Figure 8.7 Using relevance feedback to refine a search; the program now looks for articles like the ones I've specified.

we're trying to retrieve. But in practice, the system often fails. The reasons are several. For one thing, client software isn't particularly strong, at least not yet, in terms of handling relevance feedback, and it's more than possible that, having run a successful initial search, you will find yourself unable to generate any meaningful result by adding new references.

The other problem with relevance feedback is that WAIS is a new system; it is under continuous development, and while its potential is enormous, it doesn't always succeed in making the subtle distinctions we would like it to make between documents. Then, too, remember that we are dealing with a wide variety of databases of different kinds, some of them better built and maintained than others. It may be that the depth of information we were hoping to find in a particular database isn't there, at least not yet; in that case, all WAIS can do is to recycle our requests until we finally realize we are producing the same screen of results each time we go through the process.

Could WAIS be improved? Certainly, and work in that direction is ongoing. It would be useful, for example, to be able to run standard Boolean searches within these databases. In other words, we'd like to use connector words like

AND or NOT to signify relationships; for example, "show me all documents that contain the word newspaper AND the term New York but NOT the term New York Times." In Boolean terms, such a request could be phrased this way: (new york and newspaper) not (new york times).

But not all WAIS servers will support using words like AND in this special sense. As we've just seen, WAIS typically examines its databases for all the keywords you select; if you put new york and newspaper in as a search statement, the software will search for every instance of the words new, york, and, and newspaper. This limits the nature of our queries.

Nonetheless, WAIS can still take us places that no other Internet tool can. Let's run a second search to sharpen our skills, and see if WAIS can help with the history of a very remote place.

Searching for Pacific Islands

Long fascinated by the islands of the Pacific, I've always harbored the desire to visit the distant Marquesas Islands. In his book *Return to Paradise*, James Michener talks about standing quayside in Papeete, Tahiti, watching a schooner loading for the long trip to this northernmost outpost of French Polynesia. Subsequently, a local news item caught my eye with a comment about the upcoming commemoration of the settlement of the islands. I'd like to see if the Internet offers any resources about Pacific islands in general and, in particular, about the Marquesas. Can I find any history databases that talk about the islands?

The search begins with the directory of servers, as it must, since I don't yet have the names or addresses of any servers specializing in this part of the world. So I run the keyword history past WAIS to see what the directory of servers can generate. The result is shown in Figure 8.8. Notice that I've pulled up quite a few hits involving history. This is a satisfying turn of events, since not long ago, such materials were hard to come by. It's natural that WAIS servers should concentrate on computing topics, but we can expect to see broader participation from the social sciences and the humanities as educators, writers, and librarians begin to realize the potential of the system.

One source in particular catches my eye; it's called ANU-Pacific-Islands-L.src. ANU, I happen to know from other reading, stands for Australian National University, certainly a primary site for Pacific Island studies. The -L following the name tells me that we are probably dealing with the archive of a mailing list (most of which, at least in the BITNET world, are named with this suffix). Thinking that the database must hold various conversations about the islands, I elect to view its synopsis, then to use it as a source.

At this point, I have the ANU database listed as my source; any search I run will therefore query it. I could go with just this source, but it seems reasonable to search any other databases that look promising. And indeed, Australian National University seems to have been quite active in WAIS development. I

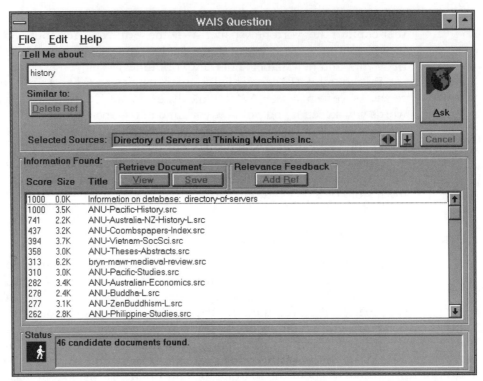

Figure 8.8 Results of a search on the keyword history; all of the hits are databases with some connection to that subject.

can enter any other sources I'd like to use from the list of history hits. I choose ANU-Pacific-History.src, which seems to be tailor-made; another choice is ANU-Pacific-Manuscripts.src.

I now enter a keyword: marquesas. Surprisingly, this search generates 76 hits. You can see the result in Figure 8.9. I learn that 1995 is indeed the four hundredth anniversary of the first European contact with the inhabitants of the Marquesas. I retrieve bibliography records of significant works about the islands, including Sharp's "Fact and Fancy in the Marquesas Group," which turns out to have been published in the Journal of the Polynesian Society, and E.S. Dodge's "An Account of the Marquesas Islands." I even learn of the existence of whaling ship records maintained at the Old Dartmouth Whaling Museum in New Bedford, Massachusetts.

Choosing among these entries, I can refine my search by telling WAIS which of these hits is the most germane. I'll leave the whaling records aside and concentrate on the material that focuses specifically on Polynesian culture and history. By highlighting each of the entries I find most useful, I can add them to the relevance feedback list (they then appear in the Similar to: field). Or, I can actually call a document up on-screen, select a portion of it, and then

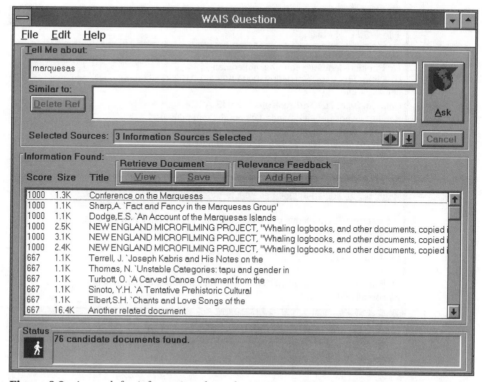

Figure 8.9 A search for information about the Marquesas Islands produces a surprising number of hits.

add that selection to the relevance feedback list. In Figure 8.10, you can see this process at work.

I have called up a document for viewing and have selected a portion of the text. All I need do now is to call down the Edit menu; there, I have a relevance feedback option that lets me select this material for inclusion in the new, refined search.

Finally, I am left with a search that basically says, "tell me about the Marquesas Islands, but come up with references that are close to the ones I have specified." When I run the new search, I get a modified list of hits. Many of the same items appear, but in new numerical ranking, indicating which are now considered the most valuable for the search, based upon the relevance feedback technique.

Adding Sources Manually

Normally, when we begin a search, we start with the directory of servers at a particular site. It's the general reference source that shows us what databases are out there, and lets us choose one or more against which to run our search.

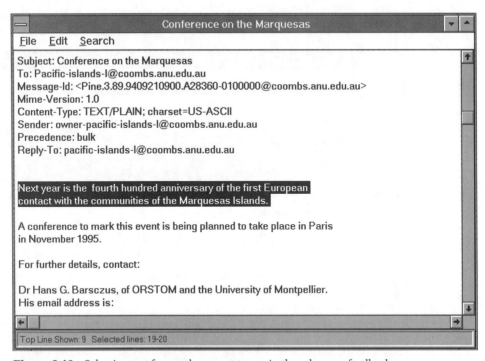

Figure 8.10   Selecting text from a document to use in the relevance feedback process.

But after you have worked with WAIS for a while, you will find that, depending on your interests, certain databases tend to be ones you return to frequently. You will want to add these servers to your list of sources so that you can get back to them quickly. After all, why go through the entire directory when you happen to know that precisely the right database is available, and that all you need to do to reach it is to click on its entry?

Note: Relevance feedback, as a concept, is one of the most exciting aspects of the WAIS project. But as it currently stands, the feedback you get may be disappointing. The system does not yet have the full battery of tools it must have to understand the kind of subtle distinctions between data sources that a good researcher must work with. In my own work, I have found that actually putting relevance feedback to work occasionally results in a tighter search, but my advice, given the current state of the art, is to simply run a basic WAIS search under your topic and go through the list of hits with great care. You will often do a better job than WAIS at discovering which of the relevant items you need, and they may be buried at the end of the listings, even though relevance feedback has suggested to you that the top items are best.

You need, then, to learn how to add a database to your server list. I already explained this with EINet WinWAIS when we chose sources for particular searches; the program simply added the source information into its own records, and we could return to that particular database whenever we wanted. Eventually, you will build up a list of databases that will allow you to tailor your WAIS environment for your specific research needs.

But what happens if you are looking through a magazine one day and come across a listing for a WAIS server you had never heard of before? To add a server to your list of sources, turn to the Sources Editor screen. This is accessible by pulling down the Edit menu and choosing Select Sources. Within the Select WAIS Sources dialog box, click on the New button. It is this dialog box that you will use to add new sources, by filling in the appropriate fields. Notice in Figure 8.11 that the Port setting has already been given; it's 210, which is the WAIS standard.

As for the rest of the information, you must specify the name of the database, the server it's located on, and the actual database file. In Figure 8.12, you see a filled-in source definition, in this case, the one for U.S. Department of State Travel Advisories. Notice that we've also got a note at the bottom telling us when this database was created. The point is, at any time you can add new servers to your list of databases in one of two ways:

- Search the directory of servers, find appropriate databases, click on them to view their contents, and add them to your list of sources.

- Add the source information manually, using the host and database name supplied by whoever told you about the new database.

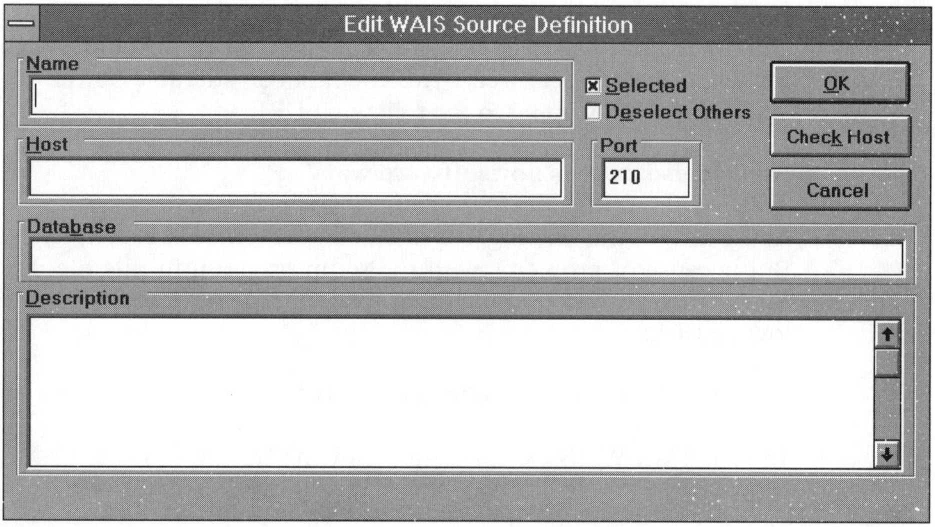

Figure 8.11   Use this screen to add a new WAIS source by filling in the appropriate fields.

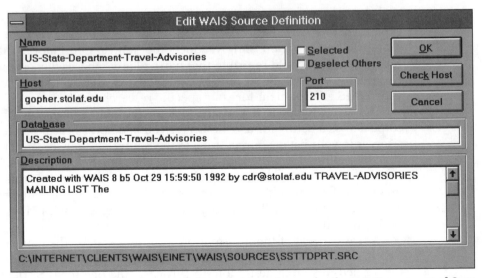

Figure 8.12 A completed source definition; this is the one for the U.S. Department of State travel advisories database.

Either will work (although adding new sources through the directory of servers is clearly faster). Both ways will let you build up a reference list you'll use frequently in your work.

WinWAIS: An Alternative WAIS Client

Good software comes from unexpected sources, as the Internet proves time and time again. The following is a program created by the U.S. Geological Survey which is a full-featured WAIS client of considerable power. You can download WinWAIS by going to the following URL:

ftp://ridgisd.er.usgs.gov/software/wais/

At the time of this writing, the filename was wwais24.exe, a self-extracting file. But because of problems with the setup program in this file, I have used an earlier version, found in the file wnwais21.zip. You can find this file at the following URL:

ftp://sunsite.unc.edu/pub/micro/pc-stuff/ms-window/apps/

To install WinWAIS, perform the following steps:

1. Move the compressed WinWAIS file to the directory of your choice (but not the same directory as the one into which you plan to install

Note: Don't be put off when you download a program and discover a problem, such as the installation difficulty I encountered in WinWAIS. Creating good client programs for an environment as rapidly changing as the Internet requires you to think on the fly. By the time you read this, the WinWAIS home site will doubtless have the problem with its setup file fixed. If it doesn't, there are always countless sites around the Internet where previous versions of any program can be found. I mention the University of North Carolina site above because it is particularly full-featured and reliable.

the program). I set up mine in a directory called */waisdist,* at the suggestion of the program's help file.

2. Run the WinWAIS setup program from within Microsoft Windows by pulling down the File menu in Program Manager and giving the Run command. The file you want to run is setup.exe.

WinWAIS will then prompt you for basic TCP/IP information, as you can see in Figure 8.13. Here the issue is simple. WinWAIS needs to know whether it will be working with Windows Sockets, and you must tell it that it will. To do so, leave the Windows Sockets box checked, and uncheck the embedded TCP/IP box by clicking on it. The WinWAIS setup program will then run through its installation routine and create the necessary files on your hard disk, as well as establish a program group for WinWAIS itself.

Setting Up Sources in WinWAIS

When you double-click on the WinWAIS icon in the new program group, the screen shown in Figure 8.14 will appear. The query screen isn't much different from the one presented by EINet WinWAIS, but then, we wouldn't expect it to be; the issues posed by WAIS remain the same no matter what the client's implementation happens to be. As you can see, we have a query field at the top, followed by a second field in which to place our relevance feedback queries. The third window will hold the responses we get from our various searches.

To get to the list of sources, pull down the File menu and choose Select Sources. You will see the screen shown in Figure 8.15. Notice that there is only one source listed, a directory of servers database. That should prove useful, since we know that we begin our queries at a directory of servers and thereby find other databases that specifically handle the kind of request we'd like to make. To view this source, highlight it, and the full information will appear, as in Figure 8.16.

The first step in running a search is to highlight the Directory of Servers and drag it into the top window, thereby selecting it as your source (you can do the same thing by double-clicking on this entry). In my own work, I prefer to

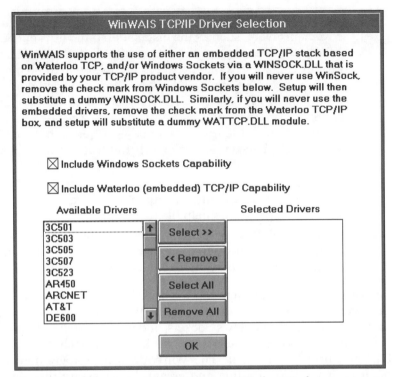

Figure 8.13   You must tell WinWAIS to use Windows Sockets to get your SLIP/PPP connection to work with the program.

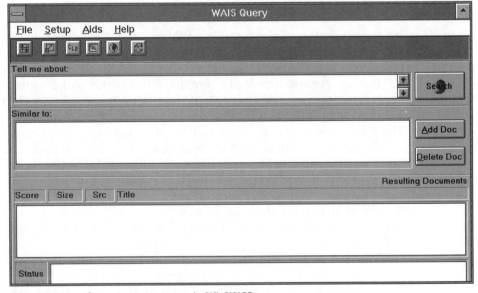

Figure 8.14   The main query screen in WinWAIS.

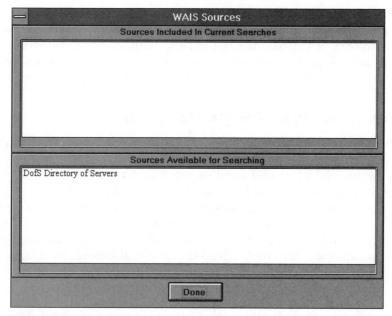

Figure 8.15 WinWAIS lets you choose sources by dragging them into the upper field in this dialog box.

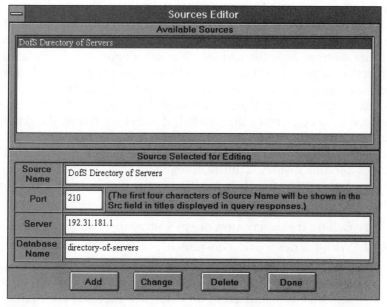

Figure 8.16 Viewing information about a particular source in WinWAIS.

go through the Directory of Servers at Thinking Machines Corp. (this is the same one we used in our searches with EINet WinWAIS). To add that directory to WinWAIS' list of sources, I used the Sources command from the Setup menu and added the necessary information. This is the same method you will use to enter any other servers to the WinWAIS list.

Step-by-Step Searching for Ancient Sites

Calling down the File menu, we can choose the Select Sources command. By double-clicking on the Directory of Servers, we then select it as our source for the search. Suppose I am interested in finding archives of information about archaeology available through WAIS databases? I'd like to learn more about the history of central Asia and its links to Europe. The best way to find out whether any WAIS resources exist that can help is to search the Directory of Servers under an appropriate term. I use the keywords archaeology history anthropology and let WinWAIS go to work. And indeed, the search reveals 59 references that use these keywords in their file descriptions.

That was step one. In step two, we must choose which of these sources are the most promising. I can call up a description of any one of them by double-clicking on its entry. In Figure 8.17, for example, I have clicked on the source called academic_email_conf.src. If you will examine this figure, you will see that we have run into one of the traps WAIS unintentionally sets for us.

The academic_email_conf.src database came up as a result of my search under the keywords archaeology history anthropology, but reading through its description suggests that it was for other reasons than the one I had in mind. In fact, academic_email_conf.src is itself a listing of academic conferences and USENET newsgroups; it is not itself a database of information about any of the three topics I chose in my keyword list, but rather, it may contain pointers to other sources of information. This, of course, can be valuable, but it is instructive to keep in mind that WAIS sources exist in a wide variety of formats, including directories to other types of information.

Two other servers look promising: bryn-mawr-classical-review.src is a database of articles from the journal of the same name; the database is full-text, so we can use it to retrieve whole articles for our work. Another useful find is ANU-Central-Asia-Studies-L.src. This is the archive of a mailing list that focuses on the history, culture, language, and economy of central Asian nations. I need to add both to my list of sources. To do so, the following steps are necessary:

1. Call up the description of any source to be added to the list.

2. With the description on-screen, pull down the File menu.

3. Choose the Save As command. This will call up the Sources Editor screen; all the necessary fields will have been added for this source, and all you will need to do is to click on Add. Then click on Done to exit the Sources Editor.

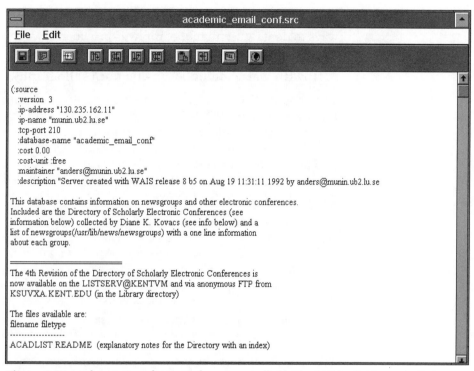

Figure 8.17 A description of a particular source, called up by double-clicking on its listing.

4. Now return to the File menu. Choose Select Sources to edit the sources you want to use for the search. In this case, we want to deselect the Directory of Servers (no point in leaving it in our search list because we've already searched it). Double-clicking on its entry deselects it; double-clicking on the two new entries places them on our search list.

I am now ready to run the next part of my search. Using the keywords silk road, I run the search, and am rewarded with nine hits. Among them is a review of a new book on Central Asia with interesting historical information about the development of trade routes between Europe and the region. There is also news of a conference in Tashkent to evaluate recent historical finds relating to ancient commerce. I also find several odd hits. A recipe for steamed buns? The reason it's there is because of the way WAIS searches. My keywords were silk road; WAIS found both words, though not in sequence, in the recipe in question, and thus thought it had found something I might like to see. But to give the system credit, it ranked the item low on the list in terms of its possible relevance. Remember to bring your sense of humor with you when you use WAIS, and keep in mind how it categorizes what it finds.

Note: Trying to keep up with WAIS issues? There are a number of ways to do it. A useful bibliography is provided at WAIS, Inc.; go to the following URL:

ftp://ftp.wais.com/pub/wais-inc-doc/bibliography.txt

You should also consider the USENET newsgroup **comp.infosystems.wais**, where WAIS issues are discussed and both users and programmers regularly gather for conversations.

A number of mailing lists are also dedicated to WAIS. You can join any of them by sending mail asking that your name be added to the subscription list. The correct address is included with each entry. They include the following:

wais-discussion	A moderated list on WAIS subjects and the world of electronic publishing. Send mail to **wais-discussion-request@think.com**.
wais-interest	A moderated list used to announce new releases of WAIS software. Send mail to **wais-interest-request@think.com**.
wais-talk	A technical list that specializes in development issues. Send mail to **wais-talk-request@think.com**.

You can also check frequently updated information about WAIS from the Clearinghouse for Networked Information Discovery and Retrieval. Contact the following URL:

http://kudzu.cnidr.org/cnidr_projects/

WAIS on the Macintosh

Two excellent Macintosh programs for WAIS access exist: WAIS for Macintosh (once known as WAIStation), a product of Thinking Machines Corp., and MacWAIS, a Macintosh version of the EINet WAIS software. For a complete list of Unix, OS/2, and other clients, check the Frequently Asked Questions document for the USENET newsgroup **comp.infosystems.wais**. You can retrieve this document by signing up for the newsgroup; the document is regularly posted there. Or you can get it from the following URL:

ftp://rtfm.mid.edu/usenet-by-group/news.answers/wais-faq/

WAIS for Macintosh

To retrieve WAIS for Macintosh, go directly to the FTP site at Thinking Machines Corp. The URL is:

ftp://quake.think.com/wais/

At the time of this writing, the filename was wais-for-mac-1.1.sea.hqx.

To use WAIS for Macintosh, you will first need to complete the installation process. Here is how to do it:

1. Put your WAIS application wherever you choose. It can go into any folder you prefer, or it can remain on your desktop as an alias. The advantage of leaving an alias on your desktop is that your Internet applications are instantly accessible without your having to go through the folder hierarchy to find them.

2. Within the WAIS folder you will find a folder called, simply, WAIS (it will probably be found within the System Folder inside your WAIS application). Copy this WAIS folder to your Macintosh's System Folder. The System Folder for your Mac must be called System Folder and it must reside on the top level of your hard disk. If it does not, WAIS for Macintosh won't be able to locate the databases and preferences it needs to find to run your searches.

3. You are now ready to start WAIS for Macintosh. Double-click on its icon to launch the program. When you do, two windows will appear, one marked Sources, the other Questions; both will be empty. Sources are the WAIS databases to be used for a particular search. Questions are the queries you frame by entering keywords into the WAIS system. To complete installation, close WAIS for Macintosh at this time and restart it. You should now see a source listed in the Sources window; this is the Directory of Servers at Thinking Machines.

Your job in using WAIS for Macintosh is to create a query. To do so, choose New Question from the Question menu. You will see the screen in Figure 8.18. The screen is not dissimilar from those created by the Microsoft Windows clients we have already examined. We will enter a question and specify a source to be searched. Let's do both now.

For the question, I will specify servers that deal with physics. We know now that WAIS is searched in a multistep process. First, we look in a directory of servers to find out which databases will be the most likely to house the information we need. Then, we move to those specific servers and search them with the same or, perhaps, more specific keywords. I will enter the keyword physics in the Look for documents about field.

Now we need to specify a directory of sources to search. To do this, drag the Directory of Servers source from the Sources window into the Sources field of the query window. Now we have a keyword and a source selected, and can proceed with the search. I activate it by clicking on the Run button. The results are shown in Figure 8.19.

I can double-click on any of these hits to view the item in question. In Figure 8.20, I have chosen the cold fusion database (cold-fusion.src). Notice that

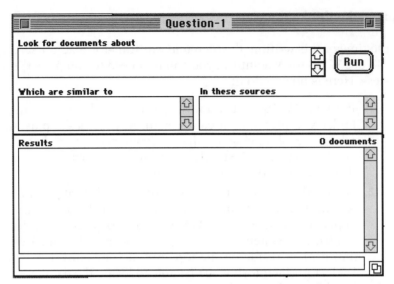

Figure 8.18 Use this screen to create new questions in WAIS for Macintosh.

the screen shows me information about the database; it is an annotated bibliography of materials relating to the so-called "cold fusion" phenomenon that so captivated researchers several years ago. If I click on the Contact box at the top of the screen, which currently says Mac TCP, I can pull up the actual server information for the site.

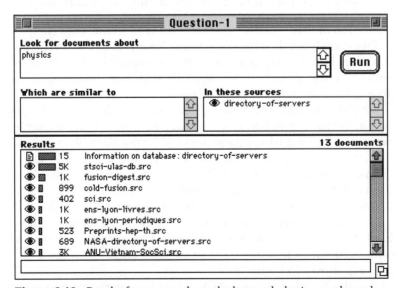

Figure 8.19 Results from a search on the keyword physics, as shown by WAIS for Macintosh.

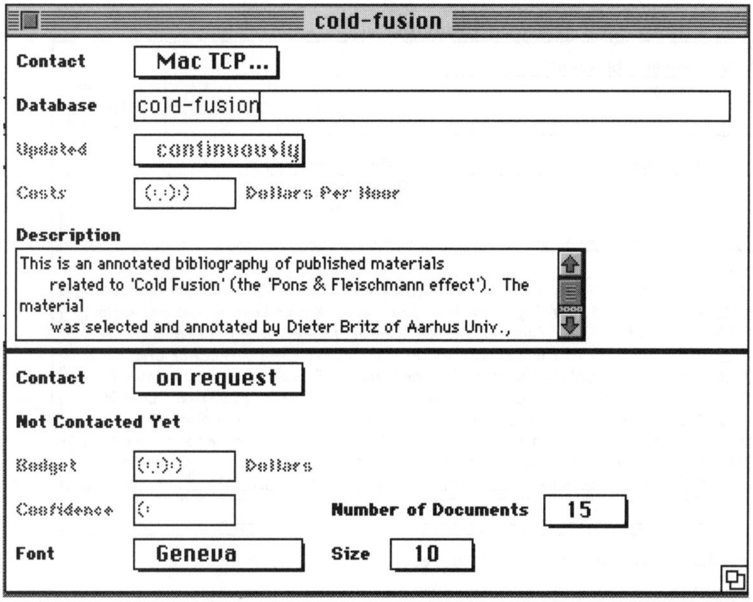

Figure 8.20 Source information about the cold fusion database.

Now we need to find out how to add sources to our list for searching. The easiest thing to do is to call down the File menu and choose the Save command for any source that you want to add to your list. Alternatively, you can highlight that source in the list of search hits and drag it into the sources window on the query screen (although this method won't automatically add the source to your Sources window for future searches). In either case, you will be prompted for a place to save the source. If you save it to the Sources folder inside the WAIS folder in your System Folder (WAIS for Macintosh prompts you to do this), you will add the source to your Sources window. You can do this for as many sources as you would like to search.

In the case of our physics search, let's assume I am looking for more information about current research into cold fusion. The first thing I need to do is to highlight and add two interesting databases—cold-fusion.src and fusion-digest.src. I use the methods just outlined to complete this procedure. The second step is to remove the directory of servers from the list of active databases; after all, I've already run a search against it. To do this, I simply drag it to the Sources window. Now I can frame my request by entering a keyword in the appropriate field on the query window. I choose several: cold fusion research. You can see my impressive list of hits in Figure 8.21.

There are a number of intriguing documents here, but if I want more, I can always highlight any items that seem particularly useful and drag them to the Which are similar to field in the query window. I can then run the search again, using relevance feedback to home in on documents that more closely meet my needs.

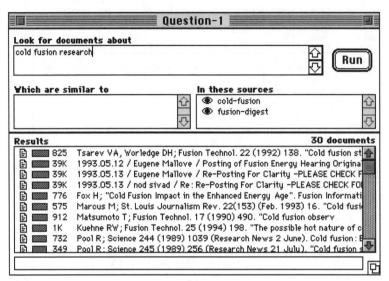

Figure 8.21 Results of a search on research into cold fusion.

MacWAIS

EINet MacWAIS is a shareware program that you are free to evaluate for up to thirty days; after that period, you are asked to register your copy with EINet. The program can be found at the following URL:

ftp://ftp.einet.net/einet/mac/

At the time of this writing, the filename was macwais1.29.sea.hqx. EINet MacWAIS costs $35, which can be sent to the following address:

EINet Mac Shareware
MCC
3500 West Balcones Center Dr.
Austin, TX 78759-5398

When you unpack MacWAIS, you can double-click on its icon to produce the screen shown in Figure 8.22. What you are seeing is the source window overlaid upon the query window (you will see in the figure that I have already added several sources; your screen will not show these). It is from this initial window that you will be able to control the sources MacWAIS uses in its searches. Like its EINet WinWAIS counterpart, MacWAIS offers two sources to begin with, a directory of EINet shareware, and a Directory of Servers. For your initial searching, choosing the Directory of Servers makes sense, because it lets you track down other sources you might like to add to your list for temporary or permanent inclusion with the program.

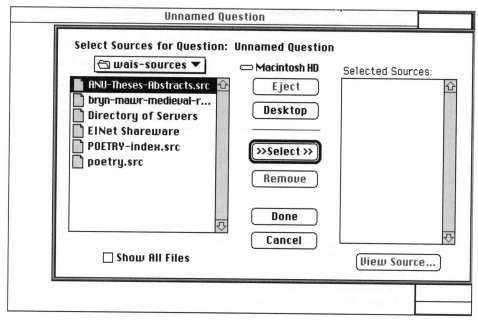

Figure 8.22 Double-clicking on the MacWAIS icon calls up the new query screen, overlaid by the sources screen.

Note that the window to the left shows the currently available sources, while the window on the right shows those that are selected at the moment. You can move between them by highlighting a source and then clicking on either the Select button to add a source, or the Remove button to take it off the list of selected sources. When you have chosen the Directory of Servers, click on the Done button to move to the query screen. You see this screen in Figure 8.23. As you can see, the basic fields here are similar to those of other WAIS browsers; MacWAIS, in fact, is drawn after the model of WAIS for Macintosh, so there are few surprises in terms of keyword entry or source selection.

To run a WAIS search with MacWAIS, simply enter your keyword(s) in the Tell Me About: field. Let's suppose I want to learn something about Geoffrey Chaucer, the English medieval author. I know that searching under this term is far too specific; there are unlikely to be any servers that specialize in Chaucer and his works per se. So I will broaden the search term, using the keyword literature. I receive a list of results, as shown in Figure 8.24.

We have several interesting hits here, and I can view any of them by highlighting the item in question and clicking on the View button; alternatively, I can simply double-click on the item I want to see. When I do this, a screen pops up with full database information. In Figure 8.25, I have chosen to examine the source called queueing-literature-database.src; I haven't the faintest idea what its title means until I examine the description. Clearly, this database, which focuses on telecommunications literature, isn't likely to have anything

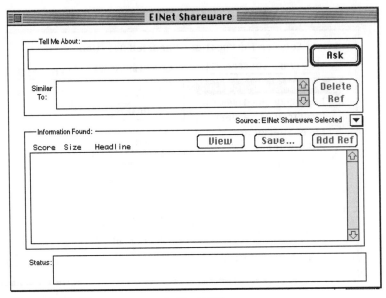

Figure 8.23   The query screen in MacWAIS.

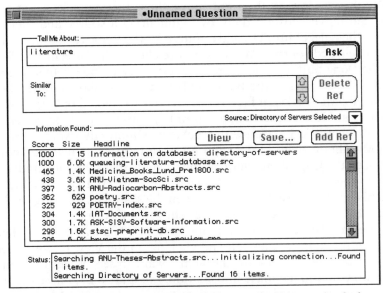

Figure 8.24   Results of a search of the Directory of Servers, under the keyword literature.

of use to a medievalist like myself. I work through the entire list now, choosing a variety of databases to use in my next search. I add them as I find them by highlighting them in turn and clicking on the Save button, which includes them in the source list.

In this way, I compile several sources: poetry.src, POETRY-index.src, and bryn-mawr-medieval-review.src. I save each to my source list using the methods just outlined. I also remove the Directory of Servers from the source list for the second part of my search. To edit the source screen at any time, it's only necessary to pull down the Sources menu and click on the Select command. Having tuned my source list as required, I run the search, using the keyword chaucer and canterbury tales. Figure 8.26 shows my list of hits. I can now page through these documents to find those that are particularly interesting. Figure 8.27 shows a brief biography of Chaucer that this list produced.

To perform relevance feedback with MacWAIS, it's only necessary to select the items that are appropriate and click on the Add Ref button. In this way, I can compile those items that are closest to my needs and then run the search again by clicking on the Ask button. In this case, the list I generate is different only in the rankings given the individual hits, an indication that I have pushed as deeply into the three WAIS sources I have selected as is possible. A rule of

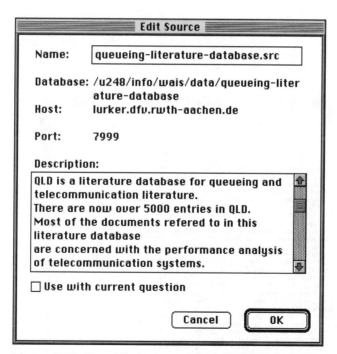

Figure 8.25 Examining a source in MacWAIS to determine whether it is relevant to our search.

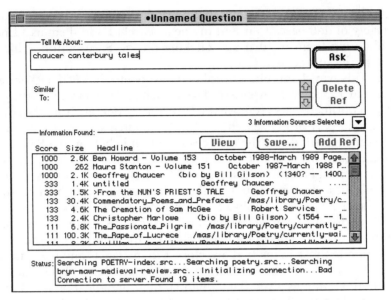

Figure 8.26 A list of hits using the search terms chaucer and canterbury tales.

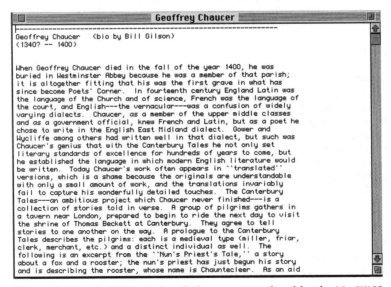

Figure 8.27 A brief biography of Chaucer, as produced by the MacWAIS search.

Note: None of the WAIS clients, either for the Macintosh or for Microsoft Windows, is particularly good at recovering from a network error. For example, it sometimes happens that when I attempt to search a particular server, the program can't make the connection, for whatever reason. Sometimes this will produce a message saying the connection to the server has failed. In other cases, the program will hang up waiting for a response that doesn't come. If this happens to you, it's only an indication that something, somewhere along the line, has broken down. Your only recourse is to exit the program (you may have to reboot) and run the search again, perhaps at a later time. It's a dismaying but true fact that the Internet works much, but not all, of the time. Get past your initial annoyance at such glitches and you will develop the imperturbable, zen-like state of mind of the true network aficionado. As in all things, persistence pays.

thumb with relevance feedback is that when the same hits continue to recycle, you have reached the end of the technique's usefulness.

MacWAIS is configurable through its Preferences menu, which is accessible from the File menu. You can see this menu in Figure 8.28. Most of these items may be left in their default state, but several deserve our attention:

Maximum Result Documents   This field allows you to specify how many hits the server should return as a result of its search. The default is 40.

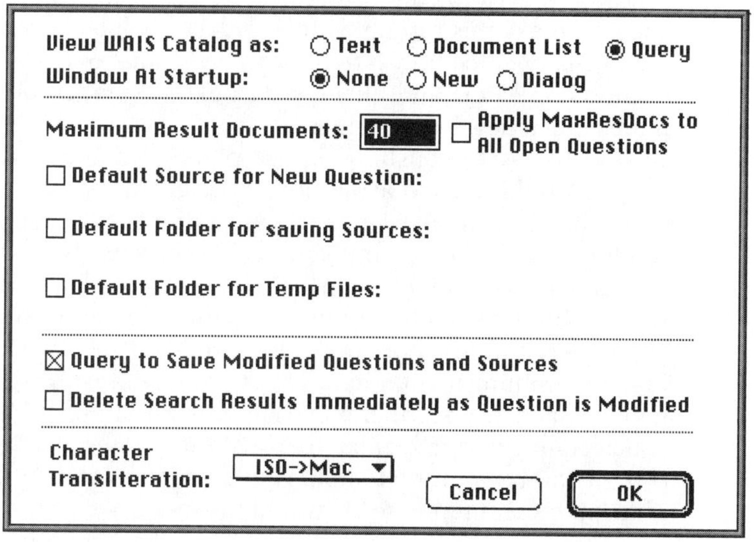

View WAIS Catalog as: ○ Text   ○ Document List   ◉ Query
Window At Startup: ◉ None   ○ New   ○ Dialog

Maximum Result Documents: [40]   ☐ **Apply MaxResDocs to All Open Questions**

☐ **Default Source for New Question:**

☐ **Default Folder for saving Sources:**

☐ **Default Folder for Temp Files:**

☒ **Query to Save Modified Questions and Sources**
☐ **Delete Search Results Immediately as Question is Modified**

Character Transliteration: [ISO->Mac ▼]   (Cancel)   (OK)

Figure 8.28   The MacWAIS Preferences menu.

Default Source for New Question

Here you can specify a source to be used as the default for any new question. The default is none (the box is unchecked); when this is the case, the first thing you see when you attempt to ask a question is the sources dialog box, allowing you to specify what you want to search. It probably makes sense for you to include the Directory of Servers as your default here, since the first search you run will doubtless be to ascertain whether there are any other databases that meet your specific needs. By clicking on this box, you cause MacWAIS to call up the sources window, from which you can select the source to use as your default.

Note: What makes a good WAIS source? The answer to this question is as varied as the people who use WAIS, and those who create the databases that will make the system into a useful research tool. What is exciting about WAIS and, in a way, is its greatest challenge, is the fact that it allows anyone with a network connection to become a publisher of information. For example, I am an inveterate collector of old movies. I specialize in the period from 1929 to 1956, working my VCR night after night recording the offerings of the various cable channels. I've accumulated a vast number of these films, and a great deal of information about them.

This is precisely the kind of thing that could be indexed with WAIS. Suppose I created a catalog of all my holdings, along with complete movie descriptions, cast lists, directors' notes, or whatever. I could set up WAIS on my own machines, indexing my database with keywords and using a WAIS client to search it. And if I chose to make this resource more widely available, I could set up a server that would allow it to be searched by anyone with an appropriate connection and client program. The endeavor gives self-publishing a new lease on life.

But like self-publishing, it also places demands upon the creators. I would have to avoid any copyrighted material in creating such a database (copyright issues are a thorny question that awaits resolution in the courts, but you don't want to be on the wrong side of this issue as it applies to networking). I would also have to take responsibility for maintaining the quality of my information; after all, there is nothing more pernicious than a database with faulty or ill-managed information in it. The Internet, unfortunately, contains many databases and other materials with questionable pedigrees. If you become interested enough in WAIS to create a database of your own, it will be your job to hold it to the highest standards as a part of helping the Internet to grow and prosper.

Default Folder for saving Sources:	Allows you to specify where new sources should be saved. The default is to leave this box unchecked, which means that when you save a source, MacWAIS will prompt you for where to put it each time. If you check this box, the program will give you the opportunity to select the folder of your choice.
Default Folder for Temp Files	Allows you to specify the folder in which documents retrieved for viewing should be saved. The default, which is to leave the box unchecked, causes such documents to be saved into the MacWAIS folder.

Z39.50 over the Web

At the Clearinghouse for Networked Information Discovery and Retrieval in Research Triangle Park, North Carolina, interesting projects in information hunting are the organization's raison d'être. Z39.50 is an information retrieval protocol standard; WAIS is one of the implementations of Z39.50, but not the only one. The standard was approved in 1988 by the National Information Standards Organization, which develops the protocols used in library and

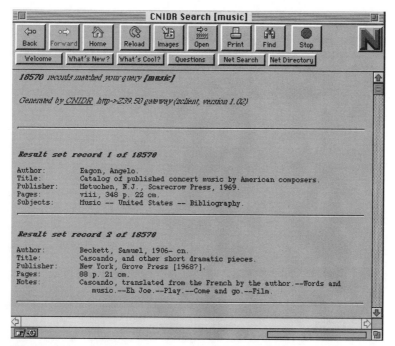

Figure 8.29 Using Netscape, a World Wide Web browser, to run a search under the keyword music.

research work. In its broadest sense, Z39.50 is designed to help computers working in the client/server model handle information requests, with the client passing queries along to an information server. An important use for this kind of engine is in the library community, where on-line library catalogs demand an efficient means of searching.

In Figure 8.29, you see an example of an information search run through a World Wide Web browser (in this case, Netscape); I have searched for a bibliographic database using the keyword music. You can see that the list of hits is extensive; we are looking at only the first two of over 18,000 references!

Anyone interested in the broad issues of information retrieval through Z39.50 methods should consult the World Wide Web page at CNIDR. It is available at the URL mentioned earlier in this chapter:

http://cnidr.org/welcome.html

Links are provided to a wealth of information about Z39.50, WAIS, and the continuing development of robust search engines. We will examine how to use World Wide Web browsers in Chapter 11.

9

Gopher as Graphical Tool

Created at the University of Minnesota, Gopher was one of the first Internet tools that met the needs of average people. By "average," I mean people whose job descriptions don't include programming in C or maintaining computer networks across widely dispersed buildings on a university campus. The Internet's roots in Unix have been such that those proficient with the operating system often forget how difficult it is to work with complicated commands and their associated parameters. But one system administrator, Mark McCahill by name, decided that the University of Minnesota's faculty and staff needed an easier way to get their bearings on the net. Gopher was the result.

Gopher's name more or less describes it. True, as any sports fan may guess, the system is named after the Golden Gophers of Minnesota. But it can also be construed as "gofer," and that is exactly what Gopher does—it allows you to point to what you want, and then goes out over the network to retrieve it. What amazes novices about Gopher is that its resources, like those of Mosaic, need not be local at all. The distributed nature of the Internet, spread through over 130 countries, allows this tool to reach halfway across the globe for a file using the same mechanism with which it pulls in the local academic schedule, a weather forecast, or on-line literary work.

Gopher running in the Unix environment simplifies users' lives considerably. Couple Gopher with SLIP/PPP and you create an even more graphical environment, with the capability of displaying on-line graphics, running multiple sessions simultaneously, keeping target lists of favorite Gophers and more. Gopher thus provides an example of how your SLIP/PPP connection can take an already useful tool and turbocharge it. In this chapter, we'll examine three interesting Gopher implementations—HGopher (a public domain program); WinGopher, a commercial product; and TurboGopher for the Macintosh. I will illustrate the principles that underlie all Gopher use using HGopher, and then examine each program in detail to show how to draw maximum benefit from it. Use one of these Gopher clients and you'll find the bare-bones Unix Gopher to be a spartan environment; you'll be unlikely to go back.

Basic Gopher Principles

A Gopher server presents information in the form of menus. Each menu, and by inference, each Gopher site, is thus as logical and informative as its system administrators have chosen to make it. Newcomers should remember that, as with FTP sites, practices may vary from location to location. What one system administrator sees as a logical presentation of data may strike another as needlessly complex. And because Gopher has now spread from Minnesota to encompass thousands of sites around the world, there is no reason to expect the menu structure on one Gopher to mimic that of another. This can be a frustrating problem for anyone looking for centralized logic on the Internet, but then, the Internet was never conceived from the top down as an information system; rather, it grew from the bottom up, by the continuing efforts of its developers.

The closest analogy would be to the multitude of bulletin board systems (BBS) scattered around the globe. They may all use similar software (with variations, of course, depending upon their implementation), but no two BBS systems are alike. There are BBSs that specialize in gardening, or rock music, or cats. There are BBSs that are more oriented to electronic messaging in conferences, while others focus on accumulating huge collections of files. And the only way to find out what is available at a given BBS is to log on to it and start exploring.

So with Gopher. What began as an attempt to systematize university-oriented materials at a specific site has become a publishing tool of considerable complexity that offers users the chance to explore the Internet at large, or to focus on particular subjects of interest. Paging through one of the rapidly proliferating number of Internet directories, I come across Gophers containing presidential documents (**gopher://jupiter.cc.gettysburg.edu/**), breaking news about telecommunications (**gopher://gopher.eff.org/**), collections of on-line literature (**gopher://wiretap.spies.com/**), data about cancer research (**gopher://istge.ist.unige.it**) and a musical archive (available as part of the vast holdings at **gopher://gopher.uwp.edu/**). Also intriguing are the all-purpose sites that are becoming prime Internet stops for newcomers, like **gopher://world.std.com/**. We'll examine some of these shortly.

Gopher is also capable of undertaking other jobs besides the retrieval of textual documents. If you double-click on a Telnet resource, Gopher will allow you to open a session with that site, in some cases prompting you for particular information you may need to complete the connection, such as a login or password. Gopher can also access files at FTP sites and retrieve them for you (in fact, running file retrievals through Gopher is probably the easiest way for beginners to download data). The important thing for the end user is that these transactions are handled without requiring you to enter complex commands. Gopher is built to know about these types of resources and to differentiate among them.

The Gopher Interface

Let's take a look at the interface issues raised by Gopher. Remember, the concept was to make using the distributed resources of the network easier by allowing users to see a list of available items and to point to what they want. What users gave up by way of choice (menus, after all, are determined arbitrarily by the administrator) they gained by way of accessibility. In Figure 9.1, you see the result, a Gopher's top menu as viewed through a Unix shell account. Here I am operating without SLIP/PPP, simply logging on by modem to a Unix machine.

The menu structure is apparent; we have twelve choices, ranging from news about the service provider whose Gopher this is (Interpath, here in Raleigh, North Carolina), to local tools like a radio station's program guide, and listings of events from a weekly news magazine. Notice, though, that we

Figure 9.1 A Gopher session as seen through a shell account.

are hardly confined to the Raleigh, or even North Carolina area. We also have the capability of moving into other Gophers, which effectively opens up the entire world for us, since Gopher systems are spread around the globe. To move to any of these choices, we use the cursor keys to reposition the marker arrow. When it is adjacent to the item we want to see, we hit a Return to retrieve it. Options are then presented for reading the material, saving it to disk or mailing it to our e-mail address. In Figure 9.2, for example, I have moved into the WCPE program schedule and have checked on what's playing the first week in November 1994. As you can see, Gopher can be a wonderful publishing tool for anyone with specialized information and a yen to reach a broader audience.

In the preceding example, we looked at textual documents that can be read on-screen. But remember: Gopher "documents" can in fact be any kind of data. Text is certainly predominant, but you will also find images, sounds, and in some Gophers, moving video. Gopher can point to a weather map or a search capability that allows you to hunt through a database using keywords. Gopher is, then, more than a textual retrieval service. It is moving along with the Internet into a world of accessible multimedia resources. And as we'll see shortly, Gopher also can tie into a service called Veronica, allowing you to search through Gopher menu items around the globe.

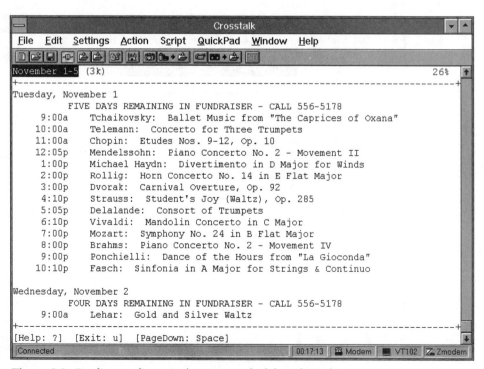

Figure 9.2 Reading a radio station's program schedule with Gopher.

Now let's look at what **SLIP/PPP** can do for your Gopher work. In Figure 9.3, I have moved into an intriguing site using WinGopher. Notice that the basic information remains on-screen just as it did with the Unix Gopher through a shell account, but the presentation differs considerably. Here, we are looking at a Gopher called Gopher Jewels; it has a long URL:

gopher://cwis.usc.edu/11/Other_Gophers_and_Information_Resources-/Gophers_by_Subject/Gopher_Jewels/

Gopher Jewels offers over several thousand pointers to information in Gopherspace by category, along with archival materials and Gopher tips. Notice the graphical touches presented by the WinGopher software, such as folder icons instead of numbers, and the menu structure, shown at the top of the screen. Obviously, WinGopher provides mouse support and allows us to choose what we want to do by clicking on what we see on the screen or pulling down a menu.

Other Gopher clients offer the same functionality. In Figure 9.4, for example, I am using HGopher, a public domain Gopher program created by Martyn Hampson. As you can see, we once again have graphical icons providing information about the files available at the site. We click on the item we choose to visit.

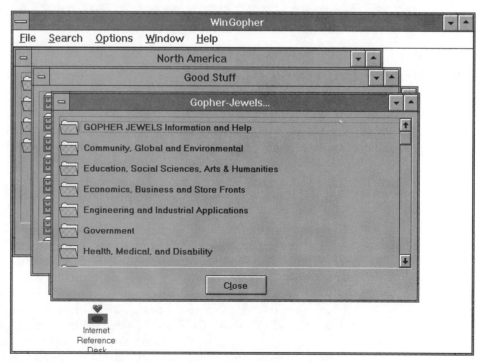

Figure 9.3 Examining the Gopher Jewels site with WinGopher.

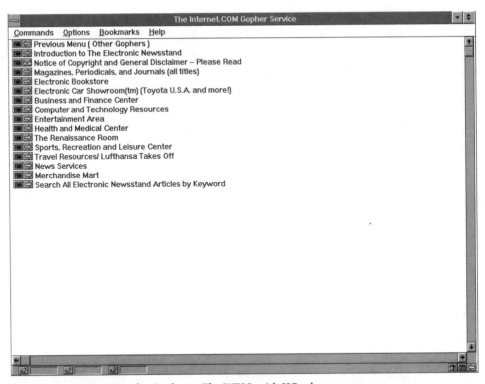

Figure 9.4   Examining the Gopher at The WELL with HGopher.

Gopher+: An Improved Protocol

Gophers work by using a protocol that allows them to communicate in workable fashion with computers around the world. The original Gopher protocol provided the basic tools, allowing Gopher clients to talk to Gopher servers using the familiar menu structure. Gopher+ is an enhancement of this original

 Note: When you retrieve a document, Gopher sends that document and then closes the connection. Although the Gopher menu remains on your screen, there is no ongoing connection between client and server. Mosaic functions in the same way, whereas FTP does not—when you are exploring the directory structure at an FTP site, your connection is live the entire time you are using FTP. Obviously, connectionless protocols like Gopher are helpful because they allow us to minimize the network's workload. You needn't feel that you are tying up a Gopher site when a Gopher menu is on your screen. You will not be generating any more network traffic until you next make a menu selection and press the Return key.

protocol that incorporates *attributes*, which means that each Gopher item has an associated attribute that flags what kind of object it is. Not all Gopher servers use the Gopher+ protocols, but those that do are able to provide a variety of new features.

Suppose, for example, that you wanted to see an image file. The original protocol could tell you that a file was an image, but which kind? There exist a variety of graphics formats, the most popular being JPEG (Joint Photographic Experts Group—the original name of the committee that wrote the standard behind such images), and GIF (Graphics Interchange Format), a type commonly found in the libraries of commercial on-line services like CompuServe, and certainly widely distributed on the Internet. Because the original Gopher protocol couldn't tell you what kind of image you were dealing with, displaying that image was a problem. Gopher+ can assign an attribute to that image so that a viewer program, either internal or external, can be set up to display it.

More significantly, from my point of view, is the ability of the Gopher+ protocol to provide background information on a document. One of the biggest problems we have in identifying resources on the Internet, and in keeping them up to date, is not having an easy way to check on when a document was created, who wrote it, how to get in touch with them, and any of the other data that can make information more reliable. Gopher+ can provide such information, and can even include an abstract of the document or prompt the user with questions before displaying that document. New client programs like HGopher, WinGopher, and TurboGopher work with Gopher+, so you will be able to use these features to your advantage.

> **Note:** As with any Internet tool, we immediately encounter new language. You'll run into the term *Gopherspace* (I used it already in this chapter), which simply refers to the universe of Gophers throughout the Internet. You are in Gopherspace when you are using any one of these Gophers. You may also hear the Gopher at the University of Minnesota (**gopher.tc.umn.edu**) referred to as the "mother Gopher," an acknowledgment that Minnesota is where Gopher began. Don't be surprised if you also see the site referred to as the "mother burrow." Internauts have long had a taste for the whimsical.

To make Gopher accessible, let's now use the HGopher program to show off its features, including those made available through Gopher+. Although I will examine Gopher's basic functions through the HGopher program, you should bear in mind that all the features shown here are available, though in somewhat differing form, in the other two clients we will discuss in this chapter. Information on WinGopher and TurboGopher follows later in the chapter (and always keep an eye out for new clients; this field is constantly evolving). Even if you intend to install one of these other programs, you should work through the following sections with me to understand the universal principles of Gopher use.

HGopher: A Public Domain Gopher Client

HGopher is a Gopher+ client for the Microsoft Windows environment. Although it is in the public domain, its author, Martyn Hampson, does ask that you donate $10 to your favorite charity if you use the program regularly, a small price to pay for so helpful a tool. The program can be retrieved from Imperial College in the United Kingdom at the following URL:

ftp://lister.cc.ic.ac.uk/pub/wingopher/

At the time of this writing, the filename was hgopher2.3.zip. The PKUNZIP program from PKware will be needed to unpack the binary file.

Note: Be careful about filenames. A file called hngopher2.3zip also exists. This is a version written for Sun Microsystems computers, and is not the program you want (unless, of course, you are using Sun's PC NFS). For your trivia file, NFS stands for Network File System; it is a file utility written by Sun that allows users to access directories and files on remote systems as easily as those on the user's own computer. Most versions of Unix now incorporate NFS. In our case, we want the version compiled for execution on a PC.

The HGopher Package

When you unzip the HGopher file, you should find the following files:

hgopher.exe   The HGopher program.

hgopher.hlp   HGopher's on-line help system. This is a crucial file, for the documentation that comes with HGopher is sparse. You will find yourself using this help file to answer most questions.

hgcso.exe   A viewer for CSO information. CSOs, as we will see below, are set up to display information from colleges and universities.

hgopher.ini   A critical initialization file. This is where the defaults for the HGopher program are located.

default.gbm   HGopher's bookmark file. Several defaults have already been set, including one at Imperial College that contains background information and viewers for HGopher.

readme.txt   A short text file with the latest news about HGopher.

Installing HGopher

HGopher is a simple program to install. To proceed, copy the files you just unpacked from the HGopher zip file into the directory of your choice. I have set up all my clients in a directory called *c:\internet\clients*, with subdirectories branching off for each type of client. Thus, HGopher resides in the *c:\internet\clients\gopher\hgopher* directory. But this is simply a system that works for me, and you should give some thought to the best file system for your purposes. There is no need to bury HGopher this deep in your directory structure if you would prefer to use *c:\hgopher* instead.

You will now need to create HGopher as an item in one of your Windows program groups. You can do this through Windows' Program Manager by using the New command from the File menu, or by dragging the filename in File Manager into an open program group. Wherever you put it, the HGopher icon, a bewhiskered gopher face, should now appear in that group.

Configuring HGopher

To configure HGopher, you must first get it up and running. Double-click on the HGopher icon to do this; the program will be launched, taking you straightaway to the Gopher site at Imperial College.

Although HGopher can now be used to move between Gopher sites and read text documents, you need to set the program up to handle other file types, and also to give it information such as which Gopher server you would like to use as your home server. The principle is this: when HGopher or any other Gopher client starts, it will contact whichever server has been established as its home server. You should choose a Gopher server close to you to minimize the load on the network. Remember that once you're in the Gopher system, you will be able to move through its menus to access Gophers throughout the world, so starting off at your home base doesn't present you with any limitations.

Gopher Setup

To set up a home Gopher server, pull down the Options menu and choose the Gopher Set Up item. This menu is shown in Figure 9.5. Notice the top item here, the field called Gopher Server. Initially, this field will be set to **gopher.ic.-ac.uk**, the home Gopher server for HGopher. I have already replaced this with the name of my local server. If you are not sure what your local server should be, contact your service provider. Chances are the provider runs a Gopher, or can direct you to the site that makes the most sense for you. Enter the address of that Gopher in this field.

Leave the Selector field blank for now. This field can be used for those occasions when you want to automatically connect to a Gopher and go somewhere other than its top menu; you may eventually want to place a value in this field (see HGopher help for more information on doing so), but for most use

Note: Adjacent to the Gopher Server field is a field called **Port.** A *port* is a software address on a server computer; it has nothing to do with hardware. Ports are used to specify to which application you want to connect on the remote computer; in most cases, Gopher uses port 70, which is why this is marked as the default. You should leave the default at 70.

this won't be necessary. Instead, move down to the section of the Gopher Set Up Options menu called Files, where you will see two fields, described here:

Tmp Directory   This is where HGopher will store temporary files. Insert the directory on your hard disk where you would like such files to go.

Save to Directory   This is where HGopher saves files when you use its save function. Be sure to add the directory you would like to use here. In a moment, we will explore how to save files during an actual session.

You can leave the rest of the items in the Gopher Set Up Options box as they are; the defaults work fine. But for the curious, here is a quick look at what they are, in case you want to tinker with them when you've had a little more experience. The first three items contain information about attributes; they apply in situations where you have already examined a Gopher menu and are now returning to it.

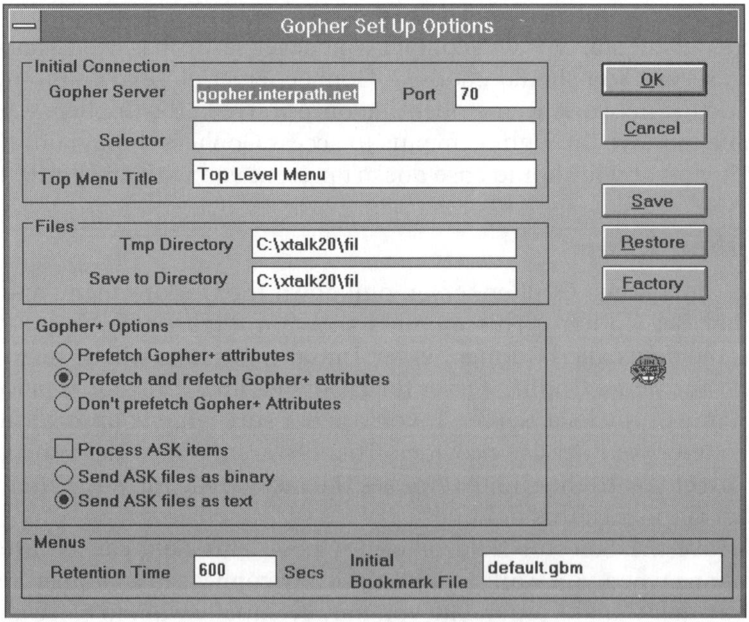

Gopher Set Up Options

Initial Connection
Gopher Server `gopher.interpath.net`   Port `70`   OK   Cancel

Selector ` `

Top Menu Title `Top Level Menu`   Save

Files
Tmp Directory `C:\xtalk20\fil`   Restore

Save to Directory `C:\xtalk20\fil`   Factory

Gopher+ Options
○ Prefetch Gopher+ attributes
◉ Prefetch and refetch Gopher+ attributes
○ Don't prefetch Gopher+ Attributes

☐ Process ASK items
○ Send ASK files as binary
◉ Send ASK files as text

Menus
Retention Time `600`   Secs   Initial Bookmark File `default.gbm`

Figure 9.5   Establishing a home Gopher server in HGopher.

Prefetch Gopher+ attributes	If HGopher knows, because you have previously examined a directory, that it contains items with Gopher+ attributes, it will attempt to retrieve all those attributes. But if it finds Gopher+ items in a non-Gopher+ directory, it will simply mark the attributes with a plus symbol (+). You can fetch the attributes again by clicking on the symbol. This tends to speed up HGopher operations.
Prefetch and refetch Gopher+ attributes	When HGopher encounters a Gopher+ directory, it will retrieve all the attributes even if this requires a second connection to the server. This is the default setting.
Don't prefetch Gopher+ Attributes	When HGopher encounters Gopher+ items, it will not fetch their attributes. Instead, it will simply mark them with a plus symbol (+), allowing you to retrieve them yourself if you choose.
Process ASK items	Gopher+ allows a server to send a series of questions to the user before presenting the information. This is called *ask processing*. With this box checked, this feature is enabled. You can turn it off if you prefer not to receive such questions. No Gopher server, incidentally, should ask you for a password. If it does, ignore the request. Your password must remain secure.
Send ASK files as binary	Allows Gopher to send binary as well as ASCII files.
Send ASK files as text	Tells Gopher to send any ASK file as text. This option is preferred as it works with the widest range of Gopher+ servers.
Retention Time	Refers to the length of time in seconds that HGopher caches menus. HGopher will retain a menu in memory in your machine, allowing you to go to any item, but opening network connections only when called for. The 6,000 second default time works fine.
Initial Bookmark File	This is the file that HGopher will load as your bookmark file when it first runs. You can edit this file as necessary to reflect your own choice of file and directory. More on bookmarks in a moment.

Network Setup

Now turn to the Network Setup item on the Options menu from the main HGopher screen. This menu is illustrated in Figure 9.6. Unfortunately, it's one of the most confusing menus HGopher provides, but there is only one operation you need to perform here. The key on this menu is to check the box marked Use Vendor provided. HGopher is referring to the Domain Name Services (DNS) provided by your service provider; by clicking this box, you specify that the program should use your vendor's DNS capability. We discussed the Domain Name Service in Chapter 6 on electronic mail. Remember that the

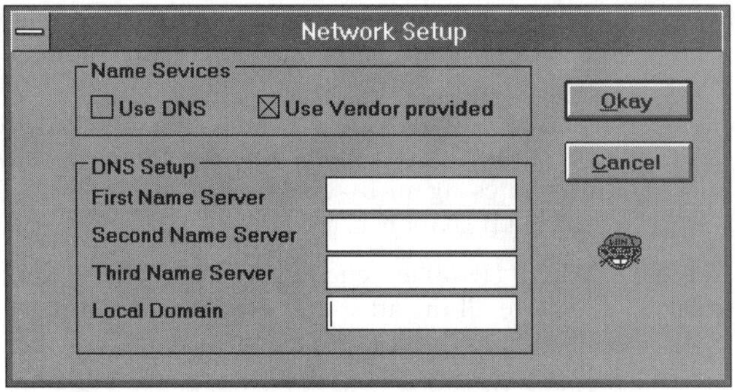

Figure 9.6 HGopher's Network Setup screen.

DNS runs on host computers or routers; its function is to turn a domain name (**harold@hastings.anglosax.gov**) into an IP address (128.241.106.2) that precisely places the computer on the Internet.

Check the Use Vendor provided box, and be sure the Use DNS box is left unchecked. This is important, because the Use DNS box enables HGopher's internal DNS, which is not reliable. When you check the Use Vendor provided box and uncheck the Use DNS box, you are set. There is no need to fill in the other fields on this menu unless you are planning to use Sun's PC NFS. If you're running Microsoft Windows on a standard PC, you won't be doing the latter.

HGopher should now be configured for use. To verify that it is, move to the Commands menu and double-click on the Go Home item. You should be taken to the Gopher server you have chosen as your home site. The program is now ready for use.

The HGopher Screen

One good place to start using HGopher is on its bookmarks page. You can reach this by pulling down the Bookmarks menu and choosing the Show Bookmarks item. HGopher will present you with a list of Gopher sites that have been set up as a default Gopher menu. You can move to any of these sites by double-clicking on the item in question. For now, let's take a look at the University of Minnesota's Gopher. Minnesota, after all, is where the entire Gopher phenomenon began. Double-click on the item marked Gopher Home (Minnesota). You should see a screen that looks like the one in Figure 9.7. Please

Note: When using HGopher, double-click on the text description of the menu item, not the icon itself. Clicking on the icon will pop up a two-part menu that allows you to retrieve information about the item and the administrator at the site.

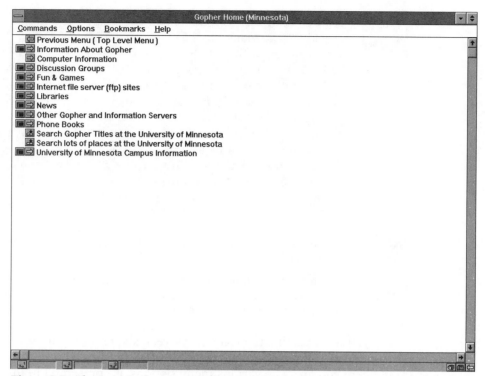

Figure 9.7   The main Gopher menu at the University of Minnesota, as seen through HGopher.

examine this figure with care. We need to explore basic HGopher usage by looking at procedures and icons.

The top-level menu at the University of Minnesota is a reflection of the kind of tool Gopher has become worldwide. We have information about Gopher itself, computer-related items, discussion groups, something called Fun & Games, Libraries, News, and a useful choice called Other Gopher and Information Servers, which, as we've already seen, can be used to connect to Gophers around the world. We also have a search capability, as shown in the items marked Search Gopher Titles at the University of Minnesota and Search lots of places at the University of Minnesota. A Gopher at any given site is usually just such a collection of local and broader-based information; each Gopher site opens out to the worldwide Internet.

Now consider the icons to the left of these menu items. Each illustrates something about the item it flags.

   A Gopher menu. When you see this icon, it means that double-clicking on the item will take you to a submenu with further choices. Notice that the icon can also be reversed, as in the first menu item on the Minnesota menu. This indicates that clicking on the item will take you to the previous menu.

Note: With any Gopher client, you have the ability to return quickly to the menu you have just visited. In the case of Figure 9.7, you will notice that the top item is marked Previous Menu (Top Level Menu). Were I to double-click on this item, I would be taken back to my home Gopher (in my case, the one at Interpath, the service provider here in Raleigh, North Carolina). Any client moves you up and down through the menu tree. Gopher's great advantage is its easy-to-follow menu structure; after using it for a time, you may also perceive this as a disadvantage, in that it is necessary to descend and ascend menu trees to get what you need. Other than Gopher's bookmark capabilities, there is no way to move *across* the menu structure.

 A Gopher item with one or more views; this indicates you are connecting to a Gopher+ item.

 A search engine. You will see this symbol associated with tools like Veronica and Jughead, which are ways you can search Gopher menus for keywords. More about how each works shortly.

If you will examine the HGopher screen shown in Figure 9.7, you will see that it contains further information. The title bar at the top of the screen tells you where you are. The various menu options are presented in the line below the title bar. At the bottom of the screen is a status bar that tells you what is happening as you attempt to establish a connection; a green light will flash as data is received. Notice that there are three status bars—you can have up to three Gopher connections working simultaneously. You can abort any transfer of information by clicking on the associated button.

The HGopher screen also contains icons in the bottom right corner. The meaning of these icons is as follows:

 A toggle between different ways of processing information with HGopher. You can choose View mode to see the document, File mode to copy it to a local file of your choice, or Directory mode to copy it to the directory you specify.

 Takes you to your home Gopher server from wherever you are.

 Takes you to the previous directory.

Moving through Gopher's Menus

Getting information out of Gopher is easy; you simply point to what you want and double-click on it. In this way, you can retrieve a Gopher menu item, or be taken to the next layer of menus beneath the current one. In Figure 9.8, for example, I have moved one layer into the menu structure at the University of

Note: A major Gopher destination will be the HGopher Information Centre, established by Martyn Hampson at Imperial College in Britain. HGopher is not strong on textual documentation, although there are a few minor items at this site including a Frequently Asked Questions list. But the real purpose of the Information Centre is to act as a repository for file viewers that are compatible with HGopher. Hampson also includes what he calls the HGopher Assault Course, which contains different kinds of documents that can be used to test your own file viewer setup. You will find the Centre already established on the default HGopher bookmark list, and you should take advantage of Hampson's work to check out the viewers here. You can also use the following URL:

ftp://lister.cc.ic.ac.uk/pub/wingopher/

Minnesota by clicking on the Information About Gopher item on its top menu. If you look back at Figure 9.7, you will see that this item contained two icons. The first is the icon associated with Gopher+ capability; the second is the arrow icon that points to an underlying Gopher menu.

Notice that we now have several new icons, each of which can tell us something about these menu items. Here are the new icons and a brief description of what they mean:

     A text file.

     A Gopher+ item for which the attributes are not yet known.

     A movie file.

    An image.

As is now obvious, HGopher makes extensive use of icons in its work. Indeed, icons and other graphical tools are one of the true advantages of a SLIP account; they get you past the character-only VT-100 interface of a straight shell account.

Knowing that the first item on the menu, called About Gopher, is a text file, we can double-click on its description to call it up. The actual file appears in Figure 9.9. Notice that this file is displayed through the Windows Notepad program. This is the common method used by HGopher in displaying the various file types; it relies upon external viewer programs to do its work. We'll see this again in a moment as we begin to look at other viewers for HGopher.

Retrieving Files with Gopher

Gopher allows us to read information readily, but it should not be construed as a display tool alone. Indeed, what we need to take advantage of from Gopher's

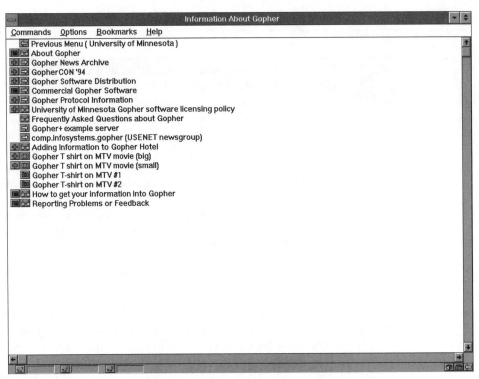

Figure 9.8 Moving deeper into the menu structure at the University of Minnesota.

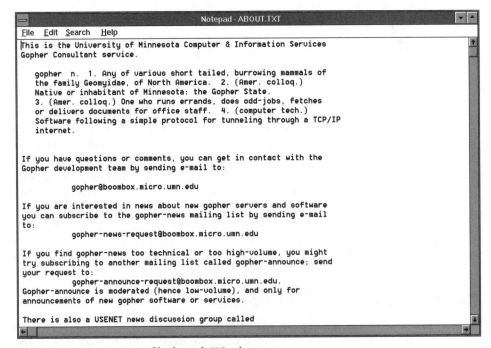

Figure 9.9 Viewing a text file through HGopher.

Note: HGopher's on-line help is quite useful. There are many other icons used by the program that are explained in the help system, and it is a good idea to consult it frequently when you run into icons that are unfamiliar. The positive side of icons is that they tag information with its obvious attributes. The negative side is that the meaning of the icons isn't always obvious; an enigmatic icon may demand a bit of research.

unusually facile browsing capabilities is the ability to move information from a Gopher to our own system. This is easily enough managed, no matter which Gopher client you decide to use. With a Unix shell account, the first step is to call up the document in question, at which point other options become available. We can request that Gopher mail a document to our electronic mailbox or save the document on disk. When I use my shell account, I frequently use the latter capability to retrieve information and print it out for later study. In fact, my office is filling up with three-ring binders full of papers collected on the net.

A SLIP/PPP account renders this process more transparent. Remember, SLIP/PPP means your computer has a place on the network; data packets are flowing between it and the Internet. Thus, any file you are examining on your screen is there for you to save. You will be prompted for a filename and directory in which to save it.

Let's take a look at this process in action. We'll move back across the country to the Interpath Gopher in North Carolina (**gopher://gopher.interpath.-net/**). In Figure 9.10, I have called up a document that intrigues me; I have retrieved it by double-clicking on its menu item. It's a tale of two boatbuilders who embarked upon a voyage down the Danube River; the story originally ran in *Spectator Magazine* here in Raleigh, and is an example of how magazines are beginning to use Gopher as a publishing tool. Because I have Interpath's Gopher set up as my home Gopher, I can move directly to it from anywhere in Gopherspace by clicking on the small house icon at the bottom right of the HGopher screen.

Gopher is an excellent publishing tool for this kind of document; however, I don't prefer to read long passages of text on-screen because of eyestrain. To get around this problem, I will download the program to my own machine. To do so, I simply pull down the File menu and choose the Save As command. In Figure 9.10, I have already highlighted this command. A click on it will pro-

Note: Here the benefits of a SLIP/PPP connection stand out. Just as with FTP, we move the file directly to our own computer, rather than having to use our service provider's machine as an intermediary. Once we have loaded the text file by double-clicking on the menu item, it is available for us to save.

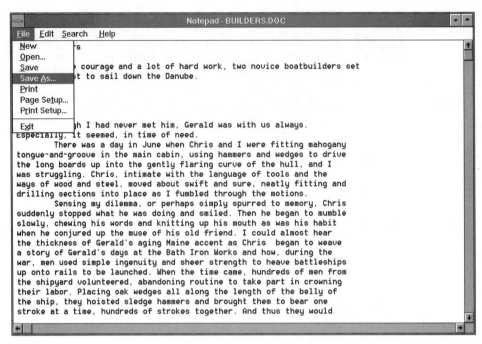

Figure 9.10   Examining a magazine article on-line through HGopher.

duce a dialog box prompting me for the directory in which I would like to store the file. The filename will be whatever I choose to insert in this box, although HGopher will supply me with a suggested title: builders.txt. Whatever title I decide to use, I soon have the file saved on my disk.

Viewing Images and Other File Types

As we've already seen, HGopher works with external viewer programs for most file types; we just examined a text file that made use of the Windows Notepad program. Despite their name, don't think of viewers as just visual in nature. An audio "viewer," for example, is a program that allows you to hear a sound file, just as an image viewer allows you to work with graphics and images. To set up the proper viewers for HGopher, we need to finish our configuration of the program by pulling down the Options menu and clicking on the Viewer Setup item. The Viewers dialog box will appear, as shown in Figure 9.11.

The method here is to select a file type that we'd like to view and then specify a viewer for that type. To tell the viewer what to display, HGopher makes use of parameters that are passed to the viewer programs. Let's now set up a viewer to handle GIF (Graphics Interchange Format) files. To do so, we need to select the file format by scrolling through the Select View type area in the

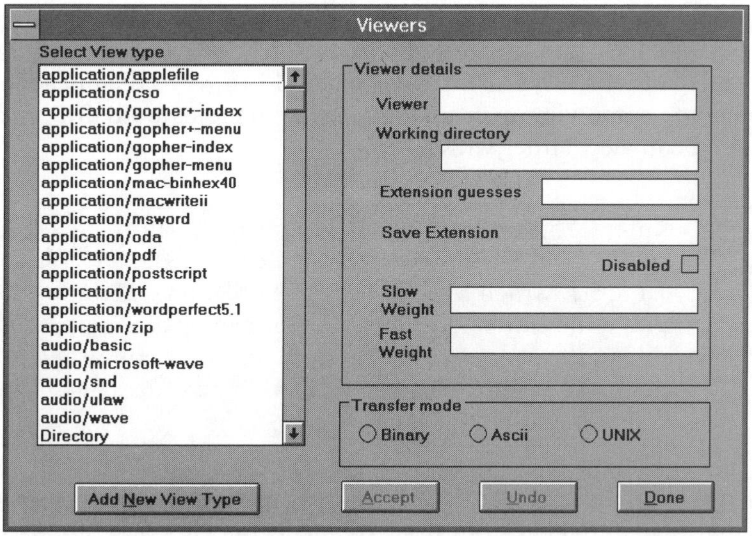

Figure 9.11   Use the Viewers dialog box to establish paths to the viewer programs you will use with HGopher.

Viewers dialog box. Doing so, we come to the file type image/gif, as shown in Figure 9.12.

Note what I have done here. The image/gif file type is highlighted, which changes the values in the rest of the dialog box. I have now inserted values in the Viewer field (I use the lview program to view GIF files), and I have placed

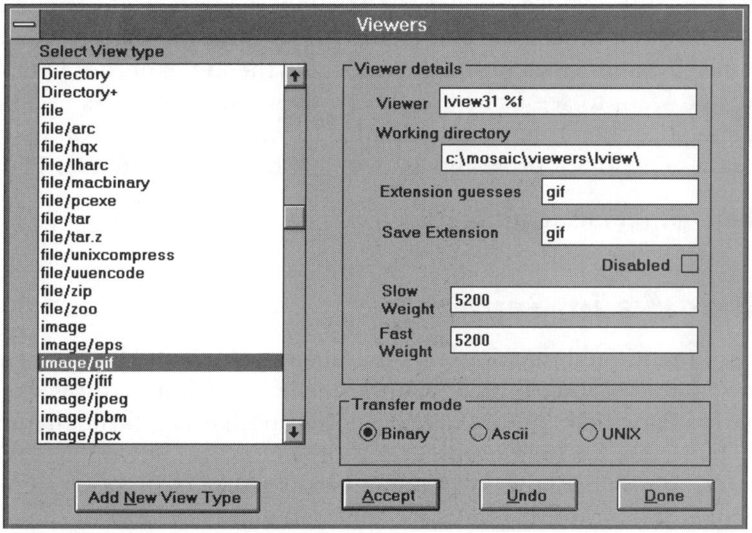

Figure 9.12   Setting up a viewer to use with GIF images in HGopher.

the proper working directory for my system in the relevant box (*c:\mosaic\viewers\lview*). By pressing the Accept button, I save this setting, and can now move on to other file types. I will, for example, move to the image/jpeg file type to place the same viewer in position (lview handles both GIF and JPEG file types so I can view either with it).

Note: You will see that HGopher uses parameters to pass information to the file viewers. In the case of the GIF file format, it is using %f, which simply passes the filename along to the program so the file can be displayed. A complete list of parameters is available in the HGopher help system. If you're confused about parameters, you needn't be concerned; HGopher uses default parameters that will work in most cases.

I can now move to the HGopher Information Centre (it's on the default bookmark page) to check out my GIF and JPEG viewer setup. As you can see in Figure 9.13, when I clicked on an image called Red Dwarf, HGopher retrieved the file and then sent it to my lview program, as set up in the Viewer Setup menu. The image then appeared on-screen; if I chose, I could manipulate it within the lview program, closing it when finished.

You will need to set up file viewers for the kind of files you want to see. Obviously, a text file editor is critical, but HGopher has already been set up to work with Windows Notepad (although you can set up an alternate viewer if you prefer). I also suggest that both GIF and JPEG viewers be enabled. The rest of the file types can be set up using the same Viewer Setup menu and the principles just outlined. You will need to make your own decisions about how many you think it necessary to enable. My recommendation would be to use HGopher for a while as is and get a feel for the kinds of files you are encountering and want to see or hear. You can then add viewers as necessary. Check in at the HGopher Information Centre for more information about viewers, and for a selection of programs known to work with HGopher. The URL is:

gopher://gopher.ic.ac.uk:71/

Using Bookmarks in Gopher

Earlier I mentioned that Gopher's menu structure could become cumbersome because it forces you to go down into the menu system to retrieve information, then to surface again before taking another path down through another menu tree. Doing this for long becomes too time-consuming, which is why we turn now to Gopher's bookmarks. A bookmark is a way of marking information; in particular, it lets you flag a useful item and add it to a list of such items. This can be handy indeed; the next time you want to see the item, you simply click on it and you are there.

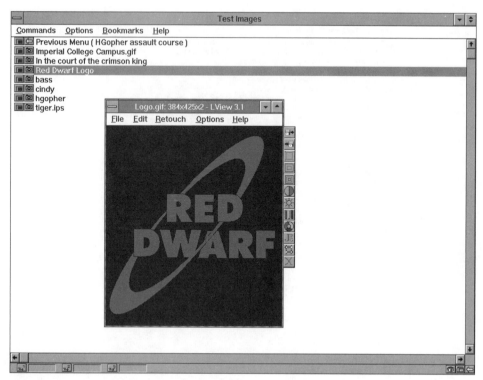

Figure 9.13 Viewing an image through HGopher.

Such customization is a valuable asset. To use bookmarks, you must first find the item you want to save. Let's suppose we are looking around at The WELL, a service provider in Sausalito, California that offers a full-featured Gopher. The home page is shown in Figure 9.14. The WELL's Gopher contains such a diversity of information that I would like to be able to call it up whenever I choose. I can do this easily by using Gopher's bookmark function. Here's how: I pull down the Bookmarks menu and choose the Mark menu item. To see the bookmark in place, I choose the Show Bookmarks item on the same menu. The menu shown in Figure 9.15 appears. HGopher comes configured with various bookmarks; in addition to these, you will find the new bookmark for The WELL's Gopher at the bottom of the list.

Now notice an important fact. When I wanted to place the entire top menu for The WELL in my bookmark page, I needed to click on the Mark Menu item. But suppose I find a particular menu item that I'd like to keep as a bookmark. To save it to my bookmark page, I simply click on Mark Item on the same menu. This menu option will not be available until you highlight an item by clicking on it once with the mouse. When you have done so, you will be able to save it to the bookmark page. Each of the bookmarks is, of course, a Gopher item; double-clicking on any of them takes you directly to the item or menu in question.

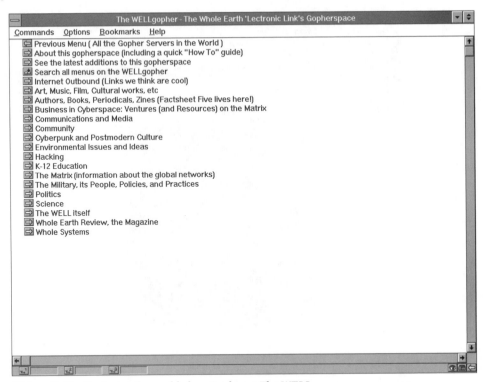

Figure 9.14   Exploring the world-class Gopher at The WELL.

Note: Want to keep up with Gopher developments around the Internet? There are several places to check. The first is a Frequently Asked Questions document about Gopher, which gives you background material and a snapshot of the current state of the art. To retrieve it, use the following URL:

ftp://rtfm.mit.edu/pub/usenet/news.answers/gopher-faq

You'll also see a list of client programs in the FAQ for various platforms like the NeXT Computer and other Unix machines.

Keeping up with Gopher, though, means watching the USENET newsgroups (we will examine newsgroups in Chapter 10). Consider subscribing to the following groups:

comp.infosystems.gopher

alt.gopher

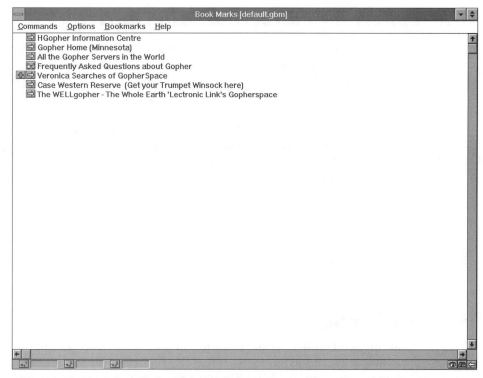

Figure 9.15   HGopher's bookmark list makes it easy to move between popular Gopher sites.

We've examined many Gopher features through the HGopher client, but as mentioned, any good Gopher client should be able to provide you with access to all the Gopher tools. We haven't yet taken a look at Gopher's ways with Telnet and FTP, or search tools like Veronica. To illustrate these capabilities, let's now look at two other Gopher clients, WinGopher and TurboGopher, and see how they handle such chores.

Note: If you're wondering whether a particular site maintains a Gopher, there's a quick way to find out. Many system administrators, when setting up a Gopher, follow the convention of naming it with the initial word "gopher." You can use this to attempt to connect to the site. Suppose, for example, that you'd like to find out whether your brother's company, Widgets, Inc., maintains a Gopher server. You know that **widgets.com** is the company's address, because it's part of your brother's e-mail address: **fred@widgets.com**. To see if there's a Gopher at this site, try to connect to **gopher.widgets.com**. It may or may not work, but chances are, if this company has a Gopher, this is its address.

WinGopher: A Commercial Alternative

Having tried out a public domain program, you may want to examine the features of the best commercial Gopher product on the market, WinGopher. Developed by Notis Systems Inc., WinGopher comes in two packages, the basic WinGopher program and WinGopher Complete, the latter of which includes a version of Distinct TCP/IP as well as the necessary SLIP and PPP drivers to complete the connection. Assuming you've already got SLIP or PPP up and running, you won't need the latter, but anyone just starting out with SLIP/PPP will find WinGopher Complete an obvious option.

You can reach Notis Systems at the following address:

Notis Systems Inc.
1007 Church St.
Evanston, IL 60201
Voice: 800-556-6847
Voice: 708-866-0150
Fax: 708-866-4970

Installing WinGopher

Getting WinGopher up and running is relatively routine, assuming you already have your SLIP/PPP account active. If you don't, the installation of the complete package, with SLIP/PPP and the TCP/IP software, proceeds through a step-by-step install program. I found the process to be seamless; the program will prompt you for the kind of installation you would like to make. Full installation includes everything, while choosing a custom installation lets you install only WinGopher and skip TCP/IP.

Assuming you already have a SLIP/PPP connection option, you will want to choose the custom installation. If you don't, WinGopher may attempt to use the wrong version of the winsock.dll file, since you will have a version of that file from Distinct TCP/IP as well as one from your other TCP/IP software. Most such software modifies the path statement in your autoexec.bat file during installation to tell your system where to find winsock.dll, and if WinGopher tries to use the wrong version of it, the program won't be able to function.

WinGopher at Work

To launch WinGopher, simply double-click on its icon with your SLIP/PPP connection running. If you are using the Distinct TCP/IP package from the complete installation, double-clicking the icon will pop up a dialog box asking if you want to place the outgoing call. An answer of Yes will take you onto the net. In either case, WinGopher's first destination is the WinGopher Test Server, which is a Gopher site stuffed with interesting Gopher resources, including background materials about WinGopher, as well as sound, graphics, and video files. These give you the chance to test out your WinGopher system. The introductory screen at this site is shown in Figure 9.16.

As with HGopher, moving around in the Gopher site involves double-clicking on a resource. A new window will pop up with the desired item in it. You will notice in Figure 9.16 that WinGopher uses icons. Although different from those in HGopher, the concept behind the icons remains the same. The file cabinet icons are an indication of further directories; double-click on one of these items and you will be taken to another set of options. Notice the image icon as well; it looks like the sun setting in the ocean. Click on this and an image appears. WinGopher comes with several built-in viewer programs, including a text viewer, an image viewer, and a Telnet application. You won't need to load anything else to view an image, whether it be in GIF or JPEG format. In Figure 9.17, you can see an infrared satellite image I retrieved from the University of Illinois. Here are a few of the most important WinGopher icons:

 A directory at the current server. This means that clicking on the icon will produce a submenu with further choices, which may include text files, images, or a number of other possibilities including Telnet sessions.

 A directory, but at another Gopher site.

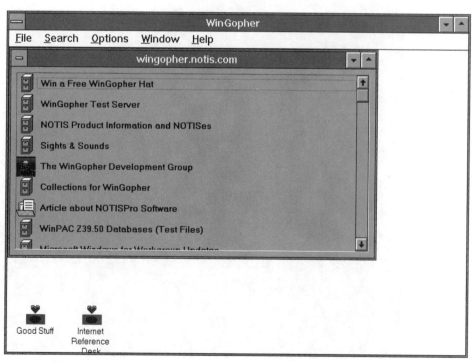

Figure 9.16   The WinGopher home site; notice the extensive use of icons.

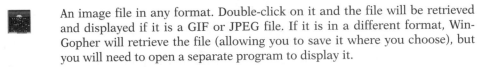 An image file in any format. Double-click on it and the file will be retrieved and displayed if it is a GIF or JPEG file. If it is in a different format, Win-Gopher will retrieve the file (allowing you to save it where you choose), but you will need to open a separate program to display it.

A search. When you click on this icon, a search box will appear allowing you to enter a keyword. This is the image that will identify Veronica servers for searches through Gopherspace.

A text file. Double-click on this icon and the WinGopher viewer will appear with the file enclosed.

A phone book, allowing you to search a directory of users at a particular site. Double-click on this icon and a query window will open, allowing you to enter information.

A sound file in any format. Double-click on this and the file will play if it is in WAV format (WinGopher will launch the WAV player program to do this). If it is in another format, WinGopher will retrieve the file but you will need to open a separate program to play it.

A binary file. Double-click on this icon and a dialog box will appear, allowing you to save the file to the directory of your choice.

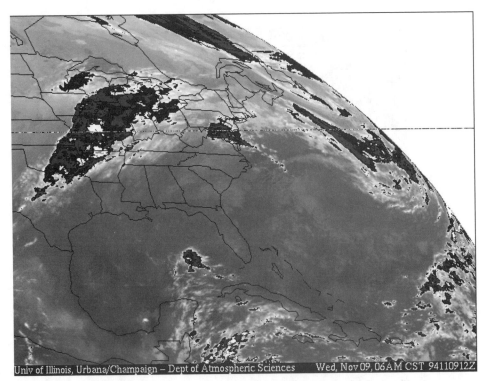

Figure 9.17 The image of a weather map retrieved through WinGopher.

WinGopher contains numerous other icons, but these are the essential ones. They quickly become second nature. I particularly like the size and clarity of WinGopher's icons.

A Telnet Session through WinGopher

Gopher lets you do much more than just read text, as we've already seen by using HGopher to retrieve an image and display it. Let's now take WinGopher into the Telnet environment. One of the major developments in the library community over the past few years has been the emergence of library catalogs from universities and colleges. These catalogs are available for searching; while we can't get into full-text displays of library holdings (at least, not yet), we can run title searches against the entire collection at a particular site.

To take a look at what is available, you might start at the University of Minnesota's Gopher and follow the menus to the various library options. Libraries from all over the world are searchable through this Gopher (and, of course, many other Gophers around the world that maintain similar links). If you will examine Figure 9.18, you will see that we run into a new icon when we start exploring the possibilities.

Here I am looking for library catalogs in Arizona. Notice the entries for Maricopa Community Colleges. We see two items listed as such—the first carries the icon for a text file, while the second icon, hitherto unfamiliar to us, shows two linked computers. This is the Telnet icon.

By clicking on the text file, we receive information about the site in question, including login instructions. But clicking on the Telnet icon also gives us login information, as shown in Figure 9.19.

Whichever client program you use, Gopher will always present you with a screen reminding you that you are about to enter a Telnet session, and con-

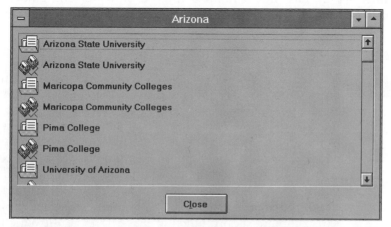

Figure 9.18 Library catalogs are well represented on the Internet. Note the linked computers icon that represents Telnet.

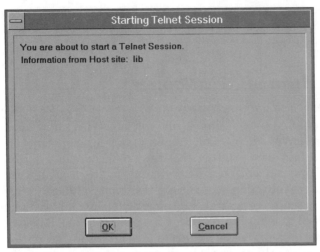

Figure 9.19 WinGopher prompts you with necessary login information when you begin a Telnet session.

taining login instructions where necessary at the site to which you intend to go. Notice that I am being told how to sign in at Maricopa Community Colleges by using lib as my login. When I click on OK, the Telnet screen appears (in this case, it shows the WinGopher Telnet screen, whereas other Gopher clients might show the Telnet client of your choice). I can log in at this site and wind up at the top menu at this library. Figure 9.20 shows me at the library prompt, ready to search.

When it is time to exit, I can type quit at the prompt and then pull down the File menu on the Telnet screen, choosing Exit to close the viewer and return to the WinGopher main screen. By prompting me with the appropriate login, the Gopher system has thus simplified my use of Telnet and guided me to the resource I needed, without my having to type in complicated commands.

Note: Telnet resources vary depending on the site you have selected. Remember, when you leave Gopher to embark upon a Telnet session, you are moving outside the Gopher program. Whatever commands are available on the remote system are the ones that you must use. Fortunately, most library sites are relatively self-explanatory. You simply have to accustom yourself to the idea that you will need to study the screen and master a few commands, commands that may vary depending upon where you have gone in your session. Above all, make sure you know what command to use to exit the remote system, so you can return to Gopher. Usually, the exit command is prominently placed on the introductory menu. Look for it each time.

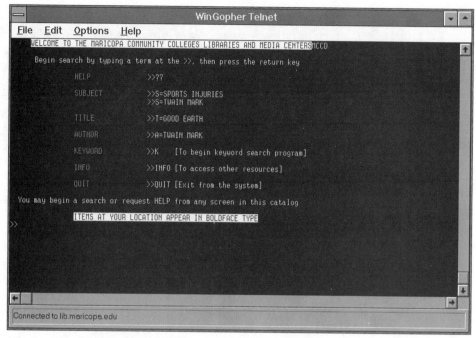

Figure 9.20   An active Telnet session to examine library resources.

Setting Up Information Collections in WinGopher

WinGopher *collections* function like the bookmarks in most Gopher client programs; you can pick items that interest you and save them to a single menu. But WinGopher ups the ante by offering multiple collections. The program ships with pointers to government materials, image files, Internet background information, books, news, and more. To reach these, you simply pull down the File menu and take the Open Collection option. You will receive a dialog box allowing you to choose which collection you'd like to see. Choosing it will cause it to be displayed as an icon at the bottom of the WinGopher screen; double-click on the icon to activate its window.

In Figure 9.21, I have called up several collections. Note their icons at the bottom of the screen; one is a collection of images, one is the Internet Reference Desk, and another is Searches. The one I have selected to display is called Good Stuff. You can see it in the most recently opened window, with menu items pointing to interesting sites. This is where I found the University of Illinois weather server I used when generating the satellite image shown earlier.

But WinGopher doesn't limit you to default collections. To create a new one, pull down the File menu and choose New Collection. The Collection Properties dialog box will appear, as shown in Figure 9.22. The Description field contains information about the collection, while the Icon Field contains the icon you want to use to represent the collection. If you click on the Browse for

Note: Each time you double-click on a WinGopher menu item, a new window appears. WinGopher makes it easy to move through these windows by providing you with a convenient Close button on each. Double-click on a text file and the text viewer is launched; you can save the file or simply close it when you've read it. The same occurs with images; you are given the option of saving them or closing them after viewing. The SLIP/PPP connection, remember, retrieves files directly to your computer's memory. You can then save any file you retrieve to the directory of your choice.

Icon button at the bottom of the box, you will be shown the various icons available in your WinGopher directory and can make a choice. When you click on OK, the collection is created.

To add items to a collection, open the collection by pulling down the File menu and choosing the Open Collection command. When you find the item you want to save, select the item by clicking on it. Pull down the Options menu and click on Add Item to Collection to call up the Add To Collection dialog box. There, you will be shown a list of the collections that are currently open. You can select the one you wish to augment and click on OK to add your item to that collection.

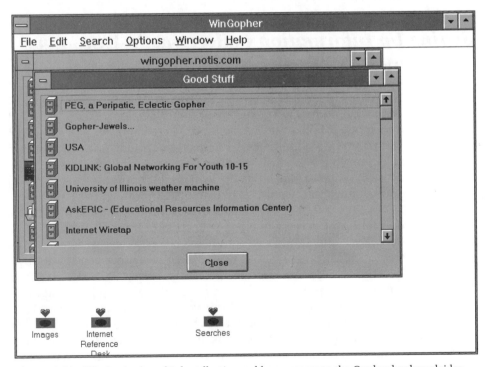

Figure 9.21 WinGopher's multiple collections add new power to the Gopher bookmark idea.

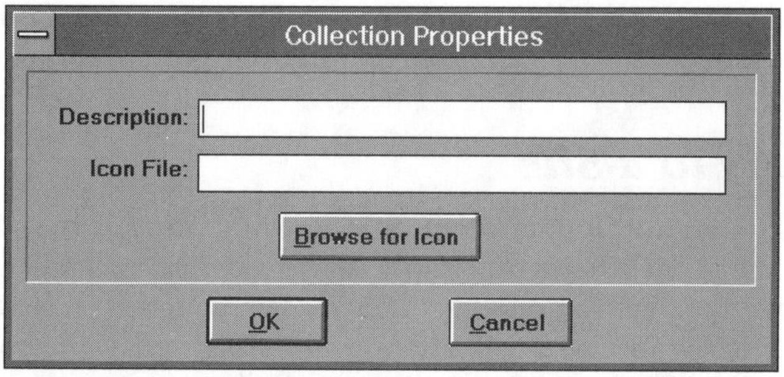

Figure 9.22   The Collection Properties dialog box lets you set up new collections for any topic you choose.

WinGopher's capabilities with collections and information management are terrific. In Figure 9.23, you see WinGopher's Collection Manager, which lets you open or delete collections, and also select the collections you want to be available when you start WinGopher. Choose multiple collections by holding down the Shift key while clicking, or click on the Select All and Deselect All buttons to deal with the entire list of collections.

You can open the Collection Manager from the Options menu. After getting a feel for collections in WinGopher, you will want to think about the best ways to archive your information. You can arrange collections by topic, by file type, or by site; it's your call. Whatever the case, WinGopher wins high marks by providing capabilities in this regard that most Internet tools lack. Indeed, the biggest problem faced by any Internet user is the sheer diversity of infor-

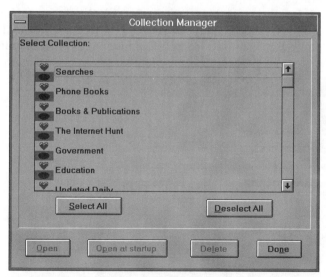

Figure 9.23   Use WinGopher's powerful Collection Manager to keep track of your information collections.

mation coupled with a lack of consistent organizing principles. Collections are one way researchers and other users can begin to impose order.

Connecting Directly to a Site

Moving up and down the Gopher menu trees is fascinating at first, but eventually you reach the point when you simply want to connect to a Gopher whose address you already have. To do this in WinGopher, you must have a collection as your active window, or else a collection icon highlighted at the bottom of the WinGopher window. Then choose the Create a Collection menu item from the Edit menu. Fill in the fields in the Create Collection Item dialog box, using Directory as the file type. You can see how I filled in this dialog box in Figure 9.24; here, I am setting up WinGopher to connect to the Gopher at Interpath. The icon for Interpath will now appear in the collection window with the name I have assigned it.

Searching Gopher with Veronica

Now that we have a way to save particular items and return to them quickly, we could also use a system that would allow us to search Gopherspace. The tool, developed at the University of Nevada at Reno by Steve Foster and Fred Barrie, is called Veronica. Veronica can't do everything; it can't, for example, dig into the text files at a Gopher site to run searches on keywords. But it can run keyword searches on Gopher *menu* items, which can be handy indeed. Such searches allow you to reduce the universe of Gophers to a select few that offer your keywords.

In Chapter 8, I mentioned the novels of Patrick O'Brian, a favorite author of mine. Because of his work, I have developed an interest in the days of sail and the Napoleonic Wars. So let's search Gopherspace for information about

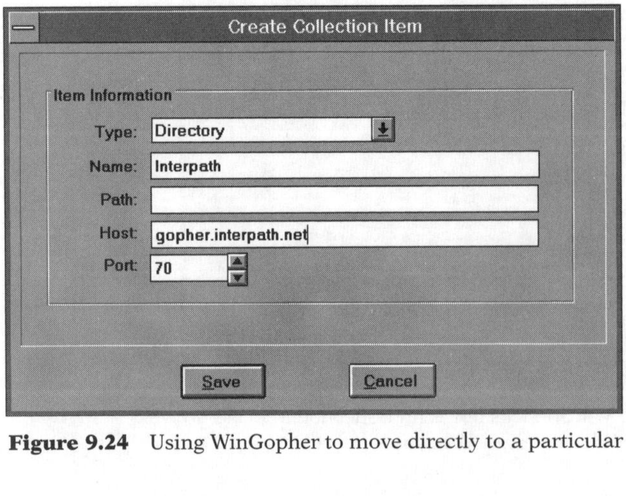

Figure 9.24   Using WinGopher to move directly to a particular site.

Note: Graphical clients pose an interesting question for Internet users. For example, I would prefer a more direct way to move to a Gopher site than either HGopher or WinGopher permits; with the former, you must set up a bookmark and then click on it to go where you choose, while with WinGopher, you create what amounts to the same thing and are given an icon to click on to move to your site. Using the character-based connection to Gopher available through a shell account, I can move around Gopherspace with considerably more convenience by simply typing in the address to which I want to connect at my service provider's prompt. To get to Interpath, for example, I would simply enter the command **gopher gopher.interpath.net**, which would take me directly to the site.

The question, then, is this: are graphical clients always superior? And the answer, I think, depends upon your own preferences and, in particular, the action you are taking at the time. WinGopher offers superb interface features, but its reliance on menus and icons without convenient shortcuts means that at times it takes you longer to do what you want than you would have preferred. Both systems work, but experienced users often look for a combination of graphical niceties with shortcuts that bypass the more obvious steps. Why not, for example, offer a simple menu item with a Go command that opens a field in which you fill in the address in one line and go?

Napoleon. To do so, I need to find a Veronica server. The closest at hand is the one at Notis, which appears on the Notis Gopher's main menu. I know that it contains search capabilities because of the icon in the shape of an eye. Double-clicking on this icon calls up the search box shown in Figure 9.25. I have already entered my search term: napoleon.

By choosing OK, I begin the search, which soon results in a window of its own. You can see in Figure 9.26 some of the resources I was able to track

Figure 9.25 A Veronica query allows you to search Gopher-space for menu items that match your keyword.

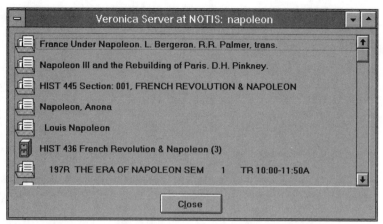

Figure 9.26 Results of a Veronica search under the keyword napoleon.

down. Each is a menu item somewhere in Gopherspace with the word napoleon in it. I find not only text files, as shown by their icons, but also menus of information at various sites and, further down this long list, a series of images of Napoleon himself, as well as several compressed files including Napoleonic materials.

How to find other Veronica sites? That one is easy. WinGopher contains among its collections a complete listing of the Veronica sites it can query. You can call up the Searches collection by using the Collection Manager. Double-click on its icon and you will see a Gopher menu with all the Veronica sites available. Another good way to keep up with Veronica and, for that matter, with Gopher developments in general, is to use the Gopher at the University of Minnesota, where all of this began. Minnesota is not the only site that offers links to a complete run of Veronica servers, but it's certainly the most authoritative.

Note: Veronica has grown increasingly difficult to use because of the intense load placed upon the system by the Internet's recent growth. I used to be able to log on to virtually any Veronica server and run my search immediately. Today, it's a rare phenomenon to get a hit at the first Veronica site I try. You will probably find it necessary to try site after site; at many, you will receive notice that the system is too busy to accept your search, and that you should try again later. The thing to do is persevere. Nothing else does the job like Veronica, even if we must exercise patience to use it.

Using Internet Phone Books

Trying to find somebody on the Internet is a frustrating experience. Given our ability to use Veronica and other tools to search throughout Gopherspace for menu items, it seems puzzling that we can't unleash some kind of digital tool to track down friends in remote cities, or acquire the e-mail addresses of people we have read about in books or magazines. But when you think about it, this lack of an overall directory structure makes a degree of sense. The Internet, after all, is decentralized; it has no main office, no single organizing body, and certainly no repository of universal address information.

What the Internet does offer are phone books for more or less circumscribed areas. The situation is not terribly different from what you find when using the telephone system today. Each city, each town, has its own telephone book. If you want a number in Poughkeepsie, you must acquire the Poughkeepsie book, or else call information in that city to ask for the number. The difference is, the Internet boasts no information number. Your job in finding someone is to go out and acquire the electronic version of a phone book for that city yourself, and then to search it to find the person you seek.

Gopher can help in this task by making phone books of various kinds available for searching. You will see such directories referred to as "white pages," a term that, in the Internet world, almost invariably refers to directories at colleges or universities, with listings of staff and students. This is a reminder that the key area of network growth in the 1980s was academic, as the National Science Foundation sought to link our schools to supercomputer sites containing the world's fastest computers; the Internet soon grew into a system of regional networks and linked universities, each of which compiled on-line information about people at its site.

I use WinGopher here only to illustrate the general principles, but any Gopher client will allow you to use these directories. To search an on-line phone book in WinGopher, double-click on the telephone icon at a particular site. The Phone Book Query window will then open, as shown in Figure 9.27. As you can see from the top of the screen, I have chosen a phone book at a particular school, Gustavus Adolphus College, and am now presented with a number of fields within which I can search. The fields defined for a particular phone book are determined at the site, so you will see variation as you move between various locations. Some of these directories will contain numerous fields, others will be relatively spartan. But the method for using a phone book remains the same. Click on the field you want to search and enter a search term in the Field Value: field at the bottom of the dialog box. Click Set to enter the term; click on Query to execute your search. Results appear in the Phone Book Query dialog box, as shown in Figure 9.28.

If there is more than one hit in your search, WinGopher will present forward and backward arrow buttons to allow you to scroll through the results. Clicking on the Next Query button allows you to perform another search.

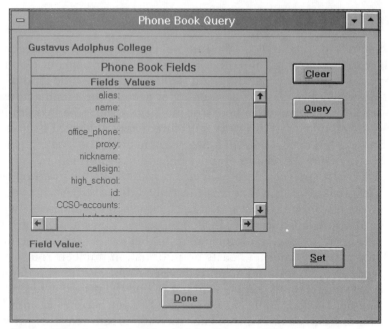

Figure 9.27 On-line phone books help us to search for information about people at various sites.

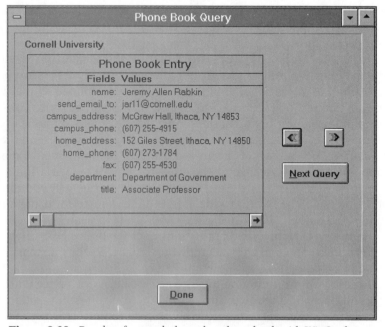

Figure 9.28 Results of a search through a phone book with WinGopher.

There are various kinds of directory options you can search with Gopher. Names you are likely to encounter include these:

CSO	A type of phone directory developed at the University of Illinois at Urbana-Champaign (the name comes from the Computing Services Office at the university, where the work took place).
WHOIS	A white pages directory for a particular organization that allows you to query a database of names and e-mail addresses.
Knowbot Information Service	A program designed at the Corporation for National Research Initiatives to search through a variety of different directories to find what you need.
X.500	An international white pages directory system designed to be a standard for directory structure, but now existing as one in a series of different approaches to finding people.

TurboGopher: A Gopher Solution for the Macintosh

TurboGopher is a Macintosh client that allows you to travel from Gopher to Gopher using familiar Macintosh file folders and icons. To retrieve it, use **FTP** to reach the University of Minnesota, where the current version is always available; it was the Gopher development team at this university that created TurboGopher. Here is the URL:

ftp://boombox.micro.umn.edu/pub/gopher/Macintosh-TurboGopher/

As of this writing, the filename was TurboGopher1.0.8b4.hqx (although a new release was in the offing).

 Note: If you examine the file directory at the Minnesota site carefully, you will notice TurboGopher versions in Chinese, Finnish, Japanese, and Spanish as well as the standard English model—quite a compliment to the worldwide proliferation of the Gopher protocols! One of the biggest challenges for the Internet in coming years will be to extend its tools into languages other than English. This gets especially interesting when dealing with ideographic languages like Japanese and Chinese; expect much development in this area.

Installing and Configuring TurboGopher

The .hqx extension to the filename tells us that TurboGopher as retrieved by FTP is in BinHex format, and can be decompressed with a tool like Aladdin

Systems' StuffIt Expander. To do so, drag and drop the downloaded Turbo-
Gopher file onto the StuffIt Expander icon. StuffIt Expander will automatically launch, decoding and decompressing the file as it goes, and place
TurboGopher on your desktop. The great thing about the Mac, of course, is
that file installation is often a snap.

   To launch TurboGopher, simply double-click on its icon. As configured by
the University of Minnesota, the program is designed to log on to the Minnesota Gopher server, displaying the window shown in Figure 9.29. Note that
TurboGopher has also opened its Bookmarks window; immediately behind is
a window with the home Gopher server. The first thing you must do is to configure TurboGopher to establish the home server you want to log on to every
time the program launches. To do this, pull down the Setup menu and choose
the Configure TurboGopher item. The window shown in Figure 9.30 will
appear. You will see fields for two Gopher servers, the primary one and an
alternate, in case you can't connect to the first; as set up by the University of
Minnesota, TurboGopher defaults to one of two Gopher servers there: **gopher.-
tc.umn.edu** or **gopher2.tc.umn.edu**. I have already changed these servers to
reflect my own setup, inserting the Gopher at my service provider, Interpath,
and falling back on the University of Minnesota Gopher as my second choice.
You should insert your own Gopher choices in this field. In general, choose as
your primary Gopher a site near to you. You can, of course, continue to use the
University of Minnesota as your primary Gopher. Port settings are standardized throughout most of Gopherspace, so it's unlikely you will have to change
the port setting of 70.

   Now let's proceed with some other TurboGopher options. Choosing the
Setup menu, click on the Options item to call up the dialog box shown in Fig-

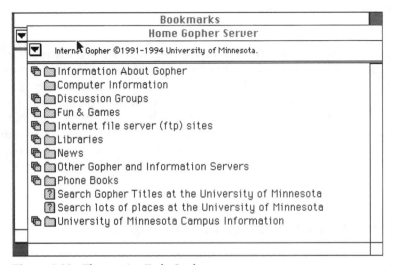

Figure 9.29 The opening TurboGopher screen.

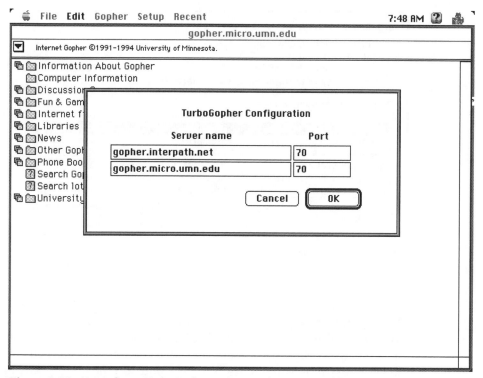

Figure 9.30   To configure TurboGopher with a new home server, fill in these fields.

ure 9.31. Notice the section of the dialog box called Gopher Helper Applications. By now we know that these are the programs that support our work in Gopher by calling up text files or images that TurboGopher can't view directly. To examine the settings for each file type and to change them, highlight the item you're interested in and click on the Set button. An Open File dialog box will then appear; you can double-click on the application you want to use for each file type.

For example, we know we will want to view image files with TurboGopher, since images are becoming so widespread around the Internet. We can highlight the Image/GIF item and click on Set to call up the Open File dialog box. There we can click on JPEGView 3.3f, a standard image viewer for the Macintosh that works quite well with TurboGopher (this assumes, of course, that you have JPEGView available; the program is shareware and can be downloaded from Mac-oriented FTP sites or commercial on-line services like America Online). Having done so, we will be able to view GIF files; we can perform the same operation to use this program for JPEG and image files in other formats as well. Figure 9.32 shows the selection process in action.

You will notice the menu in the upper right corner of the dialog box, where file types are provided. These are the types that the helper application will rec-

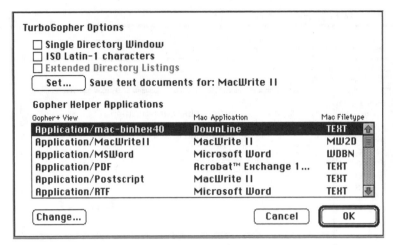

Figure 9.31 TurboGopher's Options menu lets you set up external programs for file viewing.

ognize; in most cases, you will simply be able to accept the default. Click on the OK button to do so; click on OK again when you're back at the Options dialog box. The settings you have established will be saved in the TurboGopher Settings file. By working through the entire list of applications, you can define any file type you think you will want to view and add the appropriate application.

Where do you get the helper applications you need? There are numerous FTP sites that provide such programs. Always consider the major Macintosh sites at these URLs:

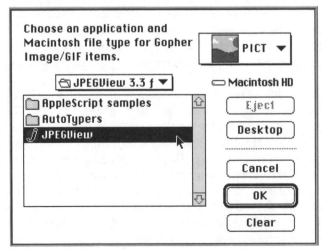

Figure 9.32 Setting up JPEGView as an external program to handle JPEG files in TurboGopher.

ftp://sumex-aim/stanford/edu/

ftp://mac.archive.umich.edu/

Macintosh files are also available at many other FTP sites, such as **wuarchive.-wustl.edu** and **oak.oakland.edu**. And, if you prefer, you can download such programs from commercial on-line services like CompuServe or America Online. America Online now makes it possible to download such a file and unstuff it automatically.

Reaching a New Site with TurboGopher

Let's take TurboGopher out onto the network by accessing the remarkable Gopher at this URL:

gopher://english-server.hss.cmu.edu/

To move directly to a site, pull down the File menu and choose the Another Gopher item. This will open up a dialog box that allows you to enter the address you would like to reach. Enter this address—**english-server.hss.-cmu.edu**—into this box, leaving the port setting at 70, the Gopher default. Click the OK button to send TurboGopher out over the net. Soon the main window at this Gopher server will appear, as shown in Figure 9.33.

> **Note:** When you enter the address to which you want to travel, remember that you don't enter the entire URL. With TurboGopher, you are entering only the address of the computer itself. It is not necessary to include the preliminary information before the double slashes, which specifies Gopher as the resource, nor do you need the final slash. These are part of the URL, and will be used with browsers like Mosaic and Netscape to specify the resource you are attempting to reach; TurboGopher needs only the machine address to reach the site.

As you can see, the list of information available here is extensive. This Gopher is maintained by graduate students in the English Department at Carnegie Mellon University. The original idea was to make available a variety of writings in the humanities, including criticism, fiction, and experiments in hypertext. But in recent days, the site has added numerous links to FTP sites, Telnet destinations, and collections of textual documents. You can look for recipes here, check the meaning of words in dictionaries, bone up on political philosophies, or read collections of on-line poetry.

Notice the two types of icons on the screen in Figure 9.33. Textual documents are shown as a sheet of paper with the corner turned down and writing

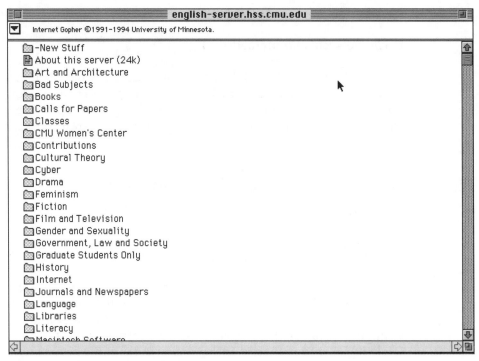

Figure 9.33   A particularly full-featured Gopher as viewed through TurboGopher.

on them, as is conventional in Macintosh work (see the About This Server document, for example, the second item on the menu). Double-click on such an icon to call the text up to the screen. The other icons are all folders; when you click on one, you open up a folder with further options. From there on, it's just a matter of exploring the Gopher site.

Searching an Index

By double-clicking the Journals and Newspapers folder on the top menu at the CMU site, I move to an underlying menu with documents, folders, and searchable indices. Let's run a search now on articles from *Communications of the ACM,* the journal of the Association for Computing Machinery. The fact that a searchable index is available is shown by the question mark in the icon next to this item. When I double-click on the item, I receive the search screen shown in Figure 9.34.

Inserting the keyword internet, I run my search against the database of holdings here, generating several screens of hits. I can double-click on any of these text files to call the item to my screen. A recent search called up an article about Internet ethics written by Vinton Cerf, a key figure in the development of the protocols that made the Internet possible.

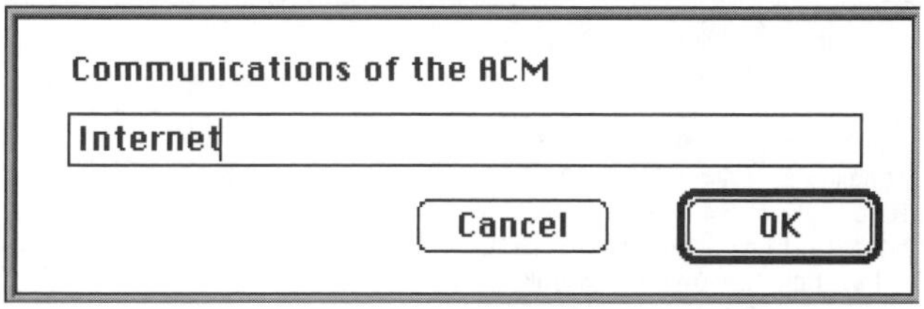

Communications of the ACM

Internet

Cancel   OK

Figure 9.34 A searchable index field in TurboGopher.

 Note: Gopher, like any other Internet tool, can be frustrating. You double-click on an item only to wait. Finally, TurboGopher tells you it couldn't connect. The fault is, most likely, not yours; it's a simple fact that Internet resources are under more of a strain than ever as huge numbers of new users have moved onto the net. When Gopher can't get you through to the site you're trying to reach, wait a few minutes and try again.

Downloading a File with FTP

Gopher makes FTP transfers a simple matter. Again, the model is point-and-click. In the case of the English-Server, I can move to the top menu item called Macintosh software, double-clicking on its folder and working deeper into the categories of available software until I find what I want. Individual program files are shown by a floppy disk icon. When I double-click, for example, on a folder called PowerMac, I move to the actual file library of programs for the PowerMac platform. Figure 9.35 shows part of this library. I have highlighted the file I intend to download, which is jpegview3.3.sit.hqx.

Double-clicking on this item will open a dialog box giving me options as to where to save the file. When I click the Save button, the file transfer begins. I can watch the status window in Figure 9.36 to keep an eye on the progress of the transfer. Upon completion of the download, the file is automatically decoded from BinHex format and decompressed. I set up Unstuffit as my decompression program when I configured TurboGopher.

Setting Bookmarks in TurboGopher

The English-Server is good enough that we'd like to be able to return there often. Fortunately, setting bookmarks remains as easy within TurboGopher as it is within any of the Windows-based Gopher clients. The key is this: to designate an item as a bookmark, you need to highlight it and then pull down the Gopher menu, choosing the Set Bookmark item. A bookmark dialog box then opens, allowing you to name the bookmark and accept it onto your bookmark page.

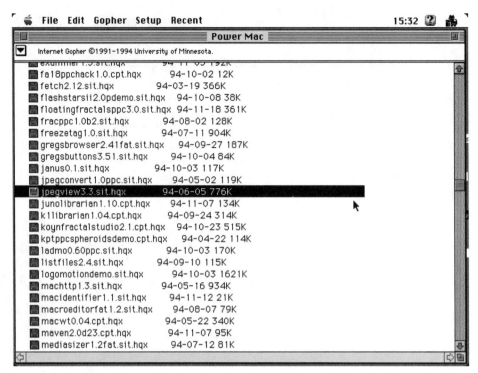

Figure 9.35 Preparing to download a file through TurboGopher.

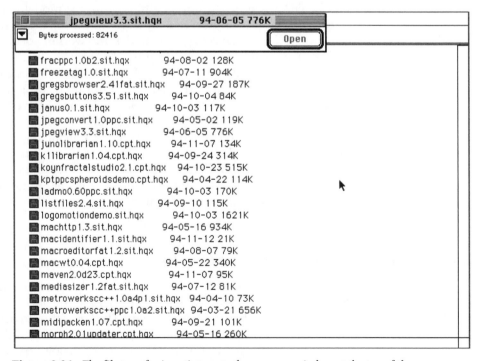

Figure 9.36 The file transfer in action; note the progress window at the top of the screen.

From the top menu at the English-Server, for example, we can highlight the menu item Journals and Newspapers, since this is the kind of resource it would be handy to return to often. Clicking on it once to highlight it, we can then pull down the Gopher menu and click on Set Bookmark. After we name it, the item will now be included as one of our bookmark items, visible when we take the Show Bookmarks option on the same Gopher menu.

Note: We have a problem if we want to set the English-Server site itself as a bookmark. To do so, we must back out of the server here and locate it as a menu item on a different server. The reason: TurboGopher assigns highlighted menu items as bookmarks; it will not assign the entire menu of a server as a bookmark (you'll recall that WinGopher and HGopher allow you to select a menu as well as an item; the Unix Gopher client also does this). But the situation is remedied by finding the English-Server on one of the Other Gophers menus at virtually any Gopher site. Select it and use the Gopher menu to establish it as a bookmark. At this point you can return to it quickly.

Of course, if you find a particular item at a Gopher site that you want to declare a bookmark, you can do so whether it's a text document, a Telnet link, an FTP library, or an entire Gopher server somewhere else. The procedure remains the same. Soon you will develop a series of bookmarks of most visited sites, and you'll use it for quick navigation. Long-time Gopher users often develop lists of such complexity that they find it helpful to share them among their colleagues. To do this, pull down the File menu and click on Save as Bookmark File. A Save File dialog box will appear that allows you to enter the name under which you would like to save your file. When you click on the Save button, the file is saved and can be mailed or given to another person on disk, like any other file. To open a bookmark file from someone else, select the Open Gopher Bookmark File from the File menu. Double-click on the bookmark file you would like to see. You can also choose to import bookmarks from a third-party file into your own bookmark file. To do so, select Import Bookmarks from the Gopher menu and double-click on the file you would like to import. The items on the new bookmark file will be added to your own.

The Gopher of Your Dreams

One of the more exciting aspects of software development is that it's never really finished. Each program moves along an arc toward greater utility and elegance; none ever achieves perfection, nor could it, given the changing nature of the technology and the evolving needs of users. Perhaps it's no surprise, then, that my ideal Gopher would combine traits from the tools we've

Note: Sometime when you have an hour or so to kill, go to the University of Minnesota's Gopher server and take the Other Gopher and Information Servers option. Spend some time browsing through the Gopher resources available throughout the world. The diversity will astound you. But bear in mind that even the University of Minnesota's Gopher doesn't list all Gophers in the world; it can only point to those it knows about. The number of new Gophers is increasing daily as people realize what an easy-to-use Internet access tool it can be.

just examined, and add a few new ones in the bargain. But first things first. Here are my picks.

For Microsoft Windows users, the clear choice is WinGopher. What I like best about the program is its ability to store and arrange information in a logical manner. My use of telecommunications grew out of a need to find and exploit information, so I am always looking for ways to improve that process. WinGopher's collections, which extend the bookmark metaphor into an archival realm, allow me to group interesting Gopher sites, either as a complete menu or a specific pointer to a resource. Thus I maintain collections of new network data, collections on literature and music, and collections on physics and astronomy.

HGopher scores high for its ease of use and certainly its price (it's freeware, after all), and the use of external file viewers makes it easy to point Gopher items like images and sound files to whatever players you choose to implement. While it lacks WinGopher's snazzy interface, HGopher actually seems somewhat more stable on my 486 than WinGopher (at least, I haven't crashed out of HGopher and had to reboot even once, while WinGopher occasionally seizes up). I wish both programs made it easier to go directly to a Gopher site, however, without wading into the menu structure to do this; a well-placed hotkey would certainly do the trick, assuming it popped up a "go" box that could be quickly filled in and executed.

Macintosh users should have no complaints with TurboGopher; I wish both the Windows Gophers could boast TurboGopher's speed. While it isn't long on bells and whistles, TurboGopher delivers every bit of Gopher functionality I could ask for and then some. All these programs use menus that are intuitive enough to allow me to move easily between my Power Macintosh and my 486 for Gopher work, but I find that in the area of system stability, TurboGopher is the best program of all. The program looks at a connection long enough to determine whether it's going to go through, and sensibly backs you out when Gopher can't connect. Increasing network traffic means we'll need programs that can handle unexpected net responses, and TurboGopher ranks high on my list for its seemingly bulletproof design.

So here's my ultimate Gopher tool: a program with the speed of Turbo-Gopher and its stability, the price of HGopher, the interface of WinGopher as well as its capabilities with collections, jazzed up with hotkeys for quick network navigation. The boundary between Gopher clients and Web browsers thus becomes less distinct, for what I have just described could be an enhanced version of Netscape or one of the other Mosaic-based browsers. These tools already handle Gopher with dispatch, and it's likely that future browsers will incorporate even more functionality. It will be interesting to see how the stand-alone Gopher client developers move to meet this challenge.

10

USENET News through SLIP/PPP

Author and critic Agnes Repplier wrote in her 1904 essay "The Luxury of Conversation": "It is not what we learn in conversation that enriches us. It is the elation that comes of swift contact with tingling currents of thought." USENET is all about that kind of elation, but don't discount the learning opportunities it presents. An enormous collection of worldwide conversations, USENET offers people the chance to converse with like-minded souls about virtually any topic under the sun. From vegetarian cookery to Icelandic literature, particle physicists to great violinists, the USENET newsgroups offer something for everyone.

Begun as an experiment in exchanging information, USENET's first traffic moved between Duke University and the University of North Carolina in Chapel Hill in 1979. The trick was to find an easy way for Unix-driven computers to move messages on a dial-up basis, calling up the receiving computer and sending current traffic in a burst of information. In this way, a message could be saved on one computer and passed along to other machines to which it connects; messages are thus duplicated and sent to machines around the world. When Jim Ellis, Tom Truscott, and Steve Bellovin connected those first two machines, they had no way of knowing they were creating a system that would push the envelope of free speech by opening a new form of communication. Out of those first two sites has grown a system comprising well over 100,000 sites, while user participation reaches into the millions. And while USENET grew up separately from the Internet, the two have coalesced to the point where anyone who is serious about the Internet will have USENET access.

Updating network information is dicey business; the numbers always change significantly by the time your words see print. But as of this writing, my local access provider, Interpath, makes available over 11,000 USENET conversations, or *newsgroups*, as they are called. I follow SLIP and PPP issues through **alt.winsock** (always pronounce the period as "dot"; thus, "alt dot winsock"). A newsgroup called **clari.local.wyoming** feeds me news items from a state whose appeal has always been its splendid isolation. Another group, **rec.radio.shortwave**, provides updated schedules for major shortwave broadcasters around the world, while **rec.humor.funny** offers the work of network comedians, some of it lame, some of it quite good.

My list of groups is always in flux; sometimes I read **comp.risks**, with moderated discussions of computer security and related issues; I also check in occasionally to **rec.music.classical** for updates on new recordings and news of the major symphony orchestras; and **alt.internet.services** is a reliable source of network information. The right *newsreader* is the key. With a good one, I can sign up or leave a given newsgroup with ease, and be alerted to the formation of new groups on a daily basis. We turn, then, to newsreaders, and how they can help you manage USENET news to maximum advantage.

USENET vs. Commercial On-Line Services

Think of USENET newsgroups as similar to the kind of forums or special interest groups (SIGs) you find on conventional on-line services like CompuServe or DELPHI. A newsgroup is simply a place where messages about a particular topic can be posted, seen by others, replied to, and folded into a continuing conversation about that topic. That being said, there are certain key differences between newsgroups and other types of discussion areas. Most newsgroups, for example, are unmoderated, meaning that no system operator (sysop) or other person in charge is filtering the messages. This is in sharp distinction to the kind of forums you find, say, on CompuServe, where several sysops keep an eye on message traffic, answer questions from new users, and ensure that conversations don't stray too far from the main topic. A certain free-form quality settles in upon USENET conversations as a result of this.

Counteracting the freewheeling nature of USENET's actual discussions is a hierarchical structure that attempts to impose order upon the network. In the commercial on-line arena, order is a result of the natural forum structure. Thus a discussion group like the Working At Home Forum on CompuServe is itself broken into sections such as Running A Business, Researching Information, and Office Hardware and Software. If you were interested in any of these areas, you could set your software to read messages within it; each of the sections acts as a subforum of its own, with a discussion that proceeds independently of that in the other sections.

USENET adopts a different model. Seven major hierarchies of newsgroups were established to handle the basic subject divisions. Within the major hierarchies, newsgroups can be created at various levels of exactitude. Thus, **misc.invest** is a newsgroup that focuses on how to invest money in a variety of vehicles. Branching off from this is **misc.invest.technical**, which takes a tighter focus as it concentrates on technical analysis and its use in forecasting the movement of stock prices. Someone intrigued by the Elliott Wave method of technical forecasting could conceivably create a group called **misc.invest.technical.elliott** or some such, leading discussions on a still more circumscribed topic.

The seven major hierarchies, all of which are distributed worldwide, feature the following issues:

comp	Computers, software, and issues relating to computer science.
soc	Society and culture; in particular, these groups provide useful discussions of events in countries around the world.
rec	Hobbies and recreational activities.
news	Issues relating to USENET and the Internet.
sci	Science in a variety of disciplines.
talk	Controversial issues and debate.
misc	Issues that don't fit readily into any of the other categories.

A variety of other hierarchies exist, the most significant of which is alt. This hierarchy, which stands for alternative, consists of discussions about many of the same topics found in the big seven, but often in a looser format. In addition, because creating alt groups is significantly easier than creating groups in the standard hierarchies, alt newsgroups tend to arise on a much wider range of subjects. Don't be surprised when you run into groups like **alt.dreams.lucid**, **alt.fan.g-gordon-liddy**, **alt.lawyers.sue.sue.sue**, not to mention a wide range of newsgroups devoted to the erotic arts. With alt in front of the name, just about anything goes.

Local newsgroups also exist to serve limited geographical areas, and specialized hierarchies like clari (for services from ClariNet, including wire service feeds), biz (for business-related material), and bit (for redistributions of selected BITNET mailing lists) offer numerous newsgroups of their own. Various companies provide their own hierarchies, adding up to a huge range of accessible topics (although many corporate newsgroups are limited to employees of the company in question). Every time I log on to USENET, it seems there are more newsgroups and my software allows me to monitor new groups as they arise and decide whether to subscribe to them.

And the choice of software is wide, thanks to the open nature of USENET communications. Remember that when you use a commercial service to engage in on-line discussions, you are necessarily locked into a specific set of commands determined by that service. Developers have been at work creating new interface possibilities (CompuServe, for example, can now be accessed with such tools as TapCIS, OzCIS, WinCIM, NavCIS, and several others, as opposed to the old command-driven, on-line method), but in general the range of software available is much wider on USENET than on any other messaging service.

Your software choices are also influenced crucially by the nature of your connection. The shell environment provides such newsreaders as tin, trn, rn, vnews, and nn, all of which have their own merits and peculiarities. The SLIP/PPP environment allows you the graphical niceties of pull-down menus, mouse support, and a variety of additional features that you can't duplicate with a character-based interface. Programs like Trumpet for Windows, Nuntius, WinVN, Newswatcher, and WinQVT give you a control over your USENET environment that adds materially to your reading experience. Let's now examine these software options in more detail, contrasting shell versus SLIP software.

Connection Options to USENET

Newsreaders that work in the Unix shell environment can be powerful, as a look at such programs as tin or nn will quickly demonstrate. What we require of a newsreader first and foremost is that it contain threading capability. Think about what happens as an on-line discussion evolves. First, someone posts a message about a particular subject. Someone else reads it and is inspired to comment. A third party comments on the comment, and soon the discussion has reached sizable proportions. Given that any newsgroup will consist of several such discussions at any particular time, we need a way to sort out one conversation from another, reading the answers to messages consecutively, and only then proceeding to the next subject. In on-line parlance, this is known as following *threads*.

Character-Based Newsreaders

The early newsreaders could show you a message but lacked the ability to follow threads. The major upgrade that trn brought to the rn newsreader was its knack for threading. I can remember sitting at my keyboard with a legal pad next to my chair. I would call up the current messages available through rn, note the ones I wanted to read in pencil, and then type in their message numbers, one at a time, to read them. Today, modern Unix newsreaders provide the threading capability that makes this method obsolete, and so, of course, do all the major client programs that run under the SLIP/PPP environment. But what a difference an interface makes.

In Figure 10.1, for example, you see the result of using a shell account and examining USENET newsgroups through a newsreader called tin. Notice that the entire display is character-based, as it must be given the fact that we are running under terminal emulation. The computer, in other words, has used software to fool the remote computer into thinking that it is dealing with a terminal connected to it. The display is correspondingly meager, but the information is available.

As you can see, tin isn't completely inscrutable. Indeed, the movement in character-based newsreaders has been toward incorporating more and more

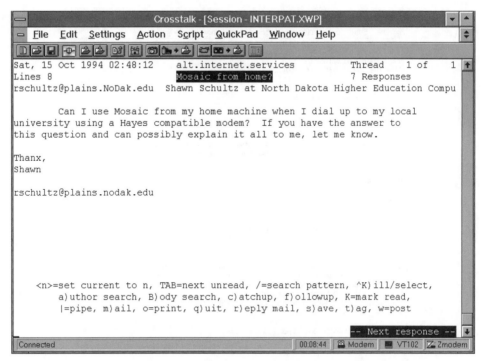

Figure 10.1 Reading USENET news with tin; note the character-based display.

user-friendly prompts on the screen. Thus at the bottom of the tin screen, you find a set of most often used current commands, while the actual message is laid out clearly, with information about the sender and the message itself presented at the top (notice that tin cleverly hides the interminable header information that takes up so much space on a less intelligent newsreader program).

SLIP/PPP Newsreaders

SLIP/PPP offers us more. In Figure 10.2, you can see a message as presented by Trumpet for Windows, a shareware product developed by Peter Tattam. Having used rn, trn, and tin for years, I found Trumpet to be something of a revelation when I came to it. I had just opened a SLIP account and had played around with several different newsreaders before downloading this fine shareware program. If you will examine the figure, I think you will understand why I found it so appealing.

Notice that we are looking at a reply to the first message. In the interval between looking at messages in the two newsreaders, someone from Italy has answered the question posed by the first poster. The original post thus appears with brackets next to it; it is being "quoted" by the responder, who then

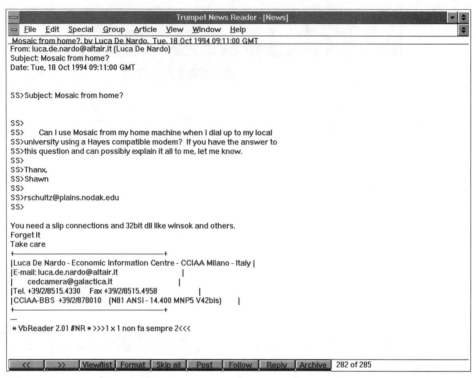

Figure 10.2 Reading a USENET message with Trumpet for Windows, a graphically oriented newsreader running under SLIP/PPP.

explains that a person using a modem to connect to the Internet needs a SLIP connection (and he could have said SLIP or PPP) to make Mosaic work. His final remark, "Forget it," presumably refers to the fact that most such university accounts offer shell access only; if our student were able to activate SLIP or PPP, however, he could certainly run Mosaic, Trumpet for Windows, Win-WAIS, or any of the other client programs I discuss in this book.

Trumpet has added much to the reading experience by giving us readily workable commands available through its menus. Across the top of the screen is a menu bar, from which we can pull down any of the menus indicated. At the bottom of the screen, the functions that tin showed to us as a series of possible commands are provided through hot buttons that we can click on to perform the desired function. For example, clicking on the Skip all button would allow us to move to the end of the current newsgroup, marking all messages as read, while clicking on Reply puts us into editing mode and allows us to enter our own response to the message. And as you'll see, SLIP/PPP provides quite a few other functions as well. In a moment, we'll examine how you can get a copy of Trumpet for evaluation. But before plunging into Trumpet, we need to consider some crucial issues of USENET participation.

USENET Rules of the Road

Perhaps no issue has so stirred controversy in recent times as the introduction of literally millions of new users to the USENET environment. First America Online, then CompuServe, joined DELPHI and BIX at offering access to the newsgroups, with the result that countless neophytes began posting and responding to messages. The influx put a strain upon a network that has always maintained itself through a spirit of cooperation and shared responsibility. This is not to say that USENET always works well, or that it ever did—there are numerous instances of people ignoring the feelings of others and needlessly using up bandwidth with postings that were less than relevant for particular newsgroups. But the more we all attempt to follow the basic USENET principles, the more powerful a service the newsgroups can be for us all.

The following guidelines, then, apply across the board, no matter what kind of newsreader you finally decide to employ. Read through them with some care, after which we will examine Trumpet for Windows for PC users and both Nuntius and Newswatcher for the Macintosh. We'll also examine alternative newsreaders for these computing platforms, and consider what issues arise as you prepare to make the choice.

- *Read before you post:* In general, read a newsgroup for at least a week before posting on it. This allows you to learn what issues have been discussed and what the tone of the newsgroup happens to be. It's also a good idea to read the **news.announce.newusers** group for background information. Many significant USENET questions are discussed and answered in this group.

- *Find the right newsgroup:* With over 11,000 newsgroups available, be sure to target your posting to the most appropriate audience. It makes no sense to post a question about your high-speed modem to a newsgroup called **soc.culture.argentina**. Fortunately, the better newsreaders provide some tools that make it possible to search the existing list at your site. We'll examine these shortly.

- *Read the FAQs:* FAQs, or Frequently Asked Questions lists, are posted in individual newsgroups and in the **news.answers** newsgroup. These documents summarize the issues that come up most frequently in the newsgroup. Before you post, check to see whether your question has already been answered in one of these lists.

- *Use mail for follow-ups:* While it is easy enough to post a follow-up message in the newsgroup, it isn't always the best solution. Consider using electronic mail to respond to questions an individual has posed; otherwise, the newsgroup may be flooded with similar answers. Context can help you decide which is best; if, in your judgment, the discussion would probably interest the majority of the newsgroup's participants, then a public response is fine.

- *Format your messages carefully:* Use lines no more than 80 characters long when you post. A length of 72 characters is even better; this makes it possible for others to quote your message inside their response. Don't right-justify text (it's harder to read), and never submit a message in all uppercase letters, which looks like shouting. Use no special control characters and avoid tabs.

- *Don't post twice:* A message to a newsgroup may take time to appear. If your message doesn't show up immediately on the group, don't assume that it has vanished and repost it. Chances are, your patience will be rewarded soon enough, and you will have avoided the embarrassment of having your message appear twice.

- *Flag your jokes:* Humor always has a place on USENET, but even the cleverest riposte can get you into trouble when someone misunderstands it. Emoticons, such as the ubiquitous smiley face—:) (read it sideways)—help take the edge off comments that might otherwise be ambiguous. Avoid sarcasm, which can land you in the midst of controversy and a potential flame war (a controversial, acrimonious discussion).

- *Don't advertise:* Advertising is off limits. Telling readers of a newsgroup about a product they might be interested in is permissible. Scattershot mailings and self-promotion of your business are not. Product announcements may be made only within the **comp.newprod** newsgroup and the "biz" newsgroups, where submission guidelines can be found.

- *No "spamming":* Flooding numerous newsgroups with copies of the same message to get wide distribution is known as *spamming,* and is not appreciated on USENET. Cross-post only to appropriate groups, usually no more than two.

- *Avoid headline news:* USENET is not a radio station. By the time you post a message about the latest development in Washington, the news will be old hat to your readers. But it is certainly kosher to post your reflections on current developments to inspire discussion, as long as you post them within a relevant newsgroup.

- *Use clear and descriptive titles:* A clear title allows people to choose threads they want to read by subject, rather than wading through irrelevant material message by message. As you will see when we tour the various newsreaders, the only way to be economical about your reading time is to work through headers; you will doubtless leave more messages unread than read in any given sweep through a newsgroup.

- *Be precise about quoting:* If you reply to a message, summarize what you are responding to so that readers will have some idea what you are talking about. A correspondent of mine sometimes sends e-mail containing nothing but the word "OK." It's often quite difficult to remember what he's talking about. If you quote a message for clarity, be sure to include only the relevant part of the text. Reposting an entire message when you are only responding to one line takes up bandwidth for everyone.

- ***Don't overdo signatures:*** A signature normally contains your name and address, and perhaps a favorite quotation. Avoid displays of ASCII art, maps, or other drawings, which simply take up storage space. Four lines should be sufficient to handle these tasks.
- ***Avoid superfluous posts:*** Messages need to have content. Don't post "Me, too" messages in response to a query. If you would like to register this kind of agreement with an author, send just him or her e-mail.

Trumpet for Windows

Programs like Trumpet for Windows go through extended evolution as users suggest new features and the developer responds with ideas of his or her own. You should not be surprised, then, to find some changes in the program between the time this book is printed and when you access Trumpet yourself (in particular, the latest beta version of Trumpet includes an extraction feature that lets you uudecode graphic images on the fly, about which more in a moment). This ability to live on the cutting edge of software development is one of the more exciting aspects of maintaining your SLIP/PPP account. You will also find that newsgroups like **alt.winsock** allow you to keep up with developments in many client programs.

Downloading Trumpet for Windows

To retrieve Trumpet for Windows, use FTP to reach the following URL:

ftp://ftp.trumpet.com.au/wintrump/

At the time of this writing, the filename was wtwsk10a.zip.

Unpacking and Storing Trumpet

Your first task is to create the necessary Trumpet directory on your hard disk, and then move to it to proceed with the unpacking procedure for Trumpet's compressed file. Follow these steps:

1. Create a *c:\wintrump* directory.
2. Move the compressed Trumpet for Windows file to the new directory.
3. Unpack the file, using **PKUNZIP** or WinZip.

You should find the following files, or their equivalent in the updated version of the Trumpet for Windows package:

disclaim.txt	A disclaimer statement from Peter Tattam, the program's author.
readme.txt	The latest information about the program, including any last minute changes and problems.
wintrump.hlp	The help file for Trumpet for Windows.
wt_wsk.exe	The executable file for Trumpet for Windows.
wtdoc.doc	The user manual for Trumpet for Windows.

At this point, you should have the entire set of Trumpet for Windows files in your *wintrump* directory.

Installing Trumpet for Windows

The installation procedure for Trumpet for Windows is cut and dried. You will first need to create a program group for Trumpet for Windows, or else place its icon in an existing group. You can perform either task from Program Manager, by pulling down the File menu and choosing the New command. Or you can drag the program from File Manager directly to the existing group within which you would like to keep Trumpet for Windows.

To run Trumpet for Windows for the first time, double-click on its icon. The copyright message box should appear, along with a notice that you will need to register your copy of Trumpet if you plan to keep using it beyond the evaluation period. Click on the OK box to continue. This action should place you into the setup routine.

Configuring Trumpet for Use

The most daunting part of any client program installation is the setup. Figure 10.3 displays the Trumpet Setup dialog box that you need to complete. Examine it with care. Let's go through the fields displayed in the dialog box.

News Host Name	This is where you enter the domain name address of your network news server (the computer that maintains USENET newsgroups at your service provider's site). Here in North Carolina, for example, my service provider's news server has this address: **news-server@interpath.net**. You can see that this is a conventional domain-format address. If you do not know what your service provider's news server's address is, simply ask. This information will doubtless have been supplied to you when you opened your SLIP/PPP account.
Mail Host Name	Enter the name of your SMTP mail server here. To refresh your memory, **SMTP** stands for Simple Mail Transfer Protocol, and refers to the standard Internet protocol for handling electronic mail messages between computers. Trumpet needs this information to know which mail server to use when you send e-mail

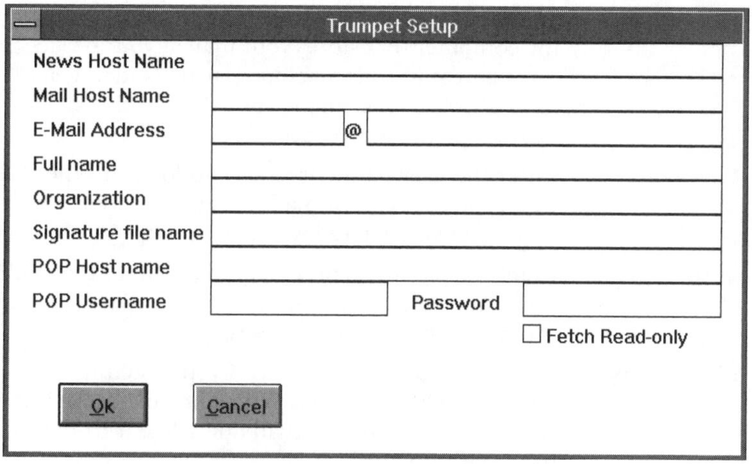

Trumpet Setup	
News Host Name	
Mail Host Name	
E-Mail Address	@
Full name	
Organization	
Signature file name	
POP Host name	
POP Username	Password
	☐ Fetch Read-only
Ok	Cancel

Figure 10.3 The setup box for Trumpet for Windows.

to the author of a USENET posting. The host name in question will have been supplied to you when you signed up for your SLIP/PPP account.

E-mail Address   Your electronic mail address goes here.

Full name   Enter your first and last name in this field; these will appear on your postings.

Organization   You can enter the name of your organization or business in this optional field. I encourage you to do so, as the more information supplied in a USENET message header, the more seriously your messages are likely to be taken. But the choice is yours.

Signature file name   A signature file contains a short text message that will be entered at the end of any posting you make. You can call this file anything you like (I call mine sig.doc). When I send a USENET message, Trumpet looks for and finds the sig.doc file and inserts it at the end of my text.

Note: Just as with e-mail signatures, USENET signature files are readily abused by making them too long. Remember that the job of a signature file is to identify you and to supply pertinent information, such as a mailing address or a telephone number. You may also want to include a favorite quotation. But making signatures needlessly lengthy by including ASCII drawings or excessive verbiage simply places an additional load upon an already overworked network. Try to keep your signature information as concise as possible. Four or five lines of text will generally be all you need.

POP Host name	We discussed mail servers in Chapter 6. The POP3 mail server is the computer that stores your mail at your service provider's site. The address for this machine is usually identical to that provided as the SMTP host name, but double-check with your service provider if you aren't sure.
POP Username	Enter the user name necessary to log in to the POP3 computer when you access your mail. This information should be identical with what you entered when you set up your mail account.
Password	Enter the password necessary to log on to the POP3 mail server. This information will appear in the dialog box as a series of asterisks for security purposes.
Fetch Read-only	This box should be checked if you would like to retrieve e-mail for previewing purposes. When the box is checked, Trumpet will retrieve your e-mail but will not delete it from the server after it has been retrieved.

Once you have filled in the information required (and remember, the organization field is not necessary), click on the OK button. Doing so will cause Trumpet to retrieve a list of the newsgroups available on your news server. Given the number of newsgroups out there, this may take some time, but remember that the entire process only occurs when you go through the setup procedure, or when you choose the Subscribe command to sign up for new newsgroups. Let Trumpet do its work; when it is through, you can decide which newsgroups to read.

Subscribing to Newsgroups

With newsgroups available in their multitudes, how do you know which ones to choose for your first subscriptions? My first experience with USENET many years ago was so daunting that I was almost scared away from the entire procedure. Using a shell account, I was automatically subscribed to all the available newsgroups, and had to learn how to unsubscribe by using a Unix text editor called vi and editing a file called .newsrc, in which subscription information was contained. I finally mastered the process, but not without some intimidation.

Trumpet does away with all that; the program makes signing on to newsgroups simple; better still, it allows you to search for newsgroups without the need to enter complicated parameters. You can use its powers and your own skills on the Internet to determine an initial set of newsgroups. My experience taught me that any newcomer to USENET will be better off by starting with a few newsgroups and following the action there for a time before signing up for more. The reason for this is that some newsgroups carry quite a bit of traffic, with the potential of overwhelming the neophyte. So my first recommendation is to pick two groups, and I would suggest **news.announce.newusers** and **alt.internet.services**. The former newsgroup is tailored for beginners, and

Note: As originally developed in 1979 by Tom Truscott and Jim Ellis, USENET used software designed to work with UUCP (the Unix-to-Unix Copy Program). UUCP was developed to handle electronic messaging between computers, but it does not include such interactive services as remote login. UUCP and the Internet are different networks, but numerous mail gateways exist between the Internet and UUCP machines. When you encounter the term NNTP (Network News Transfer Protocol), you are dealing with the protocol that allows computers to exchange USENET articles by TCP/IP connections rather than UUCP.

As a practical matter, NNTP itself need not concern the USENET enthusiast. But it is worth remarking that USENET and the Internet cannot be considered interchangeable. The two are separate networks, which give the appearance, due to the propagation of so much USENET material over the Internet, to have merged. In the same way, much BITNET traffic is now routed through the Internet's TCP/IP procedures, and for much the same reason: the propagation of information is more efficient using the well-developed TCP/IP infrastructure than by using a parallel communications network. In the case of NNTP, the overhead caused by its operations on the network is also less than that created by routing through UUCP methods.

remains a place where you can find the answers to the most commonly asked questions. The latter contains discussions about breaking news on the net and the answers to many questions.

Let's use Trumpet to sign up to **news.announce.newusers**. Moving from the setup dialog box to the subscription process should be seamless, because the first time you run Trumpet and enter the setup information, the program will take you automatically into the Subscribe to News Groups dialog box. This box is shown in Figure 10.4.

Using the dialog box is easy. We first select the top level hierarchy that we are interested in; in this case, the hierarchy is news. Notice the Top Level Hierarchy box in the figure. It contains a scrollable field that can be controlled by the up and down arrow buttons at top and bottom. Clicking on the down arrow button and holding down the mouse button allows us to move to the news hierarchy. When we do, a list of available newsgroups in that hierarchy will appear. We can then move through the lists in the Unsubscribed groups box to find the list we want. In Figure 10.5, I have highlighted the **news.announce.-newusers** newsgroup.

Subscribing to this list is simply a matter of clicking on it. When we do this, the list will be moved from the Unsubscribed groups box to the Subscribed groups box. To reverse the decision, we could simply click on it in its new position and it would be returned to the Unsubscribed groups box.

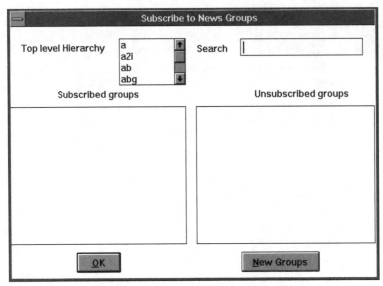

Figure 10.4 The Subscribe to News Groups dialog box in Trumpet for Windows.

Clicking on the OK button at the end of this process adds the newsgroup to our list. If you will examine Figure 10.6, you will find a list of newsgroups to which I have subscribed, as shown on the Trumpet News Reader window. This snapshot of my own newsgroups will be obsolete by the time you read this, as I subscribe and unsubscribe to groups all the time.

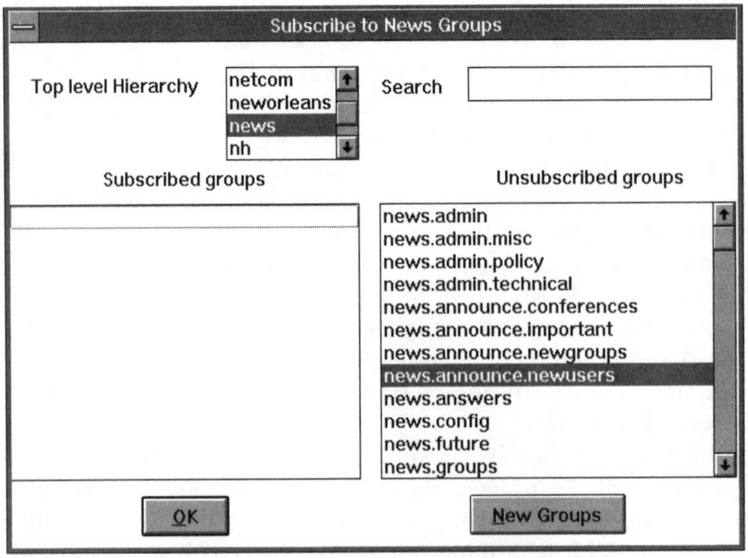

Figure 10.5 Subscribing to a newsgroup in Trumpet for Windows.

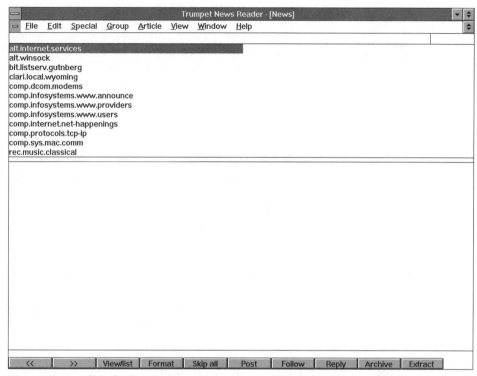

Figure 10.6   A list of subscribed newsgroups as shown by the Trumpet newsreader.

You can subscribe to as many groups as you choose, but I do recommend following through, for the purposes of this demonstration, with the **news.announce.newusers** and **alt.internet.services** groups, because the principles we examine here will apply across the entire range of newsgroups.

Reading a USENET Newsgroup

To read a newsgroup with Trumpet for Windows, simply highlight that group in the Trumpet News Reader window and click on it. When you do so, you will be presented with a list of articles currently available in that newsgroup. An example is shown in Figure 10.7. Notice that all the articles are presented to you by subject, allowing you to easily choose which you would like to read. Double-click on the article you wish to see. Alternatively, you can place the highlight bar over that article and click on the View/list button to perform the same action. Let's assume we would like to examine the useful document called Updated Internet Services List. We simply double-click on the item to retrieve it (we could also have used the Arrow keys to move the highlight bar to the appropriate document, and then pressed Return to achieve the same effect). The article is displayed in Figure 10.8.

Note: We could also have taken a shortcut to subscribe to the **news.announce.newusers** group. If you will examine the Subscribe to News Groups dialog box again, you will see that it contains, at upper right, a field called Search. This handy field allows us to type in the name of any newsgroup we wish to access. In fact, because it will search for any pattern we give it, the search function can be used by simply typing in the first part of the name. Thus, if we were to type in news, Trumpet would then display, in the Unsubscribed groups box, any newsgroups containing that string. We could quickly pick out the newsgroup we wanted by clicking on it.

The search function is useful in other ways. With newsgroups available in their thousands, we know there is plentiful information out there. The question becomes, how do we find the single newsgroup most likely to contain what we need? With the search function, we can make quick searches for key terms, pulling up the names of any newsgroups whose name contains the term in question. I have used this capability numerous times to find a particular newsgroup. I can then subscribe to it for the duration of my research into a particular issue. In this way, Trumpet allows you to tap USENET as a source of continuous, on-line information in your field.

Scott Yanoff's work has become one of the classic USENET documents. Indeed, you can learn much about the Internet and about USENET through reading regularly updated on-line postings. Remember, the great beauty of USENET, and of the Internet at large, is that so many people have contributed to the on-line resources available, greatly simplifying the task of new users. In the **news.announce.newusers** newsgroup, you will find primers on using the network, as well as wonderful documents like Emily Postnews Answers Your Questions on Netiquette, Answers to Frequently Asked Questions about USENET, What Is USENET, and more. Reading **alt.internet.services** and **news.announce.newusers** will provide a thorough grounding in network principles.

And because they are so useful, we would like to know how to save such documents. Notice the Archive button at the bottom of the Trumpet screen. We can click on it to save the article as a text file on disk. Or we could pull down the File menu and choose the Print function to send the file directly to our printer. Reading the article on-line is, of course, another alternative. Notice the scroll bar to the right of the screen. Simply clicking on the down arrow moves us down line by line into the document, or we can click on the bar itself to move down a page at a time. When we have finished reading a particular article, we can return to the list of articles available by again clicking on the View/list button at the bottom of the screen.

The basic Trumpet commands for reading articles, as presented on the button bar at the bottom of the screen, are more or less self-explanatory. Let's run through them briefly:

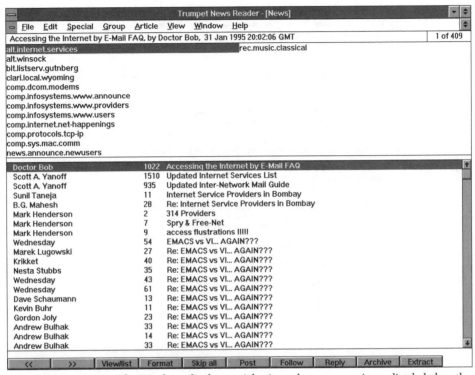

Figure 10.7 Trumpet for Windows displays articles in each newsgroup immediately below the list of subscribed newsgroups.

  <<   Scrolls through the list of newsgroups previous to the one you are currently highlighting. When a newsgroup with messages is found, Trumpet will scan the group and display the list by subject.

  >>   Scrolls through the list of newsgroups following the one you are currently highlighting.

View/list   This is in effect a toggle switch. If you are at the list of articles in a given newsgroup, clicking on this button will display the highlighted article. If you are viewing an article, clicking View/list will return you to the list of articles.

Format   Changes the format of the article list. You can move between a list showing the subject of each article only, or a list showing subject and author, with the additional ability to display article length. If you are already reading an article, clicking on the Format button will change the font being used.

Skip all   Skips all the articles in the current group and moves to the next newsgroup.

Extract   Available only in the latest beta version of Trumpet for Windows, this command allows you to highlight messages that have been saved in uudecoded format and decode them on your machine. You will be prompted

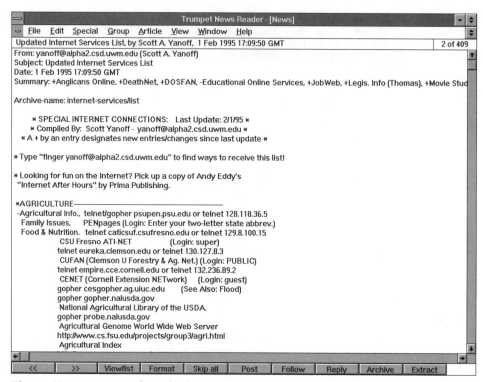

Figure 10.8   A news article on display.

for a directory in which to place the decoded file. More information on how USENET carries graphics and other binary data through encoding will appear later in this chapter.

Posting Articles to USENET

Posting articles to a newsgroup can be a powerful tool. Perhaps you have a question that network regulars can answer, or an observation that may inspire comment. Whatever the case, Trumpet for Windows makes posting relatively simple. All you need do is access the newsgroup to which you want to post; you can click on the Post button at the bottom of the screen to create and send your comment or question.

I frequently run into issues in my work that I want to submit to the combined expertise of newsgroup readers. Suppose, for example, that I wanted to find out what newsreaders were most popular for users of SLIP and PPP accounts. I could access the **alt.winsock** newsgroup, where issues relating to client software are frequently bandied about, and pose the question there.

To do so, I move to the **alt.winsock** newsgroup by double-clicking on it. I then click on the Post button to call up the Post Article window. You can see this window in Figure 10.9. In the figure, I have already filled in the necessary information, and have included my message. Let's now examine the Post Article window with this information included. Notice the top section of the window, which contains the following fields:

Newsgroups   The groups to which the article will be posted. Messages can be cross-posted to more than one group by listing the newsgroups desired, separated by a comma. But be advised that cross-posting should be done with caution. You want to be sure that the newsgroups you cross-post to really are relevant to your topic. In this example, I have posted only to the **alt.winsock** group.

Subject   The subject of the post. Choose your words with care. Readers will use your subject entry to make a decision about whether to spend their time on your article or not. Thus, subjects need to be clear and concise. A needlessly general subject like "Help" tells little; replacing it with "Problem with PPP Connection using Trumpet Winsock" makes your needs clearer, and limits your audience to those likely to have a solution.

Keywords   Appropriate keywords for the article. This is an optional field. But as with subjects, properly chosen keywords will help. The Subject, Keywords, and Summary fields are all passed from news servers to newsreader programs, where the information in them can be used to

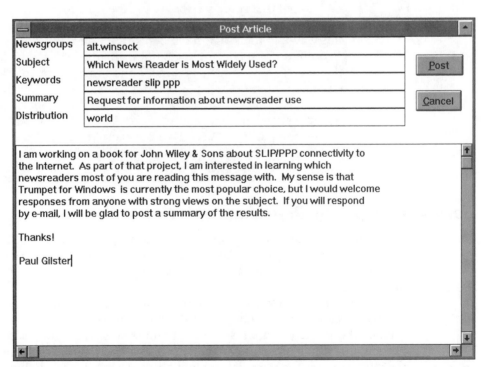

Figure 10.9   Posting an article to a USENET newsgroup; USENET is a great source for background information.

auto-select articles, or to select out articles that the user does not want to see. Choose your words with care.

Summary   An optional summary of your article.

Distribution   How widely your article will be distributed. This field deserves your careful attention. Usually, you can use the default for the newsgroup in question. You need to restrict distribution when you are aiming your message at local users yet are posting in a newsgroup that generally propagates worldwide. In such cases, using a local distribution would make sense. The local distributions made available on a particular server can only be determined by asking your system administrator; he or she may have established identifiers restricting distribution to a campus, a business, or a city. Wider distributions, which are standardized, include world, usa, na (North America), and individual states, such as nc, ny, and so forth.

Having filled in the header information at the top of the screen, I can now write my message; I can also paste text into Trumpet for Windows from a text editor. Once everything looks the way I want it to, I can click the Post button, which will post the article to the newsgroup.

Note: In my message to the **alt.winsock** newsgroup, notice that I have asked that responses be sent to me via e-mail. One way to handle this kind of request for information is to retrieve your results this way, and then to post a message summarizing what you found. In doing so, you take up less bandwidth and act as a moderator for the discussion you have created. Your summary should be as concise and as comprehensive as possible.

Incidentally, a little trolling in the **alt.winsock** newsgroup quickly revealed that Trumpet for Windows has an extremely robust competitor in WinVN, a program I discuss shortly. The continuing development of both will doubtless keep the controversy over which is best alive and well.

Following Up and Replying to Articles

To respond to an article, you have two options, posting and mailing. Be sure you understand both, as confusion can arise if you use the wrong one, thinking you have posted to the newsgroup when you have actually sent electronic mail to the article's author.

Posting an article to a newsgroup in response to something you have read involves clicking on the Follow button on the button bar at the bottom of the screen. The article you are responding to must be open. If you choose to quote particular text in a message, you can do so by selecting that text, and dragging the cursor across the material to highlight it. Then click the Follow button. If you choose to respond to the entire message, simply click the Follow button without highlighting any text, which will quote the full message.

What you will see next is the Post Article window, with either the selected text or the entire message you are responding to shown in it. Trumpet uses a right-pointing bracket, or > character, to precede each line of the original message. At the top of the screen will appear the critical header information, which you will need to examine. Most of it will already be filled out, depending upon how thorough the original poster was, but you can always add keywords or a summary of your reply, and can include a distribution as well. Clicking on Post will send your response to the newsgroup.

Trumpet also contains a Reply button at the bottom of its screen. When you click on it, you cause the Mail Article window to appear, as shown in Figure 10.10. In this figure, I have decided to reply to an article that appeared in the **alt.internet.services** newsgroup. The answer to this posting suits electronic mail rather than the newsgroup itself; it is a very specific bit of information, probably of interest only to the poster.

Note the slight differences between the Post Article and Mail Article screens. In the latter, the address is that of the original poster; your response will go to that person alone, rather than to the entire newsgroup. This is often the preferable way to handle USENET responses, since you can answer

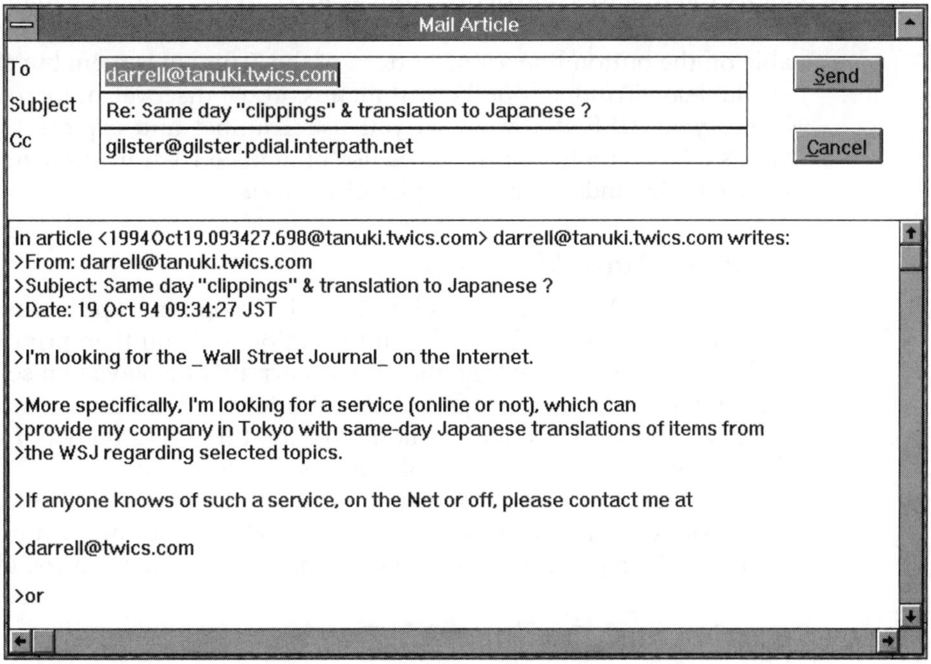

```
┌─────────────────────────────────────────────────────────────────────┐
│ ─                        Mail Article                             ▲  │
├─────────────────────────────────────────────────────────────────────┤
│ To      ┌─────────────────────────────────────────┐    ┌─────────┐   │
│         │ darrell@tanuki.twics.com                │    │ Send    │   │
│ Subject └─────────────────────────────────────────┘    └─────────┘   │
│         ┌─────────────────────────────────────────┐                  │
│         │ Re: Same day "clippings" & translation to Japanese ?  │    │
│ Cc      └─────────────────────────────────────────┘    ┌─────────┐   │
│         ┌─────────────────────────────────────────┐    │ Cancel  │   │
│         │ gilster@gilster.pdial.interpath.net     │    └─────────┘   │
│         └─────────────────────────────────────────┘                  │
├─────────────────────────────────────────────────────────────────────┤
│ In article <1994Oct19.093427.698@tanuki.twics.com> darrell@tanuki.twics.com writes: │
│ >From: darrell@tanuki.twics.com                                      │
│ >Subject: Same day "clippings" & translation to Japanese ?          │
│ >Date: 19 Oct 94 09:34:27 JST                                       │
│                                                                     │
│ >I'm looking for the _Wall Street Journal_ on the Internet.         │
│                                                                     │
│ >More specifically, I'm looking for a service (online or not), which can │
│ >provide my company in Tokyo with same-day Japanese translations of items from │
│ >the WSJ regarding selected topics.                                 │
│                                                                     │
│ >If anyone knows of such a service, on the Net or off, please contact me at │
│                                                                     │
│ >darrell@twics.com                                                  │
│                                                                     │
│ >or                                                                 │
└─────────────────────────────────────────────────────────────────────┘
```

Figure 10.10 Replying to an article by electronic mail is often the best procedure, because it doesn't tie up valuable bandwidth.

requests that might be common knowledge to the rest of the newsgroup, and thus not take up the time of your readers or the bandwidth of the network unnecessarily. You also will see a Subject field, which should already be filled in with the subject of the original post, and a Cc field, wherein you can place the address of any other parties to whom you'd like your message to be sent.

The original message appears, bracketed, in the lower part of the Mail Article screen (in USENET parlance, the message is "quoted" in your response). You can place your response after the message. Be advised that quoting entire messages isn't an effective way to proceed. In most cases, you are responding to a particular point within the message, and you can ensure that only the relevant part of the text is quoted within the message by selecting that text before clicking on the Reply button. Or you can edit the text once it has been inserted into the Mail Article button by highlighting what you want to delete and then pressing the Backspace key.

After editing the original message, enter your own comments after it. When you click the Send button, your comment will be sent to the poster of the original article.

Simplifying USENET with Trumpet

The beauty of Trumpet, and other graphical newsreaders as well, is that they allow you to have control over your USENET environment without struggling with complicated command parameters. The features just discussed are available on the button line at the bottom of the Trumpet screen, but they are also available on Trumpet's pull-down menus. You'll discover numerous shortcuts in everyday USENET work as you use Trumpet and explore these menus. Here's a look at a few of the more useful items on Trumpet's menus, with reference to the underlying principles of net use.

Printing Your Messages

Pull down the File menu and choose the Print option to print your messages; you will be prompted for further information and can then print your text. It will appear in the same font and size as currently displayed on-screen. This is a handy way to retrieve copies of useful information; I am constantly adding USENET messages to one or another of the three-ring binders I use to track developments in various areas of Internet development.

Trumpet's File menu is shown in Figure 10.11. Note the Save settings item, which allows you to save any changes you make to your newsgroups while you are inside Trumpet; otherwise, these changes are saved when you click on Exit.

Cutting and Pasting with Trumpet

Cut and paste features are critical for my USENET work. Think of USENET as a collection of information, in varying degrees of quality, from sources ranging from the expert to the meretricious. First-timers often remark on how many

| Setup... |
| Network Setup... |
| Reconnect |
| Save settings |
| Fetch mail |
| Print |
| Printer Setup... |
| Exit |

Figure 10.11   Trumpet for Windows' File menu.

time-wasting newsgroups they have discovered on a first run through the net. You may have this experience, too, but after a while, you will discover groups that become true research tools. At this point, you will want to be able to lift comments or suggestions from the text and to place them in another place for storage. One way to do this (and we'll examine other options in a moment) is by using Trumpet's cut and paste features; you do this by calling on the Copy command. The procedure is simple:

1. Choose the text you want to copy.
2. Hold down the left mouse button where you want to begin your copying and draw the mouse across the relevant text.
3. Release the mouse button when all the text you want has been selected.
4. Click on the Copy command to insert your selection in the Windows Clipboard.

From here, the selected information can be pasted into other applications as you choose. In my case, I use a program called Info Select, from Micro Logic Corp. in Hackensack, New Jersey. The program is available in both Windows and DOS versions; it is an electronic rolodex with this key difference: you can search through your electronic notes using any combination of characters, rather than being limited by keywords you have inserted in a particular field.

I maintain "stacks" of such notes on a variety of subjects. In Figure 10.12, I have selected text from a message in the **comp.internet.net-happenings** newsgroup, which I routinely use to track new network sites and other developments. Here, I'm being told about a newswire that can keep me up to speed with telecommunications news. As you can see, I have highlighted the site because I want to save this in my Info Select stack of interesting net destinations. I choose the Copy command to place it in the Windows Clipboard, from which I will go into Info Select to paste the information. You will, with some experience, quickly build a list of those newsgroups that are most helpful in your own work. My stack of notes having to do with World Wide Web sites, for example, has grown huge.

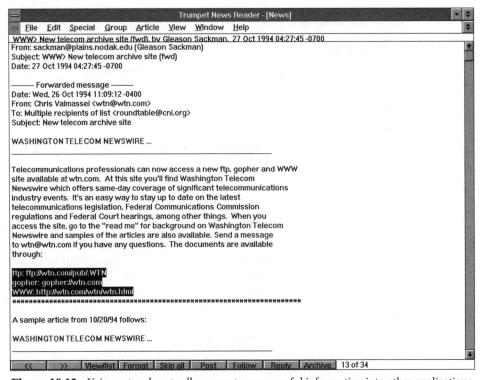

Figure 10.12   Using cut and paste allows you to move useful information into other applications.

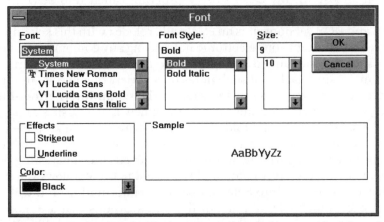

Figure 10.13   Trumpet for Windows gives you control over a wide variety of display features.

Changing Trumpet's Appearance

The Special menu allows you to manipulate the font, point size, and color of your Trumpet windows. Choose the Font option and you will see the menu shown in Figure 10.13. Note how wide your range of choices is here; you can experiment until you find the right font for your own work. Staring at computer screens all day long, I frequently suffer from eye fatigue, so the ability to change quickly between point sizes, fonts, and screen colors has proven beneficial. USENET is particularly intensive in this regard, since most of your screen activity involves reading passages of text, some of them lengthy. Notice, incidentally, that the changes you make apply to the appearance of the message viewer window; they do not affect the main newsgroup window.

Two other items may catch your eye on the Special menu, shown in Figure 10.14:

Zap all Subscribed Groups	Marks all newsgroups as unsubscribed, allowing you to start with a clean slate.
Discard Unsubscribed Groups	Deletes unsubscribed groups from the news.ini file which Trumpet uses in its work.

You will also notice the items Insert Folder and Delete Folder, which appear grayed out, and thus unusable, in this menu. To explain these, we need to examine how Trumpet handles articles, and how we can use its features for basic information management.

Manipulating Articles in Trumpet for Windows

The key to creating a good newsreader is that its designers take into account that we will need to handle separate messages in different ways. In the case of Trumpet for Windows, that means providing a variety of options for handling each. You can find the options listed on the Article menu. We have already examined how to reply to the poster of a message by mail and by following up the message within the newsgroup. But we need to examine other options on this menu in detail.

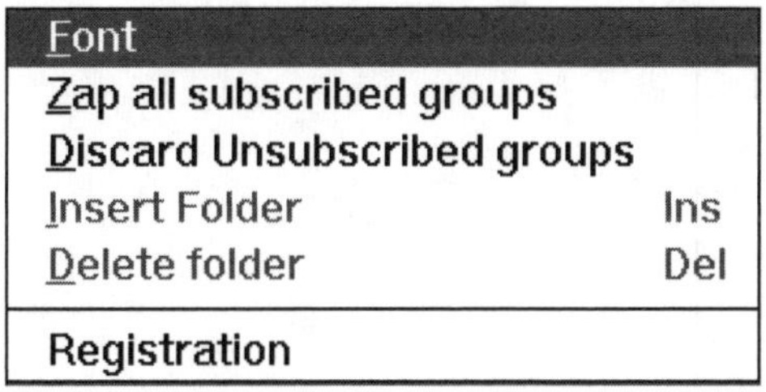

Figure 10.14 The Special menu in Trumpet for Windows.

You will find the menu shown in Figure 10.15. Note the keyboard shortcuts for each option as well.

Notice the Cancel item. This can be a useful command to know, because it enables you to cancel an article that you have written (you can't cancel an article written by anyone else).

Perhaps you doubt it would be necessary to have a cancel function, but consider what happened to me recently. While perusing the **rec.radio.short-wave** newsgroup (I'm a great fan of BBC World Service and like to get schedules here, as well as to listen to news about new receivers), I ran across several postings blasting a particular shortwave radio supply house. Having had dealings with these people in the past, I agreed with what I was reading, and posted a follow-up, adding my own comments about what had happened to me in a transaction several years back, and exhorting new customers to look elsewhere for their equipment. Almost immediately after posting this reply, however, I learned that the company was now under new management; my exhortation therefore might hurt business for an innocent party. Trumpet's Cancel option allowed me to swiftly delete this message from the newsgroup.

The Article menu also contains two critical items relating to information management:

Save to File   Allows you to save the current posting to a file of your choice. A dialog box pops up, giving you the ability to choose a filename and directory in which to put the material.

Append to File   Allows you to add the current document to a preexisting file.

The Article menu also contains several other options:

Toggle   Marks the current article as read or unread.

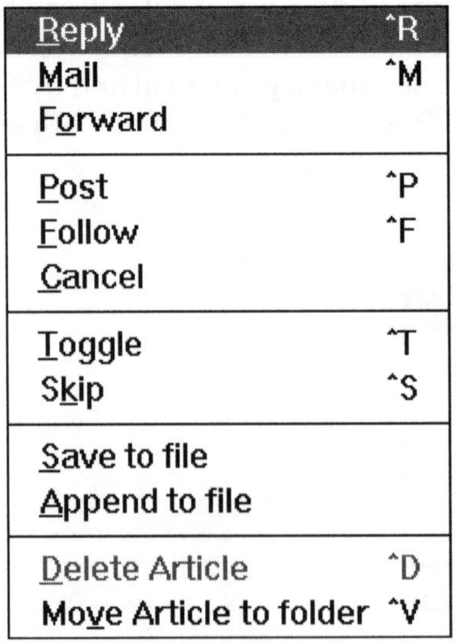

Figure 10.15 Trumpet for Windows' Article menu.

Skip	Allows you to skip the current article.
Delete Article	Allows you to delete an article or mail message. Note: this command only works while you are in the Mail window (see the next section). At other times, it is grayed out and unavailable.
Move Article to folder	Moves the current article into an archival folder for that newsgroup. To explain these latter two commands, let's move to a discussion of how Trumpet uses folders.

Managing Folders in Trumpet for Windows

The preceding suggests that good information management is the best way to keep your USENET work productive. It's all too easy to simply become overwhelmed by the sheer variety and number of messages available, until you reach the point that the most viable option seems to be to exit USENET altogether. Trumpet for Windows provides a folder feature that enhances your information management by allowing you to save messages in designated areas, for later review. You will find this feature on the Article menu under the heading Move Article to folder.

A folder is simply a place where you can put articles that have caught your attention. By default, each folder will be named for the newsgroup from which the article you are saving comes. Thus, if you are reading **alt.internet.services** and find a particularly helpful message, you can archive this with the Move Article to folder command, and it will be saved along with any other articles you have saved from the same newsgroup. It's like having a file folder set up for each newsgroup; usefully, this archival function allows you to save entire articles quickly, rather than going through the entire process of selecting text, copying it, and pasting it to another application. The latter is best used for snippets of information, like network addresses and the like; the former benefits you when you need the entire text of a posting.

Here, however, we run into a Trumpet design peculiarity. The folder function is spread confusingly over three different menus. If you are reading USENET news and pull down the Special menu, you will find the Insert Folder and Delete Folder items grayed out, which means that they cannot be used from your current position in the program. Attempt to click on them and your mouse will have no effect. To use the folder options, you must change windows in Trumpet. You can only create and delete folders while in Trumpet's Mail window, which you can access by pulling down the Window menu. Let's examine how the Mail option works.

In Figure 10.16, I have pulled down the Window menu and have clicked on the Mail option. Notice that the screen has changed from the usual newsgroup screen. The list of newsgroups is shorter than the one we viewed at the main newsgroup screen. What you are now looking at is a list of newsgroups in which I have saved messages. The other newsgroups do not appear since I have not yet saved any messages in them to a folder. The folder names correspond to the names of the newsgroups. Thus we have separate folders for **alt.inter-**

net.services, **comp.infosystems.www.misc**, **news.announce.newusers**, and
so on. In the bottom half of the screen, the messages I have saved can be found.
Each newsgroup, when highlighted, will display the saved messages. I can read
any of these messages by double-clicking on them.

Now that I am in the Mail window, I can go back to the Special menu,
where I can choose either the Insert Folder or Delete Folder items. Insert
Folder, obviously, allows me to create a new folder for a particular newsgroup, while Delete Folder will remove the folder of my choice. It is a good
idea to keep up with your folders. In my own work, I frequently fill a folder
with numerous messages pertaining to a current project; once the project is
completed, I generally delete the material to avoid taking up unnecessary
disk space.

Trumpet's Window menu, incidentally, contains two other commands that
will be familiar to Windows users:

Tile   Allows you to set up the main viewer windows in "tiled" fashion; that is,
            adjacent to each other but not overlapping.

Cascade   Sets up the main viewer windows in cascade fashion, overlapping but
            movable.

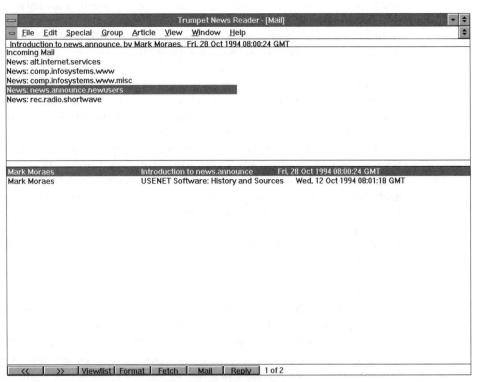

Figure 10.16   Using Trumpet for Windows to examine messages saved in individual folders.

Fast Forwarding through a Newsgroup

No matter how many times I vow to keep up with my newsgroups, it is inevitable that I miss a few days in a row and return to find a huge number of articles waiting for me. Particularly if you're going on vacation, you need to be able to mark all the articles in a newsgroup as read without having to browse through them. Trumpet makes this easy. All you need do is pull down the Group menu and choose the Catch up option. All the articles in the current newsgroup are then marked as read, and the messages themselves are not retrieved, thus saving you the time it would take to load them.

The entire Group menu is shown in Figure 10.17. Notice that you have four other options for managing a current session:

Read All   Marks all the retrieved articles in the current newsgroup as read.

Unread All   Marks all the retrieved articles in the current newsgroup as unread.

Unread 20   Marks the last twenty articles in the current newsgroup as unread.

Unread 10   Marks the last ten articles in the current newsgroup as unread.

The Group menu also contains two final options, the first of which we discussed earlier:

Subscribe   Allows you to sign up for a particular newsgroup. A list of all the newsgroups available through your NNTP server will be displayed.

Unsubscribe Marks the current group as unsubscribed.

Viewing Options

In our age of multicultural sensitivities and easily hurt feelings, wouldn't it be nice to be able to flag a possibly offensive comment so that those who might not like it would not have to read it? Ponder the dilemma of a newsgroup called **rec.humor**, wherein people post things that strike them as funny. You may think Bulgarian jokes are the hottest thing on the market, but perhaps net citizens from that country disagree. To the rescue comes a procedure known as rot13. It is a form of encryption (albeit a very simple one) that guarantees that

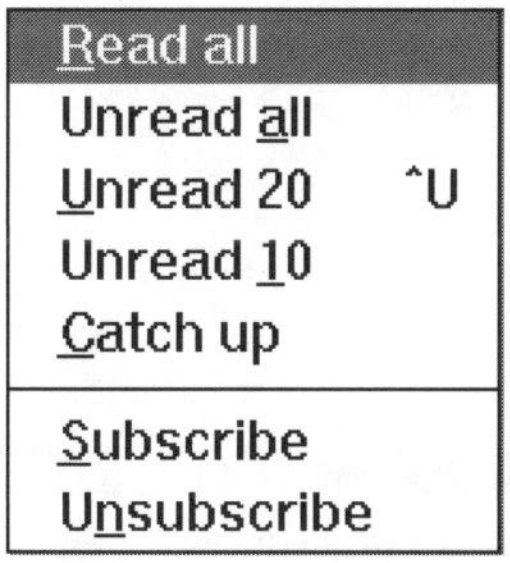

Figure 10.17   The Group menu in Trumpet for Windows.

a possibly offensive comment or joke can't be read unless the reader takes a specific action to read it. You can thus encrypt your joke so that it can be ignored by others.

The encryption method used is to move each letter by thirteen characters; a good newsreader makes it easy for the poster to do this. A "c," in other words, becomes a "p," and so on. Stumbling upon such a message in your USENET travels, you will immediately know that you are dealing with rot13. For one thing, the encryption will be obvious because the message will be unreadable. Second, the message should have the word rot13 in its Subject: line. You can see such a message in Figure 10.18. In this case, the message is not offensive; I have simply rotated a standard message about USENET via rot13 to demonstrate what the method looks like.

In actual practice, mildly offensive jokes are more likely to be tagged with descriptors identifying their content in the Subject: field, saving rot13 methods for only the truly objectionable postings (and, if you wander about USENET in certain newsgroups, you'll certainly run into plenty of material that probably should have been rotated via rot13 but wasn't). And, of course, there are other reasons for using rot13 than offensiveness. I'm reminded of the time a friend casually gave away the conclusion of Agatha Christie's *Who Killed Roger Ackroyd?* after I mentioned I had just begun reading it. To avoid such lapses on

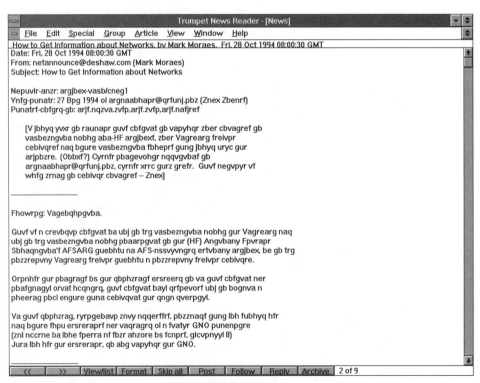

Figure 10.18 A message that has been coded through rot13 procedures.

USENET, you could always discuss plot issues in messages that had undergone rot13 conversion.

To decode rot13 articles in Trumpet for Windows, pull down the View menu and choose the Rot13 menu item. You can encrypt and decrypt any article currently on the screen using this method (though, naturally, the only time you will use this technique when reading messages is when you have a previously encrypted posting on-screen). Having used the method a time or two, see if you don't agree with me that having the visual and auditory equivalent of rot13 built into a television set would be a true breakthrough in modern electronics. Imagine being able to tell your TV to rotate all the political commercials into some digital limbo!

The View menu also contains two other items:

View Headers   Allows you to view the entire headers of articles (normally, you see only a subset of this information).

Word Wrap   Allows word wrap to work, keeping text within defined margins.

Keeping Up with New Newsgroups

So many USENET newsgroups are being constantly created that you could spend a good part of each day examining each. Naturally, we want to simplify that process. Trumpet will ignore new newsgroups until you decide to subscribe to a newsgroup. At that time, it will create a new list of available newsgroups on your local NNTP server, and will display new groups as well. You can subscribe to any newsgroup using the methods we discussed when setting up Trumpet.

Searching for Targeted Information in Newsgroups

The Internet, and by extension USENET, has always had an Achilles' heel: although information is abundant, finding it on-line is a daunting task. USENET makes this task even harder by offering thousands of newsgroups but no efficient searching mechanism across them. What we can do with Trumpet for Windows is to use its existing search functions to find the right newsgroup for our purposes. Remember that the Search box available on the Subscribe to News Groups window allows you to search newsgroup titles by keywords to find the group you need.

Here's how we can do it. Let's suppose I am interested in learning which USENET newsgroups are likely to contain information about physics. By pulling down the Group menu and choosing the Subscribe item, I call up the Subscribe to News Groups dialog box. I can now enter my search term, physics, in the Search box. The results are shown in Figure 10.19. As a matter of fact, the groups you see in this box represent only a portion of what is available under this keyword. Notice that the search term can appear anywhere in the newsgroup name; thus we get groups as diverse as **alt.sci.physics.plutonium** and **sci.physics.accelerators**. We can then subscribe to any of these groups by highlighting it and clicking on the OK button.

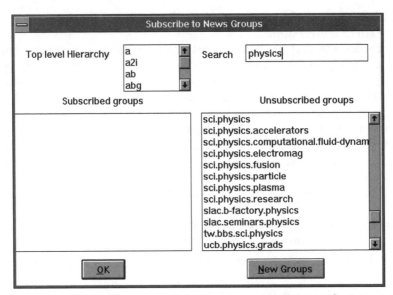

Figure 10.19   Setting up a search for newsgroups pertaining to physics.

Trumpet also makes it easy to work our way through the top-level hierarchies. Notice the Top level Hierarchy box in Figure 10.19. By highlighting any of these hierarchies, we will cause Trumpet to present a list of all the newsgroups in that hierarchy in the Unsubscribed groups box. By playing around with Trumpet's subscribe function, you can thus generate a good deal of information. This is how I ran across the following newsgroups that may be of interest to users of Trumpet:

trumpet.announce	Announcements about Trumpet for Windows and other products from Peter Tattam's Trumpet Software International (including, of course, Trumpet Winsock).
trumpet.bugs	Discussions of bugs in Trumpet.
trumpet.questions	Questions about Trumpet software.
trumpet.test	The place for test postings from Trumpet users.

Registering Trumpet for Windows

This book supports shareware programs like Trumpet for Windows for a reason. The beauty of SLIP/PPP is the wide variety of client software that becomes available to you when you enable your connection. Thus it helps to be able to shop around and try out the work of various programmers as you determine which packages are best for your purposes. Some shareware products (and Trumpet is definitely one of them) are every bit the equal of their commercial cousins; in fact, they often outdo the commercial product in terms of ingenuity and power. But shareware comes with a price: if you like the program, you need to pay for it.

Trumpet for Windows can be used for thirty days to evaluate its usefulness; after that period, you need to register your copy if you intend to keep on using it. The registration fee for the single-user version is U.S. $40, which can be sent by check or postal order to the following address:

Trumpet Software International
GPO Box 1649
Hobart, Tasmania
Australia 7001

Other Newsreader Programs for Windows

I have focused on Trumpet for Windows because I believe it to be one of the best newsreaders currently available, but there are a number of commercial, shareware, and freeware products also in the marketplace. As interest in SLIP/PPP connections grows, you can expect to see quite a few more client programs appearing from a variety of sources. Certainly you should consider commercial products if they meet your own needs, but I would also recommend evaluating the shareware and freeware alternative programs as well. Many, like Trumpet, contain all the features you are likely to need. Just remember that shareware does not mean free. It is your obligation, if you find a particular program useful, to pay the suggested shareware fee to its author. Check any program you download to see what kind of fee arrangements may be implicit in its use.

dMail for Windows

This package is distributed free and provides a number of intriguing features. Built-in uudecoding is one. When a poster wants to make a binary file available over the Internet, a problem immediately arises. The Internet works with 7-bit ASCII data only; this means that a binary file must first be translated into an ASCII format before it can be sent over network e-mail or appear in a USENET newsgroup. This explains why the newsgroups with binary files like graphics present such an odd appearance. You can see an example in Figure 10.20.

The file shown (viewed in dMail for Windows) is an ASCII representation of an image of the planet Saturn as seen by the Voyager spacecraft; it's part one of a two-part image. This image has been encoded into ASCII format with a program called uuencode, and must be decoded by the companion program, which is called uudecode. Not long ago, this would involve retrieving all the parts of a particular image (it might be spread over several USENET postings), editing them to remove the message headers, then running each through the uudecode program, which would decode and assemble the image.

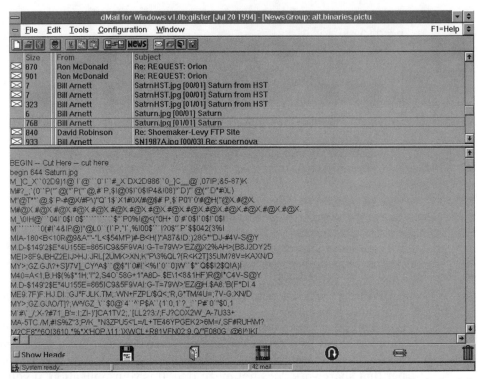

Figure 10.20   A binary message shown as coded in ASCII format. The program displaying it is dMail for Windows.

One of the beauties of the newer newsreaders is that they are beginning to include uudecode capabilities internally. dMail for Windows includes this option. You can see the result of its work in Figure 10.21. Here, I have simply highlighted the two parts of the Saturn image, then dragged them to the uudecode icon at the bottom of the screen. dMail prompts me for a destination directory and then works its magic; in a few moments, the image is ready for viewing through any graphics viewer (I use Lview).

dMail for Windows makes such operations easy with its drag and drop features, but it suffers from an incomplete menu structure that makes many commands hard to figure out. Using the function keys to run basic operations, for example, requires that you check the Help file by pressing the F1 key (there is no help option among the menus). Doing so, you can learn which keys do what, but you will also find drawbacks, such as the lack of a way to mark all messages as read without deleting them one at a time. What I do like about dMail for Windows is its easy-to-read viewing screen with gray background and various font options and, of course, its uudecode features. Another wonderful feature is its replacement for the traditional hourglass symbol; while dMail for Windows is working, it shows you a figure of a man with a shovel digging like crazy.

Figure 10.21 The uudecoding process turns ASCII soup into a stunning photograph.

You can find dMail for Windows at the following site:

ftp://ftp.cica.indiana.edu/pub/pc/win3/winsock/

The current filename is dmailwin.zip.

As always, the usual disclaimers apply about changes to network addresses, directories, and filenames. Check the login directory at the site for updated information if necessary. Figure 10.22 shows a message being read in dMail. Perhaps you can see from this image why I like the program's reading screen. If you do a lot of USENET work, you'll spend a good part of your day reading messages, and I find dMail to be unusually easy on the eyes. Program installation, I'm sorry to say, is tricky.

WinQVT

Here we have a multipurpose package, containing not only USENET news reading capability, but also send and receive functions for electronic mail, a Telnet client, FTP capability, and more (you may remember that we discussed this package in Chapter 7 on Telnet; its Telnet capabilities are superior). I mention it in the newsreader chapter because the number of shareware and freeware newsreader clients is rather small, and if you are planning to investigate different alternatives, you will want to add WinQVT to the mix.

But there is also a downside to multipurpose packages like this one. What they offer in terms of range they often lack in terms of versatility, which is another way of saying that stand-alone applications are often more powerful than application suites. I don't find the WinQVT newsreader to be as powerful as Trumpet for Windows or, for that matter, WinVN (which we are about to examine), although I do like the viewer screen, which makes it easy to work through articles by thread, saving where necessary, or following up on postings; the basic message viewing controls are laid out in a series of buttons at the top of the screen. The program does, however, seem sluggish; it can take quite a while to load a given newsgroup for viewing. The program includes a nice newsgroup search function.

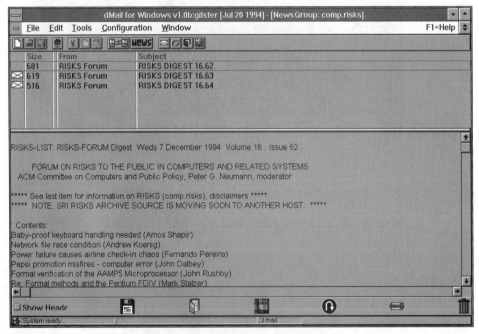

Figure 10.22   Reading a USENET message with dMail for Windows.

If you are interested in the WinQVT package, you can retrieve it at the following URL:

ftp://biochemistry.cwru.edu/qvtnet/

As we go to press, the filename is qvtws398.zip.

WinQVT is a shareware product that requires a $40 registration fee ($20 for students). Registered users will receive a user manual and upgrades for the following year. Installation is relatively simple, especially when compared to dMail for Windows.

WinVN

WinVN is a USENET newsreader with send-only mail capability; the program also includes useful uudecoding features that alone make it worth the look. I also appreciate the numerous sorting options WinVN makes available, allowing you to sort messages by sender, subject, number of lines, threads, or date. You can see WinVN in action in Figure 10.23.

You can retrieve WinVN at the following URL:

ftp://ftp.ksc.nasa.gov/pub/win3/winvn/

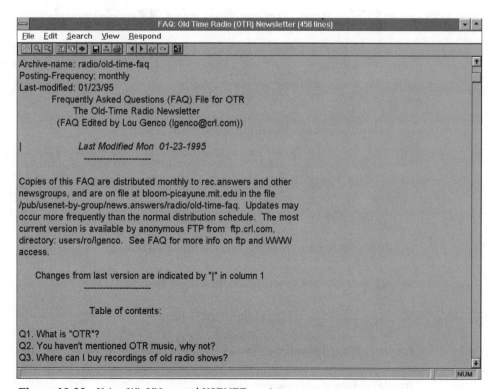

Figure 10.23   Using WinVN to read USENET postings.

At the time of this writing, the filename was winvn_92_6.zip; a new version, however, is in the works and should be available by the time you read this.

WinVN's capabilities with uudecoded files are exceptional. It is possible, as with dMail for Windows, to go through a list of binary files from a newsgroup and mark each of the files you would like to decode, running the entire decoding process in one step. This is quite a help, since many binary files, particularly graphics, come in multiple postings—a given photograph might be divided into five or six parts. With WinVN, you can mark all of these parts and then click on a single menu item to decode them to the directory of your choice and create the finished file. If you plan to do a lot of work with binary files over USENET, both WinVN and dMail for Windows will be worth a look.

What I like less about WinVN is its search capabilities. With Trumpet for Windows, you can search newsgroups and retrieve a list of only those groups that fit your search term. With WinVN, you can also search, but you are taken, group by group, through the entire newsgroup list, with a pointer showing the group that meets your search term. Both methods can be used, but I find the way Trumpet for Windows displays its search results easier to work with; WinVN's is too time-consuming.

Nuntius: A Newsreader for the Macintosh

Developed by Peter Speck, Nuntius is a freeware program, which means that while the author retains the copyright, you can use the program free of charge. You can download Nuntius from the Macintosh archive at Stanford University, among other sites. Here is the URL:

ftp://sumex-aim.stanford.edu/info-mac/comm/

I recommend, though, that you try one of its 35 mirror sites instead, to reduce the load on this overworked server. Here are some possibilities:

ftp://mrcnext.cso.uiuc.edu/pub/info-mac/

ftp://wuarchive.wustl.edu/systems/mac/info-mac/

ftp://ftp.uu.net/archive/systems/mac/info-mac/

ftp://src.doc.ic.ac.uk/packages/info-mac/

ftp://ftp.iij.ad.jp/pub/info-mac/

ftp://archie/au/micros/mac/info-mac/

At the time of this writing, two versions of Nuntius are available. System 7.5 users will want version 1.3b17, while users of earlier software can try version 1.2.

Perhaps the biggest drawback to Nuntius is its lack of an internal text editor, although the program makes it easy enough to specify an external editor for your own postings and responses to messages. But using the package otherwise is simple. By double-clicking on a newsgroup, you quickly create a window with the selected newsgroups postings in it, arranged by message threads. Another double-click on a message thread allows you to read messages within that thread. You can use the Page down button to scroll through the window. Figure 10.24 shows the Nuntius newsreader's depiction of threads in the **alt.internet.services** newsgroup.

Installing and Configuring Nuntius

It never fails to amuse my Macintosh-devoted friends when I mention to them how easy installing Mac SLIP/PPP clients seems after performing the same rites with Microsoft Windows. Configuring Nuntius, for example, is a bare-bones affair:

1. Double-click on the Nuntius icon to initiate the setup procedure. The News server dialog box will appear.

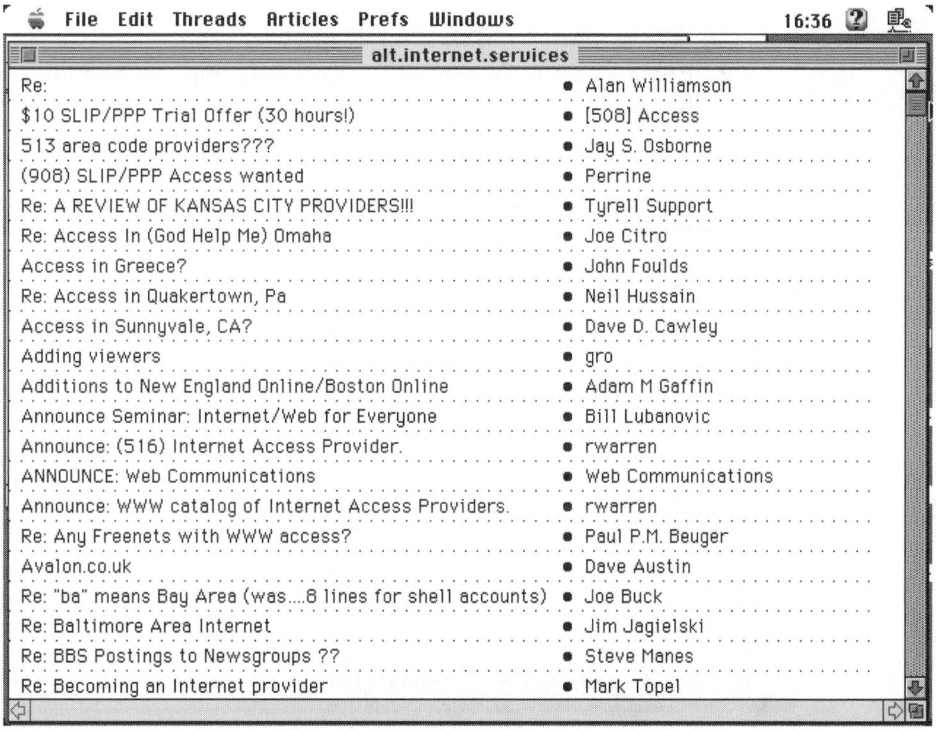

File Edit Threads Articles Prefs Windows	16:36
alt.internet.services	
Re:	● Alan Williamson
$10 SLIP/PPP Trial Offer (30 hours!)	● [508] Access
513 area code providers???	● Jay S. Osborne
(908) SLIP/PPP Access wanted	● Perrine
Re: A REVIEW OF KANSAS CITY PROVIDERS!!!	● Tyrell Support
Re: Access In (God Help Me) Omaha	● Joe Citro
Access in Greece?	● John Foulds
Re: Access in Quakertown, Pa	● Neil Hussain
Access in Sunnyvale, CA?	● Dave D. Cawley
Adding viewers	● gro
Additions to New England Online/Boston Online	● Adam M Gaffin
Announce Seminar: Internet/Web for Everyone	● Bill Lubanovic
Announce: (516) Internet Access Provider.	● rwarren
ANNOUNCE: Web Communications	● Web Communications
Announce: WWW catalog of Internet Access Providers.	● rwarren
Re: Any Freenets with WWW access?	● Paul P.M. Beuger
Avalon.co.uk	● Dave Austin
Re: "ba" means Bay Area (was....8 lines for shell accounts)	● Joe Buck
Re: Baltimore Area Internet	● Jim Jagielski
Re: BBS Postings to Newsgroups ??	● Steve Manes
Re: Becoming an Internet provider	● Mark Topel

Figure 10.24   Examining the alt.internet.services group with Nuntius.

2. In this box, enter the domain name or IP address of the news server you are using. The information is the same as that necessary when configuring Trumpet for Windows or any of the other newsreader programs. Any newsreader needs to know where to look for its news.

3. Click on OK.

When you click on the OK button, Nuntius builds a list of the newsgroups available on your service provider's news server. At the end of this process (it can be lengthy, but it only occurs when you set up Nuntius, or when you rebuild the list of newsgroups), the program will display a list of all top-level newsgroup hierarchies and present it in one window, along with an empty window called Untitled group list 1. Double-clicking on a folder icon from the former will cause a list of newsgroups to appear, along with all subcategories in the newsgroup hierarchy.

To subscribe to a newsgroup, simply click on that group and hold down the mouse button as you drag it into the Untitled group list box. Multiple newsgroups can be subscribed to by using Shift-Click on each newsgroup. Your subscribed newsgroups appear in the Untitled group list window. You can see the two windows involved in Figure 10.25, where I have dragged two newsgroups on the subjects of UFOs into the untitled group list.

Now it's necessary to save this group list and give it a name:

1. Choose Save As from the File menu.

2. Enter a name for the group in the dialog box and click on the Save button.

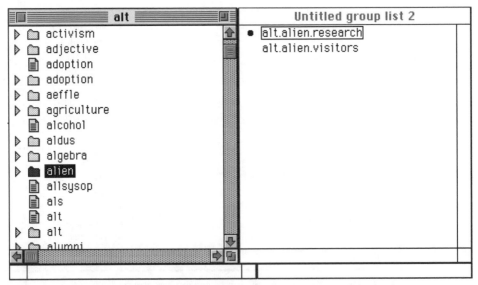

Figure 10.25 Moving selected newsgroups into the new reading list in Nuntius.

I call mine Nuntius News, to distinguish it from the other newsreaders I'm in the process of evaluating.

So far, so good; you have created your first list of subscribed newsgroups. But more information is needed. Using the Prefs menu, select the Your Name option. A dialog box will appear that gives you fields in which to enter your name, e-mail address, and organization. Fill in these fields and click on the OK button. Nuntius is now available for your USENET use.

Reading and Posting to Newsgroups

To become an active USENET participant with Nuntius, it's first necessary to get around the lack of an internal editor; otherwise, you will be limited to reading newsgroups and not responding or posting to them. We can do this easily enough by using the Prefs menu. The item to choose on this menu is Editing Articles. Choosing it will pop up the Preferences: Editor dialog box; you can see it in Figure 10.26.

As you can see from this figure, there is a Select new button under the field marked Editor of Choice. Clicking on this button will cause an Open File dialog box to appear. You can now locate the text editor you would like to use for posting and responding to articles.

Choosing a Folder for Outgoing Articles

Still using the Preferences: Editor box, we can select the folder in which to place any outgoing articles. Here's how:

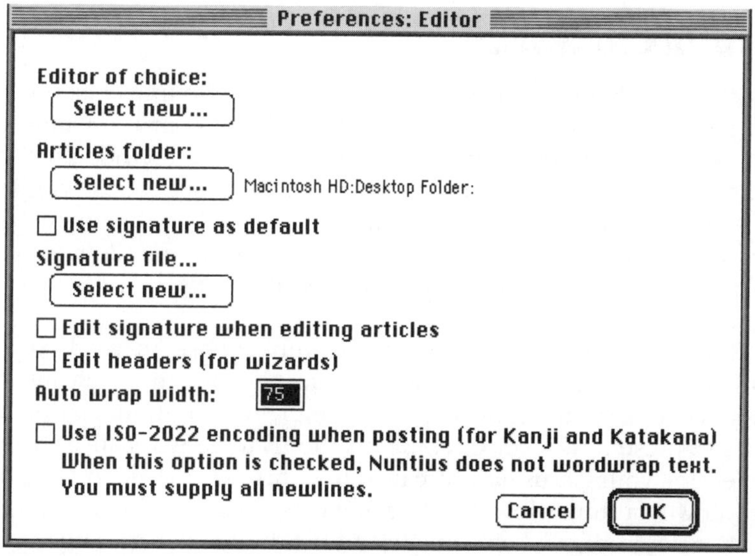

Figure 10.26 Choosing a text editor in Nuntius.

Note: There is no need to become elaborate with text editors when you're dealing with USENET newsgroups. What you want is a simple text editor for generating messages and that's it. The larger and more complicated the editor you choose, the longer it will take Nuntius to open the program (Nuntius opens your editor automatically when you reply to a posting or attempt to create a new one). Any small text editor will do; I use SimpleText.

1. Click on the Open button.
2. Click on Articles folder: Select new button.
3. Within the ensuing dialog box, choose the folder you want to use for outgoing news articles. Temporary copies of your outgoing materials will be placed here.
4. Click the Select a Folder button to make this choice.

Setting Up Your Signature

From the same Preferences: Editor box, click on Use signature as default to attach a signature to every article you post. Your signature should be no more than four or five lines long, and should be used to identify you through title, address, e-mail, or telephone number, or whatever other information you would like to include. If you click the Select new button under Signature file, you will be able to choose the signature file you would like to use (you can create a signature file using any text editor). Click on Open, then OK in the Preferences: Editor dialog box to complete your configuration of Nuntius.

Putting Nuntius to Work

To start using Nuntius in your USENET chores, double-click on its icon. This will generate the All Groups window and the newsgroup window you previously named when configuring Nuntius. Note the methodology here. Newsgroup categories are shown as folders in the All Groups window, with the individual newsgroups in that hierarchy depicted by a document icon. You can double-click on any newsgroup in your newsgroup window to read it. When you do so, the newsgroup appears in a window, with all its message threads listed.

By double-clicking on the thread you choose to read, you will cause another window to appear that contains the thread. Each message header appears with a small, right-pointing triangle next to it, indicating that the article is, at present, closed. Clicking on the triangle will cause the article to be opened for your perusal. You can move through the document by using the Page down button. How Nuntius handles message threads, and whether it opens each message when you click on the thread, depends upon how you configure it. The Prefs menu provides you with numerous options for doing so.

Posting a Message with Nuntius

To post a new message, choose the Post article in new thread command from the Threads menu. This will cause a dialog box to appear, as shown in Figure 10.27. As you can see, space is provided for a subject, and default distribution is indicated; normally, your articles will be set for worldwide distribution, but this can be altered as you see fit. Use the Edit it button to call up the text editor you established when configuring Nuntius.

When you have composed your posting, save it and close the window in your text editor. A new dialog box, called Article to post, will appear, giving you the option of adding your signature if you would like one to be attached at the end of your article. You also have the option of clicking on a Trash disk copy after posting box; this will delete the article from your hard disk after it has been posted. Clicking on the Post it button sends the article.

Replying to Postings

The procedures for replying to existing postings in Nuntius are virtually identical to those for posting a new article:

1. Choose the text within an article that you want to respond to.
2. Select the Post follow-up article item from the Article menu.

You will now be able to choose among the options just discussed with regard to signature and the disposition of the file after your message has been posted. In both cases, posting or following up to a message, you have the option of choosing the Cancel button from the Article to post dialog box if you change your mind.

Newswatcher: A Superb Take on Macintosh News

Generalizations are always dangerous, but in the current state of software development, I tend to favor the Macintosh newsreaders over their Windows-

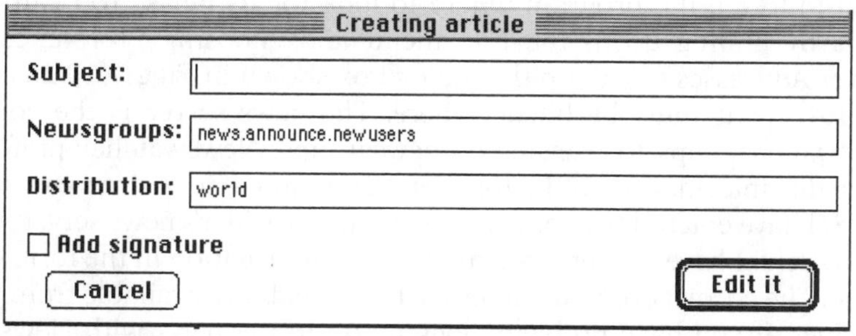

Figure 10.27 Posting a new message with Nuntius means first filling out the necessary fields.

based counterparts. My discovery of Newswatcher is a case in point. Having used almost all of the news programs for the Windows environment, I came across Newswatcher relatively late and began playing around with it out of idle curiosity (I had more or less determined to make Nuntius the primary Macintosh newsreader for this chapter, and didn't see the need to include another). But Newswatcher quickly won me over through a whole host of features.

Stability, for one. The program is rock solid and has yet to cause me the kind of network grief that all of the Windows-based programs have, at one time or another, managed to inflict. Ease of use is another. Newswatcher stays ahead of your needs by anticipating what you want to do and, more significantly, what you don't. Do I really need to see every part of a thread, or just the title? Can I retrieve that seven-part photograph of the Crab Nebula with a single mouse click, along with its description? Newswatcher delivers sensible answers to such questions, and it's also quite easy to install.

Downloading and Installing Newswatcher

Newswatcher is the work of John Norstad at Northwestern University; the program is based on an original version written by Steve Falkenburg of Apple Computer. Like many other excellent network programs, it is free software. You can retrieve it from the following URL:

ftp://ftp.acns.nwu.edu/pub/newswatcher/

The version I have been working with is 2.0b14, which is a beta version; by the time you read this, a final production version of 2.0 should be available. Newswatcher is what is known as a *fat binary,* meaning that it runs both in 68K native mode on 68K Macintoshes as well as in PowerPC native mode on Power Macs. To use Newswatcher, your Macintosh must have System 7.0 or later running with at least 2.5MB of RAM and a hard disk drive.

Double-click on Newswatcher to start the program. It will attempt to log on to your news server and, finding that it lacks the necessary address, will then make it possible for you to fill in this information. The installation of Newswatcher is relatively simple. There are certain key fields that must be filled in to tell the program where to look for its news. You can reach these fields by pulling down the File menu and choosing Preferences. Click on Server Addresses to call up the dialog box shown in Figure 10.28.

Two fields must be filled in here. The news server is the computer that Newswatcher taps to transfer its newsgroups. Newswatcher prefers that you enter this information in the form of a domain name. As you can see in Figure 10.28, I have entered the name of my service provider's news server in the appropriate field. I have also entered mail server information in the form of a domain name. The correct domain names for these fields are available from your service provider. If you have problems logging on to the news with Newswatcher, an incorrect entry in the News Server field is probably the reason.

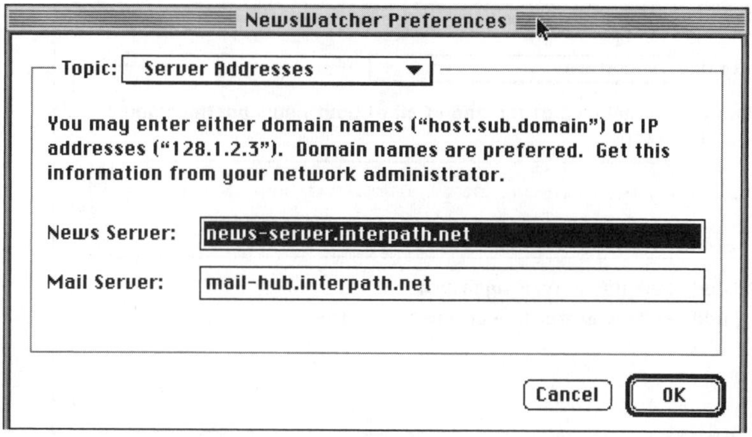

Figure 10.28 Setting up a server address for news and mail with Newswatcher.

Let's examine some other useful fields to fill in. Under the same Preferences item on the File menu you can call up a field for Personal Information. In Figure 10.29, I have filled in this field with my own values. When you enter this material, you are configuring Newswatcher so that it can insert the information in the headers of any messages you post on USENET, and in any mail you send to USENET posters.

A variety of other options are available as well, although the ones we have just set up are the most significant. Newswatcher lets you set newsreading options through a separate field from the Preferences menu, choosing a default number for the maximum number of articles to retrieve, and allowing the program to present messages and threads in a variety of ways. I recommend that you go through the options from the Preferences menu carefully to

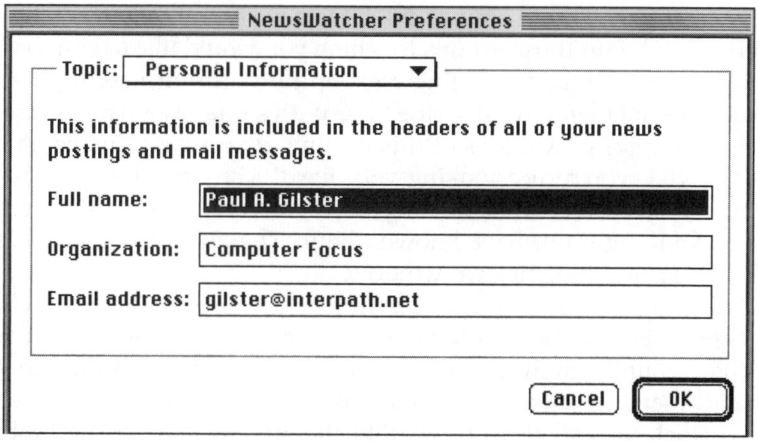

Figure 10.29 Filling in Newswatcher's fields for personal information.

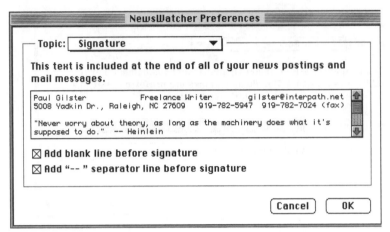

Figure 10.30   A sample signature file as set up in Newswatcher.

make sure you have Newswatcher configured to suit you. The Signature window will allow you to establish a signature text that will be included in all messages that you post. You can see an example of this in Figure 10.30.

> **Note:**   I've set up my Power Mac with aliases on the desktop, so
> that I have access to the icon for my newsgroups always available.
> A single click not only calls up Newswatcher, but also logs on to my
> service provider and begins the news reading process. This is just
> one of the ways that Newswatcher simplifies network tasks. As we
> look at the program's functions in going through article threads,
> we'll find more.

Reading and Responding to News with Newswatcher

Newswatcher will build a list of available newsgroups when you first run it; you
can then highlight those groups to which you would like to subscribe. In Figure
10.31, I have highlighted the newsgroup **news.announce.important** and can
use the Special menu to subscribe to it. With some 11,000 newsgroups available
from my service provider as of this writing, if you can't find something to read
on USENET, you're not looking very hard! The Find function from the Edit
menu can be used to track down groups you're interested in, often uncovering
groups you might not have known about. The groups you have subscribed to
will then appear in their own window.

You can either double-click on the group you want to read or else pull down
the News menu to click on Next Group, which will retrieve the current articles
for that group. Newswatcher will retrieve the articles in that newsgroup and
present them in a separate window. Figure 10.32 shows the newsgroup
alt.winsock, as called up by double-clicking on it from the Full Group List.
Most of these items are posted as single documents, but some are multipart.

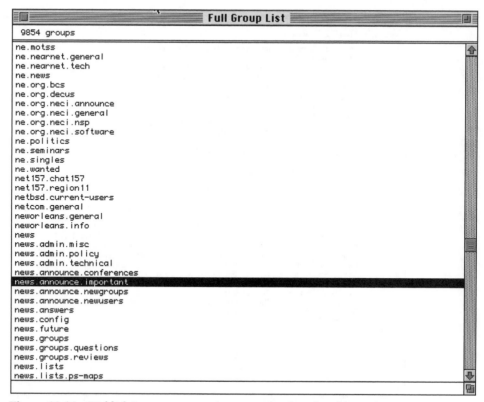

Figure 10.31 Highlighting a newsgroup in preparation for subscribing to it.

You can see which is which by examining the left-hand side of the screen. Single postings are shown by a hyphen, while multiple postings are shown with a triangle, along with a number indicating how many parts the posting contains.

Double-click on the posting you'd like to see; it will be retrieved and will soon appear in a window of its own. Figure 10.33 shows a posting that appeared in the newsgroup **comp.internet.net-happenings**; it concerns MCI's recent announcement that it would offer Internet services and tap the Netscape browser from Mosaic Communications Corp. as a key part of its package. It's a good idea to subscribe to **comp.internet.net-happenings** to stay up to the minute with recent network announcements, news of new sites, and more. You can scroll through these documents by using the scroll bar to the right of the screen.

These are the kind of touches that distinguish Newswatcher and set it above all other newsreaders I have used. Another handy feature is the way Newswatcher handles the decoding of binary files. As we saw in the section about Microsoft Windows-based newsreaders, more and more news programs are making it possible to handle such decoding, but none makes the process more seamless than Newswatcher. In Figure 10.34, I have moved into the newsgroup **alt.binaries.pictures.astro** and have clicked on a promising item. Examine the figure with care.

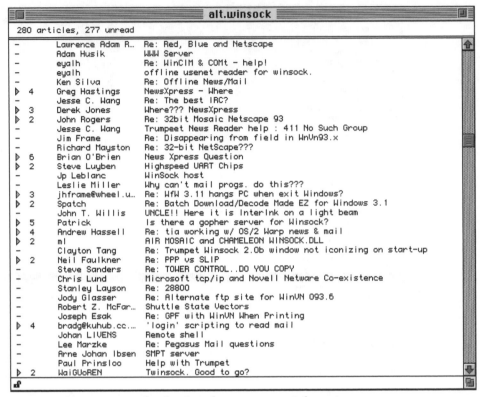

Figure 10.32 Examining the **alt.winsock** newsgroup topic by topic.

Notice that I've retrieved the first of four postings about this image; this first one explains that the image is a picture of the Horsehead Nebula, and provides background information about how it was taken. Notice that at the top right of the screen there is a page icon. By clicking on this, I begin the retrieval process. Newswatcher is smart enough to download all the necessary files in order. Not only that, it will then decode them automatically, and then leave them on our desktop ready to be viewed. You can see the image itself in Figure 10.35.

A final nice touch is Newswatcher's ability to integrate with the Netscape WWW browser. If you are reading USENET postings with Newswatcher and come across a reference to a Web document, you can hold down the Command key and click on the URL of this document. Newswatcher will then launch Netscape and tell it to home in on the home page in question. Talk about software integration!

Posting and Responding to News with Newswatcher

To post a message to a USENET newsgroup, move to that group and click on the New Message item from the News menu. A message posting screen will

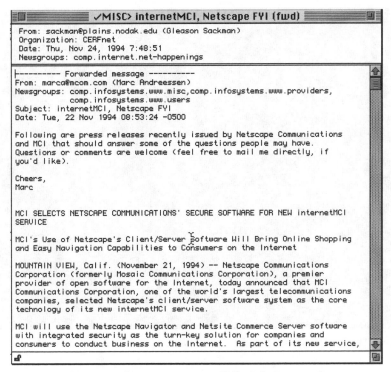

Figure 10.33 A sample message as viewed through Newswatcher.

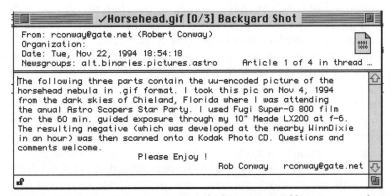

Figure 10.34 Reading a description of a binary image file in Newswatcher. Double-clicking on the icon downloads all parts of the file.

Figure 10.35   The image of the Horsehead Nebula decoded and displayed by a file viewer.

appear, as shown in Figure 10.36. In that figure, you will see that I have filled in the subject field and have written a message to the newsgroup.

Notice that I am asking in this message that people with strong thoughts on newsreader programs contact me by e-mail. I will then post a summary of responses to the newsgroup so that everyone will have the chance to see what the most popular programs were. This is one way to hold down message traffic on a newsgroup while getting the responses you need; of course, only you can decide whether your post should be answered on the newsgroup itself, for all to see, or whether it is better handled through e-mail.

Having composed my message, I can now click on OK to send it. I receive a warning screen, as shown in Figure 10.37. The message sounds intimidating, but in fact it acknowledges a basic USENET truth. Our messages are propagated all over the world; to send a message without due consideration is to be disrespectful of the bandwidth we are using. The networks are jammed with traffic, and more is coming on-line all the time. We must consider this before we post and avoid frivolous messages.

To respond to a message, you must have the message on-screen. From the News menu, choose Reply. The screen in Figure 10.38 will appear. Notice that the original message is quoted in your response; you can edit it to remove unnecessary material, supplying your own thoughts afterwards. The icons at the top of the page allow you to send your response by e-mail or as a posting to the entire group. You also have the option, from the News menu, of forwarding the message to someone else.

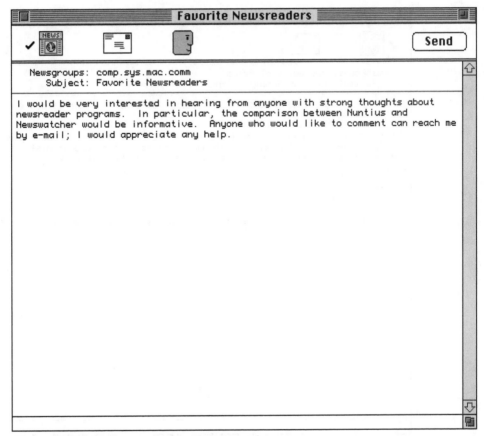

Figure 10.36　Posting a message with Newswatcher.

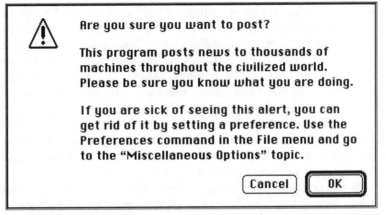

Figure 10.37　A warning message reminds you that posting to USENET newsgroups uses precious resources. Post wisely.

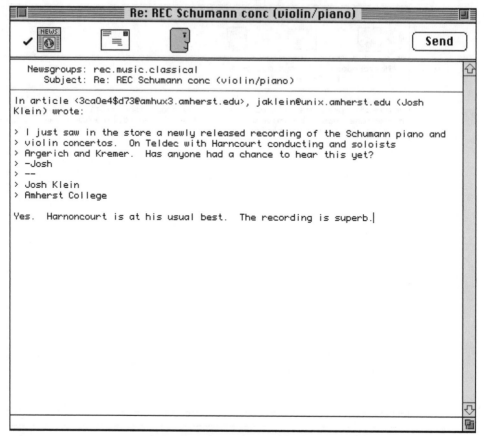

Figure 10.38   Responding to a USENET posting.

Searching Newsgroups for Information

Newswatcher makes it easy to search USENET newsgroups to find keywords in various fields. To do so, highlight the group or groups you would like to search on the Full Group List (you can highlight more than one group at a time by holding down the Command key as you click on each group). From the Special menu, choose the Search option. The dialog box shown in Figure 10.39 will appear.

You can fill in the Containing: field with the keyword you would like to search. You can also choose which field you want to search by using the pull-down menu in the Header: field. In most cases, using the Subject header is the best way to go. I have chosen four newsgroups about journalism and am about to search them under the keyword election. When I click on OK, Newswatcher will go into each of these groups and run the search.

Note the convenience of this. I don't have to be subscribed to any of these groups to search them, and I can search more than a single group at a time. Although USENET remains unwieldy, search capabilities like this give us more of a chance to use the network for targeted research. Whichever newsreader

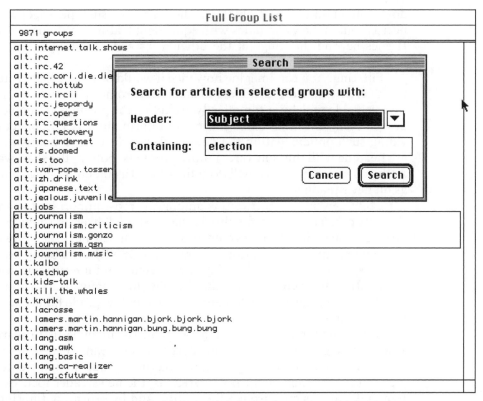

Figure 10.39 Using Newswatcher to search for articles across multiple newsgroups.

you choose, you should fully explore its capabilities to take advantage of the diverse voices available on USENET.

With its logical organization, its complete range of configuration and customization options, and its superb user interface, Newswatcher is hard to top. You will find it discussed frequently in the newsgroup **comp.sys.mac.comm**, where suggestions about future versions are frequently made, and program author John Norstad often chips in with clarifications about how the program works and news of future developments.

The Nature of Newsreader Software

If you're curious enough to try more than one newsreader package (and those of us who use the Internet daily get around to trying as many as possible), you will note one important fact. No matter what platform you use, the trend toward graphical interfaces gives newsreaders much the same look. You will find the same phenomenon in many of the all-in-one packages from various commercial houses. The Chameleon software from NetManage, for example, includes a reader that provides the same basic capabilities as Trumpet for Windows (although it's less stable). On the Mac side, such packages as TCP/Connect II contain news modules with equivalent features, although TCP/Connect II goes beyond the range of the other newsreaders with a series of filtering options that help you manage your news.

Filtering? You can imagine how nice it would be to be able to cause articles from certain valued individuals to stand out from the crowd, just as you can save valuable time by automatically excluding the postings of people who have proven themselves unreliable sources of information. TCP/Connect II, by providing such options within the newsreader environment, points to where we are heading with this software. Future products, both in the shareware as well as the commercial arena, will doubtless focus as much on news management as on news reading.

I find newsreader software is among the most important tools we use on the network. The reason for this is that USENET itself is so chaotic that we often give up on it. Countless conversations with new net users have convinced me that only the hardy continue to draw on USENET after being exposed to its more ludicrous side. On a bad day, it can seem that for every **sci.physics** there is an **alt.tv.dinosaurs.barney.die.die.die**; too many users simply dismiss USENET as a gaggle of adolescents engaged in low-grade humor and move on to other things.

A good newsreader can change all that. By allowing us to search for the kind of newsgroups that meet our needs, a newsreader can save us time and energy. By threading messages within that newsgroup so that we need only to pick out the postings that truly interest us, the newsreader focuses our attention and helps us cut through the clutter. And by providing filtering capabilities, as we will increasingly see in new software releases, a newsreader helps us to customize our USENET environment. Rather than the chaos, we begin to follow the truly helpful threads of information wherever they may lead us.

So spend some time with your choice of newsreader. If the capabilities of many such programs are identical, their implementations are not; some use menu structures that are more logical than others, and some, like Nuntius, require external programs to make them fully operational. Because you are operating in the SLIP/PPP environment, the ability to provide a genuinely helpful interface should be central to your quest.

Most of all, remember to support shareware authors. Their continuing efforts keep the Internet an exciting place for software discoveries, and the ability to try out a program before paying for it is a wonderful benefit. Nobody can afford to program at the levels that many of these program authors do without some kind of reward for their work, and the fees most are asking are minimal. We would do well to support them.

11

Browsing through the World Wide Web

Browsing is an entirely different concept from searching. We use tools like WAIS to search Internet databases, running our keyword queries past stored indices of information. Such searches are targeted; they allow us to pinpoint precisely what we're after. A *browser*, on the other hand, is a tool that lets us move through the Internet with relative ease. It's relatively difficult to run systemwide searches on a browser, although solutions to this problem are quickly being developed. What browsers do well is to present information without demanding that we learn complicated commands to access it.

Any Internet tool that simplifies access through a user-friendly front end could, in some sense or another, be considered a browser, but the term has come to have a more precise meaning. It now refers to graphical interfaces, tools like Mosaic, Netscape, and Cello, that take advantage of a system of linked information called the World Wide Web. Using one of these programs creates a drastic change in the way we look at, and present, our information. Rather than entering commands, either at a system prompt or through a menu system, we use a mouse to point at a resource we'd like to examine. The browser then goes out over the net to find it. The effect is of moving through a seamless collage of data, offering transparent access to computers that may be separated by oceans. Browsing is evidently the wave of the future, to judge from its recent success in the marketplace. And it's certainly fun.

The Nature of the World Wide Web

The World Wide Web began as a communications project in Switzerland, at the European Particle Physics Laboratory. Tim Berners-Lee, an Oxford graduate with a background in computer communications, determined to construct a system that would connect high-energy physicists around the globe so that they could keep up with the latest developments in research. It was Berners-Lee who made the mental leap that would revolutionize our view of networking. He realized that he could create documents with links to other information, using a system called *hypermedia*, and combine that with the Internet's global connectivity, to produce multimedia documents whose components could be physically located almost anywhere in the world.

Berners-Lee has now moved to the Massachusetts Institute of Technology, where he is directing development of the World Wide Web Consortium. The organization will attempt to formalize standards for the rapidly growing Web, as well as conducting research into future directions for its protocols. Berners-Lee is certainly the right man for the job, given that he is the power behind the three standards that make Web documents work. Uniform Resource Locators (URLs) are ways to specify the location of documents on the Internet. HTML, or hypertext markup language, is what developers use to create a World Wide Web document. And HTTP, or hypertext transport protocol, is the standard that allows such documents to move between clients and servers. We'll examine all of these in this chapter. But first, we need to consider the nature of the Web's core concept: hypermedia.

Hypertext and Hypermedia

To understand the World Wide Web, you must make sense out of the terms hypertext and hypermedia. Hypertext allows us to create links within a document, so that we can move directly to further information about particular words or concepts. The idea is not particularly new; think of footnotes, which mark words that are attached to additional information about them. When you read a passage marked with footnotes, you know to turn either to the bottom of the page or the end of the chapter for the extra bit of text. The author uses footnotes when he or she doesn't want to intrude upon the smooth flow of prose; the suffixed information might be interesting but not necessarily critical for your understanding; in many cases, footnotes display references to further materials on the subject.

What hypertext does is to make this kind of information easier to use. When you see a hypertext link, all you need to do is to click on it to activate the connection to it. Rather than having to manually page through text to find the joined material, you simply instruct your browser to handle the transaction for you. Now the text becomes visible by degrees; you see as much or as little of it beyond the core document as you please. If one hyperlink fails to intrigue you, you can skip it. If you find an item that does grab your attention, you can explore the link at your leisure.

Here's a passage that I have marked up with possible hypertext linkages. Take a look at it and note the underlinings, which indicate the hypertext links:

Stand outside on a moonless night this summer and you may get a feel for what galactic astronomy is all about. The belt of light running from northeast to southwest like a great bejewelled necklace is the disk of the <u>Milky Way</u>. Adrift in the <u>Orion Arm</u>, some 30,000 light-years from galactic center, we see this flattened disk from within. Look east and your view will leave the <u>galaxy</u> altogether. Turn south in the direction of Sagittarius and you'll be facing the galactic core.

If I were going to put this snippet of an article I wrote on galactic astronomy on-line, I would first mark my hyperlinks, as I have done above. I would then create the material included in each link. Reading through my passage, the reader comes to the term "Milky Way" and clicks on it. Up comes the hyperlink:

The Milky Way is a spiral galaxy, a flattened disk of stars whose thickness amounts to about one-twentieth of its diameter; the disk bulges significantly at its center. Randomly scattered around the disk in an area known as the "halo" are great clusters of stars, known as "globular clusters" because of their spherical shape.

My reader can now return to the text. The next hyperlink is set up on the term "Orion Arm." My reader clicks on this item to see the following:

The sun appears to lie near the inner edge of one of the Milky Way's spiral arms, called the Orion Arm because of the defining presence of the Orion Nebula. The Perseus and Sagittarius-Carina arms lie to either side of the Orion Arm.

Finally, my faithful reader clicks on the hyperlink for "galaxy." The following is produced:

Because the night sky is filled with light, we tend to think of the earth as surrounded by a random distribution of stars. Yet we exist within a huge structure, one that is subject to observation and analysis. The Milky Way is a spiral galaxy, a flattened disk of stars whose thickness amounts to about one-twentieth of its diameter; the disk bulges significantly at its center. Randomly scattered around the disk in an area known as the "halo" are great clusters of stars, known as "globular clusters" because of their spherical shape.

The advantage of hypertext is primarily that it conceals text you don't want to read while providing access to text that you do; it thus allows you to set your own course through a document, although, of course, you are dependent upon the skill of the person who created the hyperlinks to anticipate your needs. The alternative to hypertext would be to display the entire document as one long text, forcing you to skim through the items you don't want to see to find the ones you do. When you have a pretty good idea what you want to learn, hypertext can prove helpful, although in and of itself, it's hardly the breakthrough concept its early proponents suggested.

But hypermedia is another thing. Hypermedia refers to creating the same kinds of links between not just textual data, but any kind of digital information. Now we create something that has no precedent in written communication. If I write a passage describing the sound of a Fauré quartet, I can create a hyperlink that allows my reader to experience that sound. You click on the hyperlink and hear the ravishing interplay of piano and viola, violin, and cello. If I speak of the beauty of the Andromeda galaxy, through hypermedia I can send my reader to a stunning photograph of that distant whorl of stars.

Apply this hypermedia concept to the Internet and you have created linkages that are worldwide in scope. The World Wide Web, like the other Internet protocols we've examined in this book, can be viewed in various ways depending upon the browser you decide to use. But the key is to make information searching transparent. You see, it doesn't matter whether the hyperlink resides on the same computer as the original text. I could create a document referring to Fauré and set up a hyperlink with a computer in Japan to the recorded performance of the quartet. The reader of my document would not need to know where the sound was coming from to enjoy it. In a similar way, I could create an entire page of information with hyperlinks to other computers. This capability of ambling through an entire network of participating computers and providing a graphical interface that presents information in multimedia form is what has made the World Wide Web the hottest Internet tool of the 1990s.

HyperText Transport Protocol

How does it all work? Behind the scenes, the World Wide Web makes use of a protocol called HTTP. This is the method a Web browser uses to move hypertextual data, defining the techniques by which we move from one resource to another through hyperlinks. To make the World Wide Web function, we therefore need a system that allows us to embed the necessary commands within a hypermedia document on-line. Our software must understand that when we click on a marked resource, it should execute a command that will take us to the specified site using the specified protocol. HTML does this by associating highlighted Uniform Resource Locators, or URLs, that our browser can retrieve with HTTP. We've been using URLs throughout this book in relation to FTP sites. Let's now take a closer look at them, because they make Web browsers the most flexible interface tools the Internet has yet seen.

Uniform Resource Locators

The challenge of connecting so many computers in so many lands is to be able to find what you need. Consider how lengthy the specification of a single resource could be. Suppose I wanted to tell you about a file like the original Mosaic program, located at the National Center for Supercomputing Applications in Champaign-Urbana, Illinois. I would have to give you a complete Internet address to get you to that computer (you could reach it by FTP). But once there, my job wouldn't be ended; you would also need to know in what directory to look, and you would need to know the name of the program.

I might specify that information this way:

Site: **ftp.ncsa.uiuc.edu**
Directory: *Web/Mosaic/Windows*
Filename: mos20a9.exe

As you can see, I've consumed three lines with this chore. A Uniform Resource Locator would allow me to express the same information in a single line:

ftp://ftp.ncsa.uiuc.edu/Web/Mosaic/Windows/mos20a9.exe

You begin at the far left, where the nature of the Internet tool needed to reach the resource is located; in this case, it's FTP. The address of the computer follows after the double slashes. Then we have the directory tree leading us to the file in question. The method is simple and has the tremendous advantage of standardizing an often bewildering naming process.

The World Wide Web proceeds through such resource identification. In fact, we can use a Web browser to access any number of different resources. Each is specified by a particular statement, as follows:

- For FTP resources:

  ftp://*internet_address*/*directory_tree*/*filename*

  as in the preceding example.
- For Telnet sites:

  telnet://*internet_address:port*/

  as in **telnet://locis.loc.gov/**

  Notice here that we indicate a port if it is necessary to do so. Most Telnet sessions proceed over port 23, which is the default. In the event that a different port is indicated, it would be inserted in the position shown. Thus you might see an address like the following:

  telnet://rafael.metiu.ucsb.edu:5000/
- For Gopher servers:

  gopher://*internet_address:port*/

  as in **gopher://gopher.interpath.net/**

  Here, the only thing to note is the port designation, which in most cases will not need to be used; Gopher defaults to port 70.

- For USENET newsgroups:

news:*newsgroup_name*

as in **news:alt.winsock**

Notice the differing form of this type of URL; there are no slashes, and no server is specified in the URL. Web browsers allow you to specify a news server when you configure them.

And here is the one you will use most often with a World Wide Web browser:

- For World Wide Web pages in hypermedia format

http://*internet_address/directory_tree/*

as in **http://nsa.bt.co.uk/nsa.html**

Notice this interesting fact about URLs. We have specified hypermedia resources as only one in a series of items that can be described using a URL. And while our Web work will take us to many hypermedia sites, it is instructive to see that we can also use a Web browser to specify more "traditional" forms of Internet access, such as FTP and Telnet. Indeed, Mosaic and the other graphical browsers we examine in this chapter make it possible for us to perform multiple functions. While Mosaic doesn't make as fully featured an FTP client as, say, WS_FTP, or Fetch on the Macintosh, it does allow us to get into a remote site and download files to our hard disks. And it can be linked to a separate Telnet client of our choosing to allow us to run a Telnet session, just as it can be used to read USENET news.

HyperText Markup Language

Now that we can specify the location of the resources and services we want to access, we also need a final piece to complete the World Wide Web puzzle. We must be able to create documents in a format that a browser can understand, enabling us to display the various kinds of information that this hypermedia system can manipulate. We need to be able to see an image on the screen, and to apply textual formatting to achieve typeset-quality documents. And, of course, we have to be able to show the hyperlinks that lead us to other documents on the Web.

HyperText Markup Language, or HTML, fits the bill nicely. While the language is actually a variant of the complicated Standard Generalized Markup Language (SGML) used for electronic texts, it is considerably easier to use. Anyone with an ASCII text editor can create an HTML file with a little practice, and learn how to insert graphics and modify textual formatting to achieve beautiful visual effects. The best way to do this is to study examples of HTML files on-screen. Fortunately, the Web browsers we now turn to make it possible not only to view a Web page, but also to see the underlying HTML code and to print it out.

Ultimately, HTML produces a document that's as useful as it is aesthetically pleasing, rendered by nothing more than the application of ASCII text within a simple text editor. In Figure 11.1, you can see such a document. This page (viewed through the Netscape browser) demonstrates how powerful HTML can be in providing information in a uniquely productive format. At your fingertips, you have the entire corpus of Shakespeare's works; click on a play and you are taken to it. Within the plays, a glossary of obscure terms is provided through hyperlinks. Sites like these bring remarkable power to your computer; they point to a future where the Internet is a genuine educational tool.

NCSA Mosaic for Microsoft Windows

If there is one lesson to be learned from looking at the variety of Web browsers in this chapter, it is that all of them work in basically the same way. While user

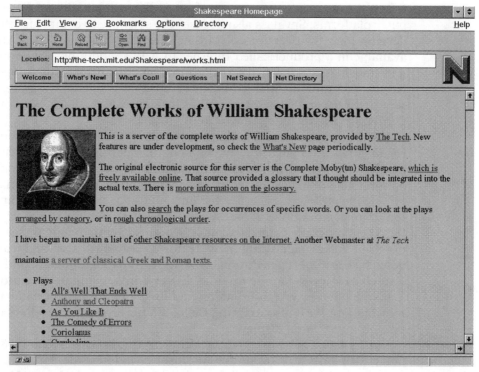

Figure 11.1 HTML can create World Wide Web pages of remarkable depth. This site contains links to the entire corpus of Shakespeare's works.

interfaces vary and the internal programming changes the way the client deals with data (this shows up particularly with Netscape, which is noticeably faster than the other browsers), the principle of using hyperlinks to move directly to data sites remains. We begin with NCSA Mosaic, which deserves its place as the patron saint of all the browsers that follow. The program, in its latest incarnation, offers menu-based installation and customization options that make it significantly easier to use.

Mosaic has received so much attention in the media that it seems difficult to believe its creation occurred as recently as 1992. At the National Center for Supercomputing Applications in Champaign-Urbana, Illinois, programmer Marc Andreessen and a talented team of associates went to work devising a networked information tool called XMosaic, designed to be run on workstations in the Unix environment. Microsoft Windows and Macintosh versions followed in short order, although the three implementations have always played tag with each other in terms of features, with slight variations occurring between Mac and Windows programs.

The Mosaic phenomenon is well attested; the program has attracted admirers from around the globe, thousands of whom continue to download and use Mosaic on a daily basis. Meanwhile, commercial spinoffs have begun. Spyglass Inc. has produced Enhanced Mosaic, available through publisher O'Reilly & Associates in a series of book/disk combinations for various computer platforms; Spyglass also licenses the software to companies that want to develop their own versions of Mosaic. Spry Inc. has developed AIR Mosaic, available in a product called Internet In A Box, and a host of companies are now moving into the market, the most significant of which appears to be Netscape Communications Co., whose browser is now in widespread use (we saw the Netscape browser in action in Figure 11.1). Both Windows 95 and OS/2 Warp will include some form of Mosaic.

For the purposes of this chapter, we examine four Web browsers in detail. NCSA Mosaic remains free for non-commercial use and is under continual development; its latest version, in fact, provides a user-friendly configuration option that eliminates the tedious chore of editing an initialization file to customize the program, as earlier versions required. Netscape is an outgrowth of the original work done at NCSA, in the sense that many of the developers of the NCSA program formed the nucleus of the team that built Netscape. But the program offers significant new features, as you'll see, and can best be described as a "next generation" browser, a Web tool rethought and built from scratch to improve on the original. EINet WinWeb and its Macintosh variant MacWeb offer easy Web browsing and links to an excellent database of Web information. We'll also examine Cello, a Web browser that offers a different take on information display.

In terms of hardware, NCSA Mosaic requires at least an 80386SX computer with 4MB of RAM on the Microsoft Windows side, but 8MB is a more reasonable minimum, and if you plan heavy use, I suggest 16MB. You will need to run Windows 3.1 in enhanced mode to make Mosaic work. The same 4MB memory requirement, with recommendation for at least 8MB, holds true for the Macintosh. Macintosh users will also need to be using System 7. In general, the more memory and hard disk space you can provide to your browser, whichever it is, the better.

Retrieving Mosaic

To retrieve a copy of Mosaic from the NCSA, use the following URL for the Microsoft Windows version:

ftp://ftp.ncsa.uiuc.edu/Web/Mosaic/Windows/

At the time of this writing, the files you need are mos20a9.exe and w32s-OLE.exe. You will also want to retrieve the documentation for the program, from the following URL:

ftp://ftp.ncsa.uiuc.edu/Web/Mosaic/Windows/Documents/

The current filename is mosdocA5.zip.

Mosaic is copyrighted by the University of Illinois, but it is available for individual use at no cost; it can also be used by academic and government organizations, as well as by business in internal use. But the NCSA does request that if you plan to profit from using Mosaic in a financial sense, you should contact the organization to obtain licensing information. You can reach the necessary contacts at **mosaic@ncsa.uiuc.edu**.

 Be advised: This site changes its directory structure with regularity. If you attempt to log on and find that the directory structure has changed, you may need to do some digging. Look for a file called README or INDEX in the root directory, which should help you to determine where Mosaic and its related files have been placed. Be aware, too, that this site is heavily trafficked, and it may be necessary to attempt logging in several times at different times of day before you are successful.

To install Mosaic, you first need to unpack the Mosaic files. You should have three:

mos20a9.exe   A self-extracting file containing the Mosaic program itself and related files.

w32sOLE.exe   A utility package that allows Windows 3.1 and Windows for Workgroups 3.11 to use 32-bit processing, and thus to be able to run programs that demand it, like Mosaic. The latest version of the win32s software is always available at NCSA. This file, like the one above, is self-extracting.

mosdocA5.zip   The Mosaic for Microsoft Windows documentation.

Unpacking the Mosaic Files

Before unpacking the software, it is necessary to set up a directory for Mosaic on your hard disk. You can place the program anywhere you want, but for simplicity's sake, it makes sense to simply create a *\mosaic* subdirectory. You can do this by using the mkdir command when you are in your root directory at the system prompt; your command would thus be **mkdir \mosaic**. This is where Mosaic will reside once you have installed it.

Several other directories need to be created:

1. Create a *c:\temp* directory.
2. Move the mos20a9.exe file into *c:\temp*. This step is necessary because you can't install Mosaic into the same directory in which its installation files are located. You will install Mosaic into the *c:\mosaic* directory. After installation is complete, you can delete the files the setup program leaves in the *c:\temp* directory.
3. Create a *\mosaic\temp* directory.
4. Move the w32sOLE.exe file to *\mosaic\temp*. This directory will be used by win32s during the unpacking process. Later, you will be able to delete it.
5. Create a *\mosaic\docs* directory.
6. Move your documentation file, mosdocA5.zip, to the new directory. This directory will be used for the Mosaic documentation.

To unpack these files, you will need to be at the DOS prompt, either by exiting from Windows altogether or by moving to a DOS window from inside Windows.

1. Move to the *c:\temp* directory, or whatever temporary directory you are using for the mos20a9.exe file.
2. At the DOS prompt, type **mos20a9.exe**, followed by a Return.
3. Move to the *c:\mosaic\temp* directory.
4. At the DOS prompt, type **w32sole.exe**, followed by a Return.
5. Move to the *c:\mosaic\docs* directory.
6. At the DOS prompt, type **pkunzip mosdocA5.zip**.

In each case, the files should unpack automatically. Note that the Mosaic documentation is presented in the form of a "zipped" file; it will require

PKware's PKUNZIP utility program to unpack it (or you could use the shareware WINZIP program, in which case you could handle the entire operation within Windows).

 Note: Before installing Mosaic, you must install Win32s, a program that allows Windows 3.1 and Windows for Workgroups 3.11 to work with 32-bit applications. The Win32s program must be installed before Mosaic, because the Mosaic installation program is itself a 32-bit application. Do not attempt to install Mosaic before installing Win32s.

Installing Win32s

Win32s is software that allows you to run 32-bit applications like Mosaic in a 16-bit environment like Windows 3.1 or Windows for Workgroups 3.11. We've just retrieved and unpacked the necessary file, w32sOLE.exe. When we executed the file (by typing **w32sole.exe**), we obtained two other files: install.bat and w32spack.exe. The install program will decompress w32spack.exe into three directories. Let's proceed:

1. Move to the *c:\mosaic\temp* directory.
2. At the DOS prompt, type the command **install**, followed by a Return. You will see the files unpack, and will also note that the install program creates three new directories, called *disk1, disk2,* and *disk3.* These directories branch off the directory the w32sOLE.exe program was placed in. You should now have three new directories as follows:

   \mosaic\temp\disk1

   \mosaic\temp\disk2

   \mosaic\temp\disk3

3. When the unpacking process is complete, change directories to *\mosaic\disk1.*
4. Run the setup program. You will need to run it from Windows' Program Manager; go to the File menu and choose the Run command. Make sure that you have closed all other programs, because the setup program will need to restart your computer when it has completed the installation.
5. Win32s will now have installed the necessary files into two directories on your hard disk: *\windows\system* and *\windows\system\win32s.* You can now delete the files in the temporary directories created by the installation program. You can also delete the *\mosaic\temp* directory and the *disk1, disk2,* and *disk3* subdirectories branching off from it.

Installing Mosaic for Microsoft Windows

Once Win32s has been installed, you are ready to proceed with the actual Mosaic installation. Follow these steps:

1. Move to the \temp directory where you have stored the files you unpacked from mos20a9.exe.

2. From Program Manager, run the setup.exe program. The Mosaic program will be installed in your c:\mosaic directory.

3. Return to the \temp directory and delete the temporary files there.

4. Delete the \temp directory.

Launching Mosaic for Microsoft Windows

To launch Mosaic for the first time, you will need to log on to your SLIP/PPP account so that your Internet connection is active. Double-clicking on the Mosaic icon will launch the program. You will see the screen shown in Figure 11.2.

You have now accessed the home page for Mosaic at the National Center for Supercomputing Applications. Take a look at this figure. The basic hypertext model is at play here. Items that are underlined are hyperlinks; if you move the cursor to one of these, it turns into a small hand symbol. Single-click on such a hyperlink and you will be taken directly to the site. In Figure 11.3, for example, I have moved to the home page NCSA maintains for the Macintosh version of its software.

Hyperlinks are shown in a different color from surrounding text, and do not have to be underlined, although I am showing them underlined here for clarity. Whether or not they appear underlined on your screen is a matter of your own preference.

The basic screen elements are the same on both the Windows and the Macintosh versions of Mosaic. We begin at the top of the screen:

Document Title	This is the name of the Web page you are accessing.
Menu Bar	These are the menus that contain the Mosaic commands available to you.
Toolbar	These are icons that contain shortcuts to basic Mosaic functions. For example, if you want to go directly to the home page you have established as your default, you can simply click on the house icon.
Location Bar	This is the Uniform Resource Locator for the site you are currently accessing. Look back at Figure 11.1, and you can see that the Web server's address is **http://www.ncsa.uiuc.edu/**. This is followed by directory information to the precise HTML document we are currently reading.

Figure 11.2　The home page for NCSA Mosaic.

Mosaic Icon	The familiar Mosaic icon becomes active when you click on a hyperlink. Double-clicking on this icon while you are attempting to connect to a site will abort the process.
In-line Image	An image that is displayed along with text.
Hyperlinks	Hyperlinks are shown in a different color text from the rest of the document; normally, this color is blue. In the examples here, I am also using underlining to show the presence of these links.
Status Bar	When you move the cursor to a hyperlink, its URL will be displayed in the status bar. You will also receive messages about Mosaic activities in this area.

Document Title

Menu Bar ———→
Toolbar ———→
Location
Bar ———→

Inline
Image ———→

Hyperlinks ———→

Status Bar ———→

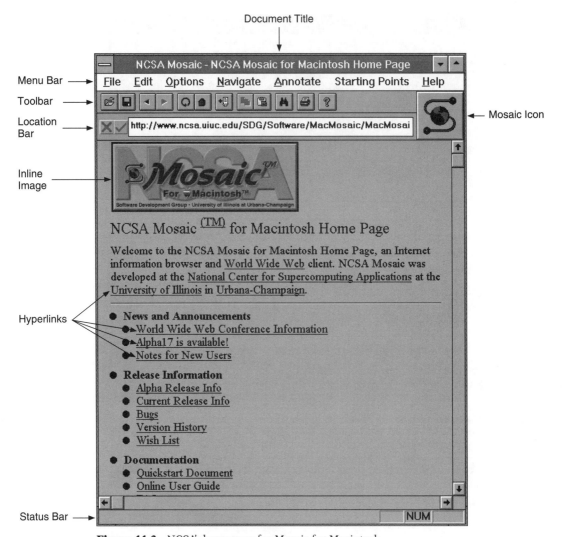

Mosaic Icon ←———

Figure 11.3 NCSA's home page for Mosaic for Macintosh.

Note: Clicking on a hyperlink is not the only way you can access a site. Another method is to pull down the File menu and choose the Open URL command. This pops up a dialog box within which you can enter the URL of your choice. Clicking on OK then takes you directly to it. A shortcut is to use the toolbar, clicking on the Open URL icon, which calls up the same dialog box.

The icons on Mosaic's toolbar are laid out as follows:

Opens a particular URL; a dialog box will appear allowing you to insert the URL of your choice.

Saves the current document to your hard disk.

Returns you to the previous document in the history list; that is, the one you accessed previous to the present one. When you launch Mosaic, this button will be grayed out, and will remain so until you move to the next hyperlink.

Takes you to the next page on the history list. If you have returned to a previous document, for example, and then want to move forward again, you can use this button. It will be grayed out until you move back to a previous document.

Reloads the current page.

Returns to the home page you have established for Mosaic.

Adds the current document to the hotlist.

Copies selected text to the clipboard.

Pastes selected text to the clipboard.

Searches for a keyword in the current document.

Prints the current document.

Opens Mosaic's help feature.

Configuring Mosaic for Windows

In the recent past, Mosaic configuration meant editing a file called mosaic.ini, which contained the basic information the program needed to function. You called the file up in a text editor and selected the items you wanted to edit. There were certain key settings that could be adjusted if you wanted, for example, to set a different default home page than the NCSA server that normally comes up when you launch the program. The latest version of Mosaic has considerably simplified the configuration process by providing you with a menu option to handle many of these chores for you. If you pull down the Options menu and click on Preferences, you will see the screen shown in Figure 11.4. Within this screen are contained all the items we need to examine to tune the program up. Let's go through the more important of these with care:

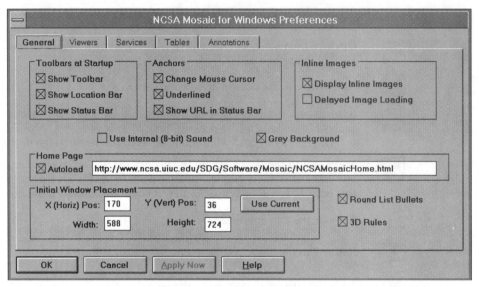

Figure 11.4 Mosaic's Preferences screen vastly simplifies the configuration process.

Toolbars at Startup

You can choose to hide any or all of the toolbars—the primary toolbar at the top of the screen, as well as the Location and Status Bar. When you make a change to any setting, the Apply Now button will become active; click on it to make your changes take effect immediately.

Anchors

Anchors are markers for hypertext; when you see an underlinked link, you are looking at an anchor. You have the option of showing these anchors under-lined or not; you can also decide whether the URL of a given hyperlink should be displayed in the status bar when you put the cursor on it. A third option is to control whether the mouse cursor changes shape when it is placed on an anchor. In the default setting, it changes to a small hand symbol when doing so.

Inline Images

Inline images are those that are displayed adjacent to text in a Web document. Mosaic needs no special tools to call these up; they load automatically if the box here is checked. The problem with inline images is that, depending upon the speed of your connection, they can take some time to load. After experi-menting with Mosaic for a time, you may decide to turn these images off to speed the loading process. In that case, Mosaic will display an icon in the doc-ument display area instead of the image; you can always choose to see such an image by clicking its icon with the right mouse button (hold down the Option key and click the image, if you're a Macintosh user).

Home Page

A home page is the place Mosaic first logs on to when it is activated. When you first start Mosaic, the program will access the home page at NCSA, either the one dedicated to the Macintosh version or the Windows version of the program. But it behooves you to change this home page. NCSA's site is under tremendous strain from the number of users trying to access it. The best thing to do is to choose another page at a less traveled site. This will benefit your own work as well, since it can be time-consuming trying to log on to NCSA during a busy period.

To change the home page setting, you must insert a new value in the Home Page field. Notice that this home page must appear in the form of a URL. The one currently enabled, for example, is the server at NCSA:

http://www.ncsa.uiuc.edu/SDG/Software/Mosaic/NCSAMosaicHome.html

You can switch this home page to any other Web document you prefer. The key principle is this: you want to find a home page that is close to you geographically and one that will load quickly. There is no point in putting a strain upon the network by choosing an obscure server half the world away as the page you will see every day by default when you load Mosaic. In my case, I have chosen the Web page at my service provider's site. Thus I have inserted a different URL here:

http://www.interpath.net/

Notice as well that you have a check box that determines whether your home page loads when you initiate Mosaic. If you leave this box unchecked, Mosaic will not look for a home page when you start it, but you can always go to the home page you've chosen by clicking on the house icon on the toolbar after the program has loaded. And if you pick up a little HTML, you may even decide to create a home page for yourself. The process isn't difficult; all it requires is a text editor and a little patience. If you're interested in HTML, see my book *The Mosaic Navigator* (John Wiley & Sons, Inc., 1994), which provides tips on setting up a home page, including linking to graphical images. When you create your own home page, all the hyperlinks can be related directly to your own interests.

Setting Up Mosaic's Viewers

Notice that at the top of the Preferences dialog box, you have a series of folder tabs, which you can use to move through the Mosaic configuration options. Let's turn now to the one marked Viewers, which you can see in Figure 11.5.

This is an important dialog box. The top field, marked Associate Mime Type of:, contains various kinds of file associations. You can see them if you click on the downward-pointing arrow to the right of the field, as I have done in Figure 11.6.

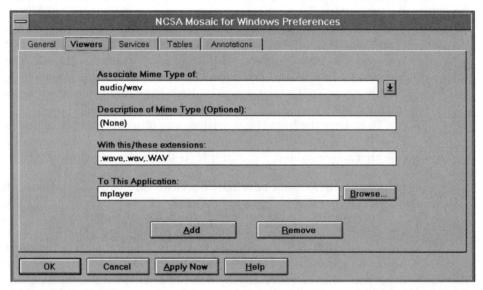

Figure 11.5 The Viewers screen lets you assign external programs to display file types that Mosaic can't handle.

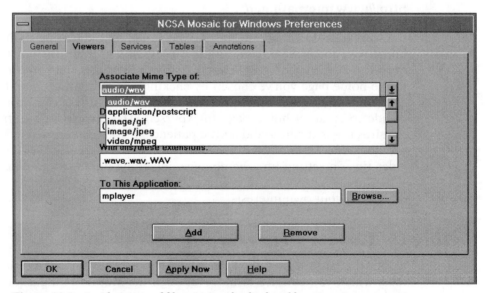

Figure 11.6 A wide variety of file types can be displayed by using viewer programs.

Why does Mosaic need viewers? We've already seen that the program can handle inline images, after all. But inline images are relatively small, and while the program can display them, it is not designed to handle larger images of the sort we find in, say, museum exhibits or other image-intensive home pages. For that kind of work, we need a separate graphics viewing program. For that matter, Mosaic isn't ready to handle such file types as .mpg movie files, or .mov (QuickTime) movie files. In each case, we need to declare an external program and a path to it so that Mosaic can send the program such files once they are downloaded, and the external program can display them for you. The Viewer screen is the place where we make these associations.

The extensions listed in this dialog box for each type of file are crucial; they let the program determine what kind of file it is dealing with and to which associated program it should send that file. You will probably not need to edit these extensions, as they are standard, but you will need to go through the list of file types and add the necessary path and program information in the field marked To This Application:. For example, I know I will be using GIF files, which are common on the Internet. Here is how I go about telling Mosaic what to do:

1. I pull down the list of file types in the Associate Mime Type of: field and click on image/gif.

2. In the To This Application: field, I place my external program information.

3. I click on OK so that Mosaic will accept these settings.

You can see my completed GIF information in Figure 11.7. As you can see, I have placed a file viewer, in this case a freeware program called LView, in a directory branching off from my Mosaic subdirectory. The directory is *c:\mosaic\viewers\lview*. The LView program is located in that directory. I could, of course, have chosen to locate the program anywhere on my hard disk, provided I told Mosaic where to find it. You can work your way through the list of file types setting up each with an external program; when you do, Mosaic will be configured for whatever it finds on the net.

But where do you get viewers? The major ones can be found at the NCSA site from which we downloaded Mosaic itself. As always, be aware that the directory structure here frequently changes, but as of now, the URL is:

ftp://ftp.ncsa.uiuc.edu/Web/Mosaic/Viewers/

Here is a list of the ones with which you should start:

LView   A fine freeware graphics viewer that allows you to view both GIF and JPEG files; both formats are found extensively at Internet sites. Notice that you will need to set up separate associations for GIF and JPEG in the Viewers dialog box.

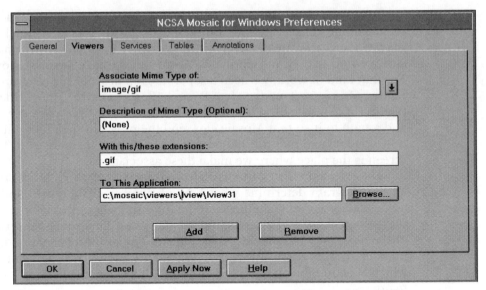

Figure 11.7   Completed information to assign an external file viewer for GIF files.

WHAM   An audio player that handles .wav files.

MPEGPLAY   A movie viewer for .mpg files.

GhostScript   An interpreter for the PostScript page description language.

Ghostview   A graphical interface for GhostScript.
for Windows

You can find all these files at the NCSA site. You will need to download them and set up directories for each. What I recommend doing is simply creating subdirectories off your *c:\mosaic* directory, as just explained. Thus I have set up the following:

c:\mosaic\viewers\lview
c:\mosaic\viewers\mpegplay
c:\mosaic\viewers\gsview

and so on. You will also find useful information about file viewers available through the Mosaic home pages at NCSA; these are included in the Starting Points menu, and provide a good place for you to begin your Mosaic explorations.

Mosaic Server Information

You must now give Mosaic some basic information about your Internet account. Click on the Services tab from the Preferences dialog box. You will see the screen shown in Figure 11.8. You will notice three major fields that demand your attention:

E-mail Address   Mosaic will need this information increasingly as electronic mail links are firmed up within the program. As of now, browsers like Mosaic do little with e-mail, but there are times when you will be able to leave a message for the creator of a home page, for example. Enter the correct e-mail information here.

SMTP Server   Enter the address of your service provider's mail server here.

NNTP Server   Enter your service provider's news server here.

Mosaic Annotations

Finally, you need to tell Mosaic what to do about any notes you may take as you work your way through the Web. The program makes it possible for you to jot down observations or any other notes about a particular site; that information is then saved and will appear on-screen as a hyperlink the next time you access the site in question. Annotations are a useful tool for anyone hoping to do research on the Web. You can move to the necessary dialog box by clicking on the Annotations tab from the Preferences box. The result is shown in Figure 11.9. What you need to do here is to enter a value in the Annotation Directory: field. Mosaic can keep your annotations anywhere you choose, but naturally, they have to be in a legitimate directory for the program to find them. I recommend setting up a *c:\mosaic\annotate* directory.

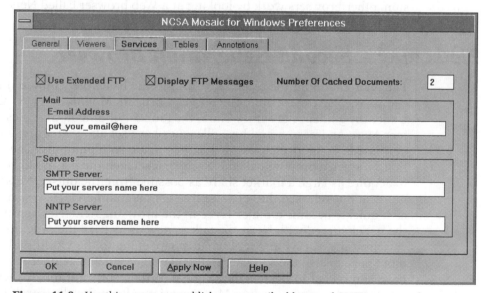

Figure 11.8   Use this screen to establish your e-mail address and SMTP server, and to enter an NNTP server for USENET news.

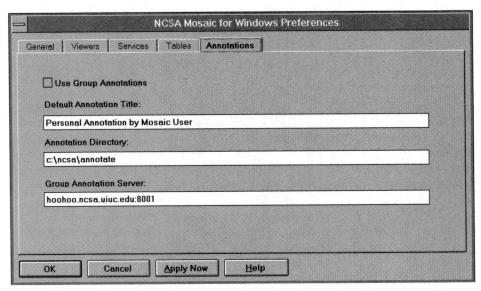

Figure 11.9 Setting up Mosaic's annotation information. Annotations allow you to make notes assigned to particular Web pages.

Mosaic for Windows is now configured for use. The best way to get a handle on its powers is to work with it, exploring hyperlinks at leisure. Because browsers tend to follow the same basic principles, as dictated by the organization of the World Wide Web itself, we will examine how Mosaic and, by extension, other browsers work by looking at a Web browser called Netscape.

Netscape: A Second Generation Browser

The team that built the original NCSA Mosaic has largely moved on to a new company, Netscape Communications Corp. in Mountain View, California. Under the guidance of James Clark, the founder of Silicon Graphics, programmer Marc Andreessen and his colleagues have set about creating a new product based on the principles Mosaic has made so ubiquitous. The company's first product, a browser called Netscape, has taken the net by storm. Deciding to acquire as large a market share as possible from the outset, Netscape Communications released the software free to non-commercial users, and watched as it quickly became a major force in the browsing field. Newsgroups all over the net chattered with Netscape talk as new users tried the program.

Netscape is a symptom of what is happening to the World Wide Web and, more particularly, the software that makes it accessible. Numerous companies have contracted to license the original Mosaic software for further development. In addition to existing Mosaic variants from Spyglass itself (Enhanced Mosaic) and Spry Inc. (AIR Mosaic), look for legions of companies to begin incorporating the technology into their own products. Digital Equipment, for example, intends to include Mosaic with all computers it sells, while NEC intends to use the software to produce graphical screens for the display of Japanese ideograms. IBM has included a version of Mosaic in its new version of OS/2 called Warp, while AT&T intends to use the software in its own desktop machines. Some form of Mosaic is slated for new versions of Microsoft Windows as well. And with thousands of Mosaic downloads continuing every month at NCSA, it is clear that interest in net browsing will stimulate the production of ever more software resources related to the Web.

That being said, why would you want to switch to Netscape if Mosaic itself provides so much functionality? The answer lies in some of Mosaic's built-in limitations. You have to remember that the original Mosaic was designed as a "proof of concept" package. Created to run over Ethernet links and still faster connections, the program was never intended to be a SLIP/PPP client working over relatively slow-speed telephone line connections. This is no surprise, given the software's connection to the supercomputing facilities at the NCSA.

Because Netscape was created with the nontechnical user in mind, the program makes intelligent use of its menus and provides configuration options that offer numerous ways to customize your environment. Knowing that their software would come into intensive use from all quarters, the developers have made Netscape much faster than NCSA Mosaic. Part of this speed difference is in user perception. Mosaic, for example, loads a home page all at once; you wait until each image has been retrieved before seeing the completed page. Perhaps sensing that the true value of most pages is in their textual documentation, however, Netscape has been designed so that you can see and move around in the text while the images are still loading. This makes moving between sites fast; and because you can stop incoming data, you can quickly decide if a site is right for you—no need to finish downloading a big image.

Downloading and Installing Netscape

To retrieve Netscape, go to the following URL:

ftp://ftp.mcom.com/netscape/windows/

At the time of this writing, the filename was ns16-100.exe; this is a self-extracting archival file.

Installation is simpler than the comparable process in NCSA Mosaic. Follow these steps:

1. Move the Netscape archive file to a temporary directory; as with Mosaic, you could set up a *c:\temp* directory for this purpose.

2. From the DOS prompt, run the program by typing out **ns16-100.exe**, followed by a Return.

3. From Windows, run the setup.exe program that was unpacked from the archive file when you ran it.

The setup program will install Netscape into any directory you choose, although the default is *c:\netscape*. The program will also add a Netscape section to the win.ini file that controls Windows operations, and will create the necessary program group and icons. You are now ready to run the program.

Running Netscape

With your SLIP/PPP connection active, double-click on the Netscape icon. You will see a screen similar to the one in Figure 11.10. As you can see, Netscape

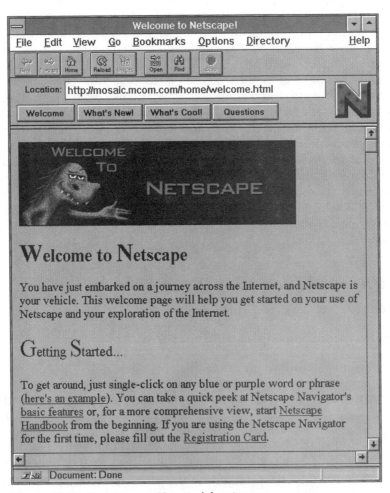

Figure 11.10   Logging on to Netscape's home page.

has logged on to the default home page at Netscape Communications itself; this home page and related links are well worth your time now, as they provide a good deal of information about the program. Notice that, as with NCSA Mosaic, hyperlinks are shown underlined. They're also in color, blue on a gray background. Clicking on any hyperlink takes you to the linked page.

And as with NCSA Mosaic, notice the page layout, starting from the top of the screen. The menu bar provides the basic menu operations for the program; the toolbar below provides quick shortcuts to primary functions, while the directory buttons beneath the toolbar provide links to frequently accessed Internet features. The location field displays the site of the current URL. The page layout is shown in Figure 11.11. Here are the toolbar icons and their meanings:

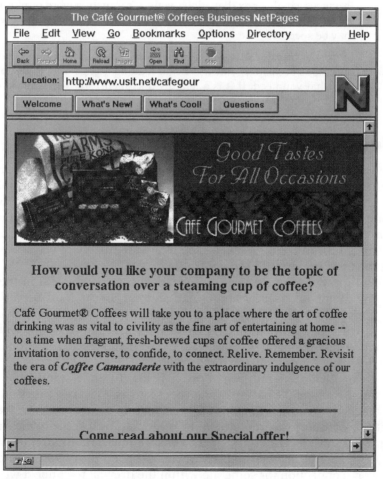

Figure 11.11   A basic Netscape page.

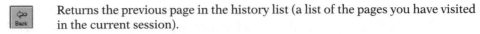

Returns the previous page in the history list (a list of the pages you have visited in the current session).

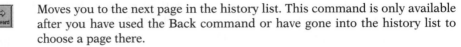

Moves you to the next page in the history list. This command is only available after you have used the Back command or have gone into the history list to choose a page there.

Returns you to the home page.

Reloads the current page.

Loads images. You will use this icon if you have turned off the option of seeing images as home pages are loading. If you have, you will see an icon instead of the image; you can click on this toolbar icon to see the image.

Lets you enter the URL of a home page you would like to access.

Produces a dialog box that allows you to search for a word or phrase within the current Netscape page. Case sensitivity and direction (up or down) of search may be specified.

Stops the transfer of page information. This is an extremely handy tool; on numerous occasions, you will begin loading a page only to discover that it is not what you need. If it is a lengthy document, you will want to click on this icon to stop the transfer process.

Configuring Netscape

Now that you've had a look at this fine program in action, let's set about configuring it for our own use. To do so, pull down the Options menu and choose the Preferences command. You will see the screen shown in Figure 11.12. Notice that the top of the screen contains a scrollable field within which is the term Mail and Proxies. If you scroll through the options in this field, you will see that you can configure Netscape in a wide variety of ways. We will examine the most important here.

Returning to Figure 11.12, it's clear that we need to fill in the fields pertaining to our mail server and e-mail address. In the Mail Server field, place the name of your SMTP server; this information should be available from your service provider. Adding this information means that Netscape will know how to handle any mail you want to send to the mail server. You should also fill in the fields for your name and e-mail address.

Below that are a number of proxy fields. To understand what they mean, we must examine the nature of Internet security. Most resources on the net can be reached by Mosaic without any problem; in some, however, the program's ability to connect to a remote server is blocked by a security measure called a *firewall*. Firewalls are established to ensure that data in an internal company network cannot be accessed. However, so-called *proxy* software can allow a network connection for someone within the firewall to connect with resources

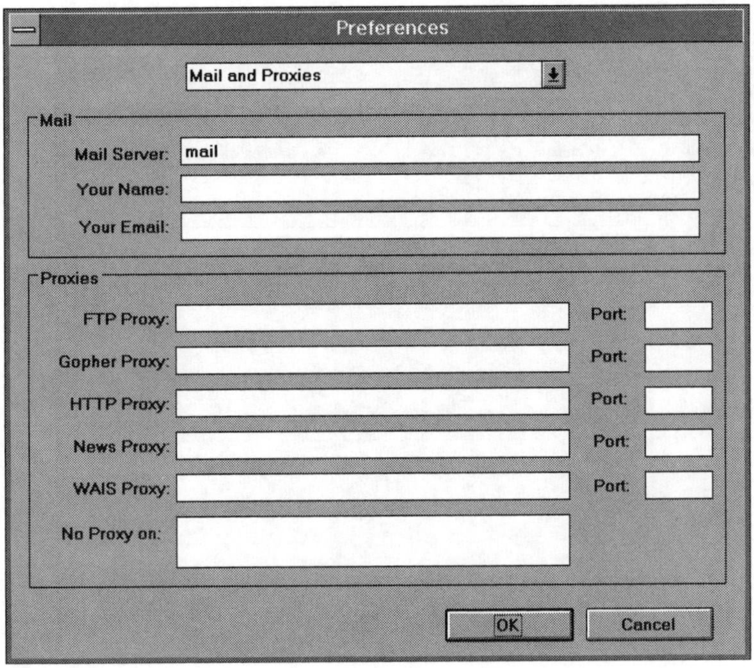

Figure 11.12 The Netscape Preferences window.

outside. Thus, if you are using Netscape from within an internal network and need to reach resources outside that network, you will have to find out from the system administrator at your site how to use this proxy software. You can then enter the relevant proxy information in this field. Because SLIP/PPP users are unlikely to be using Netscape from beyond a firewall, I will pass over this section without further comment, but full information about the use of proxies is available in Netscape's excellent help system.

Styles

If you choose the Styles option from the Preferences dialog box, you will see the screen shown in Figure 11.13. Notice that the screen is configurable from this dialog box. It is possible, for example, to show the toolbar in various ways; you can also choose to display a home page upon startup, or else go to a blank Netscape page for immediate display (at that point, you would choose the URL to which you wanted to connect, and proceed). And as you can see, you can change the home page you access by altering the information in the home page box. As with NCSA Mosaic, I recommend you leave this setting where it is to begin, but change it after you have explored the Netscape site so as to take some of the network load off this server.

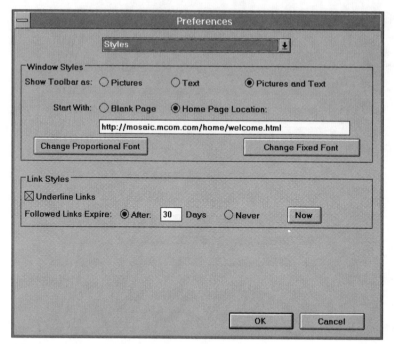

Figure 11.13 Netscape's Styles screen also allows you to choose a default home page.

Notice one other interesting point about this screen. As you use Netscape, you will learn that links that you have visited are displayed in a different color from those you haven't. This can be convenient, since there are many sites that you won't want to repeat on your journeys. On this Styles screen, you can choose a value for the number of days these "followed" links will be maintained. The default is 30; you can also choose to have them remain in effect no matter how many days pass between accesses to the site.

Directories, Applications, and News

Choosing this option from the Preferences screen presents you with the dialog box shown in Figure 11.14. We've already learned from NCSA Mosaic that a browser program frequently accesses external software to display information that it can't handle through its internal programming. This screen provides some of the information necessary for this process to work.

Temporary Directory   When Netscape runs into an item that it can't display without external help, its first action is to store this file on your hard disk as a temporary file. Such files are deleted after you exit the helper application. This field, then, allows you to control which temporary directory the program will use. As you can see, *c:\temp* is the default.

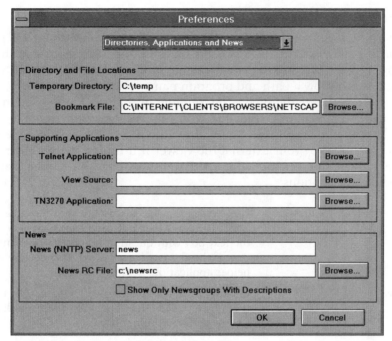

Figure 11.14 The Directories, Applications, and News screen, where you can set a path to an external Telnet or TN3270 program. You also set your news server here.

Bookmark File

This is the location of the file Netscape uses to store bookmark information. We discuss bookmarks and how they work shortly.

Telnet Application

Here you must list a Telnet program that Netscape can use to make Telnet connections. Be sure to indicate the complete path and program name for this application.

View Source

In Netscape terminology *source* refers to the HTML language that underlies a Web page. Normally, when you ask to see such a document, Netscape will show it to you as displayed by a built-in viewer. If you choose to view source documents in a different viewer, you can specify it in this field. For most uses, you can leave this field blank.

TN3270 Application

This is the path and filename of the tn3270 application you choose to use with Netscape.

News (NNTP) Server

Netscape does quite a good job with USENET news. In this field, enter the news server you are using.

News RC File

This is the file that holds subscription information about your USENET newsgroups. You should specify the directory in which your regular USENET reader maintains its files.

Helper Applications

Figure 11.15 shows the dialog box under Helper Applications. It is in this box that you establish the rest of the linkages between Netscape and the external programs you will use to display certain kinds of data. As with NCSA Mosaic, you need to show a path and program name for each application.

Here is the method: click on any line in the text field to see information about the application associated with that file type. For example, when you click on the image/gif line, you will see the linked information. Netscape will send an image to your external file viewer if it finds a file with the .gif suffix. This information is supplied in the Extensions field. But notice that you have several other options:

Use Browser as Viewer   Use Netscape itself to display the file, where possible. Those file types that Netscape can't handle are marked in the text box with question marks. If you want to display one of these types, you will have to declare a path to a helper application.

Save   Clicking this button allows you to save a file to disk after it is downloaded. Netscape will produce a dialog box to let you perform this action.

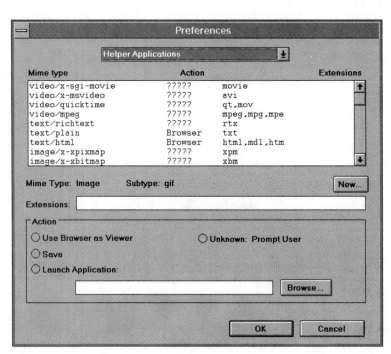

Figure 11.15 Like NCSA Mosaic, Netscape uses external helper applications to display programs it can't handle internally.

Launch Application	This is the field in which you list your associated helper application.
Unknown: Prompt User	When this button is clicked, Netscape will notify the user when it encounters an unknown file type.

Using Netscape's Bookmarks

Netscape is a joy to use because it takes the winning Mosaic concept and extends it in terms of user friendliness and capability. Bookmarks, for example, are a major addition to the pantheon of features. While NCSA Mosaic and Netscape both provide them, Netscape's editing features are superior because they are more intuitive. And make no mistake about it, you will put Netscape's bookmark resources to plentiful use. Bookmarks provide one thing the Internet sorely lacks: organization. They allow you, when you find interesting sites, to sort those sites by topic, and to return to them by clicking on the bookmark entry. Thus you are spared the chore of entering the lengthy URL, even as the hierarchical menu structure that Netscape provides allows you to categorize sites by whatever scheme works for you.

To examine how Netscape handles bookmarks, let's take the program through its paces. In Figure 11.16, I have moved to The Free On-line Dictionary of Computing. The URL is as follows:

http://wombat.doc.ic.ac.uk/

This is a free, searchable dictionary that provides an abundance of information about operating systems, networking, computer acronyms, telecommunications, and technology companies. Notice in the figure that this searchable index is presented with a field in which you can enter your query.

Let's say, for example, that I'd like to learn about V.34, the new standard for high-speed modems. I enter the v.34 keyword in the search field (notice that case is not significant in searches at this site). When I press the Return key, my request is sent out over the Internet. Soon I have a reply, as shown in Figure 11.17. The information is extensive, and made doubly useful by being provided with enclosed hyperlinks to other data. Clearly, this is a site that could be quite useful to me in my work.

When you find a site like this one, a page you will return to again and again, you can use Netscape's Bookmark feature to keep a record of it on your machine. To do so, pull down the Bookmarks menu and click on Add Bookmark. Netscape will save the necessary URL information. At any time, you can use the Bookmarks menu, clicking on View Bookmarks, to see a list of the bookmarks you have created. Figure 11.18 shows a bookmark list I put together simply by roaming about the net one afternoon. I can search this list with the Find command at the bottom of the dialog box. Notice as well that there is an Edit button. Pressing this calls up the more comprehensive screen shown in Figure 11.19.

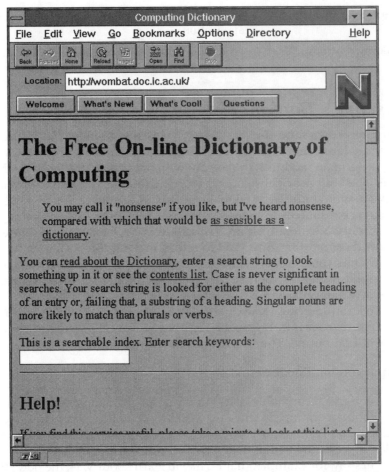

Figure 11.16 The Free On-line Dictionary of Computing, a wonderful Web resource.

Here we have quite a bit of information. Complete site data is shown to the right of the dialog box, with the URL and name of the home page displayed, along with the time the site was added to the bookmark list and the date and time of our last visit there. There is also a space to add an optional description.

You will have noticed that the list of bookmarks in Figure 11.19 is not alphabetized, as it was compiled at random, but I can use the Bookmark List dialog box to put all these entries into proper order. This is simply a matter of highlighting the item in question and clicking on the Up or Down buttons; the bookmark item then moves in accordance with my wishes. After you've added a few bookmark items, you'll soon realize how valuable it is to keep your list in an organized fashion.

As you can imagine, being able to note an interesting site and add it to your bookmark list can save time; it's also a fine way to apply your own organizing

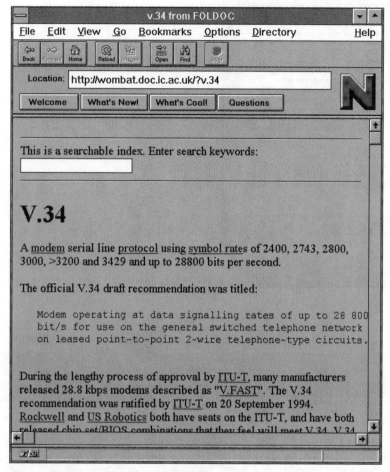

Figure 11.17 Results of a search of the On-line Dictionary using the keyword v.34.

principles to the Internet, choosing sites that fit your interests. But Netscape's Bookmark feature is even more useful when you realize that you are not confined to a single bookmark list, nor are you limited in terms of how you structure your list.

You can, for example, add header items to your bookmark list so that clicking on any of them results in a new sublist being displayed, thus creating a hierarchical menu structure of considerable complexity. You can do this in one of two ways; here's the first:

1. Click on New Header and fill in a name for your header (don't worry about its placement, as this is adjustable later).

2. Click on the New Bookmark button.

3. Provide name and URL of the new bookmark.

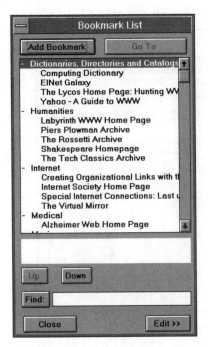

Figure 11.18 A typical bookmark list, with major topics broken out into individual listings of Web sites.

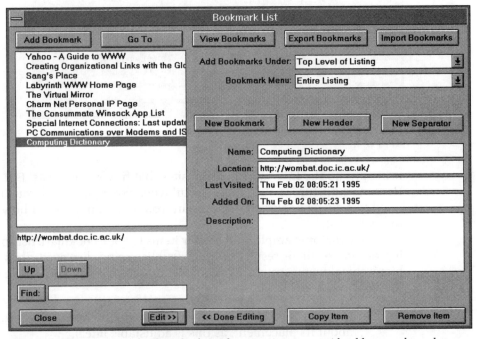

Figure 11.19 Netscape's bookmark editing features give you considerable control over how you construct and maintain your list.

4. Adjust the indentation by using the Up or Down buttons.

5. Click on Done Editing to complete the process.

Notice that, using this method, you are required to add URL and name information manually. This is what you would do if you wanted to construct a list based upon, say, resources you had read about in a magazine or book. The easier way, of course, is to add bookmarks as you journey through the net. You can create headers on the fly and adjust their placement, and the pages listed under them, as you proceed. Here's the method:

1. Move to a page you would like to add to your bookmark list.

2. Pull down the Bookmarks menu and choose the Add Bookmark command.

3. Click on View Bookmarks from the same menu.

4. From the Bookmark List dialog box, highlight the new page you have just added.

5. Use the Up and Down buttons to move the new item to the place of your choice. If you need a new header under which to list this site, click on the New Header button and it will be created. You can then move the item under the header in question.

You will now have a header you can use to separate out various bookmark items. For example, I created a header called Dictionaries and Directories by using the methods above. I then added the Free On-line Dictionary of Computing to this list in such a way that it appeared as a sub-item under my Dictionaries and Directories header. By highlighting any bookmark item and clicking on the Go To button, I can move quickly to the site.

 Note: Separators are a good way to keep your information organized. When you click on the New Separator button on the Bookmark List dialog box, you create a line that appears on your list, separating two items. You can use such separators to emphasize the distinction between different topics you may have created through your choice of headers and your placement of new sites.

We aren't through with bookmarks yet. Let's examine three important buttons on the Bookmark List dialog box:

View Bookmarks   This button allows you to create a new Netscape page containing your bookmark list in HTML format. The page can be saved by using the Save As command from the File menu.

Export Bookmarks   This button allows you to save the active bookmarks list to an HTML file. The advantage of doing this is that you can then exchange bookmark files with other users.

Import Bookmarks   This button allows you to insert a bookmark file into your copy of Netscape. Choose the file you want to import and press OK.

Notice, too, that you can use the Add Bookmarks Under item to determine where new bookmarks will be added. For example, if you would like all new bookmarks to go under your Dictionaries and Directories subcategory, you could set that value here. Then, every time you clicked on the Add Bookmark command, the new bookmark would be placed there. This is particularly useful when you are working with a number of Web sites that cluster around a particular topic; you might, for example, be researching musical subjects and want to add all new pages under your Music subcategory for the duration of your research.

Bookmarks are the acid test of any World Wide Web browser; they allow us to impose a system of order upon the flow of Internet information. It will be worth your time to master them now. As you browse through the Web, you will begin adding categories and new pages constantly, until your bookmarks become a major contributor to the success of your explorations.

Viewing HTML Code

Looking at a typical World Wide Web page through Netscape, it's hard to imagine how the combination of images and formatted text could be created over a distributed network. But in fact, despite its impressive capabilities, HTML is not terribly difficult to work with. The best way to learn about it is to examine actual code for pages that intrigue you. In Figure 11.20, for example, I have moved to the following URL:

http://www.ipac.net:80/HW/

As you can see, this is the Hidden Water page, devoted to the work of independent artists. The page is nicely formatted, with an image at the top followed by an italicized quote, then text.

How did the authors create it? To find out, I can pull down the View menu and choose the Source command. This will create the screen shown in Figure 11.21. The full range of HTML commands is beyond the scope of this book, but it is instructive to point out that if you study a few examples of HTML code, you will quickly pick up the basics. What is especially helpful is being able to see how images and links to other data are inserted in a page, as well as how HTML can control the on-screen formatting of text. Would-be home page designers will make extensive use of the source viewing feature.

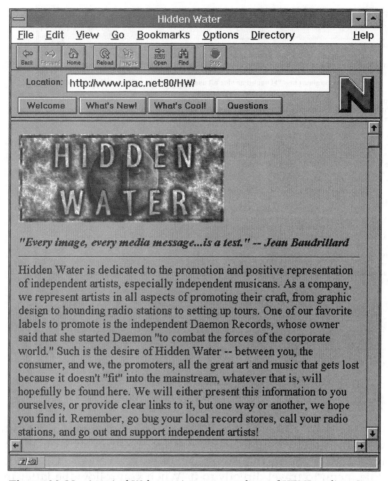

Figure 11.20   A typical Web page is constructed out of HTML coding. Compare its formatting with that in Figure 11.21.

Using Netscape to Read the News

World Wide Web browsers have a growing connectivity to the worldwide system of discussion groups called USENET. We saw in Chapter 10 how to use a variety of client programs to access USENET. What is interesting is the way in which a browser like Netscape can bring its own set of interface tools to the job. To make it all work, of course, you have to have configured the program, entering your e-mail address and news server, as discussed previously. Remember, newsgroups are not distributed through the World Wide Web per se; they travel under their own set of rules. By entering the name of your service provider's news server, you enable Netscape to access these discussions.

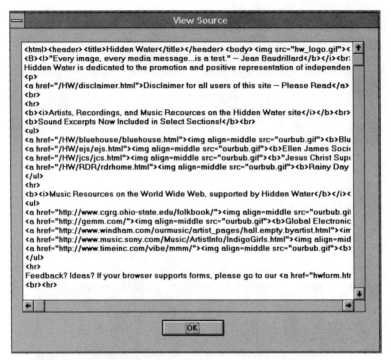

Figure 11.21 The HTML code underlying Figure 11.20; studying it will help you understand how HTML handles many display chores.

But, actually, reading USENET news is handled much the same way you move to any other resource with Netscape. You can click on a link to a newsgroup that may appear in a Web page, or you can choose Open Location from the File menu to travel directly to it. When you follow the latter method, you simply enter the name of the newsgroup as a URL. Thus, if I want to look at alt.winsock, I would enter this:

news:alt.winsock

Remember, URLs for newsgroups are different from those for other kinds of resources. Missing are the double slashes, as well as the server information, which is entered directly into your browser. When you enter this URL, you see something like what appears in Figure 11.22. Here we see the hypertext veneer imposed upon the USENET structure. Each message is set up as a hyperlink, as shown by the underlining. On-screen buttons allow us to post new articles, mark all articles as read, subscribe to the newsgroup, or go to the list of currently subscribed newsgroups.

We can click on any of these links to see the message in question. When we do so, more wonders await. In Figure 11.23, I have followed a hyperlink to a

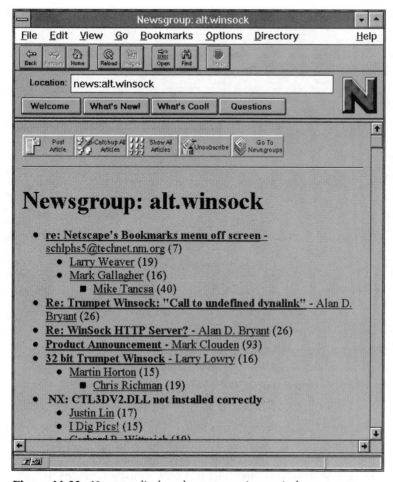

Figure 11.22   Netscape displays the messages in a typical newsgroup.

message. Take a look at the screen that awaits (I have widened the window for maximum readability). As you can see, Netscape has provided us with a full-featured newsreader interface. I have a series of buttons at my disposal to manage such tasks as posting a follow-up or replying by e-mail to the sender. I can use the icons at the top left of the screen to move to the next message in a thread, or to move to the next thread. Conveniently, the icons are located both at the top of the screen as well as at the bottom. Particularly useful as these features are, they're perhaps outweighed by the aesthetic quality of the display. Surely Netscape can qualify as one of the easiest newsreaders on the eyes! Perhaps its greatest drawback as a newsreader is its inability to work with images, as Trumpet for Windows, WinVN, and Newswatcher do so well. But the program adds a wonderful touch: When a message includes a valid URL, Netscape will display that URL as a hyperlink—click and you're there!

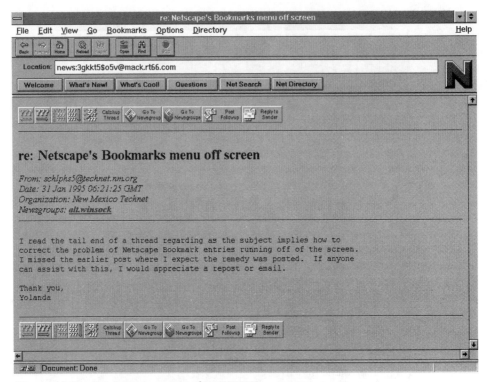

Figure 11.23   Using Netscape to read a USENET message.

In Figure 11.24, I have moved to my list of subscribed newsgroups by clicking on the Newsgroups icon. Notice that Netscape provides clickable boxes to the left of each newsgroup; by clicking on any of these, I can unsubscribe from the group. The program also tells me how many messages are waiting for me in each newsgroup, and provides the appropriate hyperlink to each. Further

Note: If you would like to examine newsgroup listings within a certain category, you can do so by using an asterisk. For example, let's assume I'd like to know how many newsgroups are clustered under the comp.internet hierarchy. I can find out by pulling down the File menu, choosing Open Location, and entering this statement:

news:comp.internet.*

I quickly receive my result; the two newsgroups in this hierarchy are **comp.internet.library** and **comp.internet.net-happenings**. Both are presented with hyperlinks to the groups so that I can read them directly.

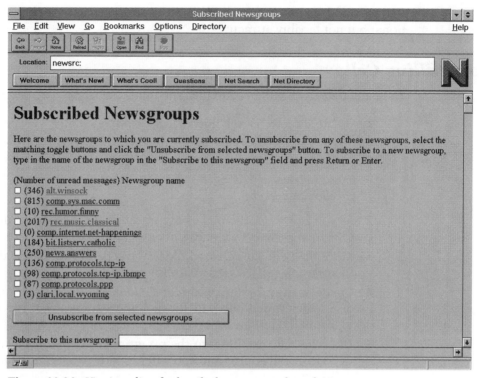

Figure 11.24   Viewing a list of subscribed newsgroups through Netscape.

down on the page (it doesn't show up in the figure), is a field within which I can subscribe to a new group.

Cello: A Different Take on Web Browsing

Although it hasn't garnered the attention in the press that Mosaic and Netscape have, Cello is a full-featured browser that offers a number of attractive capabilities. The program was created by Thomas R. Bruce, of Cornell University's Legal Information Institute. Version 1 was current as this chapter was written, but version 2 was in the offing; the latter is reputed to contain numerous upgrades. You can retrieve the program from the following URL:

ftp://ftp.law.cornell.edu/pub/LII/Cello/

At the time of this writing, the filename was cello.zip. Like NCSA Mosaic and Netscape, Cello offers you the ability to display World Wide Web data, as well as to access Gopher servers, run FTP sessions, consult X.500 directory servers, and other resources. That makes Cello a full-featured browser, though the current version lags Netscape and Mosaic in terms of its interface, which is functional but not terribly attractive.

Installing Cello

To install Cello, you will need to take the following steps:

1. Create directories for the software and associated viewer programs. The program's documentation suggests the following directories:

   c:\cello
   c:\cello\viewers
   c:\cello\download

2. As you can see, Cello makes use of external viewer programs just like the other browsers we've examined here.

3. Move the Cello compressed file to the *c:\cello* directory and unpack it there, using PKUNZIP or WinZip.

4. Create a new program group for Cello in Windows Program Manager, or else determine into which existing program group you would like to install the program.

5. Drag the cello.exe file into the program group you have chosen. The Cello icon will appear and you will be ready to configure the program.

Cello's Configuration

Double-clicking on its icon will launch Cello. Do this while your SLIP/PPP account is active, since Cello will display a helpful document that tells you more about the program and allows you to take a quick tour using the program's capabilities. You will see the screen shown in Figure 11.25.

In Figure 11.26, notice the way Cello shows hyperlinks. You can see that links are placed inside boxes made up of dashed lines. You will be able to change this format to underlining if you choose as you configure the program.

To configure Cello, simply pull down the Configure menu. Place your own information into the following fields:

Files and directories	Here you can establish a default home page if you choose, although the default page, default.htm, is a good one to start with, since it provides you with so much good information about the program. You should also fill in the directory to which you want Cello to download files.
Links Underlined Only	Click this option if you choose to see hyperlinks underlined.
Background Color	Cello provides you with the ability to tinker with a variety of color schemes. As a person whose long hours at the

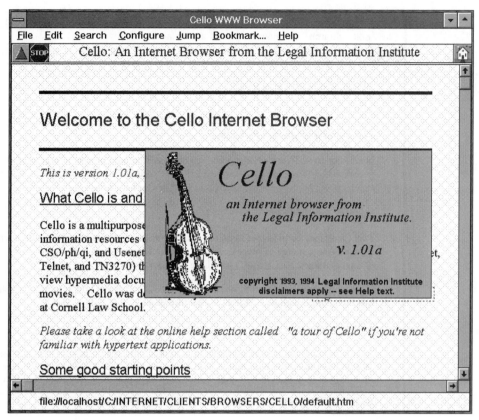

Figure 11.25 Cello's opening screen.

computer cause frequent eyestrain, I find this to be quite useful.

Your e-mail address   Enter your e-mail address here. Cello can send, but not receive, electronic mail. This is useful if you want to mail a document you are viewing to another person.

Mail relay   Enter the address of your SMTP mail server here.

News server   Enter the address of your news server here. Cello, like Mosaic and Netscape, is able to work with USENET newsgroups.

WAIS gateway   Cello has to use a gateway to send a WAIS request to a server; the program does not make requests directly. Enter the URL of the WAIS gateway you want to use here. The WAIS gateway at the following address may prove helpful: **www.ncsa.uiuc.edu:8001**.

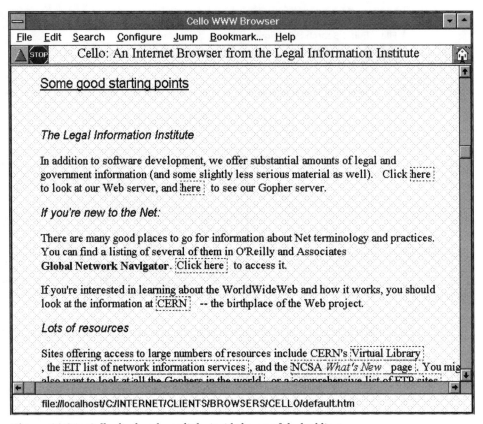

Figure 11.26 Cello displays hyperlinks inside boxes of dashed lines.

Cello's File Viewers

You can set paths and program names for several external programs to use with Cello by clicking on the Use your own command on the Configure menu. When you do so, you will be able to enter values for an external text editor, a Telnet client, and a tn3270 client (although Cello provides built-in support for both Telnet and tn3270). But setting pathnames and programs for viewing graphics or listening to sound files requires you to edit the cello.ini file that the program looks to when it initializes. This process can be managed in any text editor.

Here, for example, is the relevant part of the cello.ini file for viewing GIF files on-screen:

[Extensions]
gif=c:\wwwproj\viewers\gv057.exe ^.gif

Note: We need to discuss how Cello handles file caching, because you can juggle the variables the program uses to do this. When Cello displays a file, such as an HTML document, it keeps that file in a *cache,* which is simply a temporary storage area on your hard disk; the file is stored there under a temporary name as you proceed with your operations. Cello will discard old cached files as the space available to it on your hard disk becomes limited. By default, the program will begin eliminating the least recently used cache files so as to complete current operations and still be able to leave 500K free on your hard disk. In this scenario, 500K is called the *cache low-water mark.* You can change this setting upward or downward.

In an era of huge hard disks, it may well be that you would like to tell Cello to leave more space on your hard disk than 500K, even though these files are temporary. Or you may elect to turn caching off altogether, which you can do by entering a 0 as your cache setting. In either case, you can determine this setting by choosing the Files and directories command from the Configure menu. There you will find a menu option called Cache low-water mark. Clicking on it will call up a dialog box within which you can enter a nondefault value for the cache.

But remember this: the bigger the cache, the faster the program will run. This is because when you want to look again at pages you've recently accessed, Cello will be able to find them on disk rather than by going out over the net for them.

jpg=c:\wwwproj\viewers\gv057.exe ^.jpg
au=c:\wwwproj\viewers\wplany.exe -u -r 8000 ^.au
snd=c:\wwwproj\viewers\wplany.exe ^.snd
wav=c:\windows\soundrec.exe ^.wav
mpg=c:\wwwproj\mpeg\mpegplay.exe ^.mpg

Notice that values are suggested for the various viewers. To change them, simply enter the pathname and filename of your choice. Thus the GIF entry might read as follows:

gif=c:\cello\viewers\lview.exe ^.gif

This statement not only tells Cello where to find the necessary viewer program, but also that it should send any files it encounters with a .gif suffix to that program.

Using Cello on the Internet

Figure 11.27 shows you an example of Cello in action. Notice that I have reset the hyperlinks so that they are shown with underlining as opposed to being placed inside boxes. The major elements of the Cello screen are:

Title Field   Running across the top of the screen, this bar contains the title of the document currently being accessed. Within it are found the following three items.

This is the Backtrack Button. Clicking on it returns you to the previous document.

This is the Stop Button. Clicking on it stops the file transfer currently in progress.

This is the Home Button. Clicking on it takes you to your home page.

Status Field   The bar running across the bottom of the screen is where Cello reports on the status of current operations.

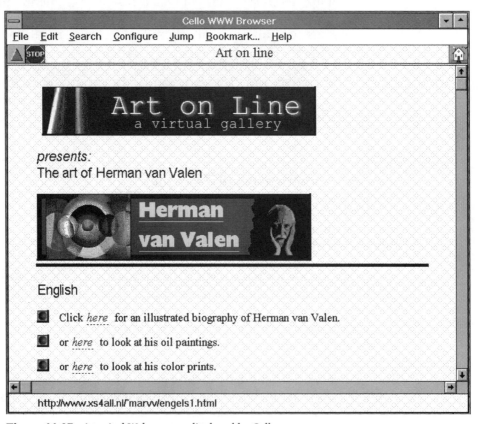

Figure 11.27   A typical Web page as displayed by Cello.

If you're interested in HTML and how to use it, Cello offers the ability to view source code from its Edit menu. It also offers a so-called "clean text" function, which renders HTML documents without their inset programming code as plain text viewed through Windows Notepad. This can be handy when you would like to print out the information from a particular page without irrelevant formatting. A built-in search function lets you examine the current page for particular occurrences of text.

In Figure 11.28, you can see Cello's Jump menu. Here you will notice the fact that Cello includes built-in support for Gopher, Telnet, TN3270, and FTP sessions. In Figure 11.29, I have clicked on the Launch FTP session command to launch a session with a remote site. Cello presented me with a dialog box asking for the address I wished to reach. Once I had filled in this information, the connection was made. As you can see, the on-screen presentation uses icons to represent directories and files; the entire FTP session is operated by point-and-click mouse commands.

Cello offers a bookmark list, accessible by pulling down the Bookmark menu from the main screen, but while the list does allow you to save URLs of frequently visited sites, it lacks the customizability built into the Mosaic variants as well as Netscape. The program also includes a History function which is built into the Jump menu.

Like most browsers, Cello provides you with the ability to turn off inline graphics if you prefer not to wait for them to download; this is particularly useful if you are running anything less than a 14.4Kbps modem (which I strongly discourage, in any case). To turn off inline images, follow these steps:

1. Pull down the Configure menu and click on Graphics.
2. Click on the Fetch Automatically toggle to remove the check mark.

From now on, Cello will not display any inline graphics it finds in Web documents, replacing them with alternate text provided by the information source.

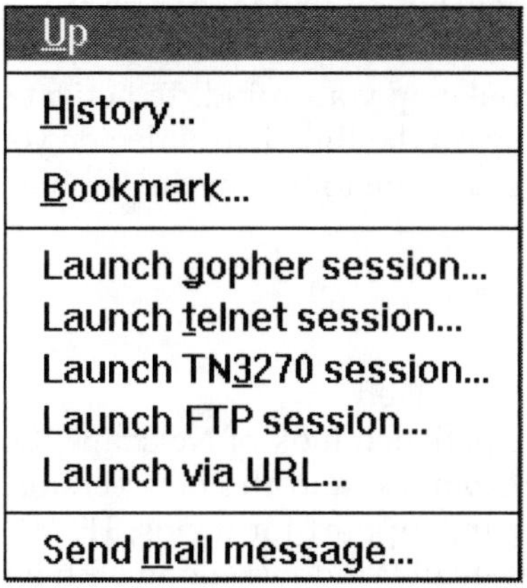

Up

History...

Bookmark...

Launch gopher session...
Launch telnet session...
Launch TN3270 session...
Launch FTP session...
Launch via URL...

Send mail message...

Figure 11.28 Cello's Jump menu allows you to use a variety of resources, including Telnet and Gopher.

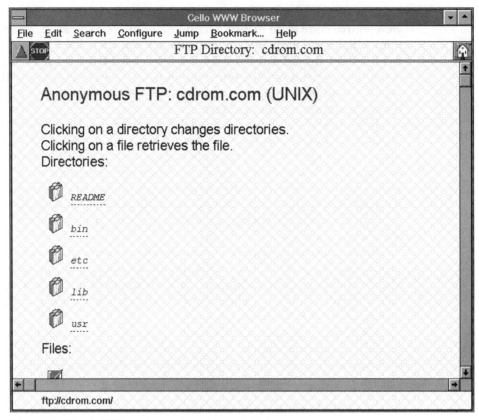

Figure 11.29 An FTP session as viewed through Cello.

Another useful Cello tool is the ability to go into "peek" mode. Perhaps you've encountered a link that looks promising, but you're not sure you want to click on it because you can't tell how long it will take your browser to download it. Using peek mode, Cello will download only the first 4,096 bytes of the linked file, to give you a chance to make up your mind. To activate peek mode, hold down the Ctrl key while clicking on the link. If you decide you would like to see the entire document, you can take the following steps:

1. Pull down the File menu.
2. Click on Reload Document.

The entire document will now be transferred.

Although the program lacks the polished look of Netscape, Cello provides quick access to World Wide Web resources, and the new version should certainly be worth a look. In the cards are support for forms, HTML editing features, and cut-and-paste capabilities in all Windows, along with improvements to the on-screen look and feel of the program. The developers are also receptive to user suggestions about future features. You can contact them at the following URL:

mailto://lii@www.law.cornell.edu

 Note: If you become a regular Cello user, you will want to subscribe to a mailing list devoted to the program. Send e-mail to the following URL:

> **mailto://listserve@fatty.law.cornell.edu**

In your message, place this text:

> **sub cello-1** *your_name*

> No other text should appear in your message.

WinWeb

The creators of EINet WinWAIS have produced a Web browser called WinWeb, which is accessible from their FTP site:

ftp://ftp.einet.net/einet/pc

At the time of this writing, the filename was winweb.zip.

Installing WinWeb

To install WinWeb, follow these procedures:

1. Create a directory for the program on your hard disk; for example, *c:\winweb*.
2. Unpack the winweb.zip file.
3. Copy all of the unpacked files except vbrun300.dll into the new directory.
4. Copy vbrun300.dll into your *c:\windows\system* directory.
5. Drag the winweb.exe file into the program group of your choice, or create a new program group for it in Program Manager by using the File menu and clicking on the New command.

Running WinWeb

Double-click on the WinWeb icon to launch the program. You will see the screen shown in Figure 11.30. This is the home page for EINet Galaxy, an

Internet directory service that includes both public and commercial information. Hyperlinks in WinWeb are shown by color changes and boldface; as with other Web browsers, the cursor changes to a small hand symbol when you place it over a hyperlink, indicating the presence of further information. A single mouse click then takes you to the linked site.

While it can be used as a full-service Web browser, EINet WinWeb is particularly well suited to tap the holdings at the company's Galaxy site. Here's how:

1. Pull down the Navigate menu.
2. Click on Search EINet Galaxy.
3. In the dialog box that appears, enter your search term.

In Figure 11.31, you see the results of a search under the keyword music. In fact, the results shown in the figure are misleading, as the site was able to come up with page after page of Web documents that fit my search term. The EINet Galaxy site is an excellent source of directory information for your Web travels.

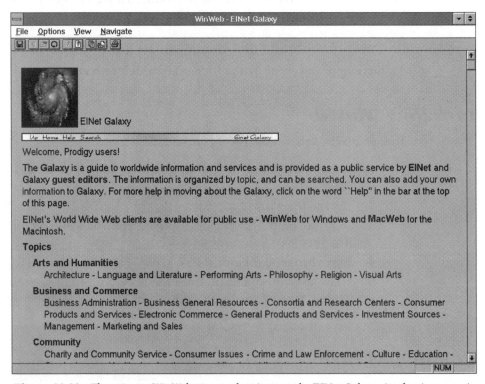

Figure 11.30 The primary WinWeb screen, showing you the EINet Galaxy site that it uses as its default.

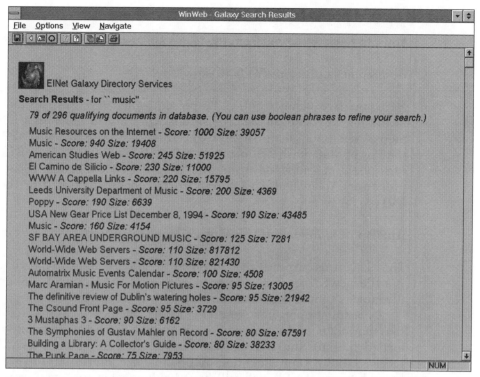

Figure 11.31   Results of a search at the EINet Galaxy site under the keyword music.

While WinWeb provides support for forms, customizing the program with external viewers requires you to edit the winweb.ini file, which the program looks to as it initializes. This is not a particularly difficult process (it can be managed in any text editor, and complete instructions are provided in the Win-Web package), but the trend is clearly toward incorporating such configuration items as menu choices. Doubtless a future version of WinWeb will move in this direction. The program does not support USENET news access.

Web Browsing with a Macintosh

The browsing clients I've discussed have their counterparts in the Macintosh world, and while you will find some differences in implementation, the basic program structures remain intact. Having used all these browsers in both environments, I can't find any compelling reason to favor one platform over the other for Web browsing, other than that installation is invariably simpler with a Mac. Experience tells me I crash as often with Mosaic on a Power Mac as I do with a Mosaic on a Windows-equipped machine, so stability doesn't seem to be a factor.

NCSA Mosaic for Macintosh

You can retrieve Mosaic from the NCSA site using the following URL:

ftp://ftp.ncsa.uiuc.edu/Web/Mosaic/Mac/

Here you have a choice of files. At present, you can retrieve a stable version 1 in the file NCSAMosaicMac.103.sit.hqx. Or you can move to a more experimental version 2; this exists in two forms: NCSAMosaic200A17.PPC.hqx (for the Power Macintosh platform), or NCSAMosaic200A17.68k.hqx (for the 68K Mac platform—machines using the Motorola 68000, 68020, 68030, or 68040 processor). You will also want to secure the documentation from the following URL.

ftp://ftp.ncsa.uiuc.edu/Web/Mosaic/Mac/Documents/

The filename is currently mac-mosaic-user-guide.cg.hqx. In the same directory is a file viewer that you can use to work with the Mosaic documentation. Its filename is common-ground-mini.hqx.

Depending upon how you downloaded them, the Mosaic for Macintosh files may not need decompressing. Clients like Fetch automatically send downloaded files to StuffIt Expander for decompression once they have been received. But if your client does not handle decompression this way (you will know because the file will still have its .hqx extension), you can always use StuffIt Expander to decompress the files yourself. Drag the file in question to the StuffIt Expander icon and release the mouse button to perform this operation.

To launch Mosaic, double-click on its icon while your SLIP/PPP connection is active. You will see a screen like the one in Figure 11.32. Notice the image icon at the top of the screen. Clicking on it will cause Mosaic to download and display the image.

Configuring Mosaic for Macintosh

Your task now is to configure the program. To do so, choose the Preferences command from the Options menu. The dialog box shown in Figure 11.33 should appear. This initial dialog box should need no changing, but you can see that it does allow you to alter to a degree the way Mosaic handles hyperlinks; they can be underlined or not as you prefer, and those that you have already explored can be marked in whatever color you choose to differentiate them from new ones.

Setting a New Home Page

Choose the Misc button now to fill in several basic fields. The Misc screen is shown in Figure 11.34. The NCSA Mosaic home page is currently selected as

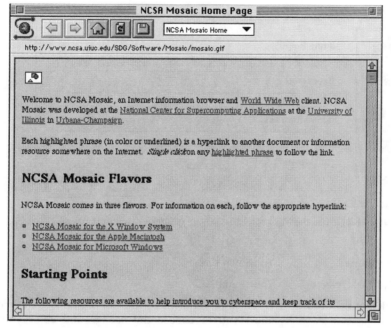

Figure 11.32   Viewing the NCSA Home Page through Mosaic for Macintosh.

the default. I would suggest leaving it as such for the time being, which will allow you to explore the site and learn more about Mosaic. But after a short time, you will want to change the setting by putting a new value in the Home Page: field. Choose a server geographically near you to minimize the load on the network. Your service provider will be able to suggest a URL for this. Fill in the other fields as follows:

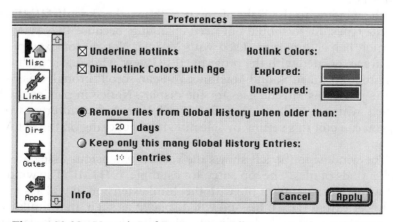

Figure 11.33   Mosaic's Preferences screen allows you to change the way you see hyperlinks.

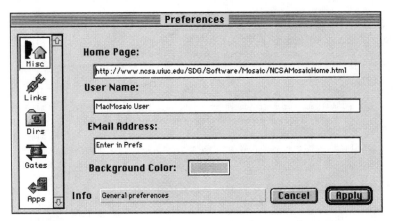

Figure 11.34   Use the Misc screen to set up an alternative home page.

User Name:	Your own name
EMail Address:	Your e-mail address
Background Color:	By clicking in this field, you can call up a color wheel that will allow you to choose the background color you prefer for Mosaic.

Linking Mosaic to Helper Applications

You will now need to set your helper applications. Helpers are those external programs that Mosaic uses to display files that it cannot display on its own, such as large images in the GIF or JPEG format, or sound and movie files. To set helper applications, click on the Apps button in the Preferences box, then the Helper Applications button that follows. You will see the screen shown in Figure 11.35.

The window to the right of the box shows the default MIME extensions and file types; these should not need changing, because they reflect the most common helper programs used with Mosaic. Notice, for example, that GIF files are associated with the program JPEGView, while basic audio is handled by a program called Sound Machine. You can scroll through this list to examine the programs Mosaic uses for file display. Notice in particular the setting for text, which defaults to Microsoft Word. If you use a different word processor, you can edit this setting by selecting it and clicking on the Set Application button.

The window to the left shows the various extensions associated with particular kinds of files. The top entry, for example, is HTML. The window tells us that when Mosaic finds a file with the .html extension, it will assume that this is a hypertextual HTML file and will display it as such. In a similar way, when it encounters a file with the .gif extension, it will assume it is dealing with an image, and will send it to the appropriate viewer, or helper, application.

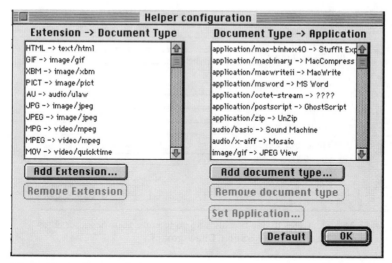

Figure 11.35   External programs can be set to display Web data that can't be handled by Mosaic itself.

You will find a set of recommended helper applications for the Macintosh at the NCSA site in the following URL:

ftp://ftp.ncsa.uiuc.edu/Web/Mosaic/Mac/Helpers/

Here are the current filenames for basic helper applications:

JPEGView   Handles a variety of file formats, including GIF, JPEG, PICT, TIFF, BMP, and MacPaint. The filename is jpeg-view-33.hqx.

Sound Machine Plays audio files in a variety of formats. The filename is sound-machine-21.hqx.

Sparkle   Plays moving video in MPEG format as well as QuickTime. The filename is sparkle-231.hqx.

These helper applications are only a few of those available at the NCSA site, but they should be enough to get you started with the major file types. Beyond these programs, there exist numerous options for configuring Mosaic with helpers. If there is another program, for graphics viewing, say, that you would like to try, you can set up a link to it and see how Mosaic handles the association. Because Mosaic can use such external programs, you have a great deal of control over how you process incoming information.

Defining Mosaic's Gateways

You're not through yet with your Mosaic configuration. In the Preferences dialog box, click on Gates. This dialog box is the one in which you will set a news

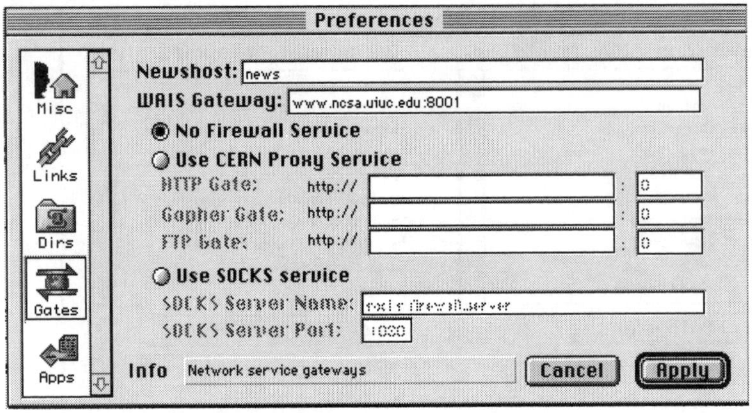

Figure 11.36 The Gates dialog box allows you to enter your news server so that you can use Mosaic to read USENET newsgroups.

server for accessing USENET newsgroups, as well as a WAIS gateway. The Gates dialog box is shown in Figure 11.36. You need to fill in these fields as follows:

Newshost: The name of your service provider's NNTP server.

WAIS Gateway: This should already be set with a default gateway: **www.ncsa.-uiuc.edu:8001**. Mosaic cannot handle direct WAIS requests, but must instead route them through a gateway.

You do not need to configure the rest of the items in this dialog box, as they pertain to using Mosaic through a network security system known as a firewall. Such systems are normally found only in large office networks, and are not germane for the individual SLIP/PPP user.

When you have completed the configuration, click on the Apply button to accept these changes. The new settings will come into effect the next time you start Mosaic.

Netscape for the Macintosh

To retrieve a copy of Netscape for the Macintosh, go to the following URL:

ftp://ftp.mcom.com/netscape/mac/

As of this writing, the filename was netscape.sea.hqx. As with Mosaic, when you download this file with a program like Fetch, the file will be unpacked automatically. But if it is not, you can drag its icon to the StuffIt Expander icon to decompress it.

To launch Netscape, double-click on its icon while your SLIP/PPP connection is active. You will see a screen like the one in Figure 11.37. Notice the large buttons at the top of the screen, which make file operations obvious and easy to effect; you could also, of course, perform the same actions by pulling down menus.

Configuring Netscape for Macintosh

From the Options menu, choose the Preferences command. You will see the dialog box shown in Figure 11.38, which is not dissimilar from the one you used to configure NCSA Mosaic. Like Mosaic's, this screen allows you to define how you want to see your hyperlinks. There is, however, one item you want to note, and that is Home Page Location:, a setting that tells you that the browser will choose as its default home page the Netscape site at **mcom.com**. You can leave this as is for the time being, because the Netscape site is filled with good information about the program, as well as numerous links to interesting World Wide Web servers. Eventually, however, you'll want to insert your own home page here to minimize the already heavy load being placed on this server.

If you click on the top field in the Preferences window, you will be able to drop down a menu with further choices on it. The Directories, Applications, and News dialog box is shown in Figure 11.39. It is here that you can set links

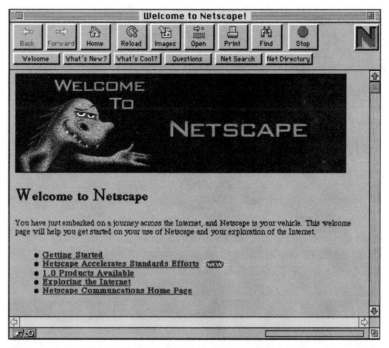

Figure 11.37 Launching Netscape on a Macintosh.

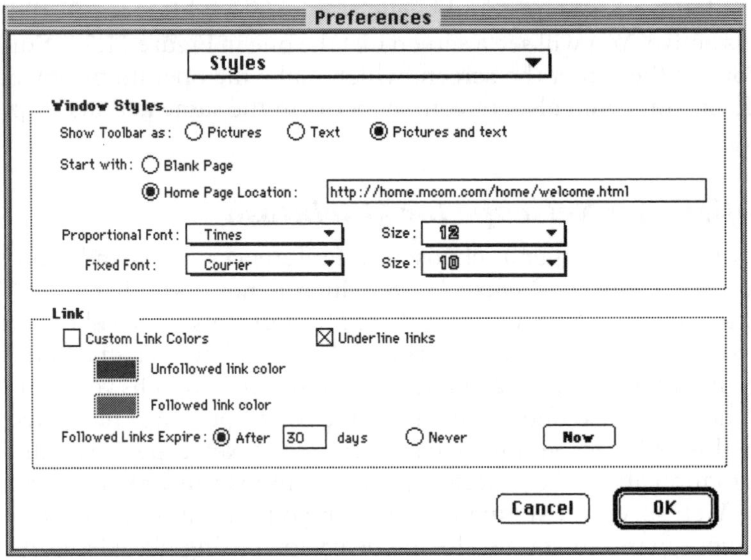

Figure 11.38   Netscape's Preferences window, from which you will control the configuration of the program.

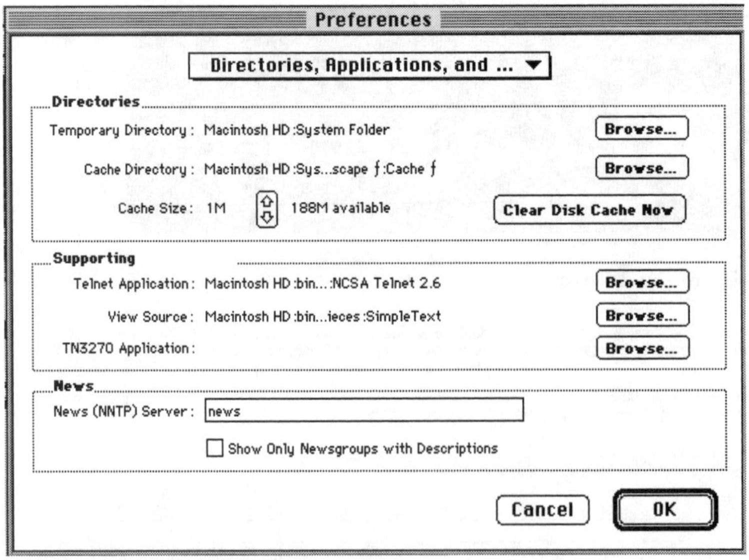

Figure 11.39   The Directories, Applications, and News dialog box.

to a Telnet application, a text file viewer, and a TN3270 program; as you can see in the figure, Netscape is linked to NCSA Telnet on my hard disk, but I can click the browse button to choose another program if I wish.

You will also need to set a news server in the News window at the bottom. Fill in the appropriate address here, so that Netscape can find the USENET newsgroups you want to read. Netscape isn't a full-featured newsreader, but its user interface is advanced enough to make reading news an enjoyable and productive experience.

We're almost through with the Netscape configuration. From the Preferences window click on Images, Network, and Mail. You will see the screen shown in Figure 11.40, with several fields that need your attention:

Display Images   I recommend you leave this value at the default, which is to display images as they are loading. Netscape is quite good at cutting off an incoming Web document when you click on its Stop button (on the icon bar of the main screen). You'll often find yourself watching an image begin to load and decide that you really don't need to see it. If you elect to see images only after they are loaded, you won't have this option.

Mail (SMTP) Server   Enter the name of your mail server here.

Your Name: Enter your full name here.

Your Email: Enter your e-mail address here.

Organization   Enter the name of your organization in this optional field.

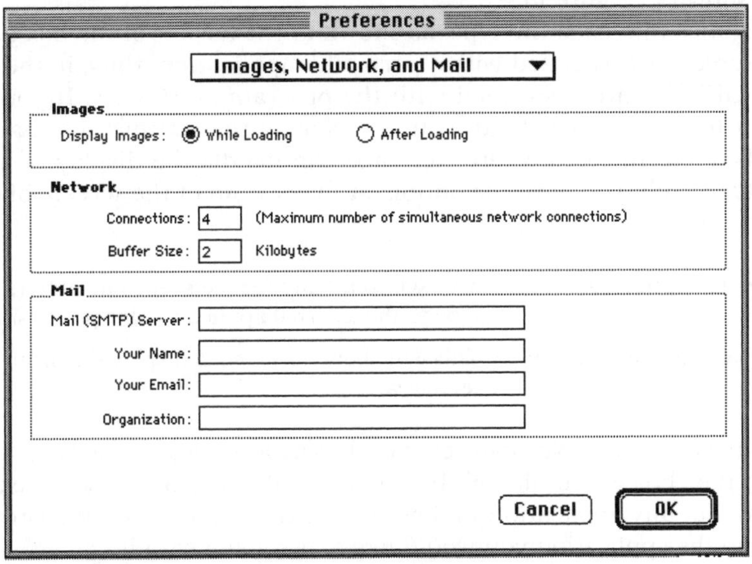

Figure 11.40   Netscape's Images, Network, and Mail dialog box, where you enter information about your e-mail address and server.

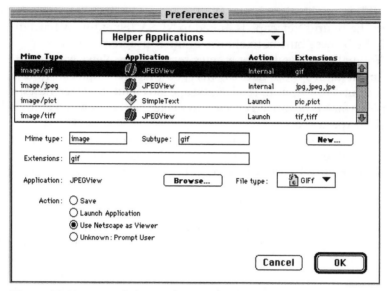

Figure 11.41   Setting helper applications in Netscape.

Finally, we come to adding the necessary helper applications to make Netscape work with various file types that it can't process internally. Click on Helper Applications from the Preferences screen; you will see a screen like the one shown in Figure 11.41.

Notice that each file type, as shown at the far left of the box at the top of the screen, is associated with a particular application; thus, in the first example, GIF files are associated with the program JPEGView. If you click on a given line in the text field, you can change the settings for that particular application. In cases where Netscape can handle the display of a particular file type itself, you have the option, at the bottom of the screen, of clicking on two buttons:

Launch Application   This will send any file Netscape encounters of the listed
                              type to the external application for processing.

Use Netscape as Viewer   This will allow Netscape to display the file in its own con-
                              tent area.

In cases where Netscape cannot display a particular file type, you will not have the choice; the file will be automatically displayed by the external program. For any application in these fields, you can click on the Browse button to find the application you would like to associate with it.

When you have completed all settings in the Preferences window, click on OK to save them. Netscape is now ready for use. But if you choose to fine-tune the program even more, examine the rest of the settings in the Options menu.

Let's run through them briefly:

Show Toolbar	Allows you to view the toolbar buttons or not as you choose.
Show Location	Allows you to control whether the URL field is visible.
Show Directory Buttons	Allows you to control whether the Directory menu buttons are visible.
Show Security Colorbar	Allows you to control the visibility of the security status bar above the content area.
Auto Load Images	Allows you to decide whether inline images should be displayed, or represented with an icon.
Show FTP File Information	Allows you to control the display of FTP file information.
Save Options	Allows you to save the changes you have made to the Options menu, other than those you have set in the Preferences dialog box (those are set by clicking on the OK button). Saved changes will remain in effect for future sessions with Netscape.

MacWeb

EINet's MacWeb is the Macintosh version of the WinWeb browser discussed earlier in this chapter. The program is easy to use and contains tight links to the EINet Galaxy home page which provides excellent directory services for the Web at large. You can retrieve MacWeb from the following URL:

ftp://ftp.einet.net/einet/mac/macweb/

At the time of this writing, the filename was macweb1.00A3.sea.hqx.

If your FTP program did not unpack the MacWeb file after it was downloaded, you can do so by dragging its icon to the StuffIt Expander icon on your desktop. You can then launch the program by double-clicking on it; this is a self-extracting file. The MacWeb 1.00A3 program and associated files will then be extracted to the folder of your choice.

Double-click on the MacWeb icon to launch the program. You will see a screen like the one in Figure 11.42. Note the image icon at the top left of the screen. A single mouse click will retrieve the linked image.

You now need to configure the program. From the File menu, choose the Preferences command, which will launch the screen shown in Figure 11.43. Here, you will need to fill in the following fields:

Home URL	MacWeb is set to load a document from your hard disk, but it can also be configured to load the URL of your choice.
Email Address:	Enter your e-mail address here.
News Host:	Enter your news server here.

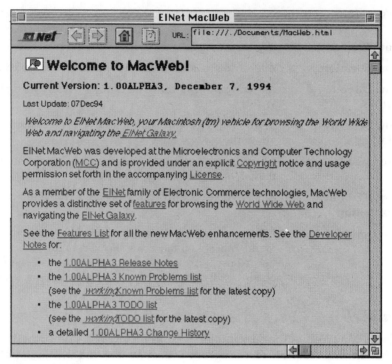

Figure 11.42   The opening MacWeb screen.

You can now move to the Edit menu where, confusingly, you will find the Helpers command. Clicking on it causes the screen shown in Figure 11.44 to appear. From this screen, you can set up associations between MacWeb and the various applications it will use to load external programs.

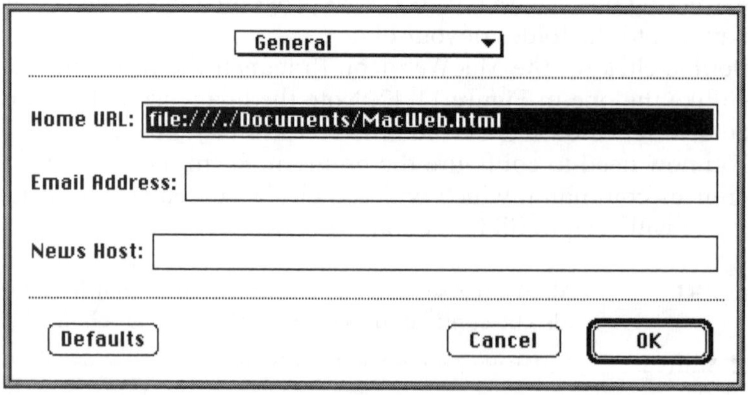

Figure 11.43   Using MacWeb's Preferences screen to configure the program.

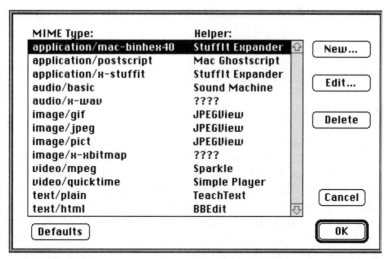

Figure 11.44 Setting up helper applications in MacWeb.

Web Browsing through TIA and SlipKnot

The World Wide Web has always been accessible to people with a shell account, through browsing programs like www and lynx, both of which work in a character-based environment. But programs like these don't support graphical browsing; the user sees nothing more than text on the screen, even if programs like lynx make this kind of browsing intuitive and powerful. And because methods of Internet access are constantly evolving, we have a large user population that continues to use shell accounts but would like to enjoy the full benefits of the Web. Without SLIP/PPP, there seemed to be no way to do this.

Enter TIA. The Internet Adapter is a shareware package from Cyberspace Development that offers graphical access through a shell account. Using it, you can log on to your service provider, run the necessary program on your service provider's machine, and click on your Web browser to make it work. The method works remarkably well, so much so that TIA has been joined by two other programs, Remsock and SlipKnot. The latter is a shareware Web browser that handles the complex translation tasks necessary to conduct graphical browsing over a shell account connection; it resides on your own computer, and requires that your service provider offer a line-mode Web browser like www or lynx (almost all of them do).

Both TIA and Remsock run on your provider's host computer, while Slip-Knot runs on your own. You can find SlipKnot at the following URL:

ftp://ftp.netcom.com/pub/pb/pbrooks/slipknot/

At the time of this writing, the filename was slnot100.zip.

For further information about TIA, send e-mail to the following URL:

mailto://tia-info@marketplace.com

The Remsock implementation can be found at:

ftp://oslonett.no/Shareware/Windows/Comm/

At the time of this writing, the filename was remsock.zip.

Exactly how the new pseudo-SLIP software packages will change the Internet's access picture is at present unclear. In the days when SLIP/PPP accounts cost considerably more than shell accounts, any software that could offer the benefits of the former at the price of the latter would be a sure success; indeed, it would almost force a drastic lowering of SLIP/PPP prices to meet the competition. Today, however, many providers are offering SLIP/PPP at prices little higher than those of a shell account, so cost may not be a deciding issue. Where this software will be valuable is in those areas where providers do not yet offer SLIP/PPP; their customers will be able to access graphical Internet tools that would otherwise be unavailable.

Afterword

Now that even shell accounts can be enlisted for graphical client software, the movement toward a user-friendly Internet interface (or, more precisely, a *series* of user-friendly interfaces in various client programs) seems unstoppable. As always, our computing resources are pushed to the limits by our new software tools; memory and hard disk space have never been at more of a premium. New communications links, and especially the broadening of the data pipeline into home and office, will ensure that we can use those tools to access network resources at higher speeds than ever before. As our tools change, so will the nature of our access and the tasks we can perform with it.

If the Internet seems balky at times, sometimes even unyielding, bear in mind that we are building it as we go. For every time you try to connect to a popular FTP site and can't get in because of the number of users already connected, there will be other times that the network provides you with a priceless insight or an exciting discovery. One or two of these moments can make up for a lot of frustration, and we can be confident that new technologies will help us speed operations, just as the legions of new users will offer a radical expansion in the network's content. Establishing a direct presence on the net through a SLIP/PPP account and pushing the envelope of software development is an absorbing challenge that may come to preoccupy you as much as it has me. In that case, I wish you a happy journey, with expectations of meeting you on the Internet.

In any case, it should be clear from our journeys that the model of networking we use every day on the Internet is vastly different from the commercial on-line services, like Prodigy and America Online, that until recently formed the model of telecommunicating by modem. What the Internet lacks by way of inherent organization it more than makes up for in the sheer diversity and breadth of its information space. True, configuring a SLIP/PPP connection has its frustrations; it is in no way as simple as loading preconfigured software like CompuServe's CIM products, or America Online's graphical interface application; likewise, the Internet has never offered a uniform access program for all categories of users.

But as we've seen, the numerous clients that perform the various tasks we run on the network do offer us an increasingly intuitive way to perform our work. And the phenomenal growth in World Wide Web sites, with the concomitant surge in the popularity of browsers like Mosaic and Netscape, clearly points to a future in which most, if not all, of our networking will be accomplished by inclusive applications. Netscape lets you send e-mail or read USENET news; you can access Gopher sites with it or download files. All of this, of course, is in addition to the Web browsing features that provide such graphical punch, and the hypermedia linkages that make information hunting effortless and global.

If you would like to explore the Internet further from the standpoint of research, my book *Finding It on the Internet* (Wiley, 1994) was written to explain how various search and browsing tools can be used to track down information. I see it as a useful adjunct to this volume, for it allows you to explore a variety of ways to search the net that aren't immediately apparent. Remember, whatever interface is provided by your client program, the underlying engine—Gopher, Veronica, WAIS—functions according to principles that should yield the same results in any client.

Or perhaps I should say, in any full-featured client. My goal in this book has been to help you assemble a collection of powerful software that could handle most any network task; a friendly interface is significant, but it must also wrap itself around an application of genuine capability. Such a toolbox is now at your disposal, but you should always be on the lookout for ways to improve it. A year ago, Netscape wasn't yet available, but it has quickly become one of the most popular browsers on the Internet, thanks to the many significant improvements it made upon the original Mosaic. Who knows what software breakthroughs we'll see in coming months? Keeping your eye on **alt.winsock** (for Microsoft Windows-equipped users) or **comp.sys.mac.comm** (for the Macintosh community) is one way to keep up with such news.

Above all, consider the need to organize and categorize your information. The best thing any network user can do is to master client capabilities that let you save frequently accessed site information. Take advantage of Mosaic and Netscape's bookmarks, for example, and add new sites to FTP programs like WS_FTP and Fetch. You'll find that, when you have network sites available at a mouse click, you'll make more frequent use of them than when you have to enter each address by hand (not to mention the problem of looking up lengthy addresses each time you need them!). If the Internet seems chaotic at times, we can organize our own usage of it by choosing the best tools and mastering their bookmark features.

Whatever shape the information highway of the future takes, the Internet today is providing access to a range of resources we would have once considered beyond possibility. Someday, network connections will be as simple as plugging a wire into a phone jack, but until that day comes, we'll continue to need access software implementing SLIP and PPP. I hope your use of the client programs we've discussed, and others you'll soon find, has convinced you that the net rewards the efforts of those who access it with an unparalleled opportunity to learn.

Glossary

anonymous FTP Entering anonymous as your login at an FTP site allows you to use resources that the system administrator has made available to the public. See FTP.

ANSI American National Standards Institute. This body is responsible for standards like ASCII (q.v.)

applications programming interface A shared subroutine that performs a function that is common across various operations. Displaying text on-screen is such a function. A program issues a call for an API, which then performs the necessary task.

archie A system of distributed computers that tracks the holdings at FTP sites throughout the world. You can use archie to search for files.

ARPA Advanced Research Projects Agency (formerly DARPA). This agency funded the original research that resulted in ARPANET, the network that validated the concept of packet switching through TCP/IP.

ARPANET Funded by ARPA to study how to make computer networks secure in the event of nuclear war, this network later split its functions, with MILNET breaking off in 1983. ARPANET was retired in 1990.

ASCII The American Standard Code for Information Interchange, which creates a standard for representing computer characters.

asynchronous The transmission of information without reference to timing factors on the receiving end.

ATM Asynchronous Transfer Mode. Perhaps the hottest news in network technology. Allows networks to move vast amounts of data, such as live video, on a switched, as opposed to a point-to-point, basis.

backbone The system of high-speed connections that routes long-haul traffic, connecting to slower regional and local datapaths.

bandwidth The size of the data pipeline; specifically, the amount of data that can be transmitted over a particular line in a given period of time. The higher the bandwidth, the faster information can flow. Bandwidth is commonly measured in bits per second.

BBS   A bulletin board system. The term usually refers to a small, dial-up system designed for local users, although some BBSs are now widely available over public data networks.

BITNET   An academic network containing mailing lists on a wide variety of subjects, often populated by scholars and experts in their various fields. Uses a different protocol than the Internet to move its data. BITNET traffic now moves almost entirely over the Internet.

browser   A program used to navigate the World Wide Web. Browsers like Mosaic and Netscape allow you to click on a link to another document, and move to a different computer where that resource is stored.

CCIRN   The Coordinating Committee for Intercontinental Research Networks, which focuses on the growth of research in the global arena. Membership includes networking organizations in numerous countries.

Class A Network   A network with an IP number beginning 1 to 127. Used by universities, government organizations and commercial organizations.

Class B Network   A network with an IP number beginning 128-191. Normally found at corporate sites and other large organizations.

Class C Network   A network with an IP number beginning 192-221. Normally used for service providers, small businesses, schools, and so on.

CNIDR   The Clearinghouse for Networked Information Discovery and Retrieval, in Research Triangle Park, North Carolina. Its mission is to support the development of network search tools.

client   Software that requests services from another computer (called the server). This model is known as client/server computing.

CMC   Computer Mediated Communication—an acronym you will occasionally encounter that refers to the entire range of networking activities.

communications driver   The software that determines how Microsoft Windows manages serial communications. SLIP/PPP work requires a more robust driver than the one supplied with Windows 3.1; a variety of freeware and commercial replacements are available.

compression   The process of squeezing data to eliminate redundancies and allow files to be stored in less disk space. In modems, data compression is used to provide higher transfer rates than would otherwise be possible.

CSLIP   A form of SLIP that compresses header information to improve performance.

CSO   An acronym (Computing Services Office) for a system that allows you to search for students and faculty members at a given school.

CWIS   Campus Wide Information Systems serve universities and colleges with local news, directories, library connections, and databases.

cyberspace   The universe of networked computers. Your electronic mail could be said to flow through cyberspace.

datagram   The standard format for a packet of data, as arranged by IP.

Domain Name System The system that locates the IP addresses corresponding to named computers and domains. A DNS name consists of a sequence of information separated by dots. Thus, mayer.hollywood.com. The Domain Name Service is a program that resolves domain names into IP addresses.

domain A part of the DNS name. The domain to the far right is called the top-level domain. In the above example, this is .com.

domain name A name that identifies an Internet host, and distinguishes it from all other computers on the network.

downloading Moving a file from one computer to another.

e-mail Electronic mail involves sending and receiving messages over the network. You use a mail program like Eudora or Pegasus to compose and read your messages.

emoticon Another term for smiley (q.v.).

Ethernet A network specification developed at Xerox Corporation's Palo Alto Research Center, and made into a network standard by Digital Equipment Corp., Intel Corp., and Xerox Corp. Connects computers in local area networks at speeds of 10 megabits per second.

FARNET The Federation of Advanced Research Networks, a nonprofit corporation promoting networking in research and education.

FAQ Frequently Asked Questions, a document that covers basic information from a particular USENET newsgroup or mailing list.

finger A program that can display information about users on a particular system. Can also be used for other kinds of data.

flame An angry response to a message posted on USENET or a mailing list. People get "flamed" for a variety of reasons, such as breaking Internet taboos against advertising over the network. Some newsgroups consist mostly of flames.

Free-Net A community-based, volunteer-built network. Free-Nets are springing up in cities around the world, as citizens work to provide free access to selected network resources, and to make local information available on-line.

FSF The Free Software Foundation is devoted to creating free software replacements for proprietary programs. Its operating system, GNU, is compatible with Unix.

FTP File Transfer Protocol is your tool for moving files from any one of thousands of computer sites to your service provider's machine. From there, you can download them to your own computer.

FYI For Your Information. Refers to a series of Internet documents containing basic material for beginners.

gateway A computer that handles moving data from one network to another. Normally used to refer to communications between two different kinds of networks.

Gopher A tool developed at the University of Minnesota that creates menus that allow you to access network resources by moving an on-screen pointer. The idea behind Gopher is to simplify the process of using network information. Gopher can point to text files, Telnet sites, WAIS databases, and a wide range of other data.

Gopherspace   A play on cyberspace. Gopherspace is a whimsical term for the world wide system of Gophers.

hardware handshaking   A method of controlling the rate of information exchange between computer and modem by using a control wire to signal changes in the data flow. Hardware handshaking must be implemented in your software and requires an appropriate modem cable.

header   A header appears as the first part of a data packet, and contains addressing information as well as providing provisions for error-checking. The word is also used to refer to the part of an e-mail message before the body of text.

hits   In network parlance, the term for "results" as applied to a database search. You might say, for example, that Veronica returned 65 hits when you searched under a particular keyword.

host   A computer directly connected to the Internet.

hostname   The name of a computer on the Internet. Could be almost anything that the system administrator can dream up.

HTML   Hypertext Markup Language. HTML is used to prepare documents that can be displayed by World Wide Web browsers. The document displays formatting, graphics, and links to other documents.

HTTP   Hypertext Transport Protocol. HTTP enables hypertextual browsing through the World Wide Web; the user clicks on links that are established in a Web document and moves to that document, even though it may be located on a different computer. HTTP provides for the specification of resources through Uniform Resource Locators, or URLs (q.z.).

hypermedia   The ability to display a range of different media through hyperlinks. A World Wide Web page, for example, may contain photographs or drawings, textual formatting, and links to audio and video sources.

hypertext   Data that provides links between key elements, allowing you to move through information nonsequentially.

Internet   The worldwide matrix of connecting computers using the TCP/IP protocols. Does not include, but often moves traffic for, other networks like BITNET and UUCP. If you see the term internet (with a lowercase i), you are dealing with a TCP/IP network that is separate from the worldwide Internet.

Internet Architecture Board   Formerly the Internet Activities Board. Coordinates research and development of the TCP/IP protocols, and oversees standards for the Internet Society.

Internet Engineering Task Force   A task force working as part of the IAB that develops standards for protocols and architecture on the Internet.

Internet Society   Promotes the growth of the Internet and works to assist those groups involved in its use and evolution.

InterNIC   Internet Network Information Center. Your first place to ask questions about the network itself. Maintains a wide variety of data that it makes accessible to all users. Run by Network Solutions, Inc., AT&T, and General Atomics.

interoperability   The ability of diverse computer systems to work together by using common protocols. Without it, the Internet could not exist.

InterSLIP   A freeware program from Intercon Systems Corporation that provides SLIP connectivity for the Macintosh.

IP   Internet Protocol defines the packet structure of a datagram; it functions at the network layer of the protocol stack. IP also defines the addressing mechanism used to deliver data to its destination.

IP Address   A network address expressed in numbers.

ISO   The International Standards Organization. Creates standards for international use, not all of which take hold (see OSI).

Knowbot   A network tool that allows you to search several different databases consecutively to find network addresses and information.

latency   The delay that occurs as data moves through a series of routers to its destination. Latency is one more factor that affects how quickly we can manipulate data on the Internet.

LISTSERV   A program that manages mailing lists by responding automatically to e-mail requests and distributing new messages.

Local Area Network   A network running, usually, in a business office, connecting multiple computers to a server computer.

MacPPP   A freeware program for PPP access to the Internet on the Macintosh.

MacTCP   The TCP/IP protocol stack for the Macintosh, as provided by Apple Computer, and included with System 7.5.

mail server   A computer that responds to electronic mail requests for information. You could ask a mail server, for example, to send you a particular file by giving a precise command, such as **send index**.

mailing list   A group discussion carried on through electronic mail. Mailing lists exist on a huge range of topics, often of a very specialized nature.

MBONE   The Multicast Backbone is a testbed for moving audio and visual information over the Internet.

metanetwork   A network that is itself made up of numerous other networks. The Internet is the prime example.

MILNET   A network run by the Department of Defense, which serves the military. Split off from ARPANET in 1983.

MIME   Multipurpose Internet Mail Extensions; the system for providing graphics and other nontextual data through e-mail.

MNP4   An error control protocol developed by Microcom.

MNP5   A data compression protocol developed by Microcom.

MTU   Maximum Transmission Unit. A measure of the size of IP datagrams. Check with your service provider to determine the proper MTU setting.

multicast   Multicasting means moving data from one point to multiple, specified network points, as opposed to broadcasting, which would send data to everyone. The term is used in connection with the operational procedures of the MBONE.

nameserver   A computer that manages Internet names and numeric addresses. A nameserver turns a domain name into an IP address.

netfind   A network search tool that allows you to track down user information.

netiquette   The etiquette of using the network. Not a trivial issue, especially now that the rise in commercial Internet sites is raising questions about advertising and other business uses of the net.

netmask   Used to divide an organization's network as necessary, creating additional destinations for routing purposes. Also called a subnet mask or address mask. Computers on the various subnets at a given site all appear to the rest of the Internet to be on a single network.

network   Computers connected to communicate information.

newsgroup   A USENET discussion about a particular topic. Some 11,000 newsgroups now exist.

NIC   Network Information Center. An organization charged with maintaining a particular network.

NNTP   Network News Transfer Protocol. The standard for the exchange of USENET messages across the Internet.

node   Any computer attached to a network can be called a node.

NSFNET   The National Science Foundation Network, an essential part of the research networking infrastructure.

OSI   Open Systems Interconnection is a standard for networking developed by the ISO (q.v.). It is used much more heavily in Europe than in the United States, where TCP/IP prevails.

packet   The basic unit of Internet data. A message sent across the net is assembled into packets, each marked with the address and other pertinent information, such as error-checking data. The TCP/IP protocols see to it that the packets are correctly routed and then rebuilt at their destination.

packet switching   The process of sending packets through the network, allowing for alternate routing if a particular network link fails.

ping   A utility that lets you check whether a given host is reachable.

POP   Post Office Protocol allows electronic mail messages to be stored on your service provider's computer until you log in to retrieve them. The protocol then downloads the messages to your computer. You use a client program like Eudora or Pegasus Mail to read and reply to messages.

port   The designation identifying the location of a particular program on an Internet host computer.

postmaster   The person who takes care of the mail system at a given site. The postmaster responds to queries about users on the system and makes sure the mail gets through.

PPP   One of two methods (the other being SLIP) for exchanging data packets wtih the Internet over a telephone line. Point-to-Point Protocol offers data compression and error correction, and remains under active development.

protocol   A protocol defines how computers communicate; it is an agreement between different systems on how they will work together. The set of TCP/IP protocols defines how computers on the Internet exchange information (a set of protocols is commonly called a suite).

public data network   A network providing local numbers by which you can access computer services in different cities, using X.25 protocols to move data.

RARE   The Reseaux Associes pour la Recherche Europeenne, an association of network organizations in Europe. Serves a function similar to that of the IETF.

resolution   The process of translating an Internet name into its corresponding IP address.

RFCs   A series of documents that describes the protocols driving the Internet, along with diverse information about its operations.

RIPE   The Reseaux IP Europeens is an organization of European Internet providers. RIPE has now been incorporated into RARE.

router   A computer system that makes decisions about which path Internet traffic will take to reach its destination. IP determines how the router will direct a data packet to its destination.

server   A computer that provides a resource on the network. Client programs access servers to obtain data.

service provider   A company that offers access to the Internet. Dial-up users obtain an account on the service provider's system and use its computers to log on to the net.

shell   A program that provides the interface that users work with on Unix systems. A variety of shells are available.

shell account   A dial-up account to a Unix-based service provider's machine. Using a shell account, you use whatever resources the provider has made available on his or her machine, but do not exchange data packets directly with the Internet. You cannot run client programs like Netscape and Eudora over a shell account; they demand a SLIP/PPP connection.

signature   A short note, usually containing your name, address, and other information (and including, often, a favorite quotation), which appears at the end of mail or newsgroup messages you send. A signature is set up by creating a special file in your home directory.

SLIP   Serial Line Internet Protocol. As opposed to a shell account, a SLIP connection allows your computer to receive an IP address. FTP sessions are thus handled directly between remote computers and your system, without going through your service provider's computers first. A SLIP account also allows you to run graphical front-end programs like Mosaic and Netscape. Despite its widespread use, SLIP is not an official standard.

smiley   Also known as an emoticon. A group of ASCII characters that provide visual references to add commentary to text.

SMTP   Simple Mail Transfer Protocol is the Internet standard protocol for handling electronic mail messages between computers.

socket   The combination of an IP address and a port address.

software handshaking   A method of controlling the flow of data between computer and modem by using control codes. In XON/XOFF handshaking, a Ctrl-S pauses the flow of transmission, while Ctrl-Q resumes it.

stack   A layered view of network operations, in which each layer is controlled by a particular protocol.

synchronous   The process of sending data communications at a fixed rate. Both sender and receiver must operate at the same rate to achieve synchronous communications.

T1   1.544 megabits per second data transfer over a leased line.

T3   45 mbps data transfer over a leased line.

tar   A method of file archiving.

TCP   Transmission Control Protocol. This is the part of the protocol stack that controls the transport of data, ensuring that it is delivered in its original form. TCP appears in the Internet's transport layer.

telnet   An Internet protocol that allows you to log on to a remote computer. Used, for example, in searching remote databases.

terminal emulation   The process of communicating with a remote computer as if your computer were actually a terminal connected to that computer. By treating your computer as a terminal, the remote machine is seldom able to tap the full processing power built into it, thus limiting the interface you work with. VT-100 is the most common form of terminal emulation.

tn3270   Works like Telnet, but designed to handle IBM systems, which require full-screen operations.

Trumpet Winsock   A shareware TCP/IP stack for Microsoft Windows.

UART   Universal Asynchronous Receiver/Transmitter. This is a chip that makes the computer's parallel data stream into a serial data stream, suitable for use in data communications. A 16550A UART is necessary for high-speed SLIP/PPP work.

UDP   User Datagram Protocol functions in the transport layer of the protocol stack. It is a connectionless protocol that cannot verify that a message has been received.

URL   Uniform Resource Locator. A standard way to refer to resources that specifies the type of service as well as the exact location of the directory or file in question.

UUCP   Unix-to-Unix Copy Program is a method of transferring files between computers that includes electronic mail. Thousands of computers around the world use the UUCP network to exchange mail over dial-up telephone lines.

UNIX   An operating system used by most service providers. Shell account users usually encounter Unix when they log on to a service provider's system, and must use Unix commands to handle routine chores like file management. Berkeley Unix comes with the TCP/IP protocols already built in.

USENET A worldwide network of newsgroups on thousands of subjects which can be accessed by newsreader programs like Trumpet for Windows and Newswatcher.

V.FAST A proprietary implementation used by some modem manufacturers to enable 28,800 bps speeds.

V.FC A de facto standard for 28,800 modems, now superceded by V.34.

V.32 A standard for 9600 bps modems adopted by the CCITT in 1984.

V.32bis A standard for 14,400 bps modems, backward compatible to V.32.

V.34 The standard for 28,800 bps modems.

V.42 An error-control standard established by the CCITT. Allows modems to maintain communications even under poor line conditions.

V.42bis A data compression standard that uses V.42 error correction.

WAIS Wide Area Information Servers, a system that allows you to search databases by keyword and refine your search through relevance feedback techniques.

WAN A Wide Area Network can be any network whose components are geographically dispersed.

Winsock A dynamic link library, or DLL, file, that contains the procedures for making Microsoft Windows work with TCP/IP. A Winsock is needed to run client programs like Mosaic or WinWAIS on a Windows-based system via SLIP/PPP.

workstation Workstations are generally more powerful than desktop IBM-compatible or Apple computers, and usually run Unix as their operating system.

worm A computer program that can make copies of itself. The Internet Worm was a program that caused network havoc in late 1988 when it duplicated itself at sites around the world.

Veronica A program that allows you to search Gopher menus for particular keywords.

WHOIS A program that allows you to search a database for people or network addresses.

World Wide Web A program that works through hypertext links to data, allowing you to explore network resources from multiple entry points.

x.25 A standard that defines how connection-based services operate. X.25 requires a connection to be made before data is transmitted.

x.500 A directory standard based on OSI (q.v.).

Index

UNITED STATES SERVICE PROVIDERS

INTERPATH

e-mail: info@interpath.net
(800) 849-6305

Provides service to:
NC (local), DC (local), and nation-wide via 800 number (extra charge)

Offering to waive the set up fee on Personal SLIP/PPP Service OR our Personal UNIX Shell Service (a $25 value).

INTERPATH • PO Box 12800 • Raleigh, NC 27605

Yes, please send me information on your SLIP/PPP accounts!

Name_____
Address_____
City _____
State/Provence _____
Zip/Postal Code _____
Country _____
Phone _____

THE BLACK BOX

e-mail: info@blkbox.com
713-480-2684 voice
713-480-2685 info

Provides service to Houston, Texas
Offering six months for $216.50 for 6 months. This is a free month, or a savings of $43.30.

Coupon MUST be redeemed for this offer.

THE BLACK BOX • PO Box 591822
Houston, TX 77259-1822

Yes, please send me information on your SLIP/PPP accounts!

Name_____
Address_____
City _____
State/Provence _____
Zip/Postal Code _____
Country _____
Phone _____

CLARKNET

e-mail : info@clark.net
410-254-3900

Provides service to: Northern VA, Washington DC, Maryland

Offering to waive the account setup fee (a $15 value).

CLARK INTERNET SERVICES, INC
10600 rt.108 • Ellicott City, MD 21042

Yes, please send me information on your SLIP/PPP accounts!

Name_____
Address_____
City _____
State/Provence _____
Zip/Postal Code _____
Country _____
Phone _____

MAESTRO TECHNOLOGIES, INC.

e-mail : staff@maestro.com
info@maestro.com
(212) 240-9600

Provides service to New York City metro area (212 and 718 area codes. Other area codes to be announced mid-1995)

Offering one free month of access + 60% off ($30.00) signup (normal $50.00) — requires a 2 month commit-ment (a $45 value).

MAESTRO TECHNOLOGIES, INC.
29 John St. Suite 1601 • New York, NY 10038

Yes, please send me information on your SLIP/PPP accounts!

Name_____
Address_____
City _____
State/Provence _____
Zip/Postal Code _____
Country _____
Phone _____

UNITED STATES SERVICE PROVIDERS

NORTH SHORE ACCESS

e-mail: info@shore.net

(617) 593-3110

Providing service to Massachusetts

Offering $10 off sign-up fee.

NORTH SHORE ACCESS
145 Munroe Street, Suite 405 • Lynn, MA 01901

Yes, please send me information on your
SLIP/PPP accounts!

Name_____

Address_____

City _____

State/Provence _____

Zip/Postal Code _____

Country _____

Phone _____

PORTAL INFORMATION NETWORK

e-mail: sales@portal.com
800.433.6444

Providing world-wide access

Offering free startup (up to $50 value) on any Portal Internet service, including SLIP, PPP. UNIX shell, and UUCP.

PORTAL INFORMATION NETWORK
20863 Stevens Creek Blvd., Ste. 200 • Cupertino, CA 95014

Yes, please send me information on your
SLIP/PPP accounts!

Name_____

Address_____

City _____

State/Provence _____

Zip/Postal Code _____

Country _____

Phone _____

TELERAMA PUBLIC ACCESS INTERNET

e-mail : sysop@telerama.lm.com
412-481-3505

Providing access to Western Pennsylvania

Offering to waive SLIP/PPP account setup fee (a $10 value).

TELERAMA PUBLIC ACCESS INTERNET
P.O. Box 60024 • Pittsburgh, PA 15211

Yes, please send me information on your
SLIP/PPP accounts!

Name_____

Address_____

City _____

State/Provence _____

Zip/Postal Code _____

Country _____

Phone _____

INTERACCESS CO.

e-mail : info@interaccess.com
800-967-1580

Providing service to Chicagoland metropolitan area.

Offering two free weeks of service (a $15 value).

INTERACCESS CO.
3345 Commercial Avenue • Northbrook, IL 60062

Yes, please send me information on your
SLIP/PPP accounts!

Name_____

Address_____

City _____

State/Provence _____

Zip/Postal Code _____

Country _____

Phone _____

UNITED STATES SERVICE PROVIDERS

SSNET, INC.

e-mail: info@ssnet.com

302-378-1386

Providing service to Delaware and Southern Pennsylvania

Offering one free month of service (a $25 value)

SSNET, INC.
1254 Lorewood Grove Road • Middletown, DE 19709

Yes, please send me information on your SLIP/PPP accounts!

Name_____

Address_____

City _____

State/Provence _____

Zip/Postal Code _____

Country _____

Phone _____

ETERNET DIRECT, INC.

e-mail : info@indirect.com

(602) 274-0100 Phoenix

(602) 324-0100 Tucson

Providing service to Phoenix and Tucson, Arizona

Offering to waive all setup and activation fees (a $15 value) and provide first month of service free (a $24.50 value)

ETERNET DIRECT, INC.
1366 E. Thomas Rd., Ste 210 • Phoenix, AZ 85014

Yes, please send me information on your SLIP/PPP accounts!

Name_____

Address_____

City _____

State/Provence _____

Zip/Postal Code _____

Country _____

Phone _____

PERFORMANCE SYSTEMS INT'L INC (PSINET)

e-mail : all-info@psi.com

interramp-info@psi.com

1-800-774-0852

Provides service to 80 local dialup cities throughout the US and access from Tokyo Japan

Offering 7 day free trial on the internet, no obligation to buy. PSInet provides the service and software (a $350 value).

PERFORMANCE SYSTEMS INTERNATIONAL INC
(PSINET) 510 Huntmar Park Dr • Herndon, VA 22070

Yes, please send me information on your SLIP/PPP accounts!

Name_____

Address_____

City _____

State/Provence _____

Zip/Postal Code _____

Country _____

Phone _____

CRL NETWORK SERVICES

e-mail : info@crl.com

415-837-5300

Provides service to National US, local to 600 cities

Offering 20 free hours at signup (a $15 value)

CRL NETWORK SERVICES
1 Kearny St. Suite 1475 • San Francisco, CA 94108

Yes, please send me information on your SLIP/PPP accounts!

Name_____

Address_____

City _____

State/Provence _____

Zip/Postal Code _____

Country _____

Phone _____

UNITED KINDOM

DEMON INTERNET LTD

e-mail: sales@demon.net
(for sales enquiries)
internet@demon.net
(for technical queries)

+44-(0)181 371 1234

Provides service to:
Local call access to most of
mainland UK. Holland coming
on-line May '95

DEMON INTERNET LTD

Gateway House • 322 Regents Park Road • Finchley
London, N3 2QQ United Kingdom

Yes, please send me information on your
SLIP/PPP accounts!

Name_____

Address_____

City _____

State/Provence _____

Zip/Postal Code _____

Country _____

Phone _____

Register with credit card details and pay a year in advance or monthly. We will waiver the sign-up fee and first month of usage (normal fees are 12.50 UK pounds sterling startup + 10 UK pounds sterling per month - NO usage fees). If the coupons is received before the 15th of the month - you get the remainder free. If after the 15th - you get the remainder and the next month free. Normal VAT rates apply at local rates.

AUSTRALIA

KRALIZEC DIALUP INTERNET SYSTEM

e-mail : info@zeta.org.au

Provides service to Sydney (02)
zone, Windsor (045) and Penrith
(047) via toll-free number

KRALIZEC DIALUP INTERNET SYSTEM
C/- Zeta Microcomputer

P.O. Box 177 • Riverstone • NSW 2765 • Australia

Yes, please send me information on your
SLIP/PPP accounts!

Name_____

Address_____

City _____

State/Provence _____

Zip/Postal Code _____

Country _____

Phone _____

Kralizec provides reliable, professional Internet connectivity for individuals and small businesses. Our standard rates are so low you don't need a discount! For an individual account the price is $15/month for up to 15 hours of connect time per month. Additional connect time is $1 per hour. For SLIP access, once only $20 charge applies. Contact us directly to discuss permanent Internet links for individuals and businesses. All amounts are in Australian dollars.

CANADA

CCI NETWORKS

e-mail: info@ccinet.ab.ca

(403) 450-6787

Provides service to Alberta, Canada. Offering 50% off the signup fee for any SLIP/PPP accounts (a $20.00 value)

CCI NETWORKS
A Division of Corporate Computers Inc.
4130 - 95 Street • Edmonton, Alberta • Canada T6E 6H5

Yes, please send me information on your SLIP/PPP accounts!

Name_____
Address_____
City _____
State/Provence _____
Zip/Postal Code _____
Country _____
Phone _____

UUNET Canada

e-mail : info@uunet.ca

(416) 368-6621
1-800-463-8123

Provides service to Vancouver, Calgary, Edmonton, London, Kitchener, Toronto, Ottawa, Montreal, Quebec City, Halifax

UUNET Canada
20 Bay Street, Suite 1910 • Toronto, Ontario
M5J 2N8 Canada

Yes, please send me information on your SLIP/PPP accounts!

Name_____
Address_____
City _____
State/Provence _____
Zip/Postal Code _____
Country _____
Phone _____

ISLAND NET

e-mail : info@islandnet.com

(604) 727-6030 (in Victoria)
(800) 331-3055 (toll free)

Provides service to Victoria, Sidney, Sooke, Duncan, Shawnigan Lake, Nanaimo, Ladysmith, etc.

Offering $25 in free usage

ISLAND NET—AMT Solutions Group Inc.
P.O. Box 6201 Depot 1 • Victoria, B.C.
V8P 5L5 Canada

Yes, please send me information on your SLIP/PPP accounts!

Name_____
Address_____
City _____
State/Provence _____
Zip/Postal Code _____
Country _____
Phone _____

EUnet

(Central European Office Address)

attn: Paul Rendek
Singel 540 • 1017 AZ Amsterdam
The Netherlands

Tel: +31 20 623 3803
Fax: +31 20 622 4657

Email: info@EU.net

EUnet is Europe's leading commercial Internet Service Provider offering the full range of Internet services including E-mail, Network News, WWW Servers, Archive Access and connectivity via leased lines, ISDN, dial-up, and X.25. Through its own infrastructure currently covering 30 countries, EUnet operates through cooperative arrangements with national and regional Internet Service Providers.

National, European, and Global—EUnet's infrastructure and support provide your best opportunity for quality service, reliability, and enterprise advantage.

EUnet Contact-Information for Austria (EUnet Austria):

ADDRESS:
  EUnet EDV Diensleistungs Ges.m.b.H
  Thurngasse 8/16
  A-1090 Vienna, Austria

CONTACT:
  Phone: +43 1 3174969
  Fax: +43 1 3106926
  E-mail: info@Austria.EU.net

EUnet Contact-Information for Belgium (EUnet Belgium):

ADDRESS:
  EUnet Belgium NV/SA
  Stapelhuisstraat 13
  B-3000 Leuven, Belgium

CONTACT:
  Phone: +32 16 23 60 99
  Fax: +32 16 23 20 79
  E-mail: info@Belgium.EU.net

EUnet Contact-Information for Great Britain (EUnet GB):

ADDRESS:
EUnet GB (GBnet Ltd)
Wilson House
John Wilson Business Park
Whitstable, Kent CT5 3QY
United Kingdom

CONTACT:
Phone: +44 227 266 466
Fax: +44 227 266 477
E-mail: info@Britain.EU.net

EUnet Contact-Information for Bulgaria (BGnet):

ADDRESS:
Digital Systems / EUnet Bulgaria
Neofit Bozveli 6
BG-9000 Varna, Bulgaria

CONTACT:
Phone: +359 52 259135
Fax: +359 52 234540
E-mail: info@Bulgaria.EU.net

EUnet Contact-Information for Czechia (EUnet Czechia):

ADDRESS:
COnet
Technicka 5
166 28 Prague 6
Czech Republic

CONTACT:
Phone: +42 2 24 31 03 37
Fax: +42 2 24 31 06 46
E-mail: info@Czechia.EU.net

EUnet Contact-Information for Denmark (DKnet):

ADDRESS:
DKnet
Fruebjergvej 3
DK-2100 Koebenhavn OE, Denmark

CONTACT:
Phone: +45 39 17 99 00
Fax: +45 39 17 98 97
E-mail: info@Denmark.EU.net

EUnet Contact-Information for Egypt (ENSTINET, EUnet Egypt):

ADDRESS:
Egyptian National STI Network
101 Kasr E.-Aini st, 12 floor
Cairo, Egypt. 11516

CONTACT:
Maged Boulos
Phone: +20 2 355 7253
Fax: +20 2 354 7807
E-mail: info@Egypt.EU.net

EUnet Contact-Information for Finland (EUnet Finland):

ADDRESS:
EUnet Finland OY
Punavuorenkatu 1
FI-00120 Helsinki, Finland

CONTACT:
Phone: +358 0 400 2060
Fax: +358 0 622 2626
E-mail: info@Finland.EU.net

EUnet Contact-Information for France (EUnet-France):

ADDRESS:
EUnet France
52, Av de la Grance Armee
75017 Paris, France

CONTACT:
Phone: +33 1 53 81 60 60
Fax: +33 1 45 74 52 79
E-mail: info@France.EU.net

EUnet Contact-Information for Germany (EUnet Germany):

ADDRESS:
EUnet Deutschland GmbH
Emil-Figge-Str. 80
D-44227 Dortmund

CONTACT:
Phone: +49 231 972 00
Fax: +49 231 972 1111
E-mail: info@Germany.EU.net

EUnet Contact-Information for Greece (FORTHnet):

ADDRESS:
KERAKLIO central office/NOC:
Foundation of Research and Technology Hellas
FORTHnet/EUnetGR
36 Daidalou str.
P.O. Box 1385, Heraklion, Crete, Greece
711110

CONTACT:
Stelios Sartzetakis
Phone: +30 81 221171, 229368
Fax: +30 31 229342, 229343
E-mail: info@Greece.EU.net

EUnet Contact-Information for Hungary (EUnet Hungary):

ADDRESS:
Computer and Automation Institute
Hungarian Academy of Science (SzTAKI)
Victor Hugo u. 18-22
H-1132 Budapest, Hungary

CONTACT:
Krisztina Hollo
Phone: +36 1 2698281
Fax: +36 1 2698288
E-mail: info@Hungary.EU.net

EUnet Contact-Information for Iceland (ISnet):

ADDRESS:
SURIS/ISnet
Taeknigardi
Dunhaga 5
107 Reykjavik

CONTACT:
Marius Olafsson
Phone: +354 1 694747
Fax: +354 1 28801
E-mail: info@Iceland.EU.net

EUnet Contact-Information for Ireland (EUnet):

ADDRESS:
IEunet Limited
Innovations Centre
Trinity College
Dublin 2, Ireland

CONTACT:
Phone: +353 1 679 9361
Fax: +358 1 679 8039
E-mail: info@Ireland.EU.net

EUnet Contact-Information for Italy (IUnet):

ADDRESS:
  IUnet c/o i2u srl
  Viale Monza
  1-20126 Milano, Italy

CONTACT:
  Phone: +39 2 2700 2528
  Fax: +39 2 2700 1322
  E-mail: info@Italy.EU.net

EUnet Contact-Information for Luxemburg (EUnet Luxemburg):

ADDRESS:
  EUnet Luxemburg
  CRP - Centre Universitaire
  162a, Avenue de la Faiencerie
  L-1511 Luxemburg

CONTACT:
  Phone: +352 47 02 61
  Fax: +352 47 02 64
  E-mail: info@crpcu.lu

EUnet Contact-Information for Netherlands (NLnet):

ADDRESS:
  NLnet
  Kruislaan 419
  1098 VA Amsterdam

CONTACT:
  Phone: +31 20 663 9366
  Fax: +31 20 665 5311
  E-mail: info@Netherlands.EU.net

EUnet Contact-Information for Norway (EUnet Norway):

ADDRESS:
  EUnet Norway
  Gaustadallen 21
  N-0371 OSLO, Norway

CONTACT:
  Phone: +47 22 95 83 27
  Fax: +47 22 60 44 27
  E-mail: info@Norway.EU.net

EUnet Contact-Information for Poland (EUnet Poland):

ADDRESS:
  PL-net Ltd
  Al. Jerozolimskie 65/79, room 16.07
  PL-00-679 Warszawa, Poland

CONTACT:
  Phone: +48 2 630 63 02
  Fax: +48 2 630 63 05
  E-mail: info@Poland.EU.net,tvd
          @Poland.EU.net

EUnet Contact-Information for Portugal (EUnet Portugal):

ADDRESS:
  EUnet Portugal
  PUUG - Grupo Portugues de Utilizadores
  do Sistema UNIX
  Quinta da Torre - building UNINOVA
  2825 MONTE DA CAPARICA, Portugal

CONTACT:
  Phone: +351 1 294 28 44
  Fax: +351 1 295 77 86
  E-mail: info@Portugal.EU.net

EUnet Contact-Information for Romania (EUnet Romania):

ADDRESS:
EUnet Romania SRL
Bd. Unirii 20, B1.5C, Ap.14
R-76105, Bucharest ROMANIA

CONTACT:
Phone: +40 1 312.6886
Fax: +40 1 312.6668
E-mail: info@Romania.EU.net

EUnet Contact-Information for Slovakia (EUnet Slovakia):

ADDRESS:
EUnet Slovakia
MFF UK, Computer Centre
Mlynska dolina
842 15 Bratislava, Slovakia

CONTACT:
Gejza Buecher / Ivan Lescak
Phone: +42 7 377 434, +42 7 725 306
Fax: +42 7 377 433, +42 7 728 462
E-mail: info@Slovakia.EU.net

EUnet Contact-Information for Soviet-Union (EUnet/Relcom):

ADDRESS:
Relcom Corp
ul. Raspletina, 4, korp. 1
123060 Moscow, Russia

CONTACT:
Dmitry Burkov
Phone: +7 095 194 2540
Fax: +7 095 198 9510
E-mail: info@USSR.EU.net

EUnet Contact-Information for Spain (EUnet Spain):

ADDRESS:
Goya Servicios Telematicos SA—EUnet Espana
Clara del Rey 8, 1-7
E-28002 Madrid, Spain

CONTACT:
Phone: +34 1 413 48 56
Fax: +34 1 413 49 01
E-mail: info@Spain.EU.net

EUnet Contact-Information for Sweden (EUnet Sweet):

(Please contact EUnet Norway for Internet services in Sweden):

ADDRESS:
EUnet Norway
Gaustadallen 21
N-0371 OSLO, Norway

CONTACT:
Phone: +47 22 95 83 27
Fax: +47 22 60 44 27
E-mail: info@Norway.EU.net,tvd

EUnet Contact-Information for Switzerland (EUnet Switzerland):

ADDRESS:
EUnet Switzerland
Zweierstrasse 35
CH-8004 Zuerich, Switzerland

CONTACT:
Phone: +41 1 291 45 80
Fax: +41 1 291 46 42
E-mail: info@Switzerland.EU.net

EUnet Contact-Information for Tunisia (EUnet Tunisia):

ADDRESS:
IRSIT /EUnet - Tunisia
BP 212, 2 Rue Ibn Nadime
1082 Cite Mahrajane
Tunis, Tunisia

CONTACT:
Mondher Makni
Phone: +216 1 787 757 / 289 853
Fax: +216 1 787 827
E-mail: info@Tunisia.EU.net